NORTEL NETWORKS
ROUTER CONFIGURATION

Nortel Networks Router Configuration

Jean-Pierre Comeau

McGraw-Hill
New York   San Francisco   Washington, D.C.
Auckland   Bogotá   Caracas   Lisbon   London
Madrid   Mexico City   Milan   Montreal   New Delhi
San Juan   Singapore   Sydney   Tokyo   Toronto

McGraw-Hill

*A Division of The **McGraw·Hill** Companies*

Copyright © 2000 by The McGraw-Hill Companies, Inc. All rights reserved. Printed in the United States of America. Except as permitted under the United States Copyright Act of 1976, no part of this publication may be reproduced or distributed in any form or by any means, or stored in a data base or retrieval system, without the prior written permission of the publisher.

1 2 3 4 5 6 7 8 9 0   AGM/AGM   0 5 4 3 2 1 0

ISBN 0-07-212533-0

The executive editor for this book was Steve Elliot and the production supervisor was Daina Penikas. It was set in Century Schoolbook by D&G Limited, LLC.

Printed and bound by Quebecor/Martinsburg.

CONTENTS

Router Hardware and Software

This chapter serves as an introduction to the rest of the book by describing the various routers available from Nortel Networks. This chapter does not cover the low-end Nautica Clam or the Marlin routers, but before we describe the various routers available, it is necessary to define just what is a router. A more detailed description of a router and how it works will be discussed in Chapter 3, "Basic IP Routing," but for all intents and purpose, a router can be defined as the following:

> *Router*   A connectivity device that uses one or more metrics (parameters) to determine the optimal path along which network traffic should be forwarded.

This definition is rather broad and leaves a lot for distinction. The competition among router makers is fierce. Everyone is trying to add more features to the router's software or streamline code to enhance performance so that they can gain more ground in the market. What I hope to do with this chapter is to provide an overview of the different routers in the Nortel line, expounding on their many features. After we become a little more intimate with the routers' capabilities, we will examine them further by discussing their particular usage of memory and how they boot.

The Nortel Networks routers provide high performance and availability for everything from remote offices to enterprise networks. They support all the popular network, routing, bridging, and *Wide Area Network* (WAN) protocols through their impressive Routing Services software (BayRS™). You will find that Nortel routers offer you the flexibility to provide strong performance for remote branch offices as well as across the enterprise without sacrificing scalability, configurability, and the availability of services.

Product Overview

The Nortel Networks router product line consists of two platform families: the *Access Node* (AN) and the *Backbone Node* (BN). The AN family of routers consists of the AN, the *Access Node Hub* (ANH), the Access Stack Node, and the Advanced Remote Node routers. Only two routers are considered part of the BN family: the *Backbone Link Node* (BLN) and the *Backbone Concentrator Node* (BCN) routers. Each of these routers has distinct configurations and capabilities. The next several sections provide brief overviews on each of the router families and their respective benefits.

Access Node (AN) and Access Node Hub (ANH)

Both the AN and ANH are fixed configuration routers/bridges that provide *local area network* (LAN) and WAN interoperability to small remote offices. The difference between the two router types is that the ANH has an 8-port or 12-port 10Base-T hub integrated into the platform. Both devices support all major routing and bridging protocols as well as data compression, traffic prioritization, and uniform traffic filters. Dynamic reconfiguration can be accomplished through the graphical configuration tool called *Site Manager* or through a console connection to the *Technician Interface* (TI). An optional *Data Collection Module* (DCM) can be added to provide full *Remote Network Monitoring* (RMON) probe capabilities according to RFC 1757. Inside each router is a Motorola MC68360 microprocessor that maintains high forwarding and traffic filtering rates regardless of the number of protocols and network interfaces used, even when processing *Simple Network Management Protocol* (SNMP) management inquiries. They can be configured with 4 MB, 8 MB, or 16 MB of *dynamic random access memory* (DRAM). Figure 1-1 shows the front view of an AN router.

The AN comes with an Ethernet or Token Ring interface (or with both). Actually, two flavors of an AN router are available, AN1 and AN2. The difference is that the AN1 does not have a removable flash card for image and configuration file storage. Since the AN1 is an older router model than the AN2, all further discussion in relation to the AN will refer to the AN2 router. Both the AN and ANH support two serial interfaces synchronous, one T1/FT1 *Data Service Unit / Channel Service Unit* (DSU/CSU), or one 56/64-Kbps DSU/CSU adapter module, and one ISDN *Basic Rate Interface* (BRI). Other capabilities include Dial Backup, Bandwidth-on-Demand, and Dial-on-Demand functionalities.

Figure 1-1
The front of an
AN router

Advance Remote Node (ARN)

The ARN is much like the AN or ANH routers in that it is crafted to provide network interoperability for remote offices. Although the AN/ANH have fixed configurations, the ARN is designed to integrate the functions of multiple devices. The goal is to decrease the number of physical devices and alleviate the duties of network management, especially in sites where no dedicated network support staff exists. The LAN interfaces that can be integrated into the ARN consist of 10/100 Ethernet and Token Ring. The two WAN interfaces can consist of a 56/64 K/T1/FT1 CSU/DSU, an *Integrated Services Digital Network* (ISDN) BRI, and/or a V.34 modem. An optional expansion slot is also provided that can accommodate an additional LAN or WAN interface. The ARN supports up to four LAN and seven serial interfaces.

The microprocessor that provides the high forwarding rates of the ARN is the Motorola MC68040 or the MC68030. Either chip is ideal for handling the computationally intensive internetwork applications, such as the *Systems Network Architecture* (SNA), *Data Link Switching* (DLSw), *Advanced Peer-to-Peer Networking* (APPN), and *Synchronous Data Link Control* (SDLC). The ARN supports WAN bandwidth optimization schemes like compression, traffic prioritization, and filters through the use of Nortel Network Routing Services (BayRS). It also can provide remote office link security by acting as a firewall as well as by using encryption.

Figure 1-2 shows the front face of an ARN. This particular ARN has an Ethernet base module located in the bottom slot (or base slot). It also has an integrated 56/64 K CSU/DSU and V.34 modem located in the two WAN slots to the left. The expansion slot is available if you need to include an additional Ethernet, Token Ring, or serial interface. Furthermore, optional

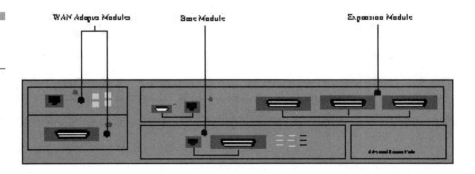

Figure 1-2
The front view of an ARN router

DCMs can be added to the configuration to provide network visibility via RMON statistics. Software RMON support is only available in the 10- or 100-Mbps systems. The flash card slot and console port are located on the rear of the router.

Access Stack Node (ASN)

The ASN is a stackable router that provides high forwarding rates to enterprise networks. The ASN is based on the FRE2 processor module found in the *Backbone Node* (BN) router family. It has a Motorola MC68060 33-MHz microprocessor capable of transmitting packets up to 30,000 per second. An optional Fast Packet Cache, using the Motorola MC68040 microprocessor, can increase this throughput to 50,000 *packets per second* (pps). Figure 1-3 shows the front view of an ASN router.

The stackable nature of the ASN enables you to add additional routers without having to replace your existing hardware. Four units can be stacked together via a specific network module called the *Stack Packet Exchange* (SPEX). The SPEX is a high-performance system interconnect (or bus) that enables the four units to act as one in a symmetrical multiprocessing architecture. It also allows each router to be removed (or hot-swapped) from the stack without disrupting the other routers. A four-unit stack supports a forwarding performance of up to 200,000 pps with 512 Mbps between each of the stack units. Figure 1-4 shows a stack of three ASN routers connected together via the SPEX network module with the SPEX cable.

The ASN accepts up to four network modules, including the SPEX, for a total of 16 network interfaces per unit (8 LAN and 16 WAN). The LAN interfaces supported are Ethernet, 100Base-T, Token Ring, and *Fiber Distributed Data Interface* (FDDI), as shown in Figure 1-5. The WAN interfaces are 56/64 Kbps, T1, ISDN BRI, and ISDN *Primary Rate Interface* (PRI). The

Figure 1-3

The front view of an ASN router

Figure 1-4
Stacked ASNs with
a SPEX-HS cable

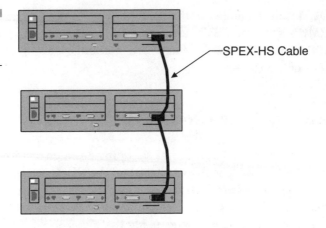

SPEX-HS Cable

Figure 1-5
The rear view of
a fully populated
ASN router

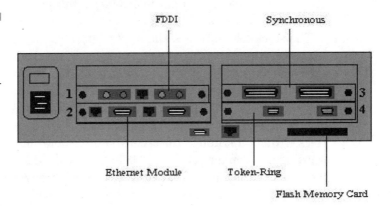

ASN supports DRAM configurations of 8 MB, 16 MB, or 32 MB. Generally, 32 MB of DRAM is not needed unless a large number of virtual circuits or more than four LAN modules exist in the stack.

All major routing and bridging protocols are supported in the Nortel Networks Routing Services (BayRS™) that runs on the ASN. BayRS contains features such as hardware fault isolation, software fault isolation and recovery, and online dynamic reconfiguration. The added features include alternate path routing and Dial-on-Demand.

The ASN incorporates a hardware-based data compression coprocessor net module that maximizes WAN use by allowing compression over all wide area interfaces. It also supports redundant nonvolatile storage through the use of multiple PCMCIA flash memory cards.

Backbone Node (BN)

Two types of routers are available in the BN family: the BLN and the BCN. They both share similar characteristics but were designed for different applications. The BLN and BLN-2 chassis supports a maximum of four *Intelligent Link Interfaces* (ILI) that have a capability of 16 LAN interfaces with a throughput of up to 150,000 pps. These routers are a good fit for medium-sized enterprises or special applications that generate high traffic through one or two interfaces, such as Internet connectivity. The BLN and the BLN-2 differ in that the BLN-2 supports power supply and cooling system redundancy. The BCN chassis supports 13 ILIs that have a capability of 52 LAN interfaces and a throughput of up to five million pps. Obviously, the BCN was designed to interconnect many networks in a large enterprise. Figure 1-6 shows the front views of the BLN and the BCN routers.

Looking internally into each system, one can see the similarities between the two members of the BN family. Both utilize Motorola-based MC68040 *Fast Routing Engines* (FRE) that connect to a one-*gigabit per second* (Gbps) internal bus called a *Parallel Packet Exchange* (PPX). The FRE processor modules are inserted into the front of the routers mating with a LAN/WAN link module inserted from the rear, making an ILI. Data received on a port on the link module are transferred to the FRE processor via the processor interconnect. The FRE decides where to send the outbound packet either

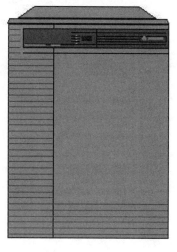

Figure 1-6
The BN router
family photo

through another network interface on the link module or to its peer processor through the PPX. The ILI forms the symmetric multiprocessor architecture of these routers, which allows multiple processors to function as a single router. Each of the routers is also equipped with a *System Resource Module* (SRM), which provides control arbitration to the PPX rails.

The BLN, BLN-2, and BCN support all major routing and bridging protocols and can support the following LAN and WAN interfaces:

LAN	WAN
Ethernet/802.3	56/64 Kbps
Token Ring/802.5 (4 and 16 Mbps)	T1/FT1
FDDI (single and multimode)	T3
100/1000 Base-T	

With the *ATM Routing Engine* (ARE), they can operate at up to 155 Mbps when connected using a Sonet/SDH STS-3/STM-1 interface. The ATM ARE supports up to 2,000 simultaneously active virtual circuits.

The layered system software architecture and extensive fault management capabilities isolate malfunctions before other router components are affected. Dynamic reconfiguration and nondisruptive operational services (or hot-swap) enable online changes in hardware and software configurations.

Product Features

The two router platform families share several common features, mainly due to the BayRS that runs on each of the different router types. The BayRS software contains traffic management features that support data compression, traffic prioritization, and uniform traffic filters. Based on the Lempel-Ziv algorithm, BayRS data compression reduces the bandwidth required to transfer LAN protocols across the wide area. Priority filters can be set for time-sensitive and/or mission-critical data to help eliminate the occurrence of session timeouts and to improve application performance.

Traffic prioritization incorporates two types of dequeuing algorithms used to transmit packets across a serial line: strict dequeuing or bandwidth allocation dequeuing. Strict dequeuing transmits all high-priority packets before transmitting any packets from the normal or low queue. Bandwidth allocation dequeuing is based on user-defined bandwidth allocation percentages for each queue. Uniform traffic filters enable inbound and outbound traffic filters to be easily established using predefined protocol-specific fields or user-defined fields.

Access Node (AN) and Access Node Hub (ANH)

Both the Ethernet AN and eight-port ANH models support an optional RMON DCM that plugs directly into the processor module of the router. This DCM contains a 25-MHz Motorola MC68040 microprocessor and a 2 MB DRAM. It provides standard Ethernet RMON capabilities plus real-time packet capture and filtering.

The AN is available in the following configurations:

- Ethernet/Synchronous
- Token-Ring/Synchronous
- Ethernet/Token Ring/Synchronous

The Ethernet/Synchronous router comes with a single 802.3 Ethernet interface supporting both Ethernet 1.0 and 2.0 frame formats as well as two serial connectors that support RS-232, RS 449/422 balanced, V.35, and X.21. An optional second Ethernet, ISDN (BRI), T1/FT1 DSU/CSU, 56/64-Kbps DSU/CSU, or a third synchronous adapter module can be installed to provide a single platform solution for applications that require a primary link, backup link, and a synchronous interface.

The Token Ring/Synchronous router also comes with dual serial interfaces supporting the various synchronous protocols. The Token Ring interface can operate at 4- or 16-Mbps ring speeds. It also supports the IEEE 802.5 *Media Access Control* (MAC) token-passing protocol, both 802.2 Type 1 (connectionless) and Type 2 (connection-oriented) protocols, and the 16-Mbps *Early Token Release* (ETR) protocol. Optional synchronous and ISDN BRI adapter modules are also available.

■ ■

NOTE: *If an ISDN BRI is configured, then only one serial interface is enabled (COM2).*

Three BayRS software options are available: IP Access, Remote Office, and Corporate Suite. Each software bundle supports the full range of WAN protocols (HDLC Encapsulation, the *Point-to-Point Protocol* [PPP], Frame Relay, and so on) as well as all of the bridging, traffic, and node management features. The differences between the software suites lie in their IBM integration features and LAN protocols. IP Access supports the IP protocol, *Source Route Bridging* (SRB), and Transparent Synchronous Pass-Through. Although Remote Office and Corporate Suite support the full range of IBM integration features, Remote Office differs from Corporate by supporting only IP, IPX, and AppleTalk Phase 2 LAN protocols. Table 1-1 shows each software suite's functionality and availability.

Advanced Remote Node (ARN)

The ARN, in most respects, is exactly like the AN router. It also has an optional Ethernet DCM that can be plugged into the processor module of the router. The DCM is a 25-MHz MC68040 processor that supports the full nine groups of the Ethernet RMON *Management Information Base* (MIB). It also monitors layer-3 traffic that it can collect and correlate over a long term. The data can then be summarized to detect trends in network performance as well as faults and traffic flows.

The base ARN model also comes with a faster chip than the AN. It is powered by the high-performance Motorola 33-MHz MC68040 processor chip, which allows higher forwarding and filtering rates. It supports dynamic RAM configurations of 8, 16, or 32 MB, while the AN only supports 8 or 16 MB. The main difference between the two routers is the amount of flexibility the ARN has for connecting devices and services. Although the AN is mainly a fixed configuration router, the ARN provides for a variety of configuration options. It supports 10Base-T, 10/100 Base-TX, 10/100 Base-FX, and Token Ring LAN interfaces, as well as PPP, Frame Relay, X.25, ISDN BI,

Table 1-1

A comparison
of BayRS for AN,
ANH, and ARN
routers

Feature	IP Access	Remote Office	Corporate Suite
BayRS Options			
Network Protocols			
IP	✓	✓	✓
Novel IPX		✓	✓
AppleTalk Phase 2		✓	✓
DECnet Phase IV			✓
Banyan Vines			✓
OSI			✓
Xerox XNS			✓
IBM Integration			
SRB	✓	✓	✓
LAN Manager Agent		✓	✓
DLSw for Ethernet and Token Ring	✓	✓	
DLSw for SDLC		✓	✓
Transparent Sync Pass-Through	✓	✓	✓
BSC Pass-Through		✓	✓
APPN			✓
Bridging			
Transparent	✓	✓	✓
Translational Bridge Ethernet to Token Ring	✓	✓	✓
Native Mode LAN (NML)	✓	✓	✓
WAN			
PPP	✓	✓	✓
Frame Relay	✓	✓	✓
ISDN BRI	✓	✓	✓

continues

Table 1-1

Continued.

Feature	IP Access	Remote Office	Corporate Suite
BayRS Options			
WAN			
SMDS	✓	✓	✓
X.25	✓	✓	✓
ATM DXI	✓	✓	✓
Dial Backup	✓	✓	✓
Bandwidth-on-Demand	✓	✓	✓
Dial-on-Demand	✓	✓	✓
Traffic Management			
Data Compression	✓	✓	✓
Traffic Prioritization	✓	✓	✓
Uniform Traffic Filters	✓	✓	✓

Switched Multimegabit Data Service (SMDS), and/or *Asynchronous Transfer Mode* (ATM) WAN interfaces. The base module in an ARN can be an Ethernet or Token Ring module allowing for either in its expansion slot. It also uses a PCMCIA flash memory card for its router software image and configuration file similar to the AN (and pretty much all the other routers).

The ARN router has an expansion slot located above the base module slot, as shown in Figure 1-2. This slot can accommodate the following LAN interface expansion modules:

- A second Ethernet or Token Ring interface
- A second Ethernet or Token Ring with three serial interfaces
- A second Ethernet with seven serial interfaces
- Seven serial interfaces

The serial interfaces can be either synchronous or asynchronous. The router can support other WAN interfaces, such as a 56/64 K DSU/CSU, T1/FT1 DSU/CSU, and an ISDN BRI adapter. The DSU/CSUs are integrated units that connect the router to a *local exchange carrier* (LEC) at speeds from 1,200 to 2.048 bps. These units also have extensive diagnostics and test functions like loopback and *bit error rate test* (BERT). Lastly, there are the X.25 pad, the ISDN BRI interface, and the V.34 modem module. The modem enables the router to take advantage of the software's dial services.

Again, like the AN (and pretty much all the other routers), the ARN uses the BayRS suite of software services. You can either implement the IP Access suite, the Remote Office suite, or the Corporate suite on this router. Refer to Table 1-1 for each suite's functionality.

Access Stack Node (ASN)

The ASN's modular design enables it to accept up to four net modules for a total of 8 LAN interfaces or 16 WAN interfaces. As with the AN and ANH, the ASN's interfaces support the 802.3/Ethernet and the 802.5/Token Ring protocols. It also supports a 100Base-T net module, complying with the *Institute of Electrical and Electronics Engineers'* (IEEE) 802.3u 100Base-T standard, as well as an FDDI net module with a 100-Mbps dual attached interface. The FDDI interface is available with a multimode and/or a single-mode connector. The multimode interface supports 62.5/125 or 50/125 micron fiber for distances up to two kilometers between stations. The single-mode fiber connectors support 9/125 micron fiber for distances up to 10 kilometers between stations.

The synchronous net modules are available with dual or quad interfaces that are capable of 1,200 to 2.048 Mbps, a full duplex operation. They support the following protocols and services:

Protocols	Services
RS-232	Dial backup
RS-422	Dial-on-Demand
V.35	Bandwidth-on-Demand
X.21	Synchronous PPP/Asynchronous PPP

The ISDN BRI interface provides two 64-Kbps D channels for data and one 16-Kbps B channel for signaling. The other available net modules are a dual *Multichannel T1* (MCT1) and a single MCE1. The MCT1 has two 1.544-Mbps interfaces allowing for high-density access to services such as a *digital cross-connect* (DACS). The MCT1 coupled with the ASN's software suite enables a connection into the ISDN switch network at a PRI. An ISDN PRI provides 23 D channels for data and one 64-Kbps D channel for signaling.

One of the big selling points of the ASN router is its stackable nature. Four ASN routers can be stacked together to function as one in a *Symmetrical Multiprocessing* (SMP) architecture. An ASN with a fast packet cache can provide a throughput of approximately 50,000 *packets per second* (pps). A stack of four ASNs will subsequently provide up to 200,000 pps. A SPEX provides the connection between the multiple routers. This SPEX is a high-performance interconnection (bus extension) that has a packet passing rate of 160 Mbps. From Figure 1-7, you can see that the SPEX cannot support online operational servicing (or hot-swapping). The SPEX connections are made from one ASN to another with terminator plugs in the end routers. This does not provide an alternate path. Removal or failure of one router in the stack will require the whole stack to be powered off.

Enter the SPEX-HS, as shown in Figure 1-8.

This net module, while still providing a high-performance interconnection between stacked routers, accommodates online operational services. The high-density D-connector cable enables the shutting down of an ASN in the stack without disrupting the other routers, and only the interfaces installed on the disconnected router are affected. Packets will continue to be

Figure 1-7
Stacked ASNs with
a SPEX cable

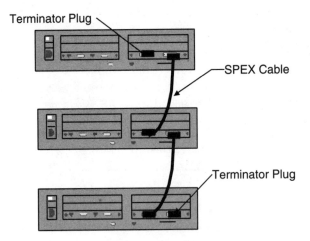

Terminator Plug

SPEX Cable

Terminator Plug

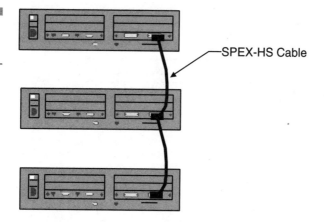

Figure 1-8
Stacked ASNs with
a SPEX-HS cable

—SPEX-HS Cable

routed across the link between SPEX-HS interfaces. Once servicing has been completed, the disabled router needs only to be plugged back into the connector cable and powered on. After the ASN performs its self-diagnosis, it joins the stack and resumes sending packets. The SPEX-HS is even faster than its predecessor operating at 256 Mbps.

Four BayRS software options are available for the ASN router: System, LAN, WAN, and Corporate. The full range of dial services, bridging options, traffic and node managing capabilities, and availability features are present in each of the four software bundles. *Native Mode LAN* (NML), however, is not available in the System and WAN software suites. The Corporate and WAN suites support all wide area protocols, while the LAN and System suite exclude Frame Relay, SMDS, and X.25. The ATM *Data Exchange Interface* (DXI) is also excluded from the System suite. Table 1-2 shows the supported LAN protocols and IBM integration features in each of the software suites.

BayRS software architecture distributes forwarding, filtering, and management functions across each unit in a stack configuration. Each network interface is directly attached to an ASN processor board that uses its own routing/bridging code, forwarding or filtering tables, and network management code to process packets coming into the interface. All updates to the routing and management tables are automatically included in the processor module's tables when they are received and then the information is passed along to the other processors modules within the stack. One caveat to be aware of is that certain computation and memory-intensive routing update protocols, such as *Open Shortest Path First* (OSPF), are activated on

Table 1-2

Comparison of
BayRS for ASN
and BN routers

Feature	System	LAN	WAN	Corporate Suite
BayRS Options				
Network Protocols				
IP with RIP, OSPF, and BGP		✓	✓	✓
Novel IPX		✓		✓
AppleTalk Phase 2		✓		✓
DECnet Phase IV		✓		✓
Banyan Vines		✓		✓
OSI		✓		✓
Xerox XNS		✓		✓
ST-II	✓	✓	✓	✓
IBM Integration				
Source Route Bridging	✓	✓	✓	✓
LAN Manager Agent		✓		✓
DLSw for Ethernet and Token Ring	✓	✓	✓	
DLSw for SDLC		✓		✓
Transparent Sync Pass-Through	✓	✓	✓	✓
BSC Pass-Through	✓	✓	✓	✓
APPN				✓
Bridging				
Transparent Bridge (Ethernet and FDDI)	✓	✓	✓	✓
Translation Bridge (Ethernet/ Token Ring/FDDI)	✓	✓	✓	✓
NML		✓		✓
WAN				
HDLC Encapsulation	✓	✓	✓	✓
PPP	✓	✓	✓	✓

Feature	System	LAN	WAN	Corporate Suite
BayRS Options				
WAN				
Frame Relay			✓	✓
ISDN BRI	✓	✓	✓	✓
ISDN PRI	✓	✓	✓	✓
SMDS			✓	✓
X.25			✓	✓
ATM DXI		✓	✓	✓
Dial Services				
Dial Backup	✓	✓	✓	✓
Bandwidth-on-Demand	✓	✓	✓	✓
Dial-on-Demand	✓	✓	✓	✓
Traffic Management				
Data Compression	✓	✓	✓	✓
PPP	✓	✓	✓	✓
X.25/Frame Relay			✓	✓
Traffic Prioritization	✓	✓	✓	✓
Uniform Traffic Filters	✓	✓	✓	✓
Multiline Circuits	✓	✓	✓	✓

only one ASN processor module within a stack, freeing the other ASNs from the processor-intensive, link-state activities.

Hardware Fault Isolation, Software Fault Isolation and Recovery, and Partial Boot are part of the ASN's fault management capabilities. A malfunctioning component or software process can be isolated from the other components or processes without disrupting the system. Any failed software process will automatically restart and if it fails to recover, it is terminated. Fault conditions on an individual processor board, flash card, or power supply will generate SNMP traps that can be sent to a network management station. A Partial Boot happens when the router determines during power-up diagnostics that a component has failed or is faulty. The ASN then bypasses the faulty component and continues its boot sequence. In case of an internal power supply failure, an external power source can be plugged into the ASN to provide redundant power.

Backbone Node (BN)

The BLN and the BCN routers each utilize an SMP architecture based on three main elements: the link modules, processor modules, and a processor interconnect. The router is split down the middle by a one-Gbps backplane called the *Parallel Packet Express* (PPX).

Link Modules   The link module is the physical network interface for connecting the BN to a variety of LAN/WAN networks. The BN routers support the following LAN interfaces:

- Gigabit Ethernet
- 10/100 Base-T
- 100Base-T
- Token Ring
- FDDI
- ATM

and the following WAN interfaces

- RS 232/422/449
- V.35
- X.21
- *High-Speed Serial Interface (HSSI)*
- ISDN PRI

Each link module connects directly to a processor module, such as a *Fast Routing Engine* (FRE) or an ARE, via the processor interconnect to form an ILI. A BLN enables up to 4 ILIs for a total of 16 LAN interfaces or 32 WAN interfaces. A BCN can have up to 13 ILIs for a total of 52 LAN interfaces (13 FDDI or ATM) or 104 WAN interfaces.

A special link module called the *System Resource Module - L* (SRM-L) is required for both the BLN and the BCN. It provides arbitration control for half of the PPX for 512 Mbps of bandwidth. The SRM-L also provides access to the TI through its console connector. In BLN routers, the SRM-L is located on the link module side of the PPX in slot 1. It is also located on the link module side of the PPX for BCN routers, but in slot 7. The SRM-L's companion is the *SRM-F*, which resides opposite the SRM-L on the processor side of the PPX or FRE side. The SRM-F controls the other half of the PPX and it is optional. With both resource modules in a BN router, full access to the one-Gbps backplane is achieved.

Processor Modules (FRE2 or ARE)   The BN platform does not utilize a central or master *Central Processing Unit* (CPU) for routing decisions. Each processor module performs the system's forwarding operations for all the protocols. The first generation of the FRE contains a Motorola MC68040 33-MHZ microprocessor with a four-Kb on-chip instruction and data cache located on an attached daughterboard. It has a module called the *Parallel Packet Express Interface* (PPXI) that provides the connectivity to the PPX. The second-generation FRE module, the FRE2-040, has the same microprocessor, but it is integrated on the processor motherboard. It also has *Single Inline Memory Module* (SIMM) slots for easy memory upgrades (up to 64 MB). The FRE and the FRE2-040 are completely compatible and can coexist in a BN router.

The next FRE that came along was the FRE2-060. This engine is based on the Motorola MC68060 60-MHz microprocessor with onboard, four-KB instruction and four-KB data caches. As with the FRE and FRE2-040, it has a high-speed packet buffer cache to optimize packet transfers. The FRE2-060 is used when high density and high bandwidth are needed, such as with ATM and multichannel T1 ILIs. These engines are fully compatible with the older FRE and FRE2-040 modules, and they can coexist in the same router.

The ARE is a high-performance processor board that performs the segmentation and reassembly functions for ATM cells. It works with the single-port SONET/SDH multimode and single-mode fiber ARE link modules that provide direct connectivity to ATM networks. Memory configurations for the ARE are 8, 16, or 32 MB of DRAM and up to 6 MB of SRAM for *virtual buffer memory* (VBM). The VBM is a memory management mechanism that enables a BN to process up to 2,000 simultaneous, active virtual circuits for cell/packet buffering.

The newest FRE on the market is the FRE4-PPC. This engine is powered by a Power PC chip and can forward packets at rates up to 400,000 64-byte pps. It is available in 32 MB, 64 MB, or 128 MB of DRAM.

These processor modules, along with the link modules, connect to the backplane (PPX) of the router to provide the intelligent link interface. The backplane effectively splits the router into two sides: a processor side and a link side. Obviously, the processor modules are inserted into the processor side, while the link modules are inserted into the link side of the router. In order to form the ILI, each module must complement each other in that a processor module in slot 1 connects with a link module also in slot 1. Figure 1-9 is a representation of the connection. How these modules communicate is described in the following section.

Parallel Packet Express (PPX)　The PPX is a fast processor-to-processor transport. It is comprised of four redundant paths (rails), each with eight

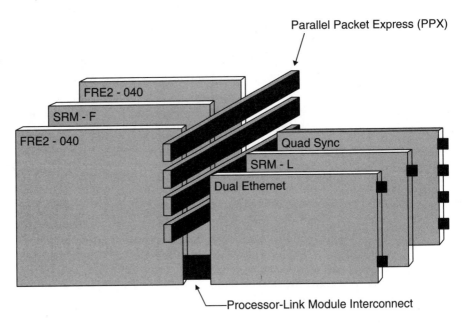

Figure 1-9
A schematic of an ILI

Note: Each resource module controls 2 rails of the PPX.
　　　SRM - F controls rails 1 & 4
　　　SRM - L controls rails 2 & 3

data lines. Each rail operates in parallel up to 256 Mbps. This configuration creates a peer relationship between all processors on the PPX. Each FRE and/or ARE can access all four paths of the PPX simultaneously. Balancing across the four rails is performed by a random path algorithm that assists in redistributing the load if a single PPX path fails. Arbitration control comes from the System Resource Module(s).

A Brief Note on Memory The internal memory of a Nortel Networks router is classified as being one of three types: global, local, or *nonvolatile memory* (NVRAM). These three types of memory are physically located on RAM chips on the processor module. For AN, ANH, ARN, and ASN routers, only one processor board exists, the BLN and BCN both accept multiple FRE2 processor modules. The global and local memory types are partitions of a single, contiguous memory address space. The size of each partition can be increased or decreased, but since they do share a single address space, increasing one automatically decreases the other. The router software plays the mediator in that it insures that the memory space is always equal to the total amount of available memory. Both memory partitions have their own specific responsibilities, as described here:

- *Global memory* This memory partition is set aside to handle buffers. All incoming and outgoing traffic is copied to these buffers.
- *Local memory* This partition of memory is responsible for storing the router software image and the routing and forwarding tables. The amount of local memory determines the maximum number of entries in the forwarding or routing table.

The third memory type stores the above partition configuration. The nonvolatile memory also exists on each processor module and it makes sure that no matter which slot the processor module is plugged into, it will retain the global and local partition configuration.

WARNING: *There should be no need to modify the default settings for the global and local memory partitions. Only change these values under the direction of a Nortel Networks Technical Service Center representative.*

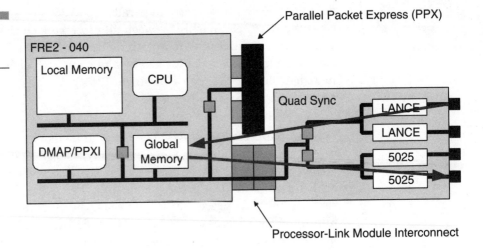

Figure 1-10
A port-to-port
data flow

The following two sections describe the flow of data into and out of a port on a link module as well as the flow as the data crosses the PPX to another link module in another slot. Figures 1-10 and 1-11 depict this process visually.

Port-to-Port Data Flow   The steps of such a data flow are as follows:

1. Data enters the interface port on a link module. The link module's firmware buffers the packet and moves it into the global memory pool on the associated FRE2 module through the processor interconnection.

2. The main CPU on the FRE2 inspects the packet for the type of routing protocol. If the protocol is not loaded in the local memory pool of the module, the CPU sends the packet to the bridging software. If no bridging software is loaded, then the packet will be dropped.

3. Assuming that the packet is routable, the CPU will compare the address information found in the packet with the address tables located in local memory.

4. The CPU will modify the packet so that it can be transferred back onto the link module to the correct port.

5. The CPU then instructs the link module's firmware to move the packet from the global memory pool to its appropriate port.

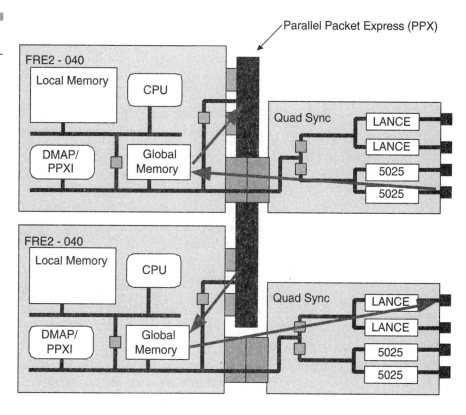

Figure 1-11

Slot-to-slot data flow

Processor-to-Processor Data Flow The data flow here consists of the following steps:

1. Data enters the interface port on a link module. The link module's firmware buffers the packet and moves it into the global memory pool on the associated FRE2 module through the processor interconnect.

2. The main CPU on the FRE2 inspects the packet for the type of routing protocol. If the protocol is not loaded in the local memory pool of the module, the CPU sends the packet to the bridging software. If no bridging software is loaded, then the packet is dropped.

3. Assuming that the packet is routable, the CPU will compare the address information found in the packet with the address tables located in local memory.

4. The CPU will modify the packet so that it can be transferred to the correct port on a link module in another slot.

5. The PPXI is then instructed by the CPU to move the packet from the global memory pool on this slot to the global memory pool on the other slot.

6. The PPXI arbitrates for the PPX and the packet is transferred (any arbitration control is done through the system resource module).

As with the other router families, the BN routers use the BayRS software to maximize LAN/WAN connectivity in a multivendor, multiprotocol environment. BayRS distributes forwarding, filtering, and management functions to multiple peer processor modules. The operating system can isolate faulting processes, thereby protecting other protocols on the same slot or other slots from being disrupted. The operating system will try to restart the failed process. If it does not restart, then it will be terminated. The BN can be partial booted when the software bypasses invalid or incorrectly configured hardware to continue the boot sequence. Other software features are online dynamic reconfiguration, nondisruptive online operational servicing (hot-swap), policy management, and differentiated services. With version 13.x of the BayRS, an embedded Web server can be implemented to extend the management and troubleshooting capabilities of the SNMP-based and command-line tools to Web browsers such as Internet Explorer and Netscape.

The Boot Image

The boot image or software image is the executable file that controls the different routers. Each type of router has a specific software image. Table 1-3 displays the router software image types.

These files are comprised of multiple executable files that contain the operating system and protocols for the router. Most executables have an *.exe* extension except for ARE router slots that denote the protocol files with a *.ppc*. For example, the IP protocol *ip.exe* is *ip.ppc* on an ARE slot. Using a Site Manager tool called Image Builder, you can customize the router's image file by adding or taking away protocols and services.

Table 1-3

Router Image files

Router	Software Image
AN and ANH	an.exe
ARN	arn.exe
ASN	asn.exe
BLN and BCN	bn.exe

The Boot Media

The software image, configuration files, and scripts are loaded on PCMCIA flash memory cards. These flash cards provide a nonvolatile medium for storage. The AN, ANH, ARN, and ASN routers support a 4-MB or an 8-MB flash card. These cards are inserted into the front of the AN and ANH routers and into the back of the ARN and ASN routers. The BN routers support 4-MB, 8-MB, 16-MB, and/or 32-MB flash cards. These flash cards fit into a slot on the FRE2 or ARE processor modules. Different sized flash cards can be used in the same BN router without conflict.

NOTE: *The use of multiple flash cards in an ASN or BN router is recommended for redundancy. If one flash card fails, the other one can be used to reboot the router.*

WARNING: *Since each processor module (or ASN router in a stack) loads a copy of the software image and configuration, make sure that the images and configurations on the different cards are of the same version and configuration level. Serious problems can arise if different versions of the software image and configuration file are loaded onto different processor modules in the same router.*

Files on the Boot Media

The basic set of files that reside on a router flash card is shown in Table 1-4.

The Boot Process

When power is supplied to a router, it follows a specific routine to load its image and configuration file. The router can retrieve its image and configuration file either locally from a flash card or from the network. It may also be desirable to have the router retrieve its startup files from a combination

Table 1-4

The basic router flash card files

File Name	Description
Common Files	
an.exe	Bootable image for the AN and ANH routers
asn.exe	Bootable image for the ASN router
bn.exe	Bootable image for the BLN and BCN routers
config	Default configuration file
ti.cfg	Configuration file that has the default TI console parameters
debug.al	Command alias* file
install.bat	Quick-start script for configuring an initial IP interface
Specific	
asndiag.exe	Copy of the diagnostic image for the ASN
bcc.help	Help file for the *Bay Command Console* (BCC)
frediag.exe	A copy of the diagnostic image resident on the *Programmable Read-Only Memory* (PROM) of the BCN and BLN
freboot.exe	A copy of the bootstrap image resident on the bootstrap PROM for the BCN and BLN routers

*An alias is a command that is created to shorten long or multiple TI interface commands.

of both local and network paths. Nortel defines the following four boot options for the AN family of routers:

- EZ-Install
- Netboot
- Directed Netboot
- Local boot

Each router in the family is configured to boot with EZ-Install as the default option. This enables the router to load its software image from its local flash card and then pull its configuration file from the network. Obviously, a network interface must be connected to the router, either synchronous, Ethernet, or Token Ring. The routers get their configuration by means of the BootP protocol, and a BootP server must be set up to receive and reply to requests from your router.

Netboot and Directed Netboot, similar to the EZ-Install process, provide the router's software image and configuration file from the network and from the local flash. Both boot options require that you connect a terminal or modem to the console port of the router. The console connection enables you to configure the IP interface that is to be used for both Netboot processes. Netboot can be configured to pull the image and configuration file from a local flash and/or a network BootP server when one file must come from the network. Directed Netboot also requires that one file come from the network, but it differs from Netboot by retrieving the file from a TFTP server.

Local boot, as its name implies, retrieves software and configuration information from a local flash card. A console connection is required to perform this boot option. The router, upon power on, looks to the local file system for its software image and its configuration file. Using the TI, you can quick-start the router using the installation script. Quick-starting the router will be covered in detail in Chapter 2, "Configure Nortel Networks Routers."

NOTE: *BN routers only support Local boot.*

Configuring Network Booting

To use any of the network boot options, you must first set up the router to participate in the process. Since the AN family of routers is the only one that can utilize the Netboot features, we will discuss each boot process as it pertains to the ASN router knowing that the AN, ANH, and ARN follow the same procedure.

EZ-Install This option is programmed into the ASN by default. The process involves the ASN loading its software image file from its local flash memory card. Then it looks to the network to get its configuration information. EZ-Install will only work if a synchronous connection exists between itself and an upstream router. The process involves the following steps:

1. Create an offline configuration for the ASN. In the next chapter, we will go into detail about creating and modifying router configurations.

2. Set up the BootP server. Unfortunately, Nortel does not provide a BootP server with its Site Manager tools. For that reason, the configuration and setup of a BootP server is not covered in this section. Suffice it to say that the configuration file created in Step 1 must reside on the server.

3. Enable BootP and set up the BootP relay interface table on the upstream router. The BootP relay interface table instructs the router as to the interface the BootP requests should be forwarded to. Since the router has no provision for transferring a configuration file, it must know where a BootP server is located in order for it to forward the request. See Chapter 3 for instructions on how to enable BootP on an interface as well as how to create a BootP relay interface table.

4. Install and boot the ASN. The router will load its local image, retrieve its transitory IP address from the upstream router, and then retrieve its customized configuration file via the BootP server.

A question should have come to mind when you read Step 4. How does the router retrieve its transitory IP address from the upstream router? Well, it depends upon the protocol configuration of the synchronous interface, either Wellfleet Standard or Frame Relay. Each protocol requires a different method for the upstream router to calculate an IP address.

Figure 1-12
EZ-Install IP address retrieval

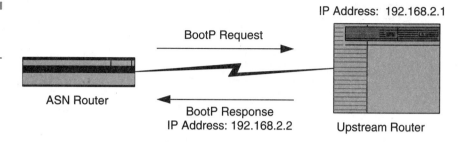

Wellfleet Standard   The upstream router will add 1 to the last octet of its IP address as the address for the requesting router. If this address is the broadcast address, then it will subtract 1. See Figure 1-12 for an example.

Frame Relay   If your Frame Relay is configured for Group Access mode, then in order for the upstream router to calculate the IP address, it must first reference its BootP client interface table. This table must be manually configured with an IP address and a *Data Link Connection Identifier* (DLCI). When the router receives a BootP request, it sends the appropriate IP address found in the BootP client interface table. Figure 1-13 shows an example of this process.

Netboot and Directed Netboot   Both the Netboot and Directed Netboot involve pulling either the image file, the configuration file, or both from the network. Unlike EZ-Install, these boot options enable you to retrieve your file via an Ethernet interface as well as a synchronous interface. The caveat is that you must first tell the router the address where the BootP or TFTP server resides. So, in order to use either Netboot or Directed Netboot, you must first connect to the router's console port and establish a TI session. The following steps summarize the Netboot and Directed Netboot configuration process. (Steps 1 through 3 are identical to the EZ-Install setup):

1. Create an offline configuration for the ASN. In the next chapter, we will go into detail about creating and modifying router configurations.

2. Set up the BootP server. Unfortunately, Nortel does not provide a BootP server with its Site Manager tools. For that reason, the configuration and setup of a BootP server is not covered in this section. Suffice it to say that the configuration file created in Step 1 must reside on the server.

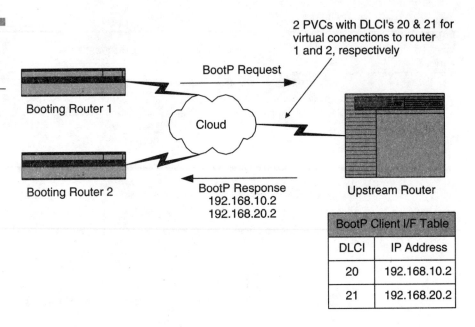

Figure 1-13
EZ-Install IP address retrieval over Frame Relay

3. Enable BootP and set up the BootP relay interface table on the upstream router. The BootP relay interface table instructs the router as to the interface where BootP requests should be forwarded to. Since the router has no provision for transferring a configuration file, it must know where a BootP server resides in order for it to forward the request. Refer to Chapter 3 for instructions on how to enable BootP on an interface as well as how to create a BootP relay interface table.

4. Establish a TI session with the router. You can either connect directly to the router or dial into a modem connected to the router. The purpose of this connection is to configure the BootP or TFTP server's address.

5. Use the `bconfig` or `ifconfig` commands to configure the synchronous or Ethernet interface. These commands will be discussed in more detail at the end of this chapter. They are used to identify the BootP/TFTP server location as well as configure an IP interface.

6. Install the `netboot.exe`, the image, and the configuration file onto the BootP server.

7. Reboot the ASN router.

The main difference between the two Netboot options is that with Directed Netboot you configure a TFTP server on your network and you define the respective parameters on the router to pull both the image and configuration file from that server. To configure the router for Netboot, you must be familiar with both the bconfig and ifconfig commands. An additional command, getcfg, is needed to verify that any configuration changes made are correct. Each command is defined next.

bconfig   This is used to specify the server where the router image and configuration file reside. Here's an example:

```
bconfig -d [image | config] [local | network] [<TFTP host><TFTP
pathname>]
```

bconfig's parameters are as follows:

- -d resets the default values for the software image and configuration file. The default values retrieve the image file locally and the configuration file over the network.
- image specifies information about the router's software image.
- config specifies information about the router's configuration file.
- local specifies that the image or config file should be retrieved off of the local flash memory card.
- network specifies that the image and config file should be retrieved from the network.
- TFTP host specifies the IP address of the TFTP server that has the image and/or configuration file.
- TFTP pathname specifies the location on the TFTP where the image and config files exist.

Table 1-5 provides some bconfig examples.

ifconfig   This configures either a synchronous or Ethernet interface for IP. Its use as a synchronous interface is as follows:

```
ifconfig [-s<slot no.>] [synchronous options] <interface> [<IP
address><Subnet mask>[<next hop address>]]
```

Its use as an Ethernet interface is as follows:

	Command	Description

Table 1-5
 	
`bconfig`
`examples`
	`bconfig image network,`
	`bconfig config network`
		Sets both the image and configuration file to be retrieved from the network

	`bconfig config network`
	`192.168.10.220 /usr/`
	`asn/config`
		Tells the router to retrieve the config file located in the /usr/asn directory on the TFTP server at 192.168.10.220

```
ifconfig [-s<slot no.>] [-d] <interface> [<IP address><Subnet mask>]
```

Here's another example of its usage:

```
ifconfig [-s<slot no.>] -disable <interface>
ifconfig [-s<slot no.>] -enable <interface>
```

The `ifconfig` parameters are outlined here:

■ `-s<slot no.>` This refers to the ASN slot ID containing the interface you want to configure. The valid values are 1 through 4.

■ `<interface>` This is the IP connector you are configuring. Use the following for each specific connector type:

```
Synchronous - com<network module no.><port no.>
Ethernet - xcvr<network module no.><port no.>
```

■ `<IP address>` This is the dotted decimal IP address for the above interface.

■ `<Subnet mask>` This is the subnet mask to use for the above IP address.

■ `<next hop address>` This parameter is used to specify a next-hop router when routers exist between the router and the BootP server.

■ `disable/enable` This enables or disables an interface for the Netboot process.

The synchronous options are as follows and are outlined in the following list:

```
[-d | -fr[-annexd | -lmi | -annexa] | -int_clk]
```

■ `-d` resets the router to its default IP setting.

■ -fr configures the sync port for the defined interface for Frame Relay. You must also specify one of three DLCMI protocols: annexa, lmi, and annexd. Annexd is the default.

■ -int_clk changes the default external clocking to internal at 1.25 Mbps.

Table 1-6 provides some ifconfig examples.

Through the TI commands bconfig and ifconfig, you can set up your router to participate in the Netboot process. To view the current configuration of you router, you can issue the getcfg command. If no interface has been configured, the output from this command shows none.

The AN, ANH, and ARN Boot Process

After powering up the router, the boot process is as follows:

1. The router runs its internal diagnostics to verify hardware integrity.

2. It then requests an IP address from an upstream router via BootP across a synchronous line. It sends the BootP request out all of its COM ports, trying COM1 and then COM2. It will attempt the following line protocols in order:

   ▪ Wellfleet Standard (point-to-point)

   ▪ Frame Relay Annex D

   ▪ Frame Relay LMI

   ▪ Frame Relay Annex A

Table 1-6	**Command**	**Description**
ifconfig examples	ifconfig -d	Resets to the default values
	ifconfig xcvr11 192.168.2.200 255.255.255.0	Configures the first Ethernet port on net module 1 with the IP address 192.168.2.200
	ifconfig -s1 -disable -com22	Disables the second com port on net module 2 in slot 1

3. Once an address is obtained, the router transmits a BootP request for its configuration file across the same sync line it received the IP address on.

4. The router retrieves its configuration file from the server using TFTP.

5. The router then looks to the local file system for its bootable image.

BN and ASN Boot Process

After powering up the router, the boot process here is as follows:

1. Each processor module (FRE, ARE, or ASN) loads its diagnostic and bootstrap programs from onboard EPROM. The diagnostic program on one processor module is run independently from any other processor module in the BN. These programs verify memory, communication paths, and communication with its associated link module.

2. Each FRE/ARE/ASN broadcasts several boot requests across the BN or ASN backbone. If, after five requests, the processor module does not receive a response, it looks locally for the boot image on an inserted flash card.

3. One processor module must have a flash card inserted to load the boot image and config file. This module becomes the boot server for all other modules requesting a boot image. If a processor module does not have a flash card to boot from, it seeks its boot image from the boot server. It does not look locally again until the router is booted again.

4. Once the boot image is loaded on the processor module, it transmits a configuration request across the backplane. Again, if no response is returned, the processor module looks to its local flash for a configuration file.

SUMMARY

Nortel routers fall into one of two router families: *Access Node* (AN) or *Backbone Node* (BN). The *Access Node* (AN), *Access Node Hub* (ANH), *Advanced Remote Node* (ARN), and the *Access Stack Node* (ASN) comprise the AN router family (as if that wasn't a given). Only two routers comprise the BN router family: the *Backbone Link Node* (BLN) and the *Backbone Concentrator Node* (BCN) routers. The AN routers, except for the ASN, are designed to deliver high-forwarding rates to small, remote offices while allowing interoperability with the larger, enterprise class of routers. The BN routers are ideal for enterprise deployment and contain multiple slots that can be populated with several processor modules to provide high performance and availability.

Each router utilizes a PCMCIA flash memory card to store its software image and configuration file. The router image contains the operating kernel as well as any protocol that is configured (or to be configured) on the router. The kernel, upon initialization, reads the configuration file into system memory in order to set up the router's interfaces and services. The system memory is divided into two memory spaces: the global and local memory spaces. It is in the global space where the buffers for all incoming and outgoing packets are stored. The local space contains the image and configuration, as well as the routing and forwarding tables. This memory space gets populated as the router boots and learns about the network.

The way these routers are defaulted to boot is by loading their software image from the local flash card and then pulling their configuration from the network. This process is called EZ-Install and it can be changed to use the network booting services, such as Netboot or Directed Netboot. The last way to boot the routers, and the only way to boot a BN router, is to load both the image and configuration file from the local flash card. This process is called a local boot.

Configuring Nortel Networks Routers

After completing the brief but informative tour through Nortel Network's router families in Chapter 1, it is time to get dirty and start configuring these devices. But (and there is always a but), before we can jump right into configuring the router, we must spend a little time discussing the various concepts that will be employed. Since routers are network devices we need to discuss the concept of a network—topology types, how they work, and the communication process that underlies them all. This book focuses mainly on the communication protocol standard TCP/IP and as we progress through this chapter, we will point out its finer details, namely addressing and communication methods. And as no network discussion can be complete without introducing the OSI reference model, it too will be presented, discussed, and compared to the TCP/IP model. Finally, we will step through the process of configuring a BLN-2 router—adding IP interfaces and global services. Protocols and services are configured on a router using the graphical router configuration program, Site Manager and its assorted tools.

Network Concepts

Networks are as common today as the telephone. In fact, the telephone system is a great example of a network. In basic terms, a network just ties things together. The things that are connected are arbitrary in that they can be anything, such as computers, printers, phones, microwaves, home entertainment systems, and video cameras. The main stipulation is that the devices must be able to communicate with each other. So, even though home appliances might be able to connect to a home network, if the devices do not share a common communication protocol (rule) then the network serves no purpose. In order to maintain the consonant premise of this book we will stick with networks as they relate to the computer industry.

There are several flavors of networks, but mainly they fall into one of three types—local area, wide area, or metropolitan are networks. *Local area networks* (LANs) connect devices within a short distance (typically within a building or campus). They are used to link computers and peripheral devices, such as printers, CDROMS, and modems under some form of standard control. Connected devices can be arranged geometrically in the form of a star, ring, or a bus. Each topological arrangement has their advantages and disadvantages but the most common configuration is that of a star. Regardless of the network topology, a LAN must satisfy three main points.

1. Anyone on the LAN can use any peripheral on the LAN.

2. Anyone on the LAN can access any client service (provided by servers) on the LAN.

3. Anyone on the LAN can message to or work jointly with others on the LAN.

As a network grows and moves away from the locality of a building or campus LAN, the need to communicate never diminishes. A *wide area network* (WAN), is employed to maintain the connections to LANs that have spread out and exist in different parts of a state or country. WANs operate over common carrier lines provided by the local exchange carrier (telephone company). The bandwidth of a WAN is much less than that which can be achieved in a LAN. LANs can accommodate rates from 10Mbps up to 1Gbps (Gigabit per second, that's one billion bits per second), while the most common WAN speeds are around 1.54Mbps. (Now, with the various Optical Carrier services, WANs can obtain truly impressive rates. But, the costs to implement such bandwidth far, far out weights their use.)

An additional network type that is offered by a local exchange carrier is a *metropolitan area network* (MAN). These are high-speed networks that connect multiple LANs within the same campus or city. They can provide real-time data access of speeds from 100Mbps up to 200Mbps. Basically, these networks are extended LANs and can come with a high price tag. Private MANs and some public MANs provide this service using the ANSI FDDI standard.

On the Wire

LANs share common physical link and data link layer protocol mechanisms with MANs as they place packets on the wire. These protocol mechanisms differ from those designed for use in WANs. Do not fret over the use of the terms physical link or data link layers, they will be described in more detail in the following sections, suffice it to say that the data must pass through several layers of rules on a computer before gaining access to the network. The last two rules before a packet hits the wire are the physical link and data link layers. There are several standards that define the rules at each of these layers. The *Institute of Electrical and Electronic Engineers* (IEEE) has defined the data link protocols that are associated with Ethernet and Token-Ring as well as several others.

Ethernet by far the most common network protocol is based on the IEEE 802.3 standard. It uses a *Carrier Sense Medium Access with Collision Detection* (CSMA/CD) technique for sharing a common channel. How this works is that every device on the Ethernet "listens" to the wire for a chance to speak (carrier sense). When the wire is not busy, the device will transmit (medium access). If another device on the Ethernet decides to transmit at the same time, their transmissions will collide. Both devices will detect the collision and each will stop transmitting for an amount of time (collision detection). After their "backoff time" has been reached, they will again listen to the wire for a chance to transmit. Ethernet is a broadcast protocol in that the transmissions from connected devices are broadcasted on to the wire.

Ethernet has grown from its first inception. It was first standardized at 10Mbps and it has since grown to surpass its 100Mbps mark to reach 1Gbps. It has even crossed physical boundaries; starting on thick, 50-ohm coaxial cable and progressing to the more flexible *unshielded twisted pair* (UTP). Its main responsibilities are to format the data in a frame, provide addressing for the frame, and pass it to the physical layer to be transmitted onto the wire. The Ethernet frame format is an encapsulation method that limits the frame's size to 1518 bytes while maintaining a minimum of 64 bytes (including error checking). Ethernet addressing is based upon a 6-byte, 48-bit address defined by the IEEE. This address is "burned" into the network interface card at the time of manufacture and it uniquely identifies an Ethernet device.

Token-Ring on the other hand, uses a token-passing scheme for network transport. A token is a small packet that transverses the network passing from one device to another. The token can be a plain "token" signifying that any device on the network can use it to transmit data. It can also be a "MAC" token, which can contain status and/or error information. Once a device gets access to the token, it then becomes an LLC token, which contains the protocol headers and user data for transmission. As its name implies, Token-Ring is usually configured in a ring topology. All stations on the ring participate in transmitting the token along by handing it off to its neighbor. The transmit wire pairs of each connected device is directly connected to the receive wire pairs of its downstream neighbor creating the ring. There exists on the ring a master device, called the Active Monitor. One of its main functions is to provide proper timing for synchronization of stations on the ring. It also has the responsibility to start the neighbor notification process called the "ring poll." This notification process allows the ring error monitor to accurately locate the fault domain in the event of an error condition.

Token-Ring LANs have been around for a long time and have been readily embraced by IBM. They can be operated at 4Mbps or 16Mbps. There have been technological advancements to the protocol that have brought the speed up to 100Mbps. But, these advancements came too late. Token-Ring vendors have dropped their product line for the more lucrative Ethernet. IBM has even announced that they will no longer develop Token-Ring solutions. Regardless, there is still a considerable amount of Token-Ring that still exists and for that reason I shall proceed. Token-Ring addressing is also delegated by the IEEE to the network interface card manufacturers. It also consists of a 6-byte, 48-bit address like its Ethernet counterpart. This address is "burned" into the network interface card at the time of manufacture and it uniquely identifies a Token-Ring device. Token-Ring addresses can also be modified by software to adhere to local constraint or standards. This function is also available with Ethernet but it is seldom, if ever, used. This practice was usually reserved for sites that incorporated older mainframe SNA controllers and gateways. The devices would be given distinct addresses in order to qualify themselves. For example, a 3172 would be given a Token-Ring address of 400031720001, which would identify it as the first mainframe gateway.

Whether we are talking about Ethernet or Token-Ring LANs, it is important to note that all connected devices share the media and in so doing "hear" all conversations. The Ethernet protocol provides for a broadcast method of transmission. This means that when a station is able to gain access to the media, it will send a packet to everyone. The only device that it is destined for will respond. All others will process the packet just enough to see if it is destined for them. If not, they drop it. The Token-Ring protocol connects everyone to each other and the token is handed off like a hot potato, in succession. Again, each device will process the packet just enough to see if it is destined for them. If not, the device will drop the packet. The next section will outline the process in more detail, focusing on the Ethernet protocol.

Can We Talk?

The way devices on a LAN talk, whether Ethernet, Token-Ring, or FDDI, is by the "burned" in address on the network interface card. This address is called the hardware, or MAC, address and it uniquely identifies a network device. Alone, this address is not sufficient for utilizing the variety of services that can be offered via a network. It must rely on communication protocols that exist above the data link layer to provide the needed application delivery and error recovery. In the next section we will discuss the TCP/IP protocols that provide these functions as well as the various layers where they reside. But, the important thing to note is that regardless of the protocols that work above the data link layer, ALL COMMUNICATION ON A NETWORK IS VIA THE 6-BYTE, 48-BIT MAC ADDRESS. It is the responsibility of the upper layer protocols to resolve to this address. Logically, the process is like this.

Scenario Two PCs, PC-A and PC-B, are connected to an Ethernet LAN. There exists on this same LAN, a server that is providing some basic service.

1. PC-A makes a call for the basic service.

   The application that is running on the PC has been programmed to send service requests onto the network to a specific application address.

2. The PC broadcasts the request onto the network.

   We are assuming that this is the first time this PC has accessed this application and it doesn't already know the server's address. It broadcast the request in hopes that the server will respond to the request. Since the PC resides on a single Ethernet network (no other device exists on the network that can forward the packet on to other LAN segments) both the PC-B and the server will get a copy of the packet.

3. PC-B processes the packet.

   The PC will look at the destination address in the packet's header to determine if it is destined for it. Since that packet is a broadcast, which is it is meant for all connected devices, the PC must process the packet further. The PC ascertains that the packet is looking for an application address that is does not have and it drops the packet.

4. The server processes the packet.

   Like previous PC-B, the server processes the packet. But, it does have the application address asked for and it responds back to the source address listed in the broadcast packet.

5. PC-A receives the response packet from the server.

The server sends the packet with a destination address of PC-A. Once PC-A receives the packet, it will cache the server's address for future requests. Although the server did not send the response as a broadcast, PC-B will still receive a copy of the packet. Since it is addressed for PC-A, PC-B will drop it.

When explaining network communication in generic forms it can become confusing. But, do not get discouraged. The next section will provide concrete examples using the IP protocol. We will also discuss the different protocol layers in detail. So, when begin to configure the router you will have a more clear understanding of the steps involved.

The TCP/IP Protocol Suite

The TCP/IP protocol suite is a group of protocols that allow computers to communicate in an effective manner regardless of the computer's hardware and software components. TCP/IP is named for two of its more important protocols—*Transmission Control Protocol* (TCP) and *Internet Protocol* (IP). With these two protocols and the several others that comprise the protocol suite, TCP/IP has evolved from its humble beginnings as a U.S. Department of Defense research project into a worldwide network communication foundation. It is not hard to see why TCP/IP has become successful despite originating from a source that seems to pride itself in its orthodoxy. Contrary to the bureaucratic trend of the time, it was designed to be open. In that anyone could use it and develop applications for it independent of specific hardware and operating systems. Not only did TCP/IP meet the need at the time, it also incorporated several important features:

■ *Open Protocol Standard* The protocols were and are freely available to everyone. Developers have complete access to the protocols through *Military Standards* (MIL STD), Engineering Notes and *Requests for Comments* (RFCs). Unlike homogeneous systems where a manufacturer can create rules that accent their specific systems, TCP/ IP allows developers to create applications that are independent of vendor-specific hardware and operating systems.

■ *Network Independence*   TCP/IP can be used with different network protocols and physical media (i.e., Ethernet, Token-Ring, FDDI, Frame Relay, and/or asynchronous dialup lines).

■ *Common Addressing Scheme*   Provisions are made so that any device, in a TCP/IP network, is uniquely addressable and can be accessed locally or across devices that provide routing information.

■ *Standardized High-Level Protocols*   Specific services were standardized to maintain consistency and availability across a wide area.

Today, TCP/IP has significantly outgrown its initial scope of providing basic data communication to geographically separate networks. It has been enhanced and expanded to provide for multimedia, hypertext, and voice. This relatively simple protocol suite has been the cornerstone of the Internet. Since TCP/IP is needed for Internet access, many companies have adopted it as their LAN protocol.

The OSI Reference Model

In data communications, ambiguity is prevalent. Someones use of syntax may not necessarily correspond with another's. To alleviate misconceptions, a common reference frame must be created in order to facilitate understanding. Terminology must coincide. As the stage was being set for a worldwide network, the *International Standards Organization* (ISO), developed a data communications reference model to define protocol functions between cooperating applications when they transfer information across an intervening network—the *Open Systems Interconnect* (OSI) Reference Model.

The OSI Reference Model is a seven-layer model where each layer defines functions to be used by any protocol as seen in Figure 2-1.

It is important to note that any protocol can take advantage of the functions in each layer and that the layer itself is not a protocol. Even multiple protocols can offer services in the same layer. As an example, the *File Transfer Protocol* (FTP) and the *Simple Mail Transport Protocol* (SMTP) both exist in the Application layer and provide user services.

On a computer, these layers form a stack where the upper layers rely on the lower layers to transfer data across the network. Data is passed down the stack, layer by layer, then onto the network where another computer receives the frame into its stack and passes the data up to be interpreted by an upper layer protocol or application. The upper layer protocol or application formulates its reply then sends it down the stack and back onto the

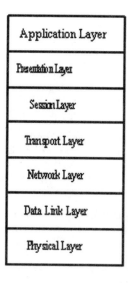

Figure 2-1
OSI reference model

| Application Layer |
| Presentation Layer |
| Session Layer |
| Transport Layer |
| Network Layer |
| Data Link Layer |
| Physical Layer |

network. Each layer protocol communicates with its peer layer protocol on a remote system and need only worry about how to pass the data to the other layers in the stack.

The ISO defined the seven layers of the OSI Reference Model to be the *Physical, Data Link, Network, Transport, Session, Presentation*, and *Application* layers. A brief description of each of these layers functions are provided in Table 2-1

The TCP/IP Model

The TCP/IP model as defined by the Department of Defense comprises only four layers. They are the *Network Access, Internet, Host-to-Host Transport*, and the *Application* layer. These layers do not exactly match the layers of the OSI model. One of the great things about the TCP/IP architecture is that is makes use of already defined lower layer protocols and begins at layer 3—Network Access. Since TCP/IP does not define the Data Link or Physical characteristics of a network it must rely on the predefined standards, such as Ethernet or Token-Ring, for transport.

As with the OSI model, data units are passed down the stack from the Application layer to the Network Access layer. Each layer adds specific control information to the front of the data unit called a header. The control information is added to ensure the proper delivery of the data. Each layer

Layer	Description
Table 2-1 OSI reference model layers descriptions.	
Physical	The Physical layer controls access to the physical media. It defines the characteristics of the hardware needed to carry the signal on to the network. It defines such items as voltage levels and pin assignments. Examples of physical layer protocols are RS232, V.35 as well as standards for local area networking such as IEEE 802.3.
Data Link	The Data Link layer is responsible for the formatting of data into defined fields to be transmitted onto the network (i.e., Ethernet, Token-Ring, etc.). It provides for reliable data delivery by detecting data corruption through checksumming and it handles addressing when multiple systems need to communicate on a LAN.
Network	The job of the Network layer is to ensure communications between any pair of nodes in the network. Of course, connecting every pair of nodes together does not scale very well. So, it is the responsibility of the Network layer to provide a path through the network. This involves route calculation, packet fragmentation and reassembly, and congestion control. The Network layer handles node addressing and data delivery.
Transport	The Transport layer is responsible for establishing a reliable communication stream between to network nodes. Errors induced by the Network layer, such as lost and duplicate packets, and packet reordering, are accounted for by this layer. The Transport layer also has provisions for a more efficient packet fragmentation and reassembly service than that of the Network layer.
Session	Session layer services offer more control over packet delivery than that of the Transport layer. Allowing a specific pattern of data to traverse the communication channel (dialog control) and combining groups of packets (channeling) are some of the Session layer's services.
Presentation	In this layer, cooperating applications agree on the proper representation of the data using standard presentation routines.
Application	User-accessed processes are handled in the Application layer. This is not the layer at which a network application resides, but the link into the protocol stack for the network application. There are some programs that do reside at this layer, as we will see as we describe the TCP/IP model.

treats its upper layer's header plus data unit as a single data unit and appends its control information as a header, Figure 2-2.

This process of adding header information onto a data unit is called encapsulation. As the data unit travels down the protocol stack it is converted to 1's and 0's for transmission onto the network. Once a station

Figure 2-2
Encapsulation
of a packet

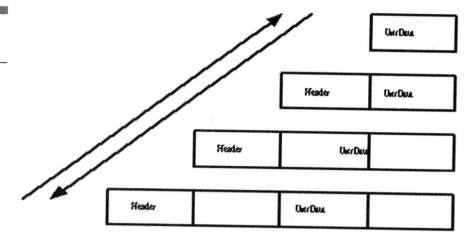

Figure 2-3
Names of data inputs
per layer and
transport

	TCP	UDP
Application Layer	Stream	Message
Host - to - Host Transport	Segments	Packets
Internet	Datagrams	
Network Access Layer	Frames	

receives the information, each layer strips off its specific header information and passes the data unit up the next layer. The process continues up
the stack until it reaches its destination where a response is generated and
the encapsulation process begins again.

These encapsulated data units have different terms depending upon
which layer of the TCP/IP model you are discussing as shown in Figure 2-3.

When applications use TCP to transfer data it is called a *stream*. If the
application uses *User Datagram Protocol* (UDP), the data unit is called a
message. On the Host-to-Host Transport layer, TCP data units are referred
to as *segments* and UDP data units are called *packets*. IP data units are
called *datagrams* and the Network Access layer data units are called
frames. Regardless of the terms used on each layer, they all mean the same

thing—data to be transmitted. Let's take a closer look at the functions of each layer in the TCP/IP model.

Network Access The lowest layer in the TCP/IP model, the Network Access layer is responsible for delivering the data from systems directly attached to the network. A function performed at this layer is the encapsulation of IP datagrams into frames. It is important that Network Access layer protocols know about the underlying network to ensure proper formatting of each frame, whether the underlying network be Ethernet, Token-Ring, or *Fiber Distributed Data Interface* (FDDI). Since all networks talk via the physical address burned into the network interface card at manufacture (granted this address can be changed), mapping to an IP address must be performed. The *Address Resolution Protocol* (ARP) as defined in RFC 826 provides a means for the physical address to be converted to an IP address. The conversions are stored in a table called an ARP Cache.

Internet Layer As we saw in Figure 2-2, the Internet layer resides directly above the Network Access layer. One of the most important protocols in the TPC/IP protocol suite functions on this layer—the *Internet Protocol* (IP). It is the core of the suite. Some of its functions include datagram addressing, routing the datagrams between remote hosts, fragmenting and reassembly of the datagrams, and moving the datagrams between the Network Access and the Transport layers.

Each datagram is defined with a 32-bit address that is unique across the Internet. IP check the destination address in the datagram to provide delivery on the network. If the host's address is not on the local network, IP provides routing of the datagram through intermediary devices called gateways or routers. Most network protocols have predefined *maximum transmission unit* (MTU) sizes that may be smaller than the originating network. In order for a large transmission unit to pass through a router it must be reduced in size to match the MTU of the receiving network. IP provides fragmentation and reassembly of a datagram to transverse varying MTU sizes. Once the datagram makes it to its destination, IP must know what protocol it must pass the data to in the Transport layer. Each Transport layer protocol has a unique number that IP needs to know in order to pass the data appropriately.

It surprises people to know that the IP protocol is actually an unreliable protocol. When I say unreliable I mean that it does not provide error detection or correction. It will accurately deliver the datagram to the network but it must rely on the upper layer protocols to handle the error recovery. IP, in and of itself, does not have a provision for sending messages that provide the needed flow control, error reporting and other informational functions. As an example, through the upper layer *Internet Control Message Protocol* (ICMP), IP can send source quench messages to ebb the sending of datagrams, detect unreachable networks and ports, and check the availability of remote hosts through a host echo or ping. One other aspect of the IP protocol is that it is connectionless. It does not provide control information for session establishment again relying on the upper layer protocols.

Transport Layer The most important protocols of the Transport layer are *Transmission Control Protocol* (TCP) and *User Datagram Protocol* (UDP). Each protocol providing delivery service from the Application layer to the Internet layer. UDP provides a low overhead, connectionless delivery service while TCP is more reliable, providing for end-to-end error detection and correction.

UDP gives applications a direct connection into the datagram delivery service. It is connectionless and unreliable. Remember that the protocol is unreliable in the sense that it does not have provision for error recovery. It is an efficient protocol when amount of data being transmitted is small. Establishing a session and breaking it down can cause more overhead than just retransmitting the message again. UDP also fits well with database applications that are "query and response." The response can be used as an acknowledgement of receipt.

TCP, on the other hand, is a connection-oriented protocol that verifies the data in each segment that is delivered. A segment is transmitted from a sending host to a receiving host. The receiving host verifies the segment's checksum and sends a "positive acknowledgement" if the segment is undamaged. Otherwise the segment is dropped and the sender retransmits the segment. This process is called *Positive-Acknowledgment with Retransmission* (PAR). TCP views the data as a continuous stream instead of as individual messages. Because of this TCP keeps track of sequence numbers in the protocol header, see Figure 2-4.

Figure 2-4
TCP communication,
3-way handshake

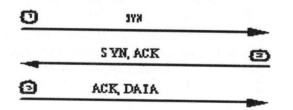

Host A

SYN

SYN, ACK

ACK, DATA

Host B

The Communication Process (The 3-Way handshake)

1. Host A sends a TCP segment to Host B with its *Synchronize sequence number* (SYN) bit set. This informs Host B that Host A wishes to establish a session and the sequence number with which Host A is going to start.

2. Host B sends a segment to Host A with its *Acknowledgement* (ACK) and SYN bits set. Host A interprets the segment as a positive acknowledgement of its session request to Host B with Host B's starting sequence number.

3. Host A sends a segment with the ACK bit set and with the beginning of the data to be sent. Communication between Host A and Host B continues with Host B acknowledging the segments from Host A.

When Host A is finished transmitting data, it will initiate another 3-way handshake where a "No data from sender" (FIN) bit is set.

Application Layer   At the top of the TCP/IP protocol stack sits the Application layer. Included in this layer are all the processes that use the Transport layer for data delivery. There are many Application layer protocols of which several provide user services. Some of the more common are *File Transfer Protocol* (FTP), Simple Mail Transport Protocol (SMTP), and Telnet. (A remote access service where you can take control of a system located miles away as if you were sitting at the keyboard.) New Application protocols have been added since TCP/IP's inception as well as improvements have been made to existing ones. The popularity of the Internet can be attributed to the Application protocol HTTP. The Internet wouldn't even work without a lesser-known protocol called *Domain Name Service* (DNS). DNS provides a mapping service that takes a system name and maps it to an IP address. Figure 2-5 is a diagram of the TCP/IP protocols and their position among the model layers.

Network Addressing

The IP protocol in the TCP/IP suite is responsible for the addressing of each device attached to a network. More specifically, each physical connection to the network must be administered a network or IP address. Network-attached devices or hosts that have more than one connection to the physi-

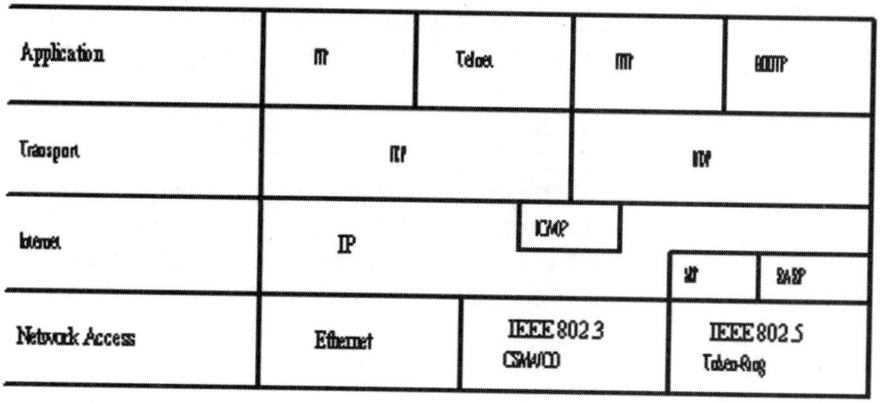

Figure 2-5
Protocol chart
per layer

Application		FTP		Telnet		FTP		BOOTP
Transport			TCP				UDP	
Internet		IP		ICMP		ARP	RARP	
Network Access		Ethernet		IEEE 802.3 CSMA/CD		IEEE 802.5 Token-Ring		

Figure 2-6
IP Address block
diagram

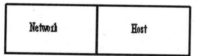

Network	Host

cal medium must have a unique IP addressed assigned for each of its connections. The IP address is a four-byte, 32-bit address consisting of a network ID and a host ID, as shown in Figure 2-6.

The network ID identifies the network segment for a particular host ID, where the host ID identifies an individual host. Routing of a datagram is based on the network ID. The datagram is forwarded through intermediary devices (routers) according to the network portion of its IP address. When the datagram reaches the destination network, the router transmits it to the host via the host ID portion of that address. What defines the separation? How does the host or routing device determine which portion of the IP address is allocated to the network and which portion is allocated to the host? The answer is a *mask*. The host device uses a mask to separate the IP address. We will discuss masking in more detail in the following sections.

The format of the IP address is a dotted-decimal notation. Each byte of the address is written as a decimal separated by decimal points, example: 172.16.2.200. Dotted-decimal notation helps us humans interpret an IP address, unfortunately computers can not benefit from the economy of base 10 numbers. Computers only understand "on or off", "1 or 0", "plus voltage or minus voltage." A base 10 numbering system, like the one we use everyday, must be converted to a binary numbering system, where two distinct states can be represented. In a binary numbering system, the only numbers that can be used are 0 and 1. A host device converts the decimal address to its binary equivalent in order for it to make its classification and forwarding decisions. Table 2-2 shows the binary equivalent of the above address.

Classification   The IP protocol defines five different classes of addresses, classes A, B, C, D, and E, each determined from the most significant bits of the first byte. Referring to Table 2-2, the left most digit in the binary representation of the address is considered the most significant and conversely, the right most digit is considered the least significant. The class distinctions are as follows:

- Class A addresses divide the network ID from the host ID after the 1st byte. A class A address is defined by having the first bit in the first byte set to zero (0). This keeps the range of possible network addresses between 1 and 127. Class A networks have less than 127 network addresses with over 16 million hosts (2^{24}) (see Figure 2-7).

- Class B addresses makes the network division after the 2nd byte. A 1 and a 0 in the first two bit positions in the first byte define the address as class B. The range of network addresses in the first byte is from 128 to 191 and from 1 to 254 in the second byte. This allows for over 16,000 networks with more than 65,000 hosts.

- Class C addresses separates the network portion from the host portion after the 3rd byte. The first three bits of byte one are 1 1 0. The range of network addresses is from 192 to 223 in the first byte and from 1 to 254 in both the second and third byte. There can be more than 2 million networks each with less than 255 hosts.

- Class D addresses are reserved for group or multicast addresses. The first four bit positions are occupied with a 1 1 1 0 sequence. Sending a datagram to a single multicast address in turn sends the datagram to a

Table 2-2

Binary equivalent of a decimal address

Format	Address			
Dotted-decimal	172	16	2	200
Binary	10101100	00010000	00000010	11001000

Figure 2-7
IP Address Class

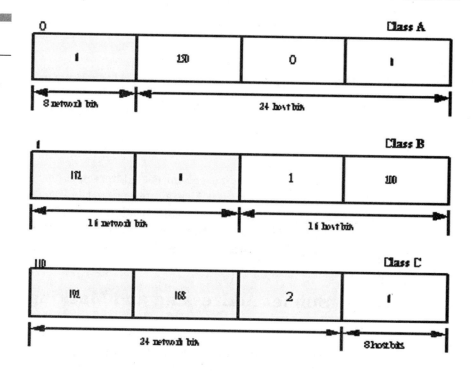

group of member addresses that can span multiple networks. The address range is from 224 to 239.

- Class E networks are labeled experimental and are not fully support in Nortel routers. These networks are numbered from 240 on up.

- Reserved addresses. Each address class has a reserved range that can be used by companies for their private networks. These addresses are not allowed onto the Internet, so Internet routers will not route a datagram with one of the following reserved addresses from Table 2-3.

NOTE: *The class A addresses beginning with 0 and 127 are reserved for special purposes and can not be used. Network 0 is reserved for the default route and network 127 is reserve for the loopback address. The default route is used to simplify the routing information handled by IP. The purpose of the loopback address is to let the local station be addressed like a remote host.*

Class	Address Range
A	10.0.0.0 to 10.255.255.255
B	172.16.0.0 to 172.31.255.255
C	192.168.0.0 to 192.168.255.255

Table 2-3

Reserved IP address ranges

There is two other special-use addresses. A host address of all 0's signifies the network. 10.0.0.0 is a reference to the 10 network. A host address of all 1's (255) signifies a broadcast address. 10.255.255.255 is the broadcast address for the 10 network. All stations on the 10 network will receive IP datagrams addressed to the 10 network's broadcast address.

Subnet Addressing and Masking

The class system of addressing was only the start of the network/host address division, bits from the host portion could be used to further subdivide the address. Partitioning the host portion into a subnet extends the *network.host* address division to the *network.subnet.host* address division. The subnetwork defines a network within a network. This is useful when you have a limited number of addresses available. For example, if you were given one class B network address of 172.16.0.0 you could extend the network portion to include the third octet (an octet is just a collection of 8 things, 8 bits, one byte). Defining the third octet for the subnetwork means that the default mask that divides a class B address must also be extended. Since an IP address and its mask are defined on an interface, routers internal to the network are able to interpret the subnet and host portions of the address. External routers will not be able to differentiate the IP address allowing you to hide the complexity of multiple LANs from the Internet.

A Brief Segue   Before we proceed to discuss subnet masking, I would like to digress a moment and talk about number systems, in particular the binary system. Feel free to skip this section. But, taking a few moments here will help you to fully appreciate the subnet masking process.

The most widely used number system is based on the number ten. I am sure having ten fingers has attributed to the base10 systems popularity. In our base10 system, each position in a number represents a power of ten. For example, the number 172 can be written in such a way as to bring out powers of ten.

$172 = 1 \times 100 + 7 \times 10 + 2 \times 1$	Bringing out the powers of ten
$172 = 1 \times 10^2 + 7 \times 10^1 + 2 \times 10^0$	Any number raised to the zero power equals one

As we can see, starting with the rightmost position in a number and proceeding left, each position is ten raised to a number starting from 0 and increasing by 1 at each position. If we take the multiplicand of the power of 10, we will form the decimal number 172. The same process can be used when using the base2 number system but instead of bringing out the powers of 10 you bring out the powers of two. An exception is that the base10 system has ten digits, 0 through 9, while the base2 system only has 2—0 and 1. For the same number, 172, it's binary or base2 representation is the following:

$172 = 10101100$ which is

$1 \times 128 + 0 \times 64 + 1 \times 32 + 0 \times 16 + 1 \times 8 + 1 \times 4 + 0 \times 2 + 0 \times 1$

Bringing out the powers of two

$1 \times 2^7 + 0 \times 2^6 + 1 \times 2^5 + 0 \times 2^4 + 1 \times 2^3 + 1 \times 2^2 + 0 \times 2^1 + 0 \times 2^0$

If we take the multiplicand of the powers of two, we form the base2 number for 172. The binary system has the same operations as our base10 system —addition, subtraction, multiplication, and division. Although performing the calculations in your head might prove to be a little more difficult that the same functions in the decimal system.

Notice that the same number in base10 only takes three digits while in the base2 system it takes eight. As the numbering system base increases, the number of digits required to represent a number decreases. For example, the same number, 172, in base16 (hexadecimal) is AC. The base16 system can represent the number with only two digits. (The letter A, in hex, is the decimal equivalent of 10. Since the hexadecimal system requires 16 single digits, letters were chosen to represent the numbers above 9.)

$$AC = A \times 16 + C \times 1 \qquad \text{which is} \qquad 10 \times 16^1 + 12 \times 16^0$$
$$160 + 12$$
$$172$$

There are as many number systems as there are numbers, albeit only two seem well suited for data communication. It so happens that the base2 and base16 number systems fit nicely into many aspects of data networking. So, as we close this segue, let us make mental notes to familiarize ourselves with the binary and hexadecimal numbering systems.

Masking

As it was stated before, a mask is used to separate the network portion of an IP address from its host portion. When subnetting is introduced, the mask is extended into the host portion to distinguish the subnetwork. The term subnet mask is defined as a 32-bit number that specifies the network and subnetwork portion of an IP address. The subnet mask is bit-oriented and is constructed by assigning a value of 1 for each position in the IP address that corresponds to the network and subnetwork. A value of 0 is assigned for each host position. Once the bits have been set, the binary number should then be converted to its dotted-decimal equivalent.

Before defining a subnet mask, you should determine the number of subnets and hosts per subnet you will require in the future. The more bits used to define the subnet increases the number of available subnets. But, increasing the number of available subnets decreases the number of available hosts per subnet. Preplanning an IP addressing scheme will allow you to efficiently assign addresses which account for growth, while preventing readdressing which can be a huge task if your enterprise is large.

To get a better understanding of how subnet masking works, let's do an example. In Figure 2-8, the two routers are connected via a point-to-point circuit. Being that the connection will only involve two devices (remember point-to-point), defining a full class B to the interfaces would result in a lot of wasted address space. If we extend the class B mask out to the third octet (a class C mask) we will reduce the number of hosts to 254. This is still a waste of address space. What we need to do is to extend the class C mask to subnetwork the host portion down to allow for only two hosts per subnet. The subnet mask used in the diagram is 255.255.255.252.

Doing the math:

Givens

Network Address:	172.16.0.0
Binary Equivalent:	10101100.00010000.0000000.00000000
Number of hosts:	2

Figuring the subnet mask:

1. Convert the number of hosts to binary

    2 hosts = 10

2. Count the number of bits in the binary conversion from Step 1.

    Starting from the right and proceeding left the number from the count, set each bit position to 0. Set the remaining bits of the mask to 1.

    Since the binary equivalent of 2 only uses 2 bits, starting from the left set the first two bits to 0. The remaining 30 bits in the subnet mask are set to 1.

    Subnet Mask: 11111111.11111111.11111111.11111100

3. Convert the subnet mask into dotted-decimal notation.

    Binary Bit Values

128	64	32	16	8	4	2	1
1	1	1	1	1	1	0	0

If all the bit positions in the previous table are set to 1, the decimal value equals 255 (Add up each value from each column). Since the last octet in the subnet mask only fills the 6 left most positions, add up just the bit values down to 4. This yields a decimal value of 252. So, the subnet mask in dotted-decimal notation is:

Subnet Mask: 255.255.255.252

In a similar vane, if you know the number of subnets you desire, you can figure the subnet mask as follows:

1. Convert the number of subnets needed into its binary equivalent.

   Suppose you needed 6 subnets. Converting the number 6 into binary yields 110.

2. Count the number of bits required to represent the number of subnets in binary.

   Three bits are required to represent the number 6 in binary

3. Place the required number of bits in the high order bit positions of the host address and convert to decimal.

   The network address, as previously given, is 172.16.0.0. The host address portion is 0.0. Placing the 3 bits in the high order of the host address portion gives:

   Binary host space: 00000000.00000000

   High order conversion: 11100000.00000000

4. Convert to dotted-decimal format.

   Dotted-decimal: 224.0

   Combining with the network mask

   Subnet Mask: 255.255.224.0 (for a class B address)

How Masking Works

Each host device filters the host, subnet, and network portions of the IP address by performing a logical AND operation on the binary bits. The logical AND is a comparison on two binary digits. If the digits are both 1, then the result from the comparison is also 1. Any other comparison will result in a 0. For our network in Figure 2.2.1, the IP segment defined between the two routers is 172.16.2.0. The subnet mask separates the host address from the network and subnetwork address as follows:

IP Address:	172.16.2.1
Binary:	10101100.00010000.00000010.00000001
Subnet Mask:	11111111.11111111.11111111.11111100

Starting from the high order bit and moving to the right, we get the following result from the bit comparison:

Network Address:	10101100.00010000.00000010.00000000
Decimal:	172.16.2.0
Host Address:	1 (determined from remaining two bits)

Because, we only needed an address space to accommodate two host devices, we chose as a subnet mask, 255.255.255.252. This gave us a space for four addresses of which we could only use two for devices. If you remember, the base network and broadcast addresses can not be used for end devices. So, in our example the address 172.16.2.0 defined the network and 172.16.2.3 defined the broadcast address. Using this subnet mask also gives us flexibility when defining more wide-area connections on the same routers. The subnet mask allows for 62 distinct subnetworks in the 172.16.2.0 address, each containing four addresses—two for hosts, one for the network, and one for the broadcast.

Configuring the Initial IP Interface

Most of the routers configuration will be done using the graphical tool called Site Manager via remote SNMP commands. In order to use Site Manager, the router's initial IP interface must be configured—a process called quick-starting the router. Quick-starting a router can be done by using a predefined script (install.bat) that steps you through the configuration process or by using a command line tool called the *Bay Command Console*, (BCC). Since the command line tool is more cumbersome than the install script, the following procedure will focus on using the install script. Figure 2-8 is the example network layout for this procedure.

Figure 2-8
Simple network
design

NOTE: *Using the install script dynamically sets the interface parameters so there is no need to reboot the router when the installation is done.*

The following is a summary of the steps that will be performed when you quick-start a router:

1. Connect to router's console port.
2. Connect the router to the network.
3. Establish a *Technicians Interface* (TI) session with the router.
4. Boot the router with the file *ti.cfg*.
5. Run the installation script (*install.bat*).

The information in Table 2-4 will be used in the following steps. It is completed with the information from Figure 2-8. Brief descriptions of each line item follows.

Line Item 1   Specify the slot number where the link module resides.
This refers to the slot that holds the particular link module that you are about to configure. The install script automatically polls your router for installed link modules and their respective processor modules. It presents this information as a list from which you must chose one item.

Line Item 2   Specify the connector, or port, on the previous link module.
This refers to the specific port on the selected link module that will be defined by the IP address. The install script will poll the router for the number of ports, or connectors, on the link module previously chosen. It will present each port, or connector, in a list from which you must choose one item.

Line Item 3   Enter the circuit name.
A topology prefix, slot number, and a port number define the default circuit name. It can be changed to a more descriptive name of your choosing. The default name that the install script displays will be dependent upon

Table 2-4

Quick start
worksheet

Network Information		Your Information
Physical Connector Information		
1	Specify the slot number where the link module resides that will hold the first IP configuration.	1
	Note: For ASN routers, also provide the module number.	1
2	Specify the connector, or port, on the above link module.	Ethernet connector 1 (XCVR1)
Circuit Information		
3	Enter the circuit name.	E11
IP Configuration		
4	Specify the IP Address of the initial interface.	172.16.1.200
5	Specify the subnet mask for this address.	255.255.255.0
6	Does the Site Manager workstation reside on this network?	Yes
IP Routing Information		
7	Specify the IP routing protocol.	
RIP Configuration		
8	Should RIP listen for the default route?	
9	Specify the RIP version.	
Static Route Configuration		
10	Specify the destination network address.	
11	Specify the destination network mask.	
12	Specify the next-hop address.	
Global Services Information		
13	Enable SNMP community management?	Yes
14	Specify IP address of Site Manager workstation	172.16.1.10
15	Specify community name.	[public]
16	Specify the TFTP default volume.	2

continues

Table 2-4

Continued.

Network Information	Your Information
Global Services Information	
17 Enable FTP?	No
18 Specify the default FTP volume.	—
19 Enable Telnet?	Yes
20 Enable HTTP?	Yes

the link module and port selected. The following are several of the topology prefixes and their meanings:

Prefix	Topology
E	Ethernet
O	Token-Ring
F	FDDI
S	Synchronous
A	ATM

The slot number indicates the slot in the router in which the link module is installed. The port number indicates the port on the specific link module.

Line Item 4 Specify the IP address of the initial interface.

This is the IP address that you would like to assign to this particular slot and port number. This address is taken from Figure 2-8. In the figure you will note that the IP network address defines the particular network segment and the interface of the router on this segment is assigned a single byte address. To clarify, Router A has an interface connected to the Ethernet segment with IP address 172.16.1.0 /24. The router's Ethernet interface has been assigned the byte address of ".200." So, its IP address is 172.16. 1.200.

Line Item 5   Specify the subnet mask for this address.

This is the subnet mask associated with the previous address. You will note in Figure 2-8 the IP address of each network segment is specified with a trailing "/" and a number. The number defines the number of bits in the subnet mask, starting from the left-most byte. A 24 signifies a 255.255.255.0 subnet mask.

Line Item 6   Does the Site Manager workstation reside on this network?

This item is added to determine if a routing protocol should be configured. For our purposes we will not configure a routing protocol on this interface. In actuality, if there are no other routers on this network segment then a routing protocol is not necessary—there will be no other devices with which to exchange route information. An answer of "yes" skips the routing protocol configuration line items (7 through 12).

Line Items 7 through 12   IP Routing Information

These line items are left blank because there will not be a routing protocol defined on the router's Ethernet interface. Chapter 3 discusses routing protocols in more detail and focuses mainly on RIP. For that reason the RIP configuration options are included in the above worksheet. The install script does support OSPF configuration information.

Line Item 13   Enable SNMP community management.

SNMP community management is required if you wish to use the Site Manager tools.

Line Item 14   Specify IP address of Site Manager workstation.

This does not have to be entered. If you know the address, then by all means add it here. The install script uses this address to test the IP connection to the workstation at the end of the script.

Line Item 15   Specify community name.

This is the "password" needed to gain access to the router's configuration information from any SNMP manager as in Site Manager. Chapter 6 covers SNMP in more detail.

Line Item 16   Specify the TFTP default volume.

The TFTP protocol is enable by default on Nortel routers. This option defines the volume to and from which the transfers will default.

Line Items 17 and 18   FTP Parameters

These two options allow you to decide if you wish to enable FTP and from which volume transfers will originate or be destined.

Line Item 19   Enable Telnet.

Enabling Telnet on the router allows for remote connections via the network. It allows you to view the router as if you were actually directly connected to it.

Line Item 20   Enable HTTP.

Version 13.x of the router software incorporates an HTTP server. This allows you to check on the router's health and status from a web browser.

1. Connect to the router's console port.

   In order to connect our computer to the router's console port we must use the console cable that came with the router. If you do not have the correct cable you will be unable to make the router connection. Router cables can be made easily enough or they can be ordered. Table 2-5 contains a list of cables according to router type and terminal or PC.

Table 2-5

Router console cables

Router	Cable	Part Number
Terminal—Local Connection		
Backbone Node	25-pin D-sub plug to RS-232 C receptacle	7525
Access Stack Node	9-pin D-sub plug to RS-232 C receptacle	7526
Access Node (Hub)	9-pin D-sub plug to RS-232 C receptacle	7526
PC w/ Terminal Emulation—Local Connection		
All Router Models	9-pin D-sub plug to RS-232 C modem plug	7527
Note: The 9-pin to RS-232 C cable comes in a kit with a null modem adapter.		
Modem—Local Connection		
Backbone Node	25-pin D-sub plug to RS-232 C modem plug	77850
Access Stack Node	9-pin D-sub plug to RS-232 C modem plug	7825
Access Node (Hub)	9-pin D-sub plug to RS-232 C modem plug	7825

There is a cable guide on the Nortel web site that contains the cable pinouts if you want to take a shot at making your own. It is fairly simple to create a 25-pin or 9-pin DIN with a RJ45 connector (one for the router and one for your computer). Then all you would need is a straight-through patch cable to join them.

2. Connect the router to the network.

Using a category 5-patch cable, connect the router to an Ethernet hub or switch. Make sure you match the speed of the router interface with the hub or switch connection.

3. Establish a *Technician Interface* (TI) session with the router.

For our example the computer with be running Windows 95 with HyperTerminal. To use HyperTerminal you must first set the communication parameters as follows:

Configuration Steps

a. Click on Start: Programs > Accessories > HyperTerminal > HyperTerminal.

Starting HyperTerminal in this way opens a new connection. Figure 2-9 is the "Connection Description" dialog box. Enter the name "Local" to describe the type of connection. You may also select an icon to represent this connection. Click [OK] to continue.

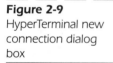

Figure 2-9
HyperTerminal new
connection dialog
box

Figure 2-10
HyperTerminal
connection
parameters dialog
box

b. Enter Connection Parameters.

Set the "Connect Using:" field, from Figure 2-10, to COM1 and click [OK]. This is assuming that your computer is connected to the router via its first COM port.

c. Modify Port Settings.

Make the following parameter changes in the "Port Setting" tab in the "COM1 Properties" dialog box: 9600, 8, n, 1, XON/XOFF. These settings are shown in Figure 2-11.

d. Click [OK] to Connect.

A login prompt and banner displays on your screen. Login to the router using the login name *Manager* with nothing as the password. (Note, the login name and password are case sensitive.)

NOTE: *The login name as well as the password is case sensitive. The previous procedure assumes that the router has never been previously assigned a password. If a password exists on the router you are quick starting, then enter that in at the password prompt.*

4. Boot the router with the file `ti.cfg`.

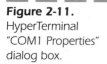

Figure 2-11.
HyperTerminal
"COM1 Properties"
dialog box.

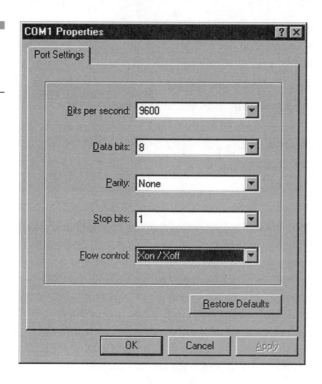

The `ti.cfg` file contains a blank configuration. Restarting the router with this file ensures that the router does not have any configured ports. The command to boot the router is

```
boot <slot_no>:<image_file> <slot_no>:ti.cfg
```

where

`<slot_no>` is the slot number of the volume that contains the image and `ti.cfg` files.

`<image_file>` is the name of the specific image file for the router to which you are connected.

a. For Backbone Node routers: image file = bn.exe

b. For Access Node routers: image file = an.exe

c. For Access Stack Node routers: image file = asn.exe

d. For Advanced Remote Node routers: image file = arn.exe

In this example, the router happens to be a BLN-2, so its image file is bn.exe. Enter the following command at the default prompt to boot the router:

[2:1]$ boot 2:bn.exe 2:ti.cfg

5. Run the installation script (`install.bat`)

Using the information from the Quick Start Worksheet, type the following at the command prompt:

[2:1]$ run install.

This command works for all routers except for an ARN router. The command to invoke the install script for them is **run inst_arn**.

Once the script begins, follow the prompts and input the desired information. The installation script will query the router to find out what link modules are available and prompt you for which link module to use (as well as which port on the link module). After the script collects all the pertinent information it will prompt you to save your changes. Accept the default configuration file name `startup.cfg`. This is to get you in the habit of keeping a previous configuration file handy in case your changes cause an adverse situation within the router. Nortel routers are programmed to boot with the file named *config*. If this file is corrupted the router will not complete the boot sequence and if an improper setting has been made the router might not function properly. So, if new changes are made and saved to an alternate file name (other than *config*) then it is easy to recover. Simply reboot the router and let it load the configuration file that was working before the changes.

NOTE: *The changes made during installation are dynamic. They take effect immediately. Do not reboot the router or you will lose all the change information that you just put in. If you made any mistake during the script execution just reboot the router with the ti.cfg file and start over.*

Now that the initial IP interface has been configured, what's next? Install Site Manager. To complete the router configuration you must install Site Manager on the management workstation. Site Manager will allow you to add protocols to the previous Ethernet interface, add another IP interface and define a multitude of other parameters. The next section will introduce you to Site Manager and how to install it on a workstation.

Site Manager Overview

Site Manager is an application that can be installed on a PC or a UNIX workstation. Site Manager's graphical user interface makes configuration and management of Nortel Networks routers easier. It was designed to centrally configure routers over IP via SNMP commands. Even though it was not designed for network management, Site Manager contains tools that allow you to poll for statistics, monitor traps and thresholds, and view router event logs. To run Site Manager on a PC you must meet the following hardware and software requirements:

- 486 PC (Pentium PC recommended)
- Microsoft Windows 95
- 16 MB of RAM (minimum)
- 60 MB of free disk space
- Microsoft TCP/IP for Windows 95 and compatible network adapters and driver
- CD-ROM drive
- VGA monitor (SuperVGA monitor recommended)

NOTE: *If you notice the requirements state the software runs on Windows 95. It will run under Windows NT 4.0. But, bear in mind that the application is a 16-bit application. Also, it is strongly recommended to run the version of Site Manager that corresponds to the version of code that is running on your routers. Corruption of the config file might happen or the router might fault (if making changes dynamically). According to Nortel, version 7.20 of Site Manager is supposed to work with all older versions of router from 11.x up to 13.2, excluding 12.04.*

Figure 2-12a
Same network
segment

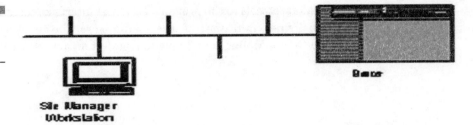

Figure 2-12b
Connection through
IP network

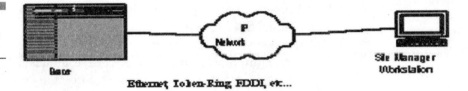

Figure 2-12c
PPP connection to
router via RAS or VPN

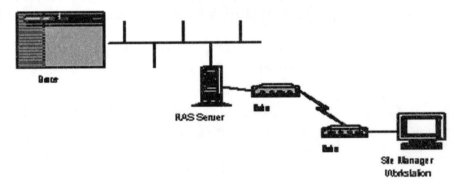

Supported Configurations (Figures 2-12a–c)

- *Same physical segment*   The Site Manager workstation can be directly connected to the same segment as the router's IP interface.

- *Connection through TCP/IP network*   A Site Manager workstation running TCP/IP located anywhere in the same TCP/IP network can remotely connect to a router.

- Point-to-Point Protocol *(PPP)*   A Site Manager workstation can dial into a network using PPP and gain access to a router. This scenario is common when not in the office and dialing into your network to make changes or check status.

NOTE: *Version 7.00 of Site Manager for Windows 95 requires the Microsoft TCP/IP protocol stack that is provided with Windows 95. It is recommended that if you are not using Microsoft's TCP/IP protocol stack to uninstall your current IP stack and install Microsoft's. I have never tried using any one else's protocol stack with Site Manager so I do not know it this is really a problem. This recommendation is mainly for those individuals that have upgraded their operating system from Windows 3.1 to Windows 95.*

Site Manager Tools

Site Manager comes with a variety of tools that can aide you in configuring and managing your router and network. These tools will be discussed in more detail later on in this chapter and in the back of this book.

- *Configuration Manager*   Creates and edits router configuration files
- *Statistics Manager*   Views router status and counters
- *Router Files Manager*   Flash file system management and TFTP
- *Event Manager*   Display window for router events
- *Trap Monitor*   A collection point for SNMP traps
- *Image Builder*   A tool for building and customizing router boot images

Site Manager also comes with tools that let you boot a specific router, reset specific router slots, set the date and time, clear the event log, and make adjustments to the routers global and local memory pools (not recommend without the specific advise of a Nortel Engineer). It also incorporates a ping facility that allows you to test IP, IPX, OSI, Vines, AppleTalk, and APPN connectivity. Fig. 2.3.2 shows a dialog box for an IP ping. To test the IP connectivity of a device or other router, put the IP address of the device in the address field and accept the default values for the other entries. Click [OK].

Installing Site Manager on a PC   Installing Site Manager onto a PC is like installing most any other application onto a PC.

1. Start by inserting the CD-ROM, labeled with the Site Manager application, into the CD-ROM drive of you PC.
2. Access the Run window from the Start menu.

3. Type the CD-ROM drive, path, and executable file:

```
<CDROM_drive>:\ms_win\setup.exe
```

The D: drive is usually the CD-ROM drive

4. Click [OK]

You can also use the browse button, Windows Explorer, or My Computer to select the CDROM drive and the path to the *ms_win* directory and click on *setup.exe*.

The installation script prompts you for the directory in which you want to install Site Manager.

5. Enter the directory in which you want to install Site Manager, or accept the default, *c:\wf*

The installation script will install the necessary files into the chosen directory. After the files have been copied, the following prompt will appear:

```
Create windows program group/items automatically?
```

6. To add Site Manager to the Start: Programs menu, click yes.

If you do not want to access Site Manager via Start: Programs menu, click on no.

The following prompt appears:

```
Do you want to start Site Manager now?
```

7. Click on Yes to start Site Manager.

The Router Connection Options window opens.

Connecting to a Router for the First Time   When you first start Site Manager the Router Configuration Options window opens, prompting you to define a router connection. This is shown in Figure 2-13.

Type in the IP address of the router you want to connect to along with the SNMP community string. During the installation of this router you chose to leave the SNMP community string to public. We will cover SNMP later in this book. You can change the other parameters or leave them at their default values. Once you click [OK] and the router is accessible, Site Manager will add it to the Well-Known Connections list, on the main Site Manager window, as shown in Figure 2-14

Figure 2-13
Router
Connection
Options window

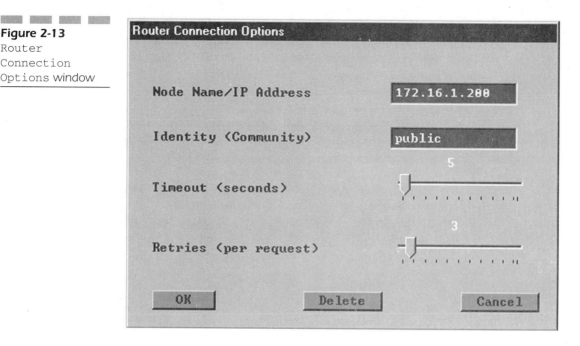

Figure 2-14
Main Site
Manager window

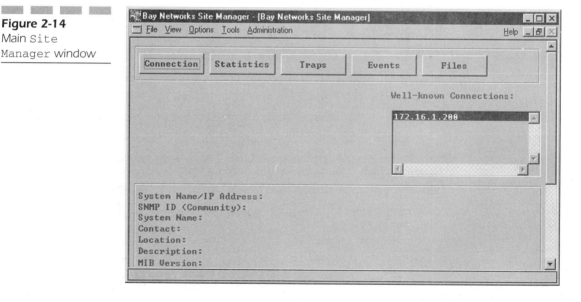

Main Site Manager Window   The first window you see after starting Site Manager is the main Site Manager window. (That is after the initial router connection has been established.) All tools are accessed through the main Site Manager window. The bottom half of the window displays basic router information such as IP address, SNMP Community ID, contact information, image and MIB versions. The top right of the window, displays routers that have been defined in the Router Connection window in a frame titled *Well-Known Connections*.

Anatomy of the Main Window   The main Site Manager window is similar to practically every other application made for Windows. It contains a menu bar and a tool/button bar. The crazy thing about Site Manager is that it actually opens as a window within a window. I find it useful to maximize the internal window to more closely mimic current Windows applications.

Menu Bar   Through the menu bar you can access a variety of options. A brief description of each menu option is provided.

- *File*   Exit Site Manager.
- *View*   Refresh the Site Manager display.
- *Options*   Allows for the connection of routers and customizing the connection list
- *Tools*   Allows access to all of Site Managers tools
- *Administration*   Through this option you can perform administration functions like booting the router or setting the router's date and time.
- *Help*   Gives you information about the version of Site Manager you are running

Button Bar   Below the menu bar is a button bar that provides access to some of the tools and options available through the menu bar. Their functions are as follows:

- *Connection*   Opens the Router Connection Options window where you can define routers to connect to as well as delete router connections.
- *Statistics*   Opens the Statistics Manager window

- *Traps*   Opens the Trap Monitor window
- *Events*   Opens the Event Manager window
- *Files*   Opens the File Manager window

Well-Known Connections lists   This list contains the IP addresses of the routers you have made a connection to using this version of Site Manager. Clicking on one of the entries in the list polls the router for its current state —up or down. To use the many functions in Site Manager, you must first select a router from this list. If one is not present it must be added in order to proceed. Routers are added to this list by clicking the [Connection] button and inputting the appropriate parameters.

Summing Up

At this point we have configured an initial IP interface on the router. We have installed Site Manager and gone over some the functions and tools contained in it. As we proceed we need to define some of the conventions Site Manager uses for it windows.

- Menu options and buttons that end with an ellipsis (. . .) open a window when selected.
- Menu options followed by a shaded arrow display a menu when selected.
- Buttons not followed by an ellipsis perform a function when selected.
- Underlined letters in menu options identify keyboard shortcuts.
- Scroll up, down, left, or right using the keyboard arrow keys.
- The PF number in a menu option identifies a program function shortcut.
- Menu options are dimmed when not active for a particular window.
- Scroll bars are located at the right side of some windows. Using these scroll bars lets you view the entire window's contents.

Referring to Figure 2-8, we see that we need to use Site Manager to configure the other interface on Router A. In order to configure the other router interfaces we need to use Configuration Manager. The next section will give you an overview of Configuration Manager its operating modes and connection parameters.

Configuration Manager Overview

Configuration Manager is the Site Manager tool that allows you to create and modify router configuration files. With Configuration Manager you can add network interfaces, based on default values, to your router. You could then customize these interfaces to you network environment by adding or deleting protocols and/or renaming circuits. Through Configuration Manager you can define the router's access security via SNMP options and parameters. You could also specify the administrative information about your router as well as its connection to the *Technician Interface* (TI). Each of these changes is reflected in the router configuration file. Recall that the configuration file is a binary file that contains the user-defined information for a router. Once a working configuration has been made it can be used to boot the router.

In order to create or modify a configuration file, a familiarization of the Configuration Manager interface is suggested. There are two ways to enter data into a parameter field in any of the Configuration Manager windows. They are as follows:

- *Values button*   This button is located in the upper right corner of a window and present different values that can be used in the parameter field. To select from the list of available parameters in the list, first click in to the field next to the description of the parameter. Click the [Values] button and select one value from the list.

NOTE: *Some parameters do not list values and will have to be typed into the field. As an example, the IP address or password parameters do not have lists associated with them.*

- *Entering values from keyboard*   This option is self-explanatory. Click into an empty field and type the desired value. Most configuration parameters have default values assigned to them. If the field is not empty, remove the default value by either double clicking into the field to select the entire word or by triple clicking into the field to select the entire field. Once the default value has been selected, type over it with the new value.

Getting Help on Parameters

One of the wonderful things about using Configuration Manager to customize the router configuration is the parameter help that is found in most of its windows. If you are unsure about a parameter function, click on help to get a description of the parameter that includes its default value, the valid options, the function of the parameter, and instructions about setting it.

Operating Modes

All configuration functions can be performed through Configuration Manager in one of following four modes:

■ Local Mode
■ Remote Mode
■ Dynamic Mode
■ Cache Mode

Each mode is identified in Configuration Manager in the top-left corner of the each window. All windows, regardless of mode of operation, contain the same information.

Local Mode is the most secure mode of operation. When creating a new configuration or editing an existing configuration file, Site Manager never accesses the router. All configuration changes are completed and saved locally on the Site Manager workstation. Access to the router is needed only when transferring a new configuration file to the flash card or when pulling the current config file down to the workstation for editing. Each instance requires using the Router Files Manager.

NOTE: *Local mode only allows you to open a configuration file that is of the same software version as Site Manager. However, you can edit existing config files from previous versions.*

Local mode is accessed through the main Site Manager window. Click on Tools: Configuration Manager > Local file . . . . The Open Configuration File window pops up (Figure 2-15) and prompts you with the name of the configuration file that you wish to modify. As with all Windows file windows, you can select from the current list of files or browse into another directory to find the file you desire.

When creating a new configuration for a router, Configuration Manager requires that you specify the router type and hardware configuration by selecting it from a list of routers and adding the installed modules. Modules installed in the router are added to the configuration by selecting the [Empty Slots] button coinciding with a particular slot. Figure 2-16 displays a blank config file when opened in local mode.

Clicking on the buttons labeled "Empty Slot" will bring up another window that lists the available modules for the specific router. Select the module from the list and it displays in the logical router view.

Figure 2-15
Local file "open"
window

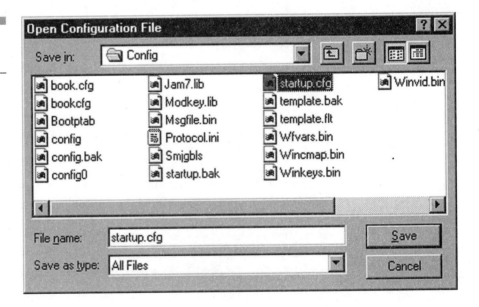

Figure 2-16

Blank configuration

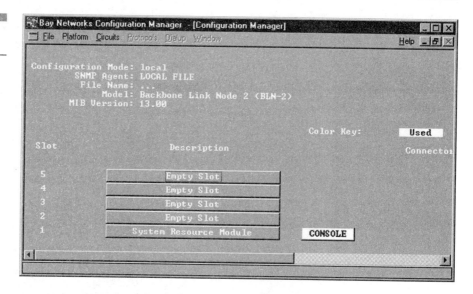

Figure 2-16

Blank configuration

Once configuration is complete, you can then TFTP the new configuration file to the router to be implemented at a later date. TFTP is controlled through the Router Files Manager tool.

NOTE: *In the file open window the option command button is "save" not "open."*

Remote Mode operation is similar to local mode operation but with the TFTP function built in. In remote mode, connection to the router is made through the network and the config file is pulled down to the Site Manager workstation for local modification. Remote mode is the preferred mode because Configuration Manager reads the hardware configuration automatically, thereby, freeing you from configuring the hardware manually.

Once the file has been modified, saving it in remote mode automatically TFTPs the file back to the router. Configuration Manager will make a back up of a local config file if it has the same name as the one chosen remotely. It will append a bak extension onto the local file. If you remotely configured the *config* file off a router and a *config* file existed on your local workstation, then the backup file will be renamed to *config.bak*.

Figure 2-17
Remote
Configuration
File window.

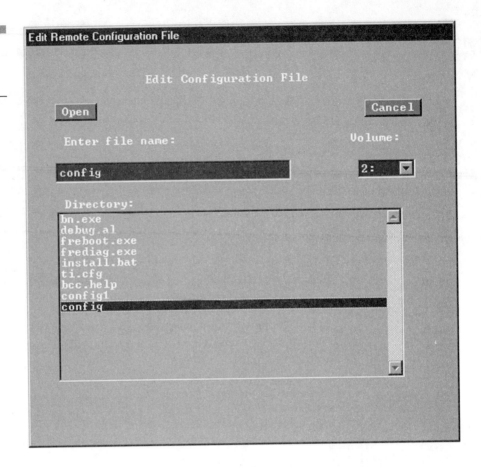

Remote mode is accessed from the main Site Manager window. Click Tools: Configuration Manager > Remote file . . . (F4). The Remote Configuration File window pops up (Figure 2-17) and prompts you for the file name of the configuration file as well as the volume number to where the file is located. Enter the information or select the file from a list.

Dynamic Mode is the "real time" operating mode for Configuration Manager. All changes done in dynamic mode take effect immediately. The changes are save to RAM but not to the config file. A word of caution about using dynamic mode to configure router. Since changes take effect immediately, disruption of service or performance issue may arise due to the type of configuration is being done. It is not recommended to create an entirely new router configuration dynamically. It is far safer to use one of the other configuration modes as well as easier to recover from erred entries.

Selecting Tools: Configuration Manager > Dynamic (F5) connects you to the router currently selected in the Well-Known connections list. Again, as in the other modes, the hardware configuration displays. Only this display is real time.

Configuring the router in dynamic mode requires SNMP *set operations* from Site Manager. The router responding to an SNMP *set* may have to read from several of its MIBs using SNMP *get operations*. If the router has to read from many MIB instances, then the response to the *set* can be exceedingly long. A way to decrease response time was to create a copy of the operational state of the router locally to a file on the Site Manager workstation.

Cache Mode is the mode in which the real time operational state of the router is saved as a file on the local Site Manager workstation. Site Manager uses this file to retrieve the values in its MIB. Configuration changes to the router are still made dynamically.

As with the other operating modes, entering this mode is through the main Site Manager window from the Tools menu. Click on Tools: Configuration Manager > Cache (F11). The Save Configuration File window pops up prompting for a filename and volume number. Site Manager uses this information to save the router's existing configuration to the name and volume given. It also downloads a copy to itself and stores it under the name given.

Adding a Network Interface

Now that we have been introduced to Configuration Manager, we will use this tool to add the serial interface from Figure 2-8. In the figure, the connection between the two routers is a point-to-point link. Since we will not be dealing with Frame Relay at this time, let us assume that the link is a T1 and that the only protocol being routed is IP. Following is a summary of the basic steps for configuring the serial interface.

Configuration Steps

1. Check the amount of free space on the router's flash card. Compact the flash memory if necessary.

2. Make a backup copy of the router's config file. In our case, we will be creating a copy of the `startup.cfg` file. This will ensure that if

anything goes wrong during the file modification, we will be able to return to a working state.

3. Start Configuration Manager in any of the desired modes. To minimize production disruption, choose local or remote modes.

4. Modify the config file.

5. Save the config file under a new name.

6. Transfer the file back to the router

7. Name boot the router with the new config file.

Using Configuration manager to configure a new interface allows us to access all the parameters associated with the interface while providing consistency checking and verification that the *Technician Interface* (TI) does not provide. These parameters consist of the physical (line) layer, data link layer, and network layer parameters of which we can modify the line parameters, edit or delete circuits, add or remove protocols, as well as perform other functions.

NOTE: *It is important to note that when configuring parameters with the TI, erroneous values can be entered without alert that can interfere with router functionality.*

1. Checking the amount of free space on a router's flash card

It is important to know the amount of contiguous free space on the router's flash card. This information can be found by using Router Files Manager from within Site Manager or via the TI. Either way, the router will display the Total Size of the flash card, the amount of Available and Contiguous Free Space. Even though the Available Free Space may allow for files to be transferred to the router, it is the Contiguous Free Space that counts. If the Contiguous Free Space is less than the size of the file that will be transferred to the router, the transfer will fail. "Compacting" the flash memory will recoup the lost space.

From the TI:

a. Connect to the router and start a TI session.

b. At the router prompt list the contents of the flash.

Type **dir** [Enter]

The screen will scroll the list of files that are on the flash card. At the end of the list will be the file system information—Total Size, Available Space, and Contiguous Space.

c. Compact the flash memory. (If needed)

Type **compact** <volume #> [Enter]

Compacting the flash memory may take a couple of minutes to complete, depending upon the type of router and the amount of non-contiguous memory locations on the card.

Within Router Files Manager:

a. Select the router in the Well-known Connections list

From the Site Manager main window, click once on the IP address, or name, of the router that you wish to configure.

b. Start Router Files Manager.

Select Tools > Router Files Manager . . .

or

Click on the Files button from the Tool Bar.

Router Files Manager displays the files on the active volume as shown in Figure 2-18.

Volumes refer to the slot where the flash memory cards are located. To change to another volume, select the volume from the volume list box at the top of the Router Files Manager window. All volumes may not display, use the scroll arrows on the right of the drop-down list to scroll through the list of available volumes. The file system information is displayed just below the files list window.

c. Compact the flash memory. (If needed)

Select Compact from the Commands menu option or press [F12]. Compacting the flash memory may take a couple of minutes to complete, depending upon the type of router and the amount of non-contiguous memory locations on the card.

It is easy to see that the Router Files Manager is a convenient tool. The graphical interface makes it easy for you to perform file management functions. To find more information about the Router Files Manager tool see Appendix B.

2. Make a backup copy Of the router's config file

During the router quick-start, we created an initial configuration and saved it to the file *startup.cfg*. We can create a backup of this file by

Figure 2-18
Router Files
Manager window

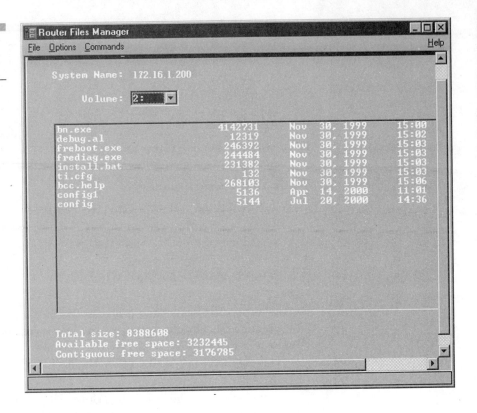

again using Router Files Manager to copy the file to our local drive or copy the file to another name on the same flash card. Since it is always safer to make configuration changes to a local copy of a config file, we will copy the file from the router.

a. Select `startup.cfg` from the list files window.

This is assuming that the Router Files Manager is still open from the previous step. If you have closed the files manager, then reopen it and continue by selecting the *startup.cfg* file in the file display window.

b. Transfer file to local drive.

Click on File: TFTP > Get File(s) . . . . The TFTP Get Files window pops up as shown in Figure 2-19.

The selected file displays in the "Proceed with TFTP Get of File(s)" list box with the default local directory entered into the

Figure 2-19
TFTP Get window.

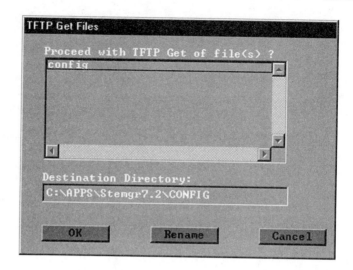

"Destination Directory" text box. If you do not wish to change any information, click [OK].

The *startup.cfg* file now resides on your local workstation in the default directory (or the directory you specified previously). Exit out of Router Files Manager.

3. Start Configuration Manager in Local Mode

As it was stated earlier, making changes to a router in dynamic mode can cause the router to become unstable. For our example, we will perform the configuration changes by accessing the config file through the Local configuration mode.

Start Configuration Manager in Local Mode.

Click Tools: Configuration Manager > Local File (or press F3).
Select *startup.cfg* from the files list box and click [Save].
Figure 2-20 displays the hardware configuration as a logical view.

4. Modify the config file

During initial configuration, the router was able to determine its hardware configuration. The hardware configuration display reflects what the router had discovered, Figure 2-20. This is the logical view of the router. Notice that the first Ethernet connector is highlighted. Since

Figure 2-20
Logical view of
the router—
Configuration
Manager main
window

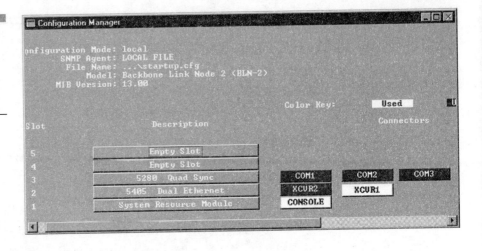

Figure 2-21
Add Circuit
window for new PPP
connection

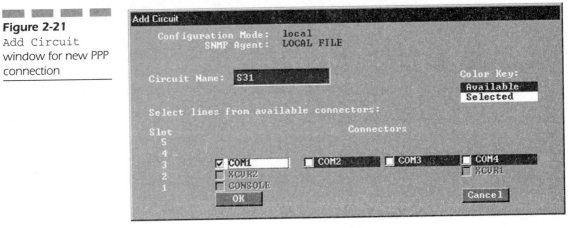

we have already configured this interface it shows up in this view as
being used. To add a serial interface we need to configure one of the
four COM ports on the Quad Sync Link Module in slot 3. The following
steps create a *point-to-point* (PPP) circuit on COM1:

a. Select a serial connector in the Hardware Configuration Display
    Locate the Quad Sync Link Module and click once on the COM1
connector button.
    The Add Circuit window opens (Figure 2-21).

Site Manager chooses a default circuit name, which can be modified if you prefer. Click [OK]. I recommend keeping the default name because in three characters it tells you the type of circuit, slot, and connector the circuit is configured on. To be a little more descriptive, you can append to the circuit name the department or segment for which this circuit is configured. For example, if this is to be the Internet circuit, you could rename the circuit to S32_Internet. This added description could only help in deciphering what the circuit is used for when viewing MIB information and statistics.

Circuit Naming Conventions   Site Manager defines the following characters to assist in maintaining a consistent naming scheme between circuit type and locations. This is a more complete list from earlier in this chapter.

Circuit Prefix	Connector
E	Ethernet
E1	E1
F	FDDI
H	HSSI
MCE1	MCE1
MCT1	MCT1
O	Token-Ring
S	Synchronous
T1	T1

Our circuit name of S32 tells us that the circuit is a synchronous circuit on slot 3, connector 2. Circuit names for ASN routers have an extra number that identifies the location in the stack. For example, an ASN circuit name of E321 designates an Ethernet circuit located on the ASN with a slot ID of 3 defined on slot 2, connector 1 of that ASN.

Figure 2-22
Wan Protocols
selection window

Figure 2-23
Select
Protocols window

b. Select the WAN and network protocols.

Since we are configuring a PPP circuit, select the PPP radio button in the WAN Protocols window, as shown in Figure 2-22.

Clicking [OK] sets all the physical layer parameters to defaults. The next window that pops up is the network protocols window (Figure 2-23).

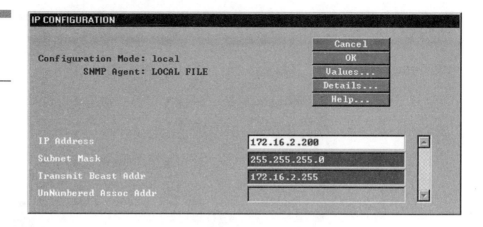

Figure 2-24
IP
Configuration
window.

IP CONFIGURATION

Configuration Mode: local
SNMP Agent: LOCAL FILE

Cancel
OK
Values...
Details...
Help...

IP Address	172.16.2.200
Subnet Mask	255.255.255.0
Transmit Bcast Addr	172.16.2.255
UnNumbered Assoc Addr	

Select the IP and RIP check boxes then click [OK]. Figure 2-24 shows the IP Configuration window that opens.

c. Configure IP for this circuit.

Using the information from Figure 2-8, enter the IP address, Subnet Mask, and Transmit Broadcast Address. The information is repeated:

IP Address: 172.16.2.200
Subnet Mask: 255.255.255.0
Broadcast Address: 172.16.2.255

Click [OK] to define the circuit with the IP information.

d. Modify IP configuration for routing.

Although Configuration Manager sets many of the parameters, you may still need to modify some of the values to fit your network. In our case we will modify the default values set for RIP, namely Poisoned Reverse and RIP Mode.

At the hardware configuration window (or the Configuration Manager main window for the router), click on Protocols: IP > RIP Interfaces . . . . The RIP IP Interfaces window opens listing the IP interface currently configured with the RIP protocol (Figure 2-25).

Select the interface in the interface list. Below the list window are the configurable parameters for this protocol. Click once into the Poisoned Reverse text box then click on the [Values] button to the upper right. The values that are currently available for this

Figure 2-25
Routing Information
Protocol parameters

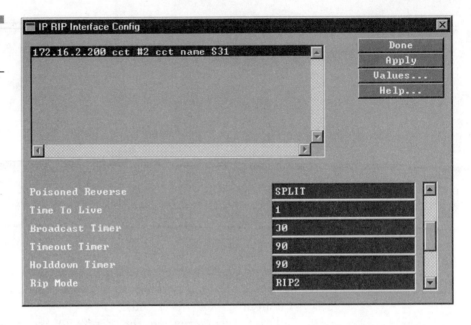

Figure 2-25
Routing Information
Protocol parameters

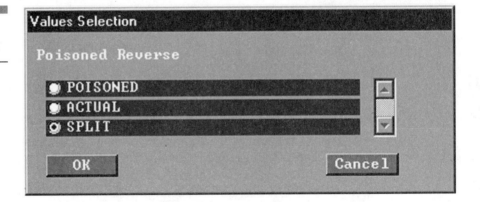

Figure 2-26
Available values for
Poisoned Reverse

parameter display in the Value Selection window shown in Figure 2-26.

Select the Split radio button, for Split Horizon, and then click [OK]. Use the scroll bars to the right of the parameter values, in Figure 2-25, to find RIP Mode. Again, click once into the parameter text box then click [Values]. Select the RIP2 radio button for RIP version 2. Once you click [OK] and return to the RIP IP Interfaces window, click [Apply] to save the changes you just made. When finished, click [Done].

If the above RIP settings are causing you some difficulty, do worry. There is an in-depth discussion of RIP in Chapter 3 that should clarify any question that may have arisen.

5. Save the config file under a new name.

In order to save the configuration file, click on File: Save As. Since *startup.cfg* is a known "good" config, we do not want to save our changes back to it in the event that something might have been in error. By choosing the Save As option, you can save the modified file with a new name. Save the file as *startup1.cfg*. Configuration Manager will save the file to your local drive.

Click File: Exit (or press F10) to close Configuration Manager.

6. Transfer new config to router.

With the router highlighted in the Well-Known Connections list, click Tools: Router Files Manager . . . . To send the file to the router you must use the TFTP "put" option.

Click File: TFTP > Put File(s) . . . (or press F4). The TFTP Put Files Selection window opens with the default path highlighted in the Path text box (Figure 2-27).

Select *startup1.cfg* from the "Files" list on the left of the window. Click the [Add ((] button to move the file to the "Files To Put:" list. Click [OK] to send the file to the router.

Click File: Exit (F10) to close Router Files Manager.

7. Name boot the router to activate the new changes.

From the main Site Manager window, select the router from within the Well-Known Connections list. Click Administration: Boot Router . . . .

Verify that the volume number is set to the correct flash card volume for both the boot image and configuration file. Change the boot image to be bn.exe if not already set. Since the whole purpose of performing the name boot is to activate the new changes, make sure the configuration file is set to *startup1.cfg*.

Click [Boot] to restart the router with the new configuration.

Figure 2-27

TFTP Put window.

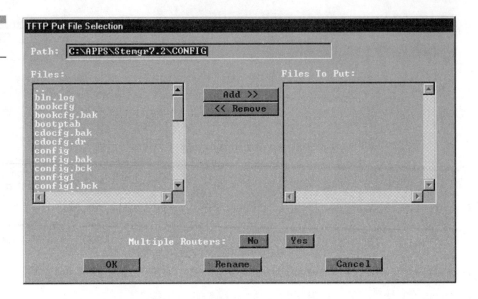

8. Save `startup1.cfg` as config and cleanup.

   Once you have determined that the router is functioning without errors, copy the `startup1.cfg` file as config. From the Router Files Manager:

   Procedural Steps

   a. Select the `startup1.cfg` file from the file list.

   b. Click Commands: Copy (F6). Make sure the source file is `startup1.cfg` and the destination file is *config*. Click [OK] to copy the file.

   Now you will have three configuration files on you flash memory card—`startup.cfg`, `startup1.cfg`, and `config`. Three configs are not needed, so delete the oldest—`startup.cfg`.

   Select *startup.cfg* and select delete from the Commands menu or press F7.

9. Archive the configuration on your workstation or server drive.

   I can not stress enough the importance of keeping an active archive of router configuration changes. There will come a time when a change is made and it faults the router. If you do not have a backup configuration file and the one on the router is outdated or lost. You will have to create the configuration again from scratch. Hoping you remembered where you put the hard copy of the configuration parameters. If you have a big enterprise the production down time can be considerable.

You do not need to keep every file that you changed, a dual file archive placed in a folder on a network server should be sufficient. One file being a copy of the previous configuration and the other being the current configuration. Every time a change is made, the current config file in the archive should be copied to the archive file name and the new config file copied to the current config file name. You can organize the archive folder by router, image version, and/or router location.

You have successfully configured the router with an Ethernet and a wide-area interface, defining the IP protocol for each. All that would be left to do is to configure the second router from Figure 2-8. There are two ways that you can do it.

1. You could follow the previous procedure.

or

2. You could modify the copy of the config from the first router and transfer it to the new flash. You want to be sure to change the IP and RIP parameters as they are identified from the figure.

Monitoring Statistics

One of the most important tools (next to Configuration Manager) that is apart of the Site Manager tools set is the Statistics Manager. This tool enables you to view the router's operational state. It enables you to gather statistical and configuration information from the router as defined by specific screens. Screens are predefined or custom built, views of the router's circuits and protocols that display a multitude of information about each. Statistics Manager uses an SNMP poll mechanism to retrieve the required information from the circuits and protocols enabled on the router. It can poll in real-time the data link layer circuit statistics as well as the network layer protocol statistics for display in the screen window.

Statistics Manager requires an active router connection. You can select a router from the Site Manager's "Well Known Connections" list before you

Figure 2-28.
Statistics
Manager main
window

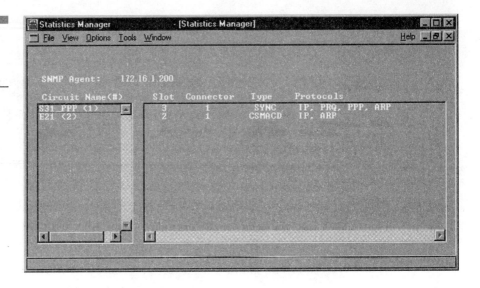

enter Statistics Manager or one can be selected afterwards. The main Statistics Manager window is shown in Figure 2-28 and it displays the connected router's current configuration.

The main window is a standard window in that it has a title bar, menu bar, and a user area. The menu bar consists of five options as described next.

■ *File*   Exits you from Statistics Manager

■ *View*   Gives you the option to refresh you display

■ *Options*   Allows you to connect to a router

■ *Tools*   Enables you access to the Statistics Manager tools

■ *Window*   Enables you to switch between different windows

The user area is split into two with circuit related information on the left side and interface and protocol information on the right side of the area. When you first enter Statistics Manager it polls the router for a list of circuit types and the location of its network interfaces as well as the bridging and routing protocols that are enabled on each.

Statistics Manager also contains four utilities that are accessed from the Tools menu bar—Quick Get, Screen Builder, Screen Manager, and the Launch Facility. A brief description of each of these utilities is offered.

■ *Quick Get*   This utility allows you to view the Nortel router's MIB for configuration parameters and statistics. It contains a MIB browser that lets you scroll through the various MIB objects and select the ones from which you want information. Quick Get retrieves all the instances of the specified MIB object and displays the statistics in a window.

■ *Screen Builder*   The wonderful thing about this utility is that it allows you to make custom screens to display the values that are not present in the predefined screens.

■ *Screen Manager*   You use this utility to select the predefined or user created screen to be added to the current screen list. There are 75 predefined screens (you can up to 4,000) of which only a small subset should be added to the current screen list (preferably the ones you will most use). You can only display statistics from windows in the current screen list.

■ *Launch Facility*   This is a program that allows you view the current screen list. Depending upon how the screens were initially defined, is how the statistics will display. There are two modes in which the screens can be defined to display statistics:

  ▪ *Circuit Mode*   Statistics Manager continually polls the router for the desired information. The poll interval is set to 5 seconds but it can be changed to match your situation.

  ▪ *Table Mode*   The statistical information is polled only once, when the window first opens. You must refresh the display to update the information.

Choosing a particular screen from the list launches the window for display.

The Quick Get and Screen Builder utilities are covered in more detail in Chapter 7. The following section will concentrate on launching the predefined screens found in the Screen Manager from the Launch Facility. Figure 2-29 shows the Screen Manager window.

The Screen Manager main window is contains three list boxes that can contain various defined screens. The top-left list holds all the predefined screens installed. These screens were installed when you installed the Site Manager program and are located in the \wf\lib\wfscrns folder, if you chose the default locations. To view any of these screens you have to add them to the "Current Screen List." To add a predefined screen, select it from the "Default Screens" list then click the [Add >>] button.

Below the list of predefined screens there is the list of "User Screens." This contains a list of custom screens that you define to suit any statistical

Figure 2-29
Screen Manager
main window

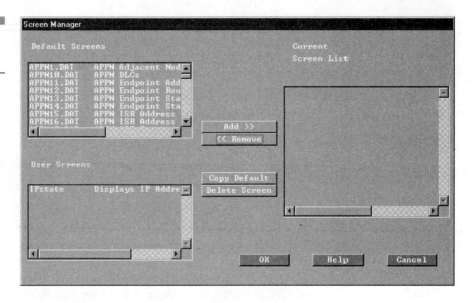

management requirements. As you can see from Figure 2-29 only one custom screen is defined—IPstate. To add this screen to the current list, select the screen then click [Add >>]. Both the predefined and user defined screen lists include the name of the screen as well as a textual message describing what the screen does or what protocols it polls.

Once you have added the screens you wish to view to the "Current Screen List," you will be able to view them by selecting them from within the Launch Facility. The Launch Facility's selection window is shown in Figure 2-30.

In this figure the IPstate screen was to the current list. To view the statistics that this screen polls you select it from the list and click [Launch]. The Launch Facility view opens formatted with the column headers defined in the screen. The Launch Facility view window is shown is Figure 2-31.

Anatomy of the Statistical View

When a screen defined to poll a router for specific statistics is launched, the Launch Facility displays the view window similar to the one shown in Figure 2-31. Even though the view pane of the launch window will be different in respect to the defined screen that was launched, the menu items of the

Figure 2-30
Launch Facility
screen selection
window.

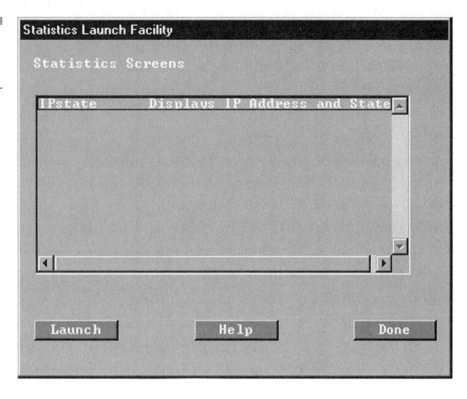

window will be identical, that is File, View, Options, Filters, and Search will
contain the same options. The Help menu item is unique to each screen due
to the "Descriptions" option. This option displays the configuration information of the specific screen. It displays the location of the screen file, the
screen type (circuit or table), its description, and the MIB objects that are
to be polled. The other menu options are described next.

■ *File*   Saves the current screen information and exits the Launch
   Facility view.

■ *View*   Allows you to refresh the view display or stop the retrieval of
   the router statistics.

■ *Options*   Allows you to change the router connection and the polling
   interval. The polling interval is used when the screen is defined in
   circuit mode. The interval is a sliding scale ranging from 1 to 120
   seconds. The Options window also allows you to zero all counters or just
   those on a specific row in the view pane.

Figure 2-31
Launch Facility
statistical view
window

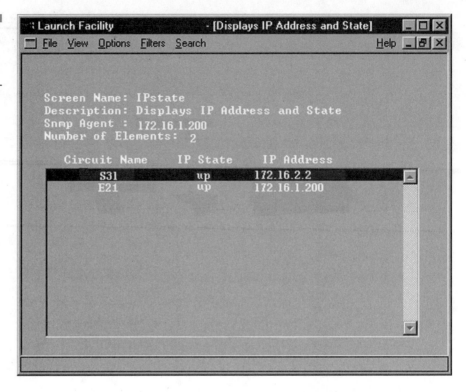

- *Filters*   Supports the use of view filters. This option allows you to apply a filter on the information in the current view. You define the text to filter on, the column to search, and whether of not you want the row containing any matches to display or hide (No Display).

- *Search*   Allows you to search for a specific text string in the current view window. The row with the matching text is highlighted.

The view pane of the window is the area below the menu bar and is where the statistics from the router display. The display is laid out in columns as defined in the screen definition. The only column that displays for all screens without specific definition is the "Circuit Name" column. The Launch Facility automatically defines this column for all views regardless of custom or predefined definitions.

The Statistics Manager is wonderful tool for troubleshooting problems that arise in your network. The amount of predefined screens give an excellent picture into the way your router is behaving. If, per chance, a predefined screen does not incorporate the information for which you are looking, you can easily create a custom screen definition. Creating custom screens is defined more fully later in this book.

SUMMARY

A network is a mechanism that ties devices together for the sake of sharing information and services. The main purpose of this chapter was to provide you with the basic concepts that are shared for most networks. Networks can be small, incorporating a building or campus as a LAN. They can stretch the length of a city while maintaining the speeds consistent of the local area. Networks can even span states and country boundaries as with private WANs and the public Internet. In all cases they exhibit one main truth; anyone connected can communicate with anyone else connected as controlled under a common standard. The standard control that we discussed in this chapter was the Ethernet and Token-Ring LAN standards.

Ethernet and Token-Ring are the rules that govern many local area networks. The Ethernet protocol defines an access technique of *Carrier Sense Multiple Access with Collision Detection* (CSMA/CD). This is also a broadcast protocol in that all transmissions are broadcasted to every station on the segment. Ethernet speeds range from 10Mbps to 1Gbps. The Token-Ring protocol uses a "token" passing technique for data transmission. Each device on the ring is directly connected to the next device on the ring forming a neighbor relationship. This knowledge of ones neighbor is a great boon for isolating Token-Ring errors. Token-Ring speeds can be 4Mbps or 16Mbps, which has been far surpassed by Ethernet. Regardless of the underlying protocol, devices communicate on a network by learning, sending, and responding to the MAC address that is defined on the network interface card.

Devices communicate on a network by addressing packets using the hardware, or MAC address of the *network interface card* (NIC). These addresses work in conjunction with addressing provided by protocols at a higher layer. By themselves, they can only get a packet to where it is going. The upper layer protocols are needed to take it several steps further and into the application. This will be evident as we continue our discussion of the TCP/IP suite of protocols in Chapter 3. In this chapter we focused our discussion on what TCP/IP was and how it addressed host devices.

A TCP/IP address consists of network and a host address. It is 32 bits, 4 bytes long and is present in dotted-decimal notation. That is, the four bytes are separated by decimal points. There are several classes of IP address each denoted with a letter. The designation specifies a range for which addresses reside. Also, in this chapter you were introduced to the concept of a subnet mask. A subnet mask is used to differentiate between the network and host portions of the IP address. It, too, is a 32-bit, 4-byte number presented in dotted-decimal notation.

Once we learned the concepts of networking and its subsequent addressing, we began configuring a BLN-2 router with its initial interface. Using Site Manager we also added an additional interface and the protocols needed for it. The initial interface configuration was performed using a terminal connected directly to the router and running a predefined installation script. This script walked us through the configuration parameters needed to create the first interface running the IP protocol. Then we had to install Nortel's graphical configuration tool, Site Manager. Using Site Manager's Configuration Manager tool we were able to access the router to perform configuration adds and changes. We were also able to create copy of the configuration file for backup by using the Router Files Manager tool. The last thing we learn was how to use the Statistics Manager tool to pull various statistical information from the router.

Basic IP Routing

In the last chapter, we learned how devices communicate when connected to each other on a single network segment. But, in reality, most networks consist of many segments, multiple networks, that must communicate with each other. Routers connect these multiple networks. They are charged with the task of maintaining accurate state information in order to provide "best" path forwarding. Each router is responsible for keeping current a table of route entries that it uses to forward packets it receives on any of its interfaces to their correct destination with the shortest delay possible. The information contained in this routing table is gained from networks that are directly attached to the router, from the manual insertion of network paths, and from information received from other routers.

When the router is first "booted," it is aware of only the networks to which it has a physical connection. It will represent these routes in the routing table with a "Local" or "Direct" designation. A Network Manager can manually add routes to a router that also appear in the routing table as "Local." These are static routes that point to networks that are accessed via other routers in the enterprise. In medium to large enterprises, static routes can become difficult to manage. Static routes are ideal for small collections of networks and for special purposes like default routes. A more efficient method of populating a routing table with routes is to learn the paths from the other routers in the enterprise. Routers use routing protocols to inform each other of the current topology of the network. Routing protocols exist to keep the information in the routing tables accurate even if the state of the network is in flux. These protocols must send advertisements (also known as route updates) from a router. These updates contain location information about networks of which the router is aware. Routing protocols also coordinate with routers to receive incoming updates and process them so the routes in the routing table are correct. With correct information in the routing table, the router can make its routing decisions based on the best path.

The Routing Process

When a router receives a packet on one of its interfaces, it must be able to extract its destination address from it. The destination address is located in the network-layer header of the incoming packet. For IP, the destination address is the 32-bit, 4-byte number located in the last portion of the IP header. Because the fields in the header are fixed length, the router can quickly skip to the point where the destination address begins and read the 4-byte address. The destination address occupies byte 17 through 20 in the IP header.

Armed with the destination address, the router divides it into its two parts—the network and host address. From Chapter 2, we learned that a subnet mask determines the break point for separating an IP address into its network and host components. Where does the router get the subnet mask it will use to divide the destination address? It will use the class designation that it interprets from the first two bits in the address, if subnet information is not known. As you might recall, the IP address can be a member of one of three major classes of addresses—class A, B, or C. If the first bit in the address is a 0 (zero), the address will have a class A (8-bit) subnet mask. If the first two bits are 1 0 or 11, the address will have a class B (16-bit) or class C (24-bit) subnet mask, respectively. The caveat to this is if the destination address is within a network about which subnetting information is known, the appropriate subnet mask is used. That is, if the network is "local" or is propagated via a routing protocol, the router will use the subnet mask as defined.

After the appropriate subnet mask has been used to separate the network address from the host address, the router can then make a decision on where to forward the packet. The router will match the network address to one found in its routing table. After a match has been found, the router forwards the packet to the next-hop address that is assigned to the route entry. The next-hop address is the address of the next router that will receive the packet as it travels a path to its destination. A packet path may include many routers before reaching the router directly connected to the destination network. Each router the packet encounters on its journey will follow a similar procedure of reading the destination address, dividing out the network portion, and forwarding the packet to the next-hop router. It is only the last router that will pass the packet to a local delivery process that will take it onto its final destination.

The local delivery process on a router is nothing more than local segment communication. As we learned in the previous chapter, local segment communication is confined to the Data Link layer protocols such as Ethernet or Token-Ring. Packets are passed from client-to-server, or client-to-client, via the device's MAC address. Every device on the segment "sees" everyone else's packets and, depending on the destination address encountered in the packets, each device will either drop them or accept them. Because a router operates in the Network layer, it has no concern for the destination or source MAC address that was originally defined in the packet. When the packet reaches the last router, the router must now retrieve the end host's MAC address in order to forward the packet to it. The router performs a local broadcast request, called an ARP (more on this later in the chapter), for the destination host's MAC. After the destination MAC is retrieved, the router enters it into the packet with its interface MAC address as the source and sends it onto the physical media.

There are two types of routing protocols—interior gateway and exterior gateway protocols. *Interior gateway protocols* (IGP) facilitate communication of routing information within an autonomous system, whereas *exterior gateway protocols* (EGP) exchange network reachability information between different autonomous systems. An autonomous system is a collection of networks and routers under a single administrative authority, as shown in Figure 3-1.

Each *autonomous system* (AS) has its own internal mechanism for collecting routing information and passing it onto other autonomous systems. Each autonomous system is given a unique number by the InterNIC that identifies the system. In order for an autonomous system to exchange information with another, it must use an external routing protocol like BGP. BGP uses path attributes to describe a route to destination networks and to keep a consistent view of the Internet's topology. RIP and IGRP are examples of Internal Gateway Protocols.

Basic IP Routing

The *Internet Protocol* (IP) is the workhorse of the TCP/IP protocol suite. Its primary function is to receive data from the Transport layer (either through

Figure 3-1

Example of two autonomous systems

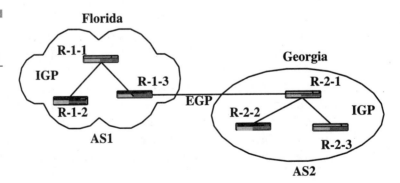

TCP or UDP), encapsulate it with addressing and control information, and route the datagram through a network to a destination host. It also handles packet fragmentation and reassembly as well as how determines how long the packet can be alive on the network (this packet-life feature is called *Time To Live* [TTL]). Figure 3-2 shows the IP header that contains all of the addressing and control information, service type, TTL, and various other options associated with datagram delivery.

The IP header is, by default, five words long (one word is 32 bits, 4 bytes) —the sixth word is optional. Because of the variable nature of the IP header, word 1 contains a field called *Internet Header Length* (IHL) that defines the length of the header in words. As we detailed the IP layers in Chapter 2, let us likewise examine the different fields in the IP header.

The information in the IP header is sufficient enough to route all protocols in the TCP/IP suite, the exception being ARP and RARP. *Address Resolution Protocol* (ARP) and *Reverse Address Resolution Protocol* (RARP) are

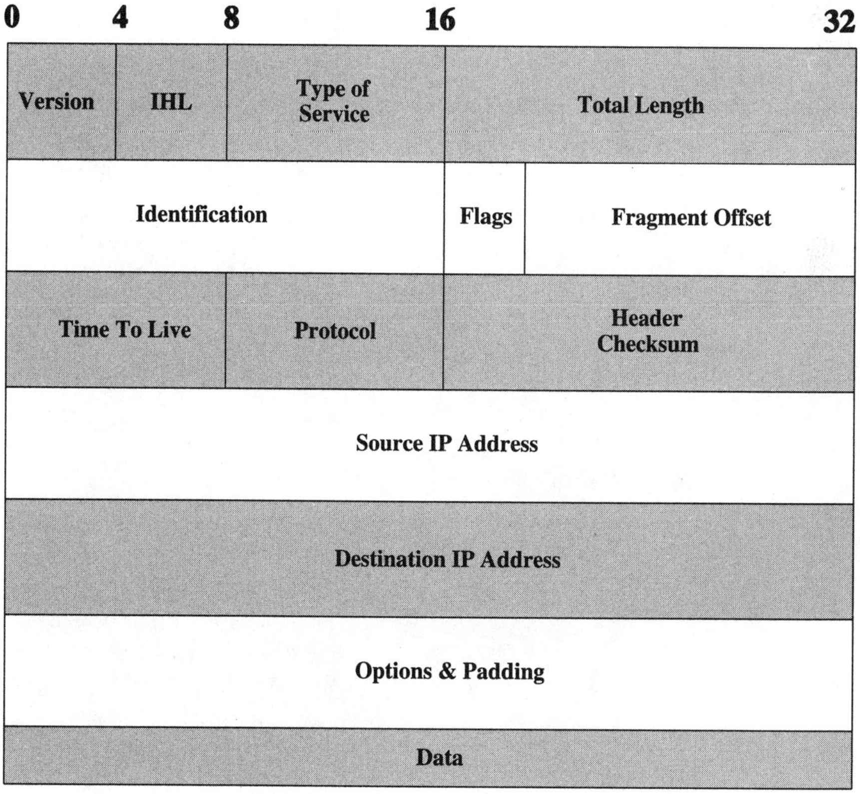

Figure 3-2
IP header format

0	4	8	16	32
Version	IHL	Type of Service	Total Length	
Identification			Flags	Fragment Offset
Time To Live		Protocol	Header Checksum	
Source IP Address				
Destination IP Address				
Options & Padding				
Data				

Field	Description
Version	A 4-bit field that identifies the IP version. Version 4 is the current IP format; the next generation is version 6.
Internet Header Length	Identifies the length of the IP header in words. This is a pointer to the start of the data. The minimum value is 5 or 20 bytes.
Type of Service	The 8 bits in this field define the quality of service. Bits 0–2 define precedence, while bits 3, 4, and 5 define delay, throughput, and reliability, respectively.
Total Length	This identifies the total length of the datagram—header plus data. This field is 16 bits long; therefore, it can specify a datagram of the size 2^{16} or 65,535 bytes. This is impractical for most networks.
Identification	A unique integer that identifies each datagram. If fragmentation of the datagram is required, this number is used in conjunction with the fragment-offset bits to determine where the datagram belongs in the original packet.
Flags	These are control bits that state whether a packet can or cannot be fragmented and if fragmented, whether more fragments are forthcoming.
Fragment Offset	A 13-bit number that identifies the fragment in the datagram. It is measured in units of 8 bytes, 64 bits.
Time To Live	This field identifies the maximum time that an IP datagram can remain on the network. It is measured in seconds but is most commonly used with hop counts. Each router will decrement this counter by 1 every time it processes the IP header. When the value reaches zero (0), the packet is destroyed.
Protocol	The value in this field identifies the upper layer protocol in the data portion of the datagram. A protocol number of 6 identifies TCP and 17 identifies UDP.
Header Checksum	Because some header fields change, a checksum on the header only is performed.
Source & Destination Addresses	This field contains the 32-bit address of the sender and receiver.
IP Options	This field contains options used for testing and debugging a network. Options may or may not appear in a datagram. Security and Record route are IP options.
Padding	Because the header is variable in length and must be within a 32-bit boundary, a padding field is incorporated to maintain the boundary.
Data	The information from the higher layer protocols.

defined in the Data Link layer below IP and provide a means for identifying IP hosts via their hardware or MAC addresses.

How IP Works

As it has been described before, data in the protocol stack is encapsulated with each layer's header information for transport across a network. Referring to Figure 3-3, we can outline the process in more detail. Assume the user on Host A is trying to send a file to Host B using the FTP protocol. Because it is beyond the scope of this text, I will not get into the specifics of FTP. Suffice it to say that the FTP protocol establishes as session using the TCP transport protocol.

1. The IP layer of Host A receives the TCP segment destined for Host B from the Transport layer of the protocol stack.

2. Host A's IP layer receives the segment as data and appends to it its header information. The IP header contains the source address of 172.16.1.1 and the destination address of 172.16.3.1 as well as information about the length of the datagram, type of service desired, and whether the packet is a fragment.

3. IP sends the datagram down the protocol stack to the Data Link layer, where it gets encapsulated into an Ethernet, 802.3 frame. From here, the frame is sent to the Physical layer and then on to Router A.

4. After Router A receives the packet, it will strip off the Ethernet header, encapsulate it with a WAN header (HDLC, X.25, or Frame Relay), and then pass it onto Router B.

5. Upon receipt of the packet, Router B will transmit the IP datagram to Host B encapsulated in an Ethernet 802.3 frame header.

The transport of an IP datagram across a network seems pretty straightforward. But, some questions should have arisen; for example, how did Host

Figure 3-3
Simple network
diagram

A know to send the packet to Router A? If all local networks transfer packets via the hardware or MAC address, how did Host A get the MAC address of Router A? Finally, how did Router A know to send the packet to Router B? These are all valid questions with two simple answers—*Address Resolution Protocol* (ARP) and *Routing Information Protocol* (RIP).

Address Resolution Protocol (ARP)

All local network communication occurs due to the "burned in" address on the *network interface card* (NIC). Now, there are provisions to manually change the "burned in" address (local administration), but for the most part, all addresses are universally administered. The company who manufactured the NIC was given blocks of addresses that they used to identify each card. This address is called the hardware or MAC address and it defines the hosts on a local area network. The hardware address is a 6-byte, 48-bit address that is controlled by a portion of the Data Link layer called the *Medium Access Control* (MAC) layer.

From Chapter 2, we know that the Data Link layer is responsible for connection control and addressing. In fact, the *Institute for Electrical and Electronic Engineers* (IEEE) "802" committee has subdivided the Data Link layer into two sublayers—the *Logical Link Control* (LLC) and the *Medium Access Control* (MAC) sublayers, as shown in Figure 3-4.

Figure 3-4
Data Link split

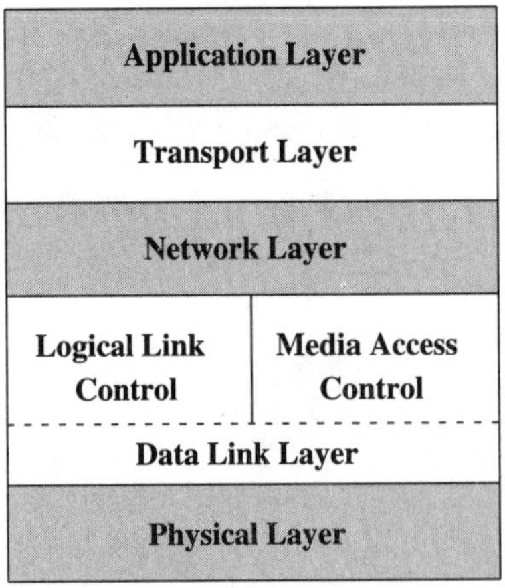

Application Layer	
Transport Layer	
Network Layer	
Logical Link Control	Media Access Control
Data Link Layer	
Physical Layer	

Through the LLC, higher layer protocols gain access to the Data Link while issues specific to a particular LAN type are handled in the MAC sublayer. In this layer, the hardware addresses, both source and destination, are mapped into frames for transmission onto the network. In our network example in Figure 3-1, we have two Ethernet 802.3 networks separated by a point-to-point WAN link. It is the responsibility of the MAC layer to properly format the IP datagram into an Ethernet frame to be sent onto the network. Figure 3-5 is an example of an Ethernet 802.3 frame that Host A would send to Host B. Notice that the first bits onto the wire (disregarding the preamble) are the bits for the destination address. But, if all we know is the IP address, how does this field get populated? How does an IP address get paired up with a hardware address?

Address Resolution Protocol, ARP, is how IP addresses get mapped to hardware addresses. On every IP host, a table exists that contains IP-to-LAN address assignments called the ARP Cache. The ARP Cache, on a host, can be created manually through static entries or dynamically through ARP queries and responses. In host-to-host communication, if an IP address is not present in the device's local ARP Cache, it will send out a broadcast address to find it. The ARP query is a Data Link broadcast message that requests the hardware address from whomever may have the particular IP address mentioned in the message. All stations receive the message, but only the host with the matching IP address will respond. It will send an ARP response that contains its hardware address. In our example, Host A is trying to send a packet to Host B.

1. Host A will look into its local ARP cache to find the hardware address that corresponds to 172.16.3.1. Host A does not find it and transmits an ARP query onto its Ethernet segment.

   As we can see from Figure 3-3, Host B will not respond back because it is on another network.

2. Host A will broadcast the ARP query three times before giving up. But, the communication does not fail. Why?

Figure 3-5

802.3 Ethernet frame

		0	**6**	**12**				
Preamble 7 bytes	**S F D**	**Dest. Address** 6 bytes	**Source Address** 6 bytes	**Length** 2 bytes	**Logical Link Control** 3 or 4 bytes	**Data** 43 - 1497 bytes	**FCS** 4 bytes

3. In the IP configuration of Host A, there is an entry called the "Default Gateway." Host A knows to forward all requests to this address if it can not find out where to send it directly. So, Host A looks into its local cache for an entry for 172.16.1.200—Router A's IP address. If it is not in the cache, Host A will broadcast another ARP query to find it.

4. Host A retrieves the router's hardware address and sends the packet to it in hopes that the router will know how to get to the network where Host B resides.

Figure 3-6 shows an ARP frame and its message format. Note the ARP message is not encapsulated within an IP datagram it occupies the data portion of a frame. Brief descriptions of the fields in the message are provided in the table on the following page.

After the packet gets to the router, the router must make a decision concerning sending the packet on to its destination. The router contains an ARP Cache and a routing table that it can use to move the packet on. As

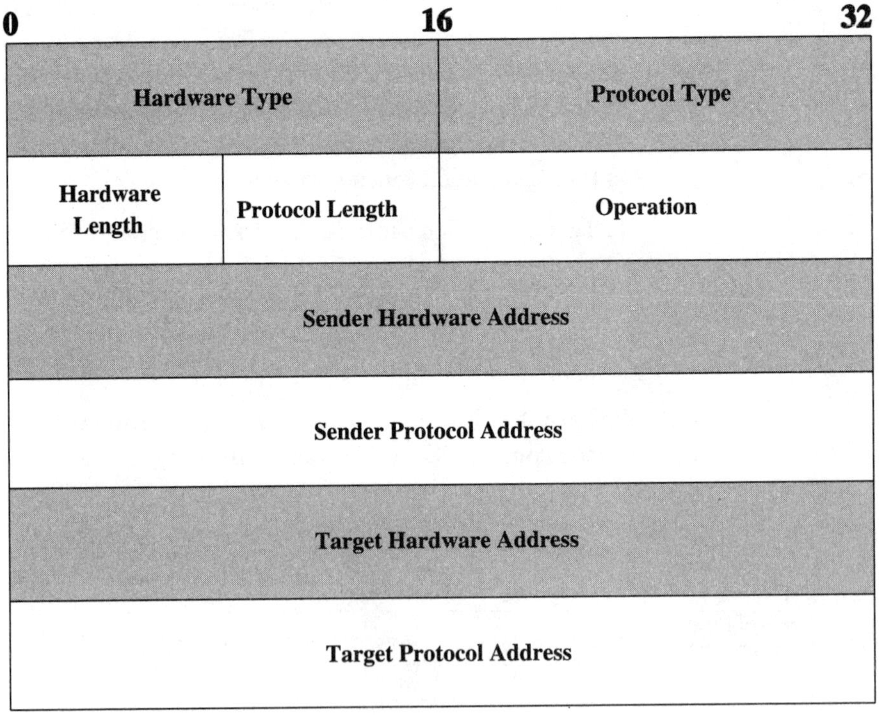

Figure 3-6
ARP header format

0	16	32
Hardware Type		Protocol Type
Hardware Length	Protocol Length	Operation
Sender Hardware Address		
Sender Protocol Address		
Target Hardware Address		
Target Protocol Address		

Field	Description
Hardware	Specifies the hardware interface type for which the sender requires a response. A value of "1" is used for Ethernet.
Protocol	Specifies the high-layer protocol address the sender has supplied. A value of "0800" represents an IP address.
Hardware and Protocol Length	Specifies the hardware and protocol address length
Operation	Specifies the function of the ARP message. A value of "1" represents an ARP request.
Sender Hardware Address	Specifies the hardware address of the sender
Sender Protocol Address	Specifies the protocol address of the sender
Target Hardware Address	This field is reserved for the hardware address of the target.
Target Protocol Address	This field contains the protocol address of the target.

before, manual entry or dynamic queries populate the ARP Cache. Routing protocols are needed to populate the routing table. A routing table contains route designations and costs associated with these designations. In the next section, we will discuss various types of routing protocols and how they are implemented in a Nortel Networks router.

Routing Protocols

The router in our example, Router A, knew how to get to Host B by way of its network address. Locally stored in the router's memory was the reachability information it needed to get the packet to Router B that it in turn passes onto the network where Host B resides. Both Router A and Router B must know how to get to the networks each other serve. They are able to learn this information by way of routing protocols. Routing protocols let routing devices dynamically learn about each other's networks and exchange the information between them. The information exchanged is used to keep the routing tables updated when changes in the network environment occur.

There are several routing protocols and they differ in scalability and performance. Some are designed for small networks, whereas others were designed for use in large intranets. The protocols used in smaller networks usually send complete routing tables and have a modest convergence time, whereas others send periodic "hello" packets to maintain their peer router status and converge relatively quickly. Regardless, there are two parts to each protocol—the transmission of routing updates from a router concerning the location and number of networks for which it has responsibility and the processing of the received updates to efficiently direct network traffic.

Each routing protocol can be included into one of two classes—distance-vector or link-state routing protocols. A distance-vector protocol sends and maintains a routing table that lists known networks and the distance to each. Link-state protocols do not send a routing table; rather, they send information concerning the status of their directly connected links. Comparison of the two would yield that link-state protocols do converge quicker than distance-vector protocols, yet they are more complex and are harder to implement than their counter parts. Surprisingly, differences in CPU and bandwidth utilization are minimal.

Distance-Vector Routing Protocols

Distance-vector protocols, as their name implies, send routing information based on the distance between networks usually denoted as a *hop count*. A *hop count* refers to the number of routers that must be traversed before reaching the destination network, as shown in Figure 3-7.

These routing protocols send a broadcast message onto each of their configured interfaces to all routers on a local subnet (or hosts acting as routing devices). The message can include a full routing table or just updates after the first full transmission of the routing table. The following are examples of distance-vector protocols:

Figure 3-7
Route table example

Network	Distance	Next Hop
172.16.2.0	1	172.16.2.2

- IP Routing Information Protocol (RIP) versions 1 and 2
- IP *Interior Gateway Routing Protocol* (IGRP)
- Novell NetWare *Internetwork Packet Exchange Routing Information Protocol* (IPX RIP)
- AppleTalk *Routing Table Maintenance Protocol* (RTMP)
- IP Enhanced IGRP
- IP *Border Gateway Protocol* (BGP)

Routing is disrupted when topological changes occur, and the speed at which all routers can recompute their tables can greatly effect network performance. It is vital to keep the routers in a "converged" state as much of the time as possible. Techniques like poisoned-reverse, split horizon, and hold-down timers increase convergence time and minimize transitional routing loops.

Transitional Loops   Loops can occur between routers when a router loses a local interface and before it can send out an update stating that the network is now unreachable. When a router loses a connection, it will remove the route from its table. However, previous broadcasts can lead another router to advertise a route to the lost connection through itself. When it propagates its table, the router with the initial lost connection can populate its table with the route through the other router. The following outlines the sequence that can lead to a routing loop (see Figure 3-8a).

Figure 3-8a
Router A and B
before the loss of
router A's Ethernet
interface and after
routes have
converged

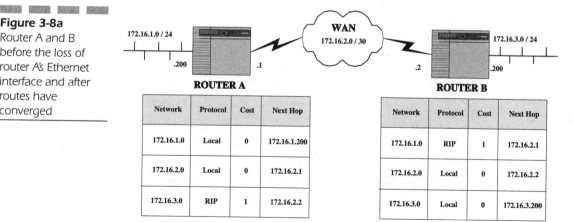

Network	Protocol	Cost	Next Hop
172.16.1.0	Local	0	172.16.1.200
172.16.2.0	Local	0	172.16.2.1
172.16.3.0	RIP	1	172.16.2.2

Network	Protocol	Cost	Next Hop
172.16.1.0	RIP	1	172.16.2.1
172.16.2.0	Local	0	172.16.2.2
172.16.3.0	Local	0	172.16.3.200

Figure 3-8b
Router A loses
connection to its
local network
interface for the
172.16.1.0 network

Network	Protocol	Cost	Next Hop
172.16.2.0	Local	0	172.16.2.1
172.16.3.0	RIP	1	172.16.2.2

Network	Protocol	Cost	Next Hop
172.16.1.0	RIP	1	172.16.2.1
172.16.2.0	Local	0	172.16.2.2
172.16.3.0	Local	0	172.16.3.200

Figure 3-8c
Router A updates its
route table with the
learned information
for the 172.16.1.0
network from
router B

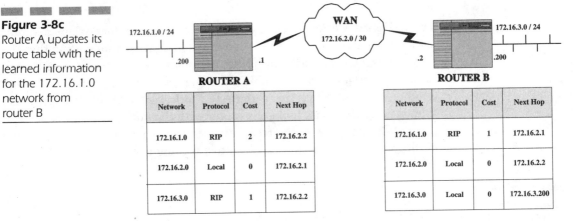

Network	Protocol	Cost	Next Hop
172.16.1.0	RIP	2	172.16.2.2
172.16.2.0	Local	0	172.16.2.1
172.16.3.0	RIP	1	172.16.2.2

Network	Protocol	Cost	Next Hop
172.16.1.0	RIP	1	172.16.2.1
172.16.2.0	Local	0	172.16.2.2
172.16.3.0	Local	0	172.16.3.200

1. Router A loses its connection to 172.16.1.0.

2. Router A removes the route to 172.16.1.0 from its routing table, Figure 3-8b.

3. Router B, using information from previous announcements from Router A, broadcasts that the route to 172.16.1.0 can be reached through itself.

4. Router A receives the update and adds the network 172.16.1.0 to its table with the next hop as Router B, Figure 3-8c. The distance value is increased by one to equal two hops from Router A to 172.16.1.0.

5. Router A receives a frame destined for 172.16.1.0 on one of its interfaces and forwards it toward Router B.

6. Router B sends the frame to Router A.

The frame will loop between the two routers until the IP *time-to-live* (TTL) value has been reached. At some point, Router A will send a route update stating that it can get to the 172.16.1.0 network through Router B. Router B will recalculate its entry for 172.16.1.0 with a hop count value of 3. Both routers will send and process each others route updates until the hop count reaches infinity, at which point the routers would remove the route.

NOTE: *The value of infinity is arbitrary and decided by the particular routing protocol (RIP uses a value of 16 to represent infinity).*

Using techniques like split horizon or split horizon with poisoned-reverse can prevent transitional loops and the "count-to-infinity" problem. *Split horizon* is simply a method by which a router omits routes learned from a neighbor router in its updates back to it. *Split horizon with poisoned reverse* includes these routes in updates, but with the their metrics set to infinity. Referring to Figure 3-9, if router A believes that it can reach D through C, A should indicate that its route to D is unreachable. By telling C that a route to D through A is unreachable, A can be assured that in the event that C loses connection to D, it won't get confused and think that it still has a path. On point-to-point links, this is easily seen. But consider if A, B, and C are on the same broadcast network. Because B can talk directly to C, A should also report to B that a path to D through itself is unreachable. Similarly, B would report that a path through itself to D is also unreachable. Using split horizon with poison reverse, router A will send a route with infinity as its distance to D to Router C. If the connection between C and D is severed, C will have no alternate path and notify A that D is unreachable. Router A now knows that the path to D is down. With Split horizon, router A would simply omit that it knew a route to D in its update to C.

Unfortunately, split horizon does have its flaws and cannot stop all occurrences of the "count-to-infinity" problem. Take for instance the scenario if

Figure 3-9
Routers A, B, C,
and D

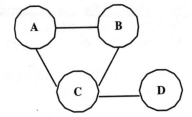

Figure 3-9, router A could believe that it had a path to D through B, B through C, and C through A. This loop would only stop when "count to infinity" was reached and only then would the route to D be deemed unreachable. Triggered updates were implemented in order to speed up this convergence. *Triggered updates* allow a router to immediately send out an update when a metric is recalculated on any of its interfaces. The update only contains the routes that have changed. When a neighbor router receives this update and the result is that its metric must be changed, it will send a triggered update to its connected neighbors. The result is a cascade of triggered updates. Due to the dynamic nature of computer networks, there is still a possibility that a loop can form. As the triggered updates are propagating to the further routers, normal updates are taking place. It is possible that after the triggered update has passed through a router that it can receive a normal update from a router that has not yet received a triggered event. This could reestablish the faulty route.

Routing Information Protocol (RIP)

RIP is one of the earliest dynamic routing protocols used in the Internet. It can trace its ancestry back to Xerox Network protocols that were adopted for the *Xerox Network System* (XNS). RIP was intended to allow routers to exchange information for computing routes in an IP-based environment—mainly the Internet. Like other distance-vector protocols, RIP makes its routing decisions based on distance only. Metric for measuring this distance is the *hop count,* where a *hop count* is a measure of how many routers a message must pass through to get to its destination. Plagued with the "count to infinity" problem, RIP's designers had to come up with a value of infinity that would be small enough to stop the "count" as soon as possible, while being large enough to accommodate real network routes. Thinking it impractical that networks would be larger than 15 hops, the value for "infinity" was set to 16. RIP is a simple protocol and, with its ease of configuration, has become one of the most well-known routing protocols.

The first version of RIP (RIPv1) was developed as a technique to pass reachability information across simple topologies. It is termed a "classful" protocol in that it relies on the predefined class (A, B, or C) of network address to determine the subnet mask. RIPv1 broadcasts two types of packets, updates and requests, every 30 seconds. Update packets carry routing information gleaned from a routing table on the router. The routing information contained in an update packet includes

■ Destination address of a host or network

■ The IP address of the gateway sending the update

■ The route metric or cost

The metric or cost of a specific route can be from 1 to 15. Routers with directly connected networks usually carry a cost of 1. When a router receives an update packet, it initializes a "timeout" timer. If the router that sent the update has not sent another one within the timeout period of 180 seconds, the route is deemed unreachable. Although the route is unreachable, it still resides in the routing table with a metric of 16. It stays in the routing table until the "garbage-collection" time has expired. This second timer is defined as 120 seconds. Request packets are sent from a RIP-aware router to other RIP-aware routers on the network. The request is for a full or partial copy of the router's routing table.

Still prevalent is the "count to infinity" problem inherent in all distance-vector protocols. RIPv1 incorporates split horizon or split horizon with poisoned reverse to speed convergence time and to reduce routing loops.

The information contained in version 1 of RIP was limited. It didn't consider autonomous systems and their interactions. It also doesn't have a facility for subnetting or authentication. Granted, these technologies were not available at the time RIPv1 was developed. An update to version 1 was needed. *RIP version 2* (RIPv2) was created to overcome the scalability and performance problems that were apart of version 1. Built over the top of version 1, RIPv2 still maintains a maximum *hop count* of 15 and sends out unsolicited updates every 30 seconds. Each update can only contain 25 routes. RIPv2 uses the multicast address of 224.0.0.9 to transmit its updates instead of a broadcast, thereby reducing network communication between devices that are not interested in receiving RIP updates. The biggest improvement comes in RIPv2's ability pass along in its updates subnet mask information. In this vane, RIPv2 is considered a "classless" routing protocol. It is not limited to the predefined classes (A, B, or C) to separate the non-host portion of a network address. The subnet mask information is included in the RIP header mentioned below. Below are the extensions added to version that are included in RIPv2.

- Routing tag—The routing tag is used to distinguish between internal and external routes and facilitates merging RIP and non-RIP networks.
- Subnet mask—The subnet mask field contains the subnet mask used to denote the network or non-host portion of an IP address.
- Next hop entry—The next hop field is used to specify the IP address to which packets to the destination should be forwarded.

RIPv2 also supports triggered updates and authentication. If authentication is implemented, one entry in the RIP packet is used for a password reducing the number of routes to 24. A plain-text password is currently the only authentication supported.

As stated earlier, RIP is a simple protocol and is easy to configure. Following are some considerations that you should be aware of before implementing it:

- The maximum amount of networks that a message can traverse is 15. As networks get larger this can pose a problem, especially if you define a cost higher than 1 to a route.
- The simplistic hop count does not take into account routes with lower delay. The router is only concerned with the number of routers between source and destination.
- RIP can use a fair amount of bandwidth because it sends a full routing table in its updates. Also, because the maximum amount of routes per update is 25, in large networks, multiple updates will have to be sent.

The RIP packet format is shown in Figure 3-10. The field explanations are shown on the next page.

In our example, Router A and Router B are both configured using RIP version 2. After each other's routing tables have been calculated, the packet from Host A can be transmitted from Router A to B thanks to the learned

Field	Description
Command	This field specifies the purpose of this datagram—request, response, traceon, traceoff, or reserved.
	Request—A request to send all of part of a routing table
	Response—This is a message containing all or part of a routing table. This can be sent in response to a request or poll, or it may be an update generated by the sending router.
	Traceon and Traceoff are obsolete.
	Reserved—A reserved field used by Sun Microsystems
Version	The RIP version number
Address Family Identifier	Because RIP2 can carry information for several protocols, a value in this field will specify the address type. IP has an address type of 2.
Route Tag	This attribute specifies that a route is to be preserved and re-advertised with the route. This is used to distinguish between internal RIP routers from external RIP routes that may have been reported by EGP or another IGP.
IP Address	The IP address of the destination
Subnet Mask	This value applied to the IP address to yield the network portion
Next Hop	The address of the immediate next hop IP address where datagrams should be forwarded
Metric	The total cost of getting the datagram from the host to the destination. This represents the sum of all costs associated with the networks that must be traversed.

information in A's routing table. Figure 3-8 shows the routing tables for Router A and B.

Link State Routing Protocols

The second class of routing protocols is called *link state* routing protocols. They are called "link state" protocols because each router keeps track of the state of all links in the network. The "state" is the specific well-being of a

Figure 3-10
RIP header format

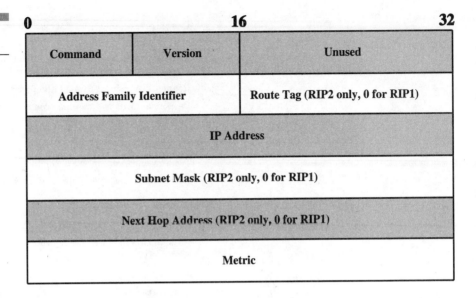

0	16	32
Command	Version	Unused
Address Family Identifier		Route Tag (RIP2 only, 0 for RIP1)
IP Address		
Subnet Mask (RIP2 only, 0 for RIP1)		
Next Hop Address (RIP2 only, 0 for RIP1)		
Metric		

router interface. Each router, in the link state routing domain, creates neighbor relationships called *adjacencies*. Link status updates, or *link state advertisements* (LSA), are only sent between these adjacent routers. A router populates an LSA packet with the name and cost to each of its neighbors before transmitting it out its interfaces. These advertisements are forwarded throughout the routing domain where each router stores the most recent generated packet from each other router. The router uses the stored advertisement packets to build the link state database. After a router has built the link state database, routes can then be computed using a specific mathematical algorithm called Dijkstra's Algorithm. Some of the main features of link state routing protocols are

- Hierarchical
- Supports *Variable Length Subnet Masks* (VLSM)
- Fast convergence
- Low network utilization
- Use of multicast packets

In multi-access networks where there is a potential for many neighbor adjacencies, a single designated router is defined to build them all. The designated router also ensures that the communication between neighbors is bi-directional. Support of variable length subnet masks allows for route summarization. Route summarization means that complete routing information can be sent to other routers in a smaller table format. As an easy example of this, if you have a router with multiple interfaces addressed as 172.30.16.10, 172.30.17.10, and 172.30.18.10, you can summarize these to an external router as 172.30.16.0 with a 22-bit subnet mask. A 22-bit subnet mask (255.255.252.0) encompasses networks 172.30.16.0 through 172.30.19.0.

Link state protocols do not send periodic updates like their distance vector counter parts. Each update is sent in response to a change or adverse circuit condition on one of the routers in the routing domain. On average, routers using a link state routing protocol will adjust to changes (converge) quicker than routers that do not. These incremental updates also lend to keeping network utilization low.

Nortel Routers

For our small network example in Figure 3-3, RIP would be the desired routing protocol to implement for the reasons we have previously discussed. RIP is added onto a circuit either during the initial configuration or later. In Chapter 2, we added a network interface that used the IP protocol and we selected RIP for that interface. When RIP is added to an IP interface, it is enabled with default values for all global parameters. The following section details the interface parameters used for RIP.

Configuration Steps—RIP Interface Parameters

1. From the Configuration Manager Main Windows, select Protocols: IP > RIP > Interfaces (Figure 3-11).
2. Select Interface in the RIP Interface list from the IP RIP Interface Config window (Figure 3-12).

The parameters listed in the IP RIP Interface Config window are defined on the following page. You will need to use the scroll bar, located at the bottom right of the window, to view most of these parameters.

Parameter	Description
Enable	Specifies whether RIP is enabled or disabled on this interface. Default is Enable.
RIP Supply	Specifies whether RIP transmits RIP updates to neighbors. Default is Enable.
RIP Listen	Specifies whether RIP receives RIP updates from neighbors. Default is Enable.
Default Route Supply	Specifies whether RIP advertises a default route in it updates to neighbors. Default is Disable.
Default Router Listen	Specifies whether RIP adds a default route to its routing table. Default is Disable.
Poisoned Reverse	Specifies whether RIP will use Poison Reverse or Split Horizon when advertising routes to neighbors. On certain interfaces, a router with the Actual cost might be desired. Default is Poisoned.
Time to Live (TTL)	This value is inserted into an IP header for RIP updates. Setting this value to one hop keeps the update on the local network and reduces the possibility of the update being forwarded around the network. Default is one hop.
Broadcast Timer	Specifies how often the RIP transmits a full routing table update. The default is 30 seconds.
Timeout Timer	This value tells RIP how long to wait for an update before declaring the particular network unreachable. Default is 90 seconds.
Holddown Timer	This value specifies the amount of time a route will be advertised after it has become invalid. Default is 90 seconds.
RIP Mode	Specifies the version of RIP to run (RIP1, RIP2, or RIP2) with subnet aggregation. Default is RIP1.
Triggered Updates	With this parameter enabled, RIP sends an update on a specified interface when it recalculates a route metric. Default is Disable.
Authentication Type	This parameter is only valid for RIP2 and it can be set to simple or left at none. When set to simple, RIP drops all packets that do not have a valid password. Default is none.
Authentication Password	A 1-to-16 character password
Initial Stabilization Timer	This is the time that RIP allows for itself to learn all routes from its neighbors before sending full updates. Default is 120 seconds.

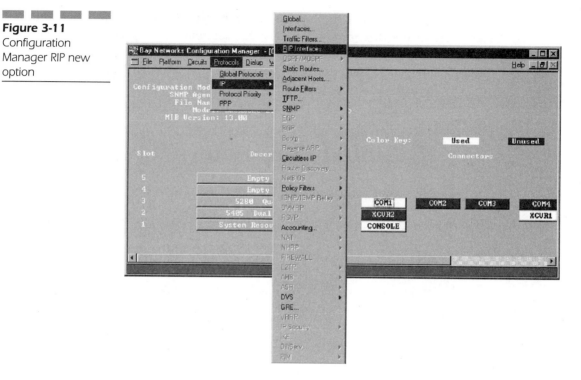

Figure 3-11
Configuration
Manager RIP new
option

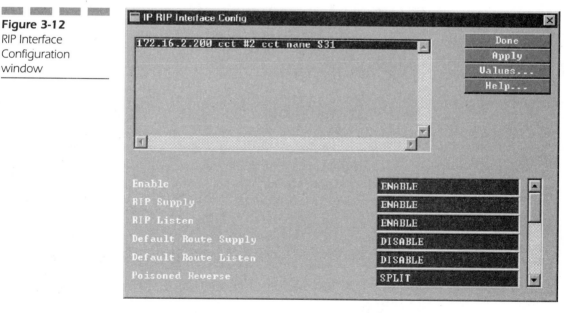

Figure 3-12
RIP Interface
Configuration
window

Most of the RIP parameters can be left at their default values. For our network in Figure 3-3, I chose to customize RIP by setting the "Poisoned Reverse" parameter to Split Horizon and changing the "RIP Mode" to RIP2. There are a couple of other parameters that affect RIP and they are located in the IP Global parameters.

IP Global Parameters for RIP

From the Configuration Manager main windows, select Protocols, IP, Global.

Parameter	Description
RIP Diameter	The value that RIP uses to calculate infinity. All routers must have this value set the same in order for RIP to function properly. Default is 15 hops.
RIP Maximum Equal Cost Paths	This parameter sets the maximum number of equal-cost paths for a network that has been installed in the routing table by RIP. Default is 1.
Multiple Nexthop Calculation Method	There are three methods that can be selected for routing between equal-cost paths—round-robin selection, selection based on source address, and selection based on both source and destination address. This parameter enables or disables multipath support. Default is Disable.

The Routing Table

In our explanation of RIP, we used Figure 3-8 as the routing table for routers A and B. In actuality, the IP routing table includes more information than just the network address, hop count, and next hop address. Figure 3-13 shows a routing table from a BLN-2 router. Notice that there are five

Figure 3-13
Nortel router routing table

Destination	Mask	Proto	Age	Cost	NextHop Addr / AS
172.16.1.0	255.255.255.0	Local	6110170	0	172.16.1.200
172.16.2.0	255.255.255.252	Local	6110170	0	172.16.2.1
172.16.3.0	255.255.255.0	RIP	9	1	172.16.2.2

more fields in the table—mask, type, protocol, ages, and index. The following explains the routing table fields:

- Destination—This is the dotted-decimal IP address of the destination network.
- Mask—This value is the corresponding subnet mask for the destination network.
- Proto—The protocol by which this route was learned. Manually configured routes are considered "Local."
- Age—This value is the number of seconds since this route has been updated.
- Next Hop Addr—This is the dotted-decimal address of the interface that would be used to forward a packet toward the network.
- AS—*Autonomous System* number (used for BGP or EGP)

A router places its own interfaces into the routing table as Type "Direct" and with "Local" for Protocol. Other entries are added from information learned from the updates from adjacent routers. Static and default routes are also added to the routing table as Type "Direct" and Protocol "Local."

Static Routes

If you want to restrict RIP updates from specific subnets or if you have a router that doesn't use a routing protocol, you must configure static routes. Static routes are manually configured on a router and they specify the next hop address to which a datagram will be forwarded. Because it is impractical to list every possible network in RIP updates, a special static route of 0.0.0.0 is used to define a default route. A default route informs a router how to handle traffic for which it does not have a route. When an unknown network is encountered, the router will forward the packet to the next hop address defined for the default route.

One reason to implement a default route is to forward packets out of your private network to the Internet. When a router on your internal network is presented with a destination network that it has no knowledge of, it would forward the packet out the defined interface that could point to your Internet gateway. The default route will allow you to keep your internal routing tables free from the many networks that are routed in the Internet.

Configuring a static route is accomplished through either the *Technician Interface* (TI) or through Configuration Manager. The following steps use Configuration Manager to create a static route that will be a default route through our synchronous interface.

NOTE: *This will only be an example and will not apply to the configuration we made in Chapter 2.*

Configuring a Default Route

Start Site Manager and select the router from the Well-Known Connections list (Figure 3-14).

Start Configuration Manager by either pressing [F3] or by selecting Tools: Configuration Manager > Local File. It is always better to work from a back or copy of a config file. Making dynamic changes may disrupt the router.

1. Open the IP Static Routes window.

   Select, from Configuration Manager, Protocols: IP > Static Routes (Figure 3-15).

   The IP Static Routes window opens displaying any static routes that may have been configured.

2. Click Add to enter the static route information.

3. Enter Static Route information.

   Destination IP Address: 0.0.0.0

   Address Mask: 0.0.0.0

   Cost: 1 (default)

   Next Hop Address: 172.16.2.2

   Next Hop Mask: 255.255.255.252

   Preference: 16 (default)

   Unnumbered Cct Name: -blank-

Figure 3-14
Site Manage main
window

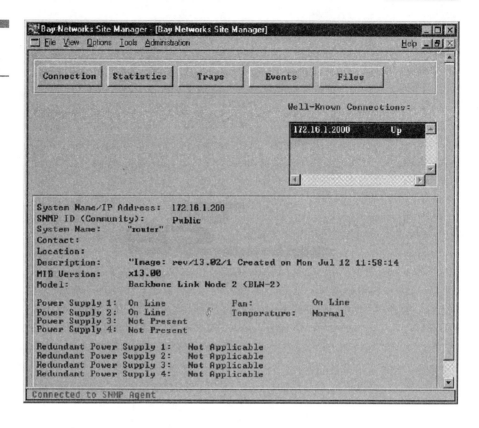

The *Destination Address* is simply the network address that you want
to configure for the static route with its corresponding subnet mask in
the *Address Mask* field. The *Cost* is the number of hops it takes to get
to the destination address. The default value is set to 1, but it can be as
high as the RIP diameter. The *Next Hop Address* is the address of the
router that will transfer the packet to the destination network with its
corresponding subnet mask in the *Next Hop Mask* field.

IP allows for multiple default routes to the same destination address.
The *Preference field* is used to weight each route. The higher the
number, the more preferred the route. When specifying a static route
for an unnumbered interface, the local route interface circuit name
needs to be included in the *Unnumbered Cct Name* field.

4. Click OK when finished entering the static route information.

Figure 3-15
Configuration
Manager Static
Routes option

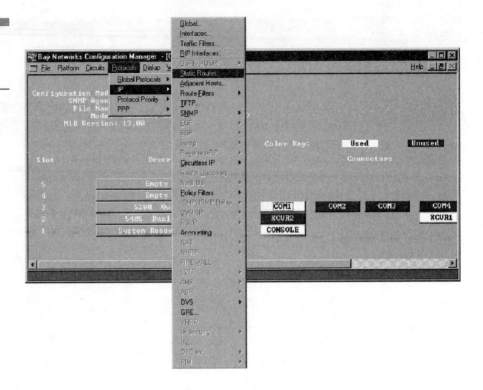

You will be returned to the IP Static Routes window, as shown in Figure 3-16, where the new static route appears in the list box.

5. Click Done to return to the Configuration Manager main window.

The above static route will tell the router to forward all unrecognized packets out its interface that points to the next hop address of 172.16.2.2.

IP Global Parameters

When IP is configured on a slot on a Nortel router, default values are automatically globally configured for the slot. Accessing the IP Global Parameters window from Configuration Manager can modify these values. Figure

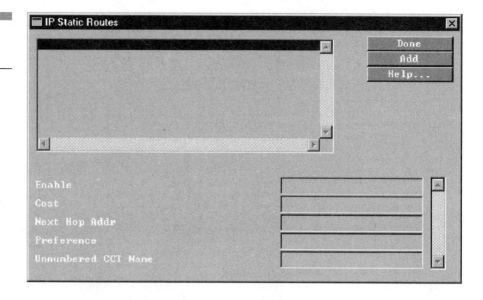

Figure 3-16
IP Static Routes
window

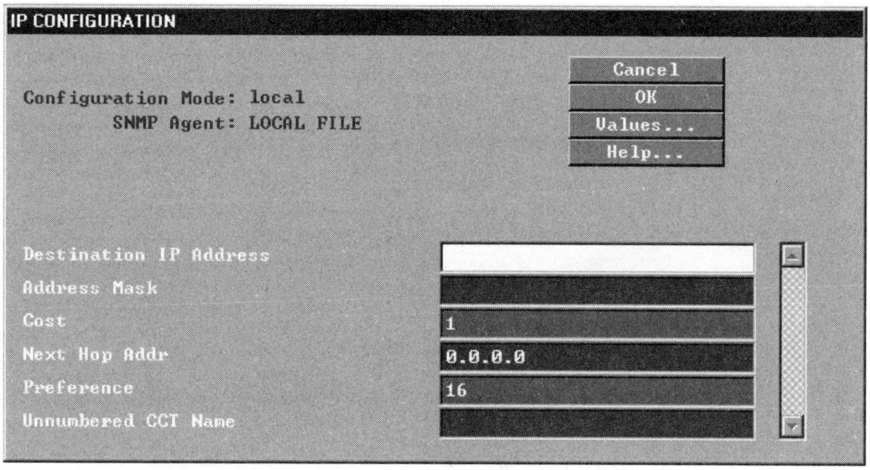

Figure 3-17
IP Configuration
window for static

3-17 displays part of the global parameters available for editing. Use the scroll bar on the right to scroll through the rest of the values. Select Protocols: IP > Global from the Configuration Manager main window.

The Edit IP Global Parameters window opens Figure 3-18. The table below outlines the IP global parameters that pertain to the routing as previously discussed.

Figure 3-18
IP Global Parameters,
part 1

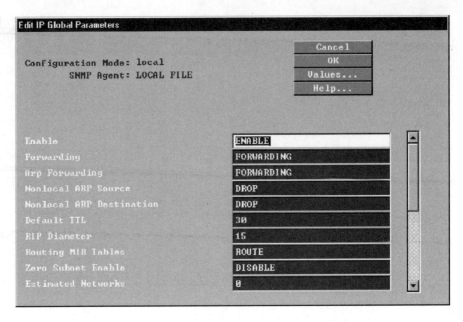

Parameter	Description
Enable	This parameter enables or disables IP on the router. It is set to "enable" by default. Note: *Disabling* IP in dynamic mode will stop all communication to and from Site Manager.
Forwarding	In forwarding mode, the router will accept all IP traffic addressed to itself and forward all others. If this value is set to non-forwarding, the router acts like a host and drops all packets not specifically addressed to it. The default is forwarding.
ARP Forwarding	Specifies how ARP works on this router in relation to the above "Forwarding" parameter. If set to forwarding, all ARP requests destined for it will be consumed. Any others will be dropped. When set to non-forwarding, specific ARP requests will still be consumed but all others will be bridged. The default is to set this parameter as is the Forwarding parameter.
Default TTL	This is the Time To Live value that is part of the IP header. The router and other routers use this value as a counter to prevent IP packets from circulating through the network forever. This value, measured in hops, is the starting value that routers decrement when transmitting an IP packet. The default value is 30 hops.

Figure 3-19
IP Global Parameters,
part 2

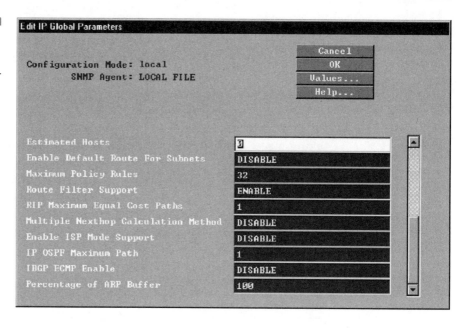

Parameter	Description
Estimated Networks and Estimated Hosts (Figure 3-19)	These values allow you to preallocate memory for the routing routing table. By estimating the number of networks and hosts you will have, you can increase the speed by which the router learns its routes. This is because the router does not need the overhead caused by dynamic routing. A default value of 0 (zero) means that the router will preallocate 500 networks and hosts.
Enable Default Route For Subnets (Figure 3-19)	This parameter determines whether the router will use a default route for unknown subnets. The default is to disable default routes. Note: A default route must be present in the routing table in order for this value to be set to enable.

SUMMARY

In this chapter, we explored the mechanisms involved with multi-segmented networks. Because practical networks rarely involve a single subnet, devices known as routers must be employed to pass traffic throughout the enterprise.

Routers determine a "best" path from a source location to a destination. They can compute these routes by using a routing protocol or they can be given a route manually. Routing protocols have the distinct benefit of scalability over manually entered routes. As a network grows, so does the management task of changing or adding routes.

There are two classes of routing protocols—interior gateway or exterior gateway protocols. This class distinction simply states where the routing is taking place. Interior gateway protocols contain the rout information for routers inside a autonomous system. Conversely, exterior gateway protocols contain the routing information required to transfer packets between autonomous systems. Despite the class of protocol, there are two main types of routing protocols—distance vector and link state. Distance vector routing protocols rely on a single metric for determining best path—*hop count*. Updates are broadcast periodically (usually every 30 seconds) and contain a full routing table. Link state routing protocols only send advertisements (LSAs) to neighbor routers when a change in the environment is detected. These protocols converge much more quickly than distance vector routing protocols and have the added benefit of affording every router in the enterprise a complete copy of the network topology. From information gleaned in these LSAs, each router computes its "best path" using the Dijkstra Algorithm, taking into account parameters such as bandwidth and priority.

We completed the chapter by discussing the methods involved in adding a distance vector protocol, namely RIP, and the parameters governing the underlying network protocol—IP. Using Site Manager and a backup copy of the router's configuration file, we added RIP to an interface and discussed the various global RIP and IP parameters used by Nortel routers in their routing decisions. Link state protocols, like *Open Shortest Path First* (OSPF), are more complex than their distance vector counterparts and are beyond the scope of this book.

IP Services

As we venture forward and deeper into configuring Nortel Network routers, you will begin to see the robustness of the TCP/IP suite of protocols that were discussed in Chapter 2, "Configure Nortel Networks Routers." In this chapter, we will discuss the IP-related services that are provided in the BayRS™ software. Most of the topics we will discuss, such as BOOTP, *File Transfer Protocol* (FTP), and Telnet, you will want to employ. Other topics, such as Circuitless IP, Proxy ARP, and RARP, you will find equally as informative, but you might want to wait as your network grows before you implement these features. The services discussed in this chapter represent a subset of the IP services provided in Nortel Network routers.

Setting up network architecture requires planning. You have to plan the physical layout. How will devices communicate (Ethernet, Token Ring, and so on)? Where will these devices be located? You also decide on a network protocol, which will influence your address structure. When you have decided on the network protocol and address structure, you will need to decide how you will go about implementing your decision. Are you going to manually configure each device or will you use an automatic method? Manual configuration, as we know, does not scale well. When the number of end devices increases, so will the amount of time needed to make changes. The BOOTP service provided in the BayRS software will allow you to use an automatic protocol to ease this configuration burden.

Among the other services provided by the BayRS software, the FTP and Telnet protocols will be extremely important to you as you manage your network architecture. FTP is a protocol that allows you to send and retrieve files from FTP servers. It is important on the router because it allows you to *get* files, such as the router's configuration file or a saved log file, from the Flash card. You can also *put* files such as scripts that allow you to pull statistics and configured parameters from the router's MIB from the *Technician Interface* (TI). In order to use the scripts *put* on the router, you would have to connect to the router via its console port or through a remote connection over the network. The Telnet protocol facilitates an "in-band" connection to the router. An in-band connection is one that uses the connected network for transport. When using Telnet, your terminal screen displays as if you were directly connected to the router's console port. A Telnet connection to a router opens up a TI where commands can be input for management and inspection, of course, after your security has been authenticated. This brings up another point: security.

Each of these services has weaknesses that can be exploited. Although these services offer a lot of functionality and convenience, you should be aware of when to implement them. Not all installations call for the full gambit of services to be configured. For instance, routers that connect you to an ISP need not have Telnet or FTP running. These protocols could be implemented on an "as-needed" basis by turning them "off" and "on" using Site Manager. One of the best methods of providing security on the router is by utilizing traffic filters.

Traffic filters, mainly IP filters, allow you to block addresses and upper layer applications from entering, or leaving, your network. You can define a range of IP addresses, or a specific address, to be prohibited from traversing the router. If you want to prevent port scans, you could implement a filter that blocks port 1. In this way, you can set up your router to mimic a firewall. We will not delve deeply into IP traffic filters, but we will get involved enough to implement some of the predefined filters as well as create one of our own.

Configuring Circuitless IP

A circuitless IP interface on a Nortel router is one that is not mapped to a specific circuit. Traffic is delivered and transmitted the same for a circuitless IP interface as it would be for an IP address mapped onto an interface. This allows the router to be reachable even if multiple IP interfaces have become disabled, that is, as long as connectivity to the router is still valid.

Several rules govern a circuitless IP interface:

■ Only one circuitless IP interface can be configured on a router. If others have been created, they will not initialize.

■ A unique IP address and subnet mask must be defined for a circuitless IP interface.

■ A circuitless IP interface *cannot* be configured in nonforwarding mode.

A circuitless IP interface is useful for remote applications like Nortel Networks' Optivity and/or HP Openview. You need only define one interface per router for a management connection. Also, these applications can maintain the management connection to a router even if the router loses several of its interfaces. Circuitless IP is a good fit for BGP as a local peer or as a DLSw slot. It can also serve as a source address when configuring a *Network Time Protocol* (NTP). Configuring a router for circuitless IP is straightforward and is described next.

Configuring the Circuitless Interface

Start Configuration Manager using a local copy of the configuration file. Although this configuration can be completed dynamically, it is recommended that you use a backup config file or a remote copy. Then follow these steps:

1. Create the Circuitless IP Interface.

   From the Configuration Manager main window, click Protocols, IP, Circuitless IP, Create (see Figure 4-1).

   The IP Configuration window opens (see Figure 4-2), prompting you for the IP address and subnet mask that will define the circuitless interface.

2. Enter a unique IP address and subnet mask for this interface.

3. Define a slot mask.

   The slot mask defines on which slots the interface will be active. A bit-value of "1" enables the interface on the respective slot.

   Let's say we are defining a slot mask for the BLN-2.

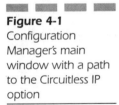

Figure 4-1
Configuration Manager's main window with a path to the Circuitless IP option

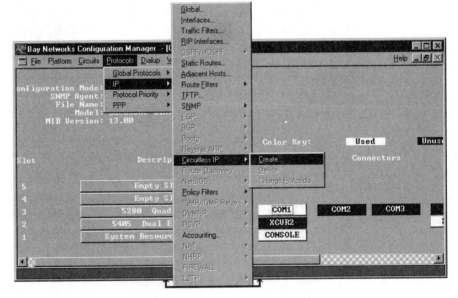

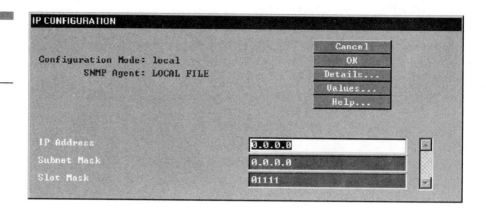

Figure 4-2
Circuitless IP
configuration
window

Because there are five slots in a BLN, there will be five bit values in this field (Configuration Manager will insert a default bit mask when this interface is added). If you wish to have all slots enabled except number 1 (the SRML), the slot mask will be

Slot Mask: 01111

Enabling the interface on a *System Resource Model* (SRM) or a slot that does not support IP will not affect the circuitless IP interface. For our purposes, we will be using another non-routable address from the class C address range (see Chapter 2). Enter the following information in the spaces provided:

IP Address: 192.168.1.1

Subnet Mask: 255.255.255.0

Slot Mask: 01111 (default)

Click OK when finished. This will open the Select Protocols window (see Figure 4-3).

4. Select Protocols for this interface.

Click the check box beside the protocol to enable it on this interface. IP is checked by default due to the type of interface. If you so desire to enable BGP, OSPF, and/or BOOTP, you will need to provide the additionalinformation required for those protocols. BOOTP will be discussed later in this chapter. Click OK to enter the additional information or to add the circuitless IP interface.

Figure 4-3
Protocol selection
window for
Circuitless IP

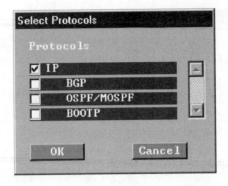

Figure 4-4
Circuitless IP menu
path for modification
of selected protocols

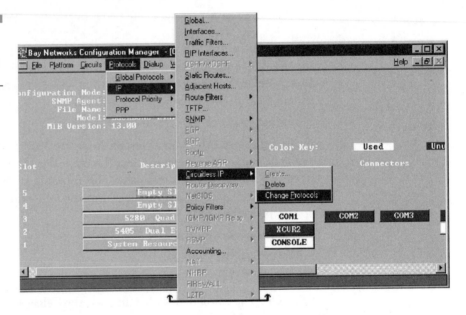

Configuration is complete. The interface is added to the router's routing table and will be propagated in its RIP updates. If you wish to remove or add a protocol to the interface, follow this path: Protocols: IP > Circuitless IP > Change Protocols (see Figure 4-4).

To remove a circuitless IP interface, completely, follow this path: Protocols: IP > Circuitless IP > Delete (see Figure 4-4).

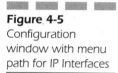

Proxy ARP

Proxy ARP defines a technique that enables the router to reply to an ARP request when the destination and source addresses are on different networks or subnetworks. The router can reply to the local ARP request as long as there is a valid route to the destination. If the valid route is a default route, the "Enable Default Route for Subnets" in the IP global parameters must be enabled.

To enable an interface to respond to nonlocal ARP requests, the Proxy parameter must be enabled as well as the Nonlocal ARP Destination parameter.

Enabling Proxy

1. From the Configuration Manager main window, click Protocols: IP > Interfaces (see Figure 4-5).

Figure 4-5
Configuration window with menu path for IP Interfaces

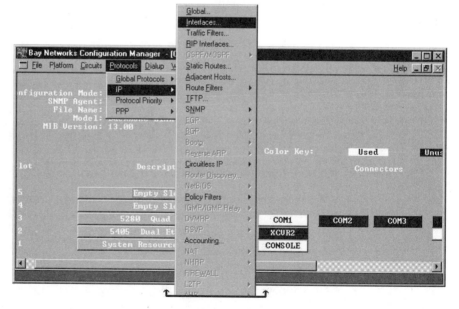

Figure 4-6
IP Interface list

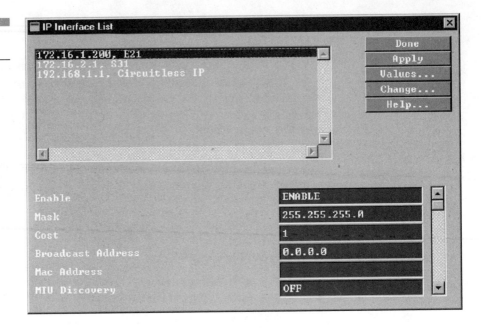

2. Select the IP interface from the IP Interface list (see Figure 4-6).

3. Scroll the list of parameters to find Proxy and set to Enable (see Figure 4-7).

   Click in the field next to Proxy and then click **Values**. Select On and then OK (see Figure 4-8).

4. Click Done.

Setting Nonlocal ARP Destination

To configure the nonlocal ARP destination, perform the following steps:

1. From the Configuration Manager main windows, click Protocols: IP > Global. The Edit IP Global Parameters window opens, as shown in Figure 4-9. Click once into the field next to Nonlocal ARP Destination and then click Values.

2. Click the Accept radio button and then OK from the Values Selection window (see Figure 4-10).

3. Click OK in the IP Global Parameters window to save changes.

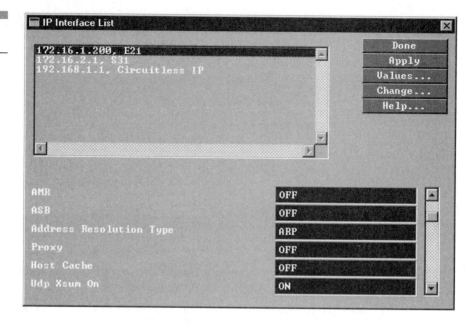

Figure 4-7
IP Interface list

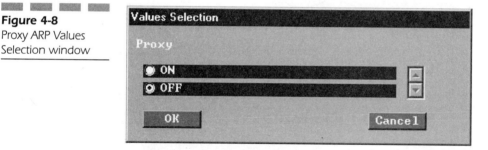

Figure 4-8
Proxy ARP Values
Selection window

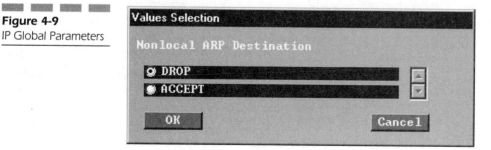

Figure 4-9
IP Global Parameters

Figure 4-10
Non-local ARP
Destination Values
Selection window

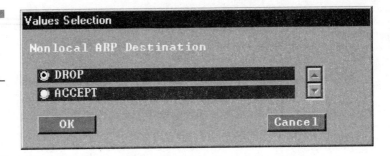

Figure 4-11
Practical example

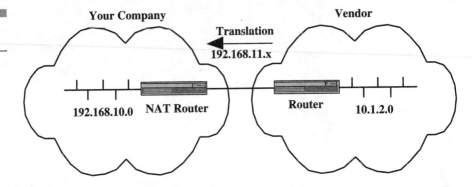

Although some people might use Proxy ARP as a means for workstations to determine a gateway, a practical example of its use follows (see Figure 4-11).

Practical Example

Suppose you are setting up a network that you want to isolate from your internal enterprise. This network could be used as a common access network for vendors—like a vendor demilitarized zone. You learn during planning that the vendor only has a few workstations that will be accessing services on your network. These workstations all have 10.x.x.x addresses, specifically 10.1.2.1, 10.1.2.2, and 10.1.2.3. It so happens that you have this very same network already defined at another location internal to your enterprise. So, you decide to hide the addresses behind *Network Address Translation* or NAT. You define a translation for these addresses of 192.168.11.1, 192.168.11.2, and 192.168.11.3. If a server on the 192.168.10.0 (Vendor DMZ) were to be accessed by these stations, the communication would fail because the ARP requests would go unanswered. With Proxy ARP enabled on the router, the server would send an ARP request requesting the hardware address associated with 192.168.11.1. The router would respond with its hardware address and the IP address of 192.168.11.1. The server would then make an entry into its ARP cache so all future communication to 192.168.11.1 would be sent to the router's hardware address. You can see how people could use this feature for discovering routers.

NOTE: *The above example mentions NAT. This will not be discussed further in this book. Suffice it to say that there are many uses for address translation—the above is just one. If your company, like many companies, uses valid Internet addresses that have not been assigned to you, you would have to incorporate some type of address translation if you were to connect your enterprise to the Internet. Configuring NAT on your border router would be one way of masking your internal addresses into ones that you have been assigned.*

Reverse Address Resolution Protocol (RARP)

RARP is a Data Link layer protocol much like ARP. Instead of converting IP addresses to MAC addresses, it does the reverse (hence the name). RARP has the same message format as ARP with the exception of the Type field value set to 8035. A client broadcasts an address request to an RARP server that is located on the same local subnet. This broadcast message contains the client's hardware (or MAC) address that the server matches with an IP address from its MAC-to-IP mapping table. After it is matched, the server sends a directed response to the client, which inspects the message for its IP address. A Nortel router, when configured for RARP, acts as the RARP server responding to RARP requests with values matched from its mapping table. The MAC-to-IP mapping table is a manually configured table that contains a list of client MAC addresses and their corresponding IP addresses.

Enabling RARP

Adding the protocol to the specific interface enables RARP. Select an Ethernet, Token Ring, or FDDI circuit connector from the Configuration Manager main window (see Figure 4-12) and then follow these steps.

1. The Edit Connector window opens (see Figure 4-13). Click Edit Circuit to open the Circuit Definition window (see Figure 4-14).

2. Click Protocols: Add/Delete to add the Reverse Address Resolution Protocol.

   The "Select Protocols" window opens (see Figure 4-15). Select the Reverse ARP check box in the protocol list.

Figure 4-12
The Configuration Manager main window

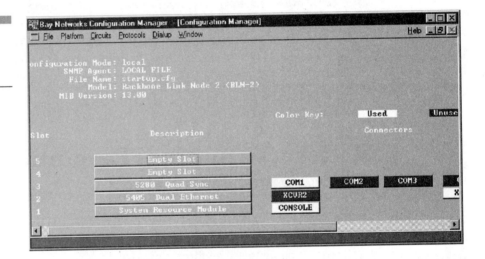

Figure 4-13
Edit Connector window

Figure 4-14
Circuit Definition
window

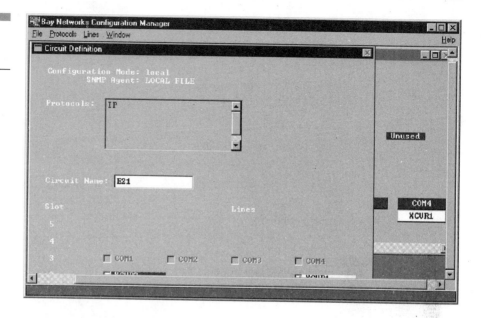

Figure 4-15
Select Protocols
window

3. Click OK and then select File: Exit in the Edit Circuit Definition
   window (refer to Figure 4-14) to return to the Configuration Manager
   main window.

4. Verify the interface has RARP enabled.

   From the Configuration Manager main window, select Protocols: IP >
   Reverse ARP > Interfaces.

Figure 4-16
RARP Interface table

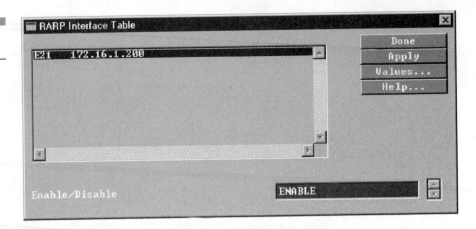

Figure 4-17
RARP map table

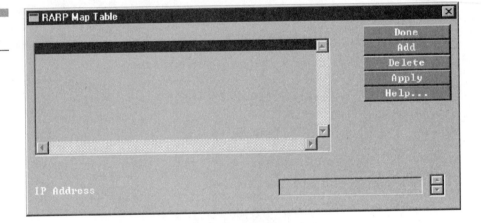

The RARP Interface Table window opens (see Figure 4-16). Select the RARP interface from the list and verify the Enable/Disable field is set to Enable. Click Done.

5. Add entries to the MAC-to-IP Address mapping table.

   The mapping table, shown in Figure 4-17, is accessed by selecting Protocols: IP > Reverse ARP > Map Table.

6. Click Add to add a new entry. Enter the MAC address and its corresponding IP address in their respective fields in the RARP Addresses window (see Figure 4-18). Click OK to save this entry.

7. Click Done to finish or click Add to add another entry.

Figure 4-18
RARP map table
address entry
window

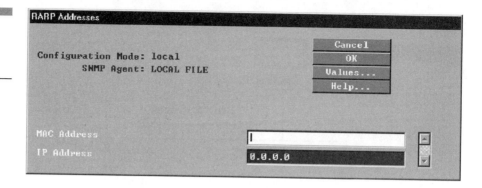

Because you are entering a MAC address/IP address pair, the workstation must be on the same local segment as one of the router's interfaces. The current supported segments are Ethernet, Token Ring, and FDDI. It is easy to see that as the number of workstations increases on a segment along with the number of segments in the enterprise, the amount of time for maintenance increases. What is needed is an automatic process that allows workstations to request configuration information, thereby reducing the amount of maintenance and administration on the network. Fortunately, there is BOOTP and DHCP to provide such a service.

Bootstrap Protocol (BOOTP)

BOOTP, like RARP, allows workstations to receive an IP address based on its MAC address. But, instead of operating in the Data Link layer, BOOTP uses the UDP Transport layer protocol. This allows BOOTP to offer IP addresses across routers. Designed as a client-server model, BOOTP clients broadcast a request message, called a BOOTREQUEST, to a BOOTP server that replies with a BOOTREPLY. Unlike RARP, BOOTP packets can contain more information than just the IP address, such as the gateway address and the address of the BOOTP server, as well as other vendor-specific information. Figure 4-19 is an example of how BOOTP works when the client and server are on the same network.

The workstation broadcasts a BOOTREQUEST packet on the network segment using the IP broadcast address of 255.255.255.255. The server responds to the request by transmitting to the workstation a BOOTREPLY

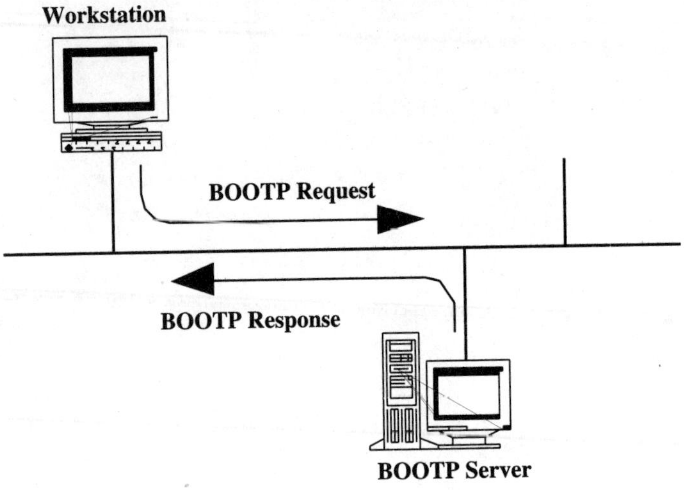

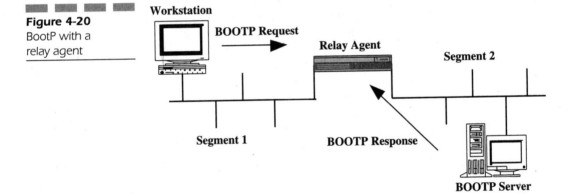

Figure 4-19
BootP on some segment

Workstation

BOOTP Request

BOOTP Response

BOOTP Server

Figure 4-20
BootP with a relay agent

Workstation

BOOTP Request

Relay Agent

Segment 2

Segment 1

BOOTP Response

BOOTP Server

packet. If, however, the client and server are not on the same physical network, a BOOTP relay agent must be configured. A BOOTP relay agent forwards a BOOTREQUEST to an interface that contains a BOOTP server. Nortel routers act as a BOOTP relay agent when BOOTP services are configured. In order for the relay agent to know to which interface a request must be sent, a forwarding table must be manually created. Each circuit defined for the Boot protocol must have an entry in the forwarding table corresponding to the network interface that contains the BOOTP server. Figure 4-20 shows the communication when the BOOTREQUEST must forwarded by a router.

Again, the workstation broadcasts a BOOTREQUEST packet to the IP broadcast address of 255.255.255.255. The router, being configured as a BOOTP Relay Agent, will receive the packet. It will then examine the BOOTP header to determine whether it should forward or drop the packet (the BOOTP message format is discussed below). The router examines the seconds and hops field in the header and compares them to defined values configured on its receiving interface. It checks for the following:

■ Seconds

This value is the minimum time the router must wait before forwarding the packet. If the value in the header is smaller than the Timeout Seconds value configured on the router interface, the router will drop the packet.

■ Hops

This value specifies the maximum number of hops that the packet can travel between the source and destination devices. If the value is greater than the value defined on the router interface, the router will drop the packet.

If both parameters meet the router's configuration, the router will accept the packet. It will increment the *hops* value by 1 and insert the IP address of its interface that received the packet into the *gateway IP address* field in the BOOTP header. After the router accepts the packet and makes its adjustments, it must determine to which network the packet must be forwarded. The router consults its forwarding table to make the necessary forwarding decision. Instead of a forwarding table, a specific server can be configured. The router would then unicast the BOOTREQUEST packet to the server through normal IP services.

After the server on the other network receives the BOOTREQUEST, it will reply with a BOOTREPLY to the IP address defined in the *gateway IP address* field it found in the request packet. The router that receives this reply packet will verify that the *IP destination address* matches the *gateway IP address* and forwards it onto the client as determined by the value in the *flags* field as follows:

■ Flags set to 1

This indicates that the client does not know its own IP address and the router must broadcast the BOOTREPLY to the IP broadcast address of 255.255.255.255.

■ Flags set to 0

This indicates that the client knows its own IP address and the router will transmit the BOOTREPLY to the address found in the *client IP address* field of the packet.

BOOTP Message Format

The BOOTP message format is displayed in Figure 4-21. The field descriptions are outlined in Table 4-1.

Enabling the BOOTP Relay Agent

In order for the router to relay BOOTP requests, it must have the BOOTP protocol loaded on the interface from which it will be receiving the BOOTP requests and replies. When a circuit is created, you have the opportunity to add the BOOTP protocol when you add the network and routing protocols. Use the following method to add BOOTP if it was not added when the circuit was created:

1. From the Configuration Manager main window, select the connector for the IP interface that will be receiving the BOOTREQUEST and BOOTREPY packets.

    If the router will be receiving boot requests on its LAN interface, select the XCVR1, Token, or FDDI connector. The Edit Connector window opens.

2. Click the **Edit Circuit** button.

    This will open the Circuit Definition window where you can add, modify, or delete protocols from this circuit.

3. Add the BOOTP protocol to the circuit.

    Select Protocols: Add/Delete, or press F4. From the Select Protocols window, select the BOOTP check box and then click OK. BOOTP has now been added to the circuit.

4. Select File: Exit to return to the Configuration Manager main window. Repeat for all interfaces that will pass the BOOTP requests and replies.

    After the BOOTP protocol has been added to all interfaces that require it, you must configure the route to the BOOTP server. To configure the

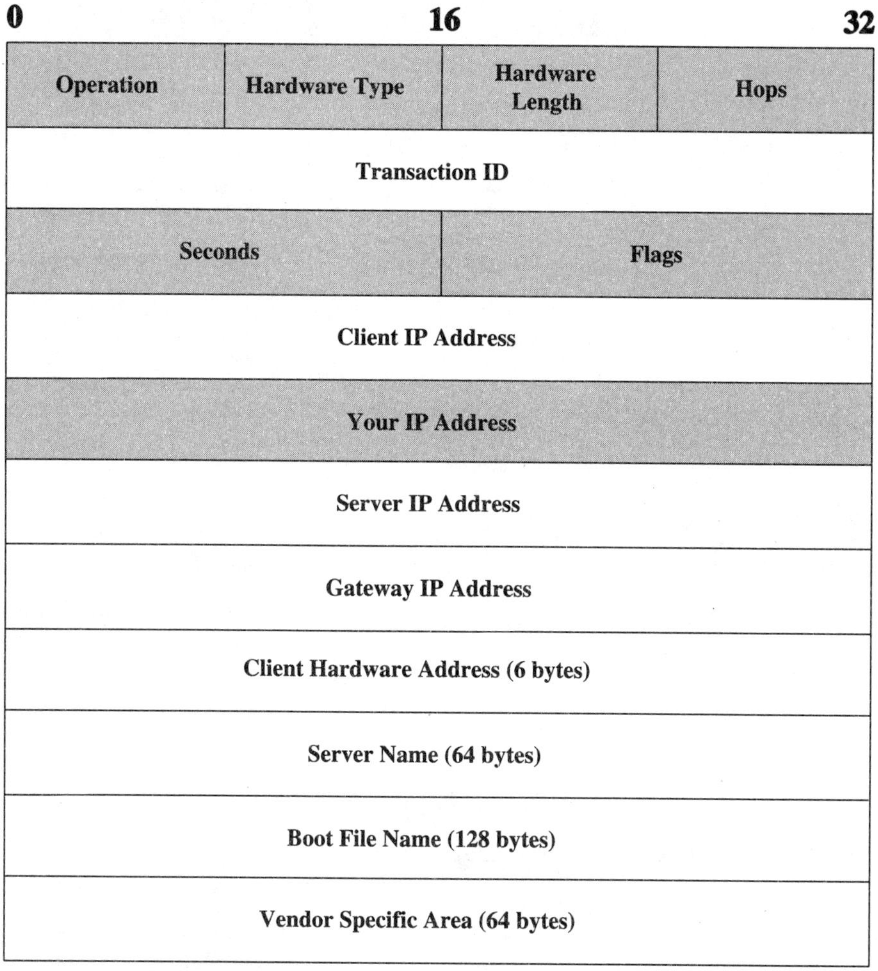

Figure 4-21
BOOTP message
format

0		16	32
Operation	Hardware Type	Hardware Length	Hops
Transaction ID			
Seconds		Flags	
Client IP Address			
Your IP Address			
Server IP Address			
Gateway IP Address			
Client Hardware Address (6 bytes)			
Server Name (64 bytes)			
Boot File Name (128 bytes)			
Vendor Specific Area (64 bytes)			

route, you must create an input/output address pair in the Relay Agent Forwarding Table.

To define the BOOTP route, follow these steps:

1. Select Protocols: IP > BOOTP > Relay Agent Interface Table.

   The BOOTP Relay Agent Interface Table window opens. A list of all interfaces configured with BOOTP is shown in the list box on the left. Below the list are the parameters for each interface (see Figure 4-22).

2. Open the BOOTP Forwarding Table.

Table 4-1

BOOTP field
descriptions

Field	Description
Operation	This is the message operation code. A "1" signifies a BOOTREQUEST and a "2" signifies a BOOTRE-PLY.
Hardware Type	This field specifies the hardware address type—Ethernet, Token Ring, and so on.
Hardware Length	This field specifies the length of the hardware address.
Hops	The value in this field is incremented by each router that forwards the BOOTP packet. Initially set to "0" by the client, each router adds "1." Default is 4.
Transaction ID (XID)	An integer value used by nodes to match the response with the request.
Seconds	The amount of seconds the router must wait before forwarding the BOOTREQUEST. Default is 0.
Flags	The flags field that, among other things, alerts the server as to whether the client knows its IP address.
Client IP Address (Ciaddr)	The IP address of the client. If it knows its IP address, it places the value in this field. If not, the client places a "0."
Your IP Address (Yiaddr)	This value is the return address if Ciaddr is "0."
Server IP Address (Siaddr)	The address of a BOOTP server. A value of "0" is taken to mean any server.
Gateway IP Address (Giaddr)	The address of the relay agent. The client sends a BOOTREQUEST message with a nonzero value in this field. The first router fills it with the interface address that received the request.
Client Hardware Address (Chaddr)	The client's hardware address.
Server Host Name	The name of the BOOTP server.
Boot File Name	The name of a file the workstation can request, from the BOOTP server, to run at boot.
Vendor Specific Area	Optional information that can be passed from the server to the client.

Figure 4-22
BOOTP Relay Agent
Interface Table
parameters window

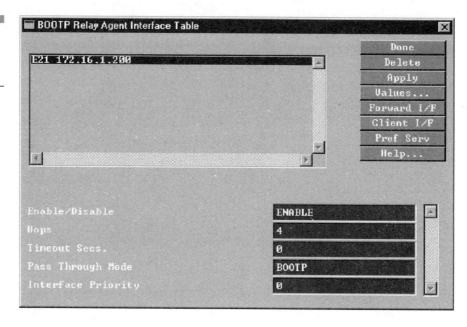

Click **Forward I/F**. This opens the BOOTP Relay Agent Forwarding Table (see Figure 4-23). If no address pairs have been entered, the list box on the left will be empty.

3. Add an Input/Output address pair.

Click the Add button to open the BOOTP Addresses window and set the addresses that will be receiving and forwarding the BOOTPREQUESTs (see Figure 4-24).

Click OK to return to the BOOTP Forwarding table window. Click OK again to return to the BOOTP Relay Agent Interface Table.

4. Define the Pass Through mode.

The BOOTP Relay Agent can forward both BOOTP and DHCP packets. Setting this parameter allows the router to exclusively forward BOOTP or DHCP or allows the router to forward both. This setting is set to BOOTP by default.

5. Save changes and then exit.

Click Apply to save your configuration changes and then click Done to exit to the Configuration Manager main window.

Figure 4-23
BOOTP Relay Agent
Forwarding Table

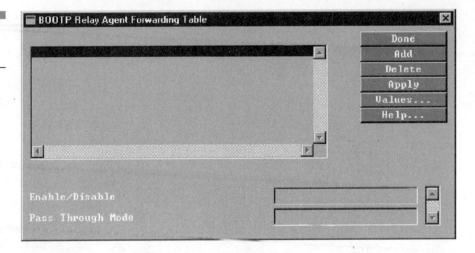

Figure 4-23
BOOTP Relay Agent
Forwarding Table

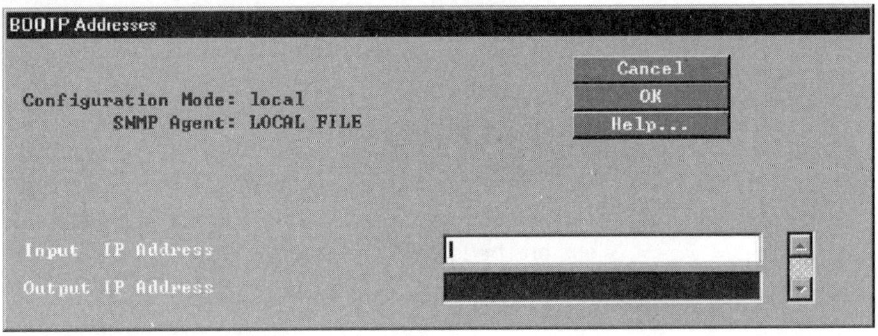

Figure 4-24
BOOTP Input/Output
Addresses window

When BOOTP is configured on an interface, the router software assigns default values for the BOOTP parameters. Most of these values will not need to be changed. Table 4-2 details the BOOTP parameters.

Client Interface Table

The **Client I/F** button in the BOOTP Relay Agent Interface Table is used to configure an *Access Node* (AN) or *Access Stack Node* (ASN) to use EZ-Install over a Frame Relay PVC. To use EZinstall, you must be using Frame Relay in Group Access mode. The Client Interface Table allows you to define an IP

Table 4-2

BOOTP parameters

Parameter	Description
Enable	Enables or Disables BOOTP on the interface.
Hops	The maximum number of hops from the client to the server. If the value in the *hops* field of the request packet is greater than this value, the router will drop the packet. The default is four hops.
Timeout Secs.	The amount of time the router will wait before it forwards a request packet. If the value in the *seconds* field is less than this value, the router will drop the packet. The default is 0 seconds.
Pass Through Mode	The parameter allows the router to forward DHCP packets as well as BOOTP packets. The default is BOOTP only.
Interface Priority	A value from 0 to 16 that defines the priority of an interface on a multinetted interface.

Figure 4-25
BOOTP Client
Interface Table
window

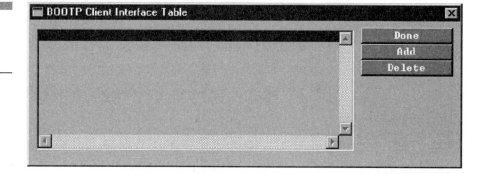

address and DLCI pair for a remote AN or ASN router. You create the Client Interface Table by selecting Protocols: IP > BOOTP > Relay Agent Table.

Click **Client I/F** to bring up the BOOTP Client Interface Table and then click Add (see Figures 4-25 and 4-26).

Enter the IP address of the remote router and the DLCI that has been assigned by your Frame Relay provider. The above is added as a reference to the additional button found in the BOOTP Relay Agent Table window. A discussion of Frame Relay will not be included in this installment of this book.

Figure 4-26
BOOTP Client
Interface Address
window

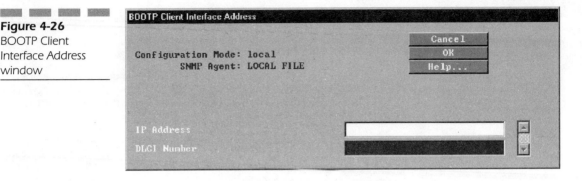

Figure 4-27
BOOTP Relay Agent
Preferred Server table

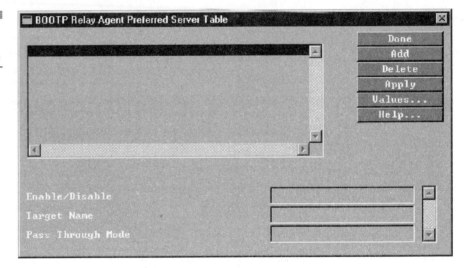

Preferred Server Table

Another way of defining a route for a request packet is by configuring a preferred server. A preferred server allows the router to send a unicast request packet to a BOOTP server. The relay agent on the router can send the BOOTREQUEST to the server using normal IP services (see Figure 4-27).

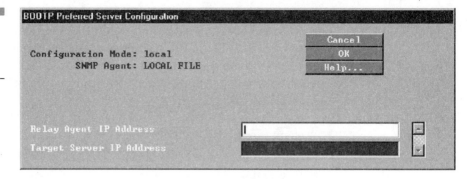

Figure 4-28
BOOTP Preferred
Server Configuration
window

From the BOOTP Relay Agent Interface Table, click **Pref Serv** and then Add to configure the relay agent IP address and the target server address (see Figure 4-28). Configuring a preferred server also allows the router to forward a BOOTREQUEST out an unnumbered interface.

Dynamic Host Control Protocol (DHCP)

As BOOTP was an enhancement to RARP, DHCP is an enhancement to BOOTP. DHCP is a protocol that can provide dynamic IP addressing to clients as well as other configuration parameters. It is a client/server protocol that allows servers to provide the addressing in one of three modes —automatic, dynamic, or manual. In automatic mode, the server assigns a permanent address to a workstation. Similarly, in manual mode, a workstation receives an IP address as provided by a Network Manager manually configuring the information into the server. The most effective use of DHCP is in its capability to dynamically allocate reusable IP addresses. In dynamic mode, DHCP servers "lease" addresses to hosts for a fixed length of time. The length of time can be from one minute to 99 years. This leasing allows for hosts that do not need permanent addresses to receive one from a limited pool of addresses. When the lease expires, the server can reallocate the address to another host on the network.

The DHCP packet format is based on the BOOTP format with the exception of an increased options field. A larger option field lets DHCP servers provide more than just the IP address to requesting clients. Because the packet types between DHCP and BOOTP are similar, DHCP servers can service both BOOTP and DHCP clients. In either case, the BOOTP Relay Agent uses the same criteria and methods for forwarding each packet type. The interaction between DHCP clients and servers with a Relay Agent in the middle is outlined here:

1. A client identifies DHCP servers.

   A client broadcasts a DHCPDISCOVER packet in hopes that a server will respond.

2. The Relay Agent receives the "discover" packet.

   The BOOTP Relay Agent, using the same criteria as that outlined previously for BOOTPREQUEST packets, determines whether to accept or drop the packet. If the Agent accepts the packet, it transmits it to DHCP servers on other networks.

3. DHCP servers respond to the discover packet.

   A server may respond with a DHCPOFFER packet that contains an available IP address. The server marks this address as temporarily unavailable. If the client does not respond within a set time or it rejects this address, the server reclaims it. The address is again available for other clients.

4. The Relay Agent receives the "offer" packet.

   Again, the Agent examines that packet. If it accepts it, it forwards it to the client.

5. Client receives the "offer" packet and targets a server.

   Because the DHCPDISCOVER packet is broadcast to many servers, each of these can respond with an offer. The client chooses a server based on configuration information it finds in the offer packet.

   Note: If the client does not receive a DHCPOFFER within a specific amount of time, it will retransmit its DHCPDISCOVER. It will rebroadcast the packet up to 10 times.

6. The client sends a request to the target server.

   The client sends a DHCPREQUEST to the target server. This request packet contains the target server's IP address. The router sends this packet to all servers.

7. The target server receives the request and sends a response to the client.

All servers that were passed the DHCPREQUEST examine the *server IP address* field for their address. Servers with an IP address that does not match the IP address in the request packet reclaim their offered IP addresses for use for other clients. Only the target server will respond to the client with a DHCPACK or DHCPNAK stating whether it can supply the configuration information or not, respectively.

8. Client responds back to the target server.

If the client finds fault in the configuration information in the DHCPACK, it will send a DHCPDECLINE back to the server and will broadcast another DHCPDISCOVER. Otherwise, it will record the information and join the network.

Although DHCP and BOOTP share a similar message format and communication mechanism (they both use UDP port numbers 67 and 68), they differ in the following ways:

- DHCP leases IP addresses to clients, allowing for reassignment as the addresses expire.
- DHCP can also provide a client with all IP configuration parameters needed for network communication.
- DHCP has a longer packet length than BOOTP.
- DHCP is more complicated than BOOTP. It has seven message types instead of two.

Telecommunications Network Protocol (Telnet)

Telnet is a client/server application that allows remote hosts to be accessed as if directly connected. The Telnet client establishes a virtual connection to a Telnet server across the network. On a Nortel router, Telnet is used to establish connections to the Technician Interface (TI). The router must be configured as a Telnet server, whereas a workstation (or another router) must be configured as a Telnet client. Connection to the TI can be established by

■ A workstation running a Telnet client connecting to the router running its Telnet server.

or

■ A workstation connected to the router via a terminal cable or modem. The router would be running its Telnet client, which can then be used to access another router running its Telnet server.

To enable Telnet services on a Nortel router, you must first have an IP interface configured. After an IP interface has been created, a TCP socket must also be created.

Creating a TCP Socket

From the Configuration Manager main window, select Protocols: Global Protocols > TCP > Create TCP (see Figure 4-29). The TCP socket will be cre-

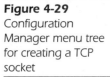

Figure 4-29
Configuration Manager menu tree for creating a TCP socket

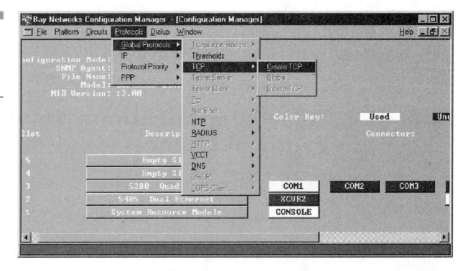

ated with default values for minimum and maximum timeouts as well as for the maximum window size.

To change any other these default parameters, select Protocols: Global Protocols > TCP > Global (see Figure 4-30).

Enabling Telnet Server

When you enable the Telnet server, you allow the router to accept incoming Telnet requests from a Telnet client. After a Telnet session is established, the client will be able to access all TI commands as if directly connected to the console port on the router.

▪ From the Configuration Manager main window, select Protocols: Global Protocols > Telnet Server > Create Telnet Server (see Figure 4-31).

The Telnet Configuration window opens (see Figure 4-32), prompting for the Manager's and User's login script. You can accept the default values or input the name of a login script that you have created. If you want to prevent a user from canceling out of the user login script, enable the Force User Logout parameter.

▪ Click OK to return to the Configuration Manager main window.

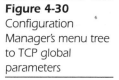

Figure 4-30
Configuration Manager's menu tree to TCP global parameters

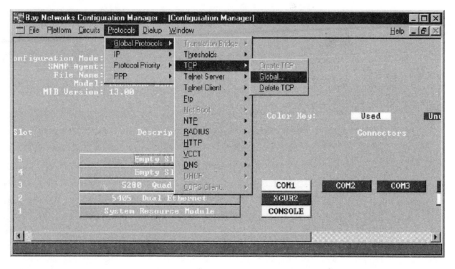

Figure 4-31
Configuration
Manager menu tree
to enable Telnet
server

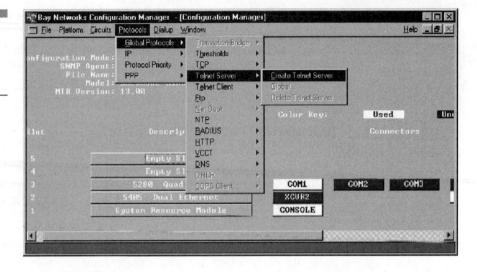

Figure 4-32
Telnet Configuration
window

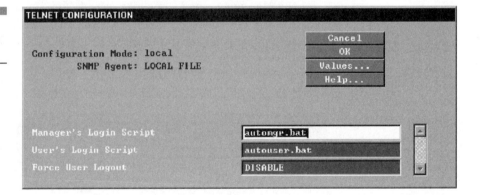

The router software assigns default values to the Telnet server. Usually, the default values will be sufficient, but if you need to change any of the values, you can access the Telnet Global Parameters by selecting Protocols: Global Protocols > Telnet Client > Global (see Figure 4-33). Some of the parameters that you might want to change would be the login, password, and command timeouts. These parameters set the amount of time the router will wait until the session times out for a login entry, password entry, or any command typed from the keyboard, respectively.

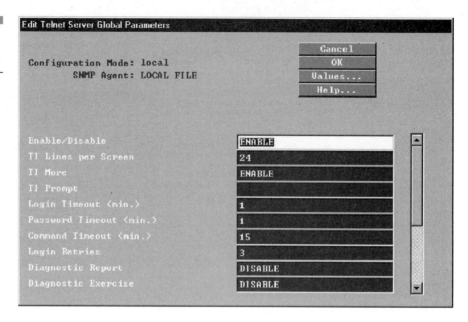

Figure 4-33
Telnet Server Global
Parameters window

Enabling the Telnet Client

Enabling the Telnet client allows the router to send outbound Telnet requests to a Telnet server. If the Telnet server is a remote router, a TI session can be established.

From the Configuration Manager main window, select Protocols: Global Protocols > Telnet Client > Create Telnet Client.

The Telnet client will be created with default values. In order to change these parameters, select Protocols: Global Protocols > Telnet Client > Global . . . . If you wish to define an alternate port for Telnet communication, you can change the "Remote Port" value from its default of 23.

Trivial File Transfer Protocol (TFTP)

As its name implies, TFTP is a simple protocol for transferring files between network devices. It has minimal capabilities and overhead. To keep

Figure 4-34
Configuration
Manager's menu tree
to enabling Telnet
client

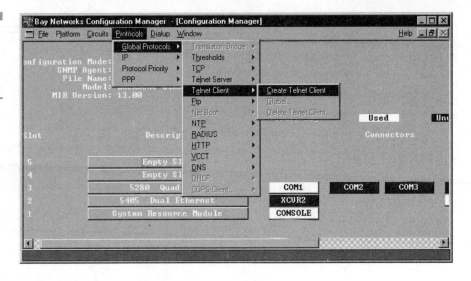

it trivial, TFTP does not list directories on remote machines nor does it perform any authorization. It is extremely restrictive when compared to *File
Transfer Protocol* (FTP).

How It Works

- TFTP clients initiates a file read or write to a TFTP server. This
  request also servers as a connection request.

- A connection is established and the file is sent. TFTP transfers data in
  fixed-length blocks of 512 bytes.

- If the client requested to read from a file on a server, the server would
  send the data to the client one block at a time, waiting for an
  acknowledgement from the client each time a block is to be sent.

- The client upon receiving the data will send an acknowledgement to
  the server. A packet containing less than 512 bytes will terminate the
  transfer.

TFTP Parameters

If you remember from Chapter 2, we configure the router with its initial IP interface using Quickstart. During the "Install" script, we were prompted for the default volume for TFTP. The default volume is one of the configurable parameters for TFTP and points to a valid file system on a flash card. Table 4-3 shows the five parameters that control TFTP.

TFTP from the Technician Interface (TI)

The TI is the command line interface into a Nortel router. Many configuration and management functions can be accessed through the TI—including TFTP transfers. To send a file from the router to another device you will need to type the following commands:

The command syntax for TFTP is

```
tftp {get|put} <address> <vol>: <file_spec> [<vol>: <file_spec>]
```

where

get & put   Retrieves and sends a file to the router, respectively

<address>   Is the address of the device from where the file will
be sent or transmitted

Table 4-3

TFTP parameters

Parameter	Description
Enable	Enables or disables TFTP
Default Volume	This parameter defines the slot that TFTP will run on. Default is slot 2. For AN routers it is slot 1.
Retry Time out	This is the amount of time TFTP waits for an acknowledgement before it retransmits the last packet. The default is 5 seconds.
Close Time out	This is the amount of time TFTP waits before it closes a connection. By default, TFTP waits 25 seconds.
Retransmit	The number of times TFTP will retransmit an unacknowledged packet before abandoning the attempt

Figure 4-35
Configuration
Manager's menu
tree to TFTP

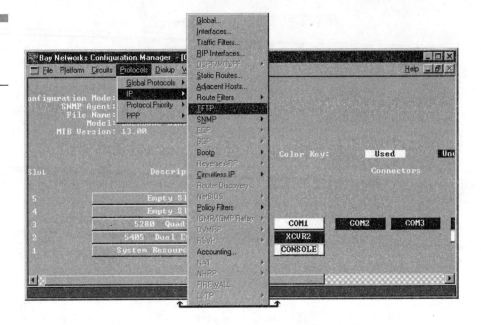

`<vol>`　　　Is the volume of the file system

`<file_spec>`　Is the name of the file to be retrieved or sent

Transferring the config file from the router to a host.

From the [2:1]$ prompt: **tftp put 172.16.1.1 1:config**

Transferring the config file from a host to the router.

From the [2:1]$ prompt: **tftp get 172.16.1.1 config**

The previous examples show the necessary commands to initiate the TFTP commands from a router. TFTP commands can also be initiated from the host's command prompt as long as the host provides TFTP support.

TFTP from within Site Manager

Using TFTP from within Site Manager requires the use of the Router Files Manager tool. We used Router Files Manager in Chapter 2 when we added an additional IP interface to the router. TFTP was used to "get" the backup configuration file from the router so that the changes we were making would not effect the working configuration file. As a recap, the procedure is repeated in the following list.

1. Select the router from the "Well-known Connections" list from the Site Manager main window.

2. Select Tools > Router Files Manager . . . .

3. Transfer the configuration file from the router to your local workstation.

   In the files list box, select the *config* file. Once selected you can transfer the file using a TFTP "get" command. Select File > TFTP > Get File(s) . . . . The TFTP Get Files window pops up with the selected file displayed in the "Proceed with TFTP Get of File(s)" list box. The default local directory is entered into the "Destination Directory" text box. If you do not wish to change any information, click **OK**. The "config" file now resides on your local workstation.

4. Transfer the configuration file from you workstation to the router.

   From the Router Files Manager main window, select File > TFTP > Put File(s) . . . . The TFTP Put Files Selection window opens with the default path highlighted in the Path text box. Select the *config* file the "Files" list on the left of the window. Click the **Add** button to move the file to the "Files To Put:" list. Click **OK** to send the file to the router.

File Transfer Protocol (FTP)

FTP is a more robust protocol than TFTP for transferring files between hosts. FTP, like TFTP, uses TCP to establish a session between an FTP client and an FTP server. The main difference between the two protocols is that an FTP client makes two separate connections to an FTP server—a control connection for sending and receiving commands and a data connection for transferring data. The following are some of the features of FTP:

- User authentication
- Directory listings
- File maintenance (copying and deleting of files)

- File transfer
- Remote command execution

In order for FTP to be configured on the router, a TCP socket must be created which was discussed in the previous section. Enabling the FTP server is detailed next.

Enabling FTP

To enable FTP, select Protocols: Global Protocols > FTP > Create FTP from the Configuration Manager main window. The FTP server will be loaded with default parameters. These parameters can be modified by selecting Protocols > Global Protocols > FTP > Global.

IP Traffic Filters

As we embrace the Internet and its potential for global communication and commerce, a need arises to protect internal infrastructure and information

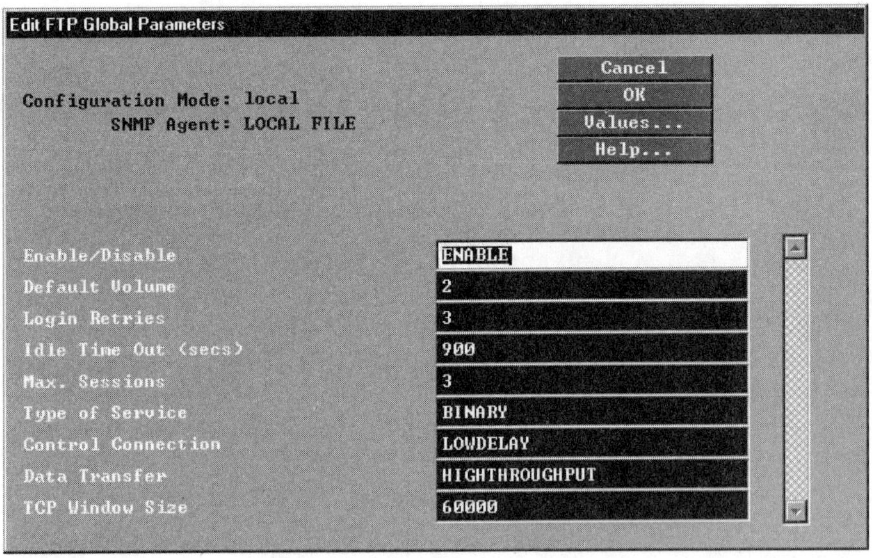

Figure 4-36
FTP Global
Parameters window

```
Edit FTP Global Parameters

                                              Cancel
Configuration Mode: local                       OK
        SNMP Agent: LOCAL FILE                Values...
                                              Help...



Enable/Disable              ENABLE
Default Volume              2
Login Retries               3
Idle Time Out (secs)        900
Max. Sessions               3
Type of Service             BINARY
Control Connection          LOWDELAY
Data Transfer               HIGHTHROUGHPUT
TCP Window Size             60000
```

Table 4-4

FTP parameters

Parameter	Description
Enable	Enables or disables FTP
Default Volume	This volume is where FTP reads and writes transferred files.
Login Retries	The number of times a user can attempt a login before being locked out. Default is 3 retries.
Idle Time Out	The amount of time FTP waits until it closes an idle connection Default is 900 seconds.
Max Sessions	Defines the number of simultaneous FTP sessions running Default is 3 simultaneous sessions.
Type of Service	The type of data transmission—ASCII or Binary. Set to Binary by default
Control Connection	Specifies the IP Type of Service value TCP will use on the control connection. Default is "low Delay."
Data Transfer	Specifies the IP Type of Service value TCP will use on the data transfer connection. Default is "high throughput."
TCP Window Size	Specifies the size of TCP windows. Default is 60,000 bytes.

from harm or unauthorized access. This need can be accommodated using protocol traffic filters. Traffic filters are created using a specific protocol. In the global network, the dominant protocol is IP and is the protocol that we will focus on in this section. In addition to security, traffic filters can be used to limit network congestion and prioritize specific types of traffic.

Traffic filters are files that tell the router to perform specific tasks on traffic it receives or forwards on an interface. Based on the information fields in the protocol headers, routers can selectively block, forward, log or prioritize network traffic. There are two types of filters that can be applied —inbound and outbound traffic filters. Inbound filters, as their name implies, act on packets the router receives. Conversely, outbound filters act on packets the router forwards. These filters are supported on the following interfaces:

- Ethernet
- Token-Ring

■ *Fiber Distributed Data Interface* (FDDI)

■ *High Speed Serial Interface* (HSSI)

■ MCT1/E1

■ Synchronous

Table 4-5 compares both types of filters. In order to use outbound traffic filters protocol priority must be enabled on the interface. Protocol priority is the mechanism by which the router sorts traffic into separate outbound queues of varying priority. There are three priority levels to which outbound traffic can be sorted—high, normal, or low.

Nortel routers support multiple filter types on a single interface. There can be 31 inbound and outbound filters defined on an interface. The filter location in the filter list determines the execution order and affects the filter result.

Anatomy of a Traffic Filter

The actual traffic filter applied to an interface is derived from traffic filter templates. These templates provide the majority of the configuration for the filter. BayRS™ provides many predefined templates that can be used for each supported protocol. Once a template is added to an interface, you can use it as is or you can adjust the parameters to suit you specific requirements. There are three components to a traffic filter template:

Table 4-5

Inbound and Outbound filter comparison

	Inbound Filters	Outbound Filters
Primary Use	Security	Traffic Direction
Bridge or Routing Protocol Support	Yes	No
Protocols Supported	Transparent Bridge, Native SRB, IP, IPX, XNS, OSI, DECnet Phase IV, Vines, DLSw, and LLC2	(Only dependent upon DLC or IP header)
Prioritization	No	Yes
Number of filters	31 per interface	31 per interface

1. *Criteria*   This is the location in the packet or frame header that is to be examined.

2. *Ranges*   As the criteria points to the specific location within a packet or frame header, the range is the numeric value, at the location, by which the frame is to be matched.

3. *Action*   The action tells the router what to do with a packet or frame that matches the filter criteria and range. It defines whether the router accepts, drops, or logs the incoming packet.

To understand each of these components more fully, split a packet into its three components. A packet can be divided into a *Data Link Control* (DLC), upper layer, and a user data portion as seen in Figure 4-37.

It is in the DLC portion where we see the headers for Token-Ring, Ethernet, FDDI, PPP along with Wellfleet standard, Frame Relay, etc. The upper layer protocols are defined by the multitude of network layer and above protocols. For our purposes and to maintain consistency with support Nortel protocols, we will limit our focus to IP, TCP and UDP. The third component of the packet consists mainly of user data. The criterion defines the location in the DLC or upper layer portions of a packet. It consists of a byte length and an offset measured from a common reference point. The common reference point or bit pattern, for IP is either the *header_start* or *header_end*. It is from this point that the offset is measured. If you were looking to filter IP traffic on "Type of Service," you would define the offset from *header_start* as 8 bits. This is because 8 bits into the IP header is the "Type of Service" field. As for length, 8 bits will suffice because it defines the length of the "Type of Service" field. Fortunately, there are predefined filter criteria that make implementing traffic filters easy. These predefined criteria consist of predefined offsets and lengths for some of the most common filter criteria. The following lists the predefined criteria for IP:

- Type of Service
- IP Address (Source and/or Destination)
- UDP Port (Source and/or Destination)

Figure 4-37
Three components of a packet

Data Link Control	Upper Layer	User Data

- TCP Port (Source and/or Destination)
- Established TCP
- Protocol Type

Once a location in a packet is defined, we must also define the ranges to which the packet will be compared. There must be at least one range defined per criterion and it must have a minimum and a maximum value. If you wish the range to be a single value, enter the numeric value in both the minimum and maximum fields. (Note: entering the value in the minimum field and leaving the max value field blank accomplishes the same thing. Configuration Manager automatically enters the same value for both fields. If, for example, you wished to filter traffic on a range of IP addresses, you could enter 172.16.3.1 as the minimum value and 172.16.3.10 as the maximum value. This tells the router to look into each packet for the above addresses and perform whatever action was defined. The actions that can be applied to traffic that matches the criterion and the range can be of the following types:

- *Accept*   Allows any and all traffic that matches the criteria
- *Drop*   Drops any and all traffic that matches the criteria
- *Log*   Sends an entry to the system event log for every match

NOTE: Only use the log action when diagnosing a problem. The event log could fill up with these filtering messages not leaving room for any critical log messages.

There are also predefined actions besides the basic three that can be applied to complete the traffic filter. For inbound filters the following predefined IP actions can be used:

- Forward to Next Hop
- Drop If Next Hop is Unreachable
- Forward to IP Address
- Forward to Next Hop Interface
- Forward to First Up Next Hop Interface
- Detailed Logging

Outbound actions tell the router to sort the traffic into high or low priority queues. As we started out this section, I remarked that the actual filter is derived from a template. These templates must be defined before they can be added to an interface. They exist as files on the Site Manager workstation and end with a *.flt extension. The beauty of creating a single template or using an existing template is that it can be applied to multiple interfaces with little or no changes. Thereby creating a reusable predefined specification that can ease management burden. In the next section, we will create a filter template and apply it to an interface to create a traffic filter.

Creating a Filter Template

Since a filter template is the building block of a traffic filter, it must contain a complete filter description. The main difference between a template and a filter is that the template is not associated with a circuit. In this section we will create a template and apply it to a circuit to create a traffic filter. In order to keep the complexity down we will be creating a filter that allows access to a single device on a network. The simple network diagram from Chapters 2 and 3 is repeated here.

Scenario   There exists a server on the 172.16.1.0 network that provides information needed by users on the 172.16.3.0 network. The server address is 172.16.1.210. Create a filter on Router A that will allow all access to this server for users on Router B's Ethernet segment while preventing their access to the rest of the network.

Configuration Steps

There are several ways this can be done. Although the following steps may not present the optimal solution, they will provide an understanding of how to implement a traffic filter.

Figure 4-38
Simple network
diagram

1. Select the incoming interface on the router from the Configuration Manager main window.

   For our example, we will elect the serial interface that connects Router A with Router B—slot 3, COM1. When the "Edit Connector" window opens, click on the **Edit Circuit** button, Figure 4-39.

2. Select Protocols: Edit IP > Traffic Filters . . . from the "Circuit Definition" menu (see Figure 4-40).

   Selecting the Traffic Filters option from the IP menu will open the "IP Filters" window (see Figure 4-41). This is the main filter window. From here, you will be able to create new template files, edit existing template files, and apply these templates for use as a filter. Since order is important in how the router interprets the filter result, you can reorder the filters to accomplish your filter goal.

3. Open Template Management window.

Figure 4-39
Edit Connector window

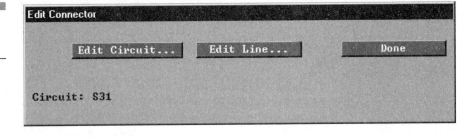

Figure 4-40
Traffic filter menu option

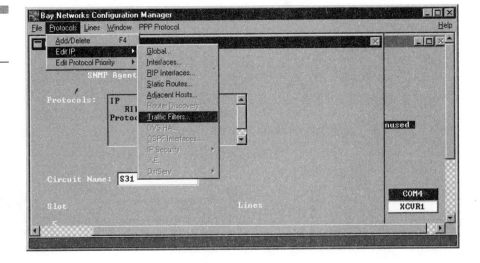

Figure 4-41
IP Filters main window

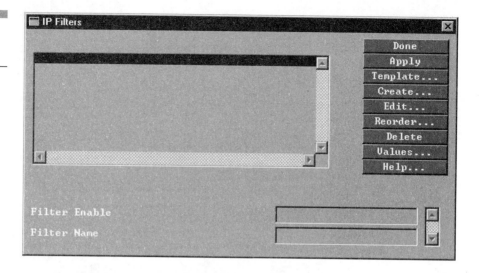

Figure 4-42
Filter Template Management window

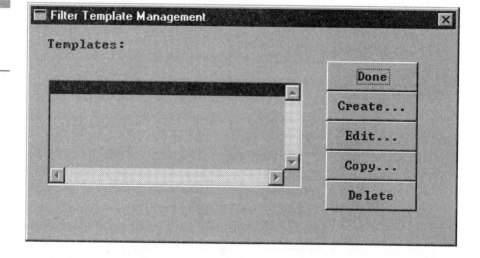

Click the **Template** button in the "IP Filters" main window (see Figure 4-41) to open the "Filter Template Management" window. This is where we will create the templates that will be used in this example and in future filter creation. Figure 4-42 shows the "Filter Template Management" window.

4. Create the access template by clicking on **Create**.

The "Create IP Template" window opens as shown in Figure 4-43.

5. Enter the Filter Name.

Figure 4-43
Create IP Template
window

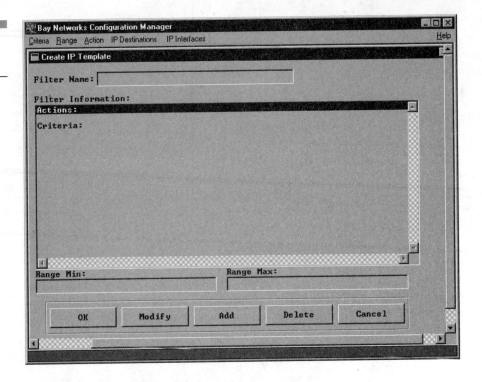

In the "Filter Name:" field, type a descriptive name for this filter. This filter is being created to allow access to the server on Router A's Ethernet, so pick a name that would describe this purpose.

6. Enter the Actions and Criteria that will govern how the router will respond to incoming packets.

In the "Create IP Template" window, Actions are displayed first in the "Filter Information" list. It matters not the order in which you assign criteria or actions as long as they match the result you are trying to achieve. Since Actions are listed first, we will define the desired Action first.

Defining an Action

This filter will allow all incoming packets to access the server. From the menu bar in Figure 4-43, click on Action > Add > Accept. The Action is displayed in the "Filter Information" list.

Defining the Criteria

We will restrict this incoming traffic to only one destination address—the IP address of the server. Add the criterion by selecting Criteria > Add > IP Destination Address from the menu bar. To complete the criteria we must add the ranges to which this traffic will be restricted. Figure 4-44 shows the "Add Ranges" window.

The minimum value in our scenario is 172.16.1.210. Since this is the only address to which we will be granting access, leave the maximum value blank. Configuration Manager will automatically interpret a blank maximum value as a single range and it will fill in the blank accordingly.

Click **OK** to return to the "Create IP Template" window.

7. Make sure all criteria have been entered and entered correctly.

   There are five buttons along the bottom of the "Create IP Template" window. The **OK** and **Cancel** buttons commits and saves changes to a template file or abandons changes without saving, respectively. You can select any criterion in the "Filter Information" list and click **Modify** to make a change to that specific entry. The **Add** and **Delete** buttons allow you to input or remove criteria from the list, respectively.

   Once you are satisfied that the template is correct, click **OK** to save and exit to the "Filter Template Manager" window (see Figure 4-42).

8. Repeat Steps 4 through 7 to add another template to drop all traffic.

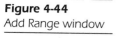

Figure 4-44
Add Range window

Add Range

Name: Server_Allow
Criteria: IP - IP_DESTINATION_ADDRESS

Minimum value

Maximum value

OK   Cancel

The scenario stated that traffic to the server should be the only traffic allowed on the Router A's Ethernet. In order to fulfill this requirement we need to "drop" all other incoming traffic on this interface.

Define Filter Name

Again, use a distinctive name that tells what the template is supposed to do.

Defining an Action

From the "Create IP Template" window, select Action > Add > Drop from the menu bar. The "drop" action is now displayed in the "Filter Information" list.

Defining the Criteria

Router A's Ethernet should only receive traffic bound for the server's address. If we restrict all other addresses on that Ethernet we will fulfill our requirement. Select Criteria > Add > IP Destination Address. Enter the following for the range:

Minimum Value: 172.16.1.0
Maximum Value: 172.16.1.255

NOTE: *We could have used the range 0.0.0.0 to 255.255.255.255, but that would prevent all incoming traffic to be dropped. Although this would achieve our desired result, if other interfaces existed on this router then traffic to them would also be dropped. If our goal is to create a firewall then this drop range would be necessary. Of course, accept templates would need to be created to allow only authorized traffic.*

Click **OK** to return to the "Filter Template Management" window.

9. Once all templates have been created, click **Done**.

10. Create Filter using the templates that were just created.

Figure 4-45
Filter creation
window

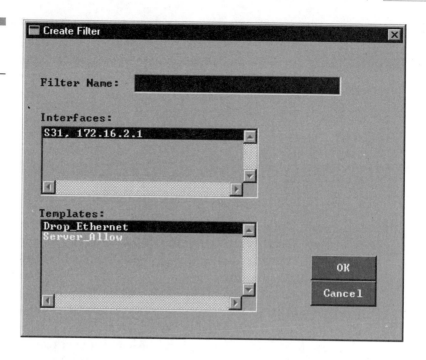

Click **Create** from within the "Filter Template Management" window. Figure 4-45 displays the "Create Filter" window that opens.

Enter a name for this filter in the "Filter Name" field. It is recommended that you include the interface designator in the filter name. So, from Figure 4-45, our first filter could be named S31_Server_Allow.

Select the "Server_Allow" template from the template list. Clicking **OK** will assign this filter to filter #1 and return to the "IP Filter" main window.

11. Repeat previous step for the drop filter.

Click **Create** and name this filter using the interface designator— S31_Drop_Ethernet. Save this filter by clicking **OK**.

12. Verify the order of the templates in the filter will provide the correct results.

Filter #1 will accept all traffic destined for the server while all others will be dropped according to filter #2. If a reorder is required, click **Reorder**. Also, if you need to edit a template, click the **Edit** button and make any adjustments that are needed.

The previous example is just one filter that the router can perform. There are seemingly an endless number of filters that can be applied using a combination of the predefined criteria as well as using user-defined criteria. A sound knowledge of the protocol header bit positions can lead you to creating vary specific filters that can permit or block all manner of packets.

SUMMARY

In this chapter we discussed several IP services provided by Nortel Network routers. Most important to many Network Administrators is the router's ability to act as a BootP Relay Agent. As many networks incorporate automatic methods for configuration, such as DHCP, it is good to know that their investment in a routing architecture will be compatible. Not only is the Nortel router compatible with DHCP, BootP, and RARP, it also provides file transfer services and Circuitless IP.

Reverse Address Resolution Protocol (RARP) provides address information to disk-less machines on the same network segment. To accommodate multiple segments, BootP was implemented. What BootP allowed was for the configuration information from client-to-server and from server-to-client to cross a router or multiple routers. As BootP replaced RARP, DHCP is steadily replacing BootP by providing more complete configuration information along with the devices IP address. Nortel routers support the *File Transfer Protocol* (FTP) as a means for *putting* and *getting* files from the router. It also supports the less rigid transfer protocol, *Trivial File Transfer Protocol* (TFTP). Authentication is not required when using TFTP to move files to and from the router.

If you desire a management interface that is independent of a router's specific physical interface, you could configure the router with a circuitless IP interface. That way you could configure a management platform to key on this virtual interface and as long as one interface to the router is good you will still be able to manage the router.

Technician Interface (TI) Software

In Chapter 2, "The TCP/IP Protocol Suite," we briefly noted the use of the *Technician Interface* (TI) when we restarted the router with a blank configuration and ran the Install script. Because none of the router's interfaces had been configured, it was the only way to access the router to begin the install process. The main purpose of the TI is to make the initial connection to the router in order to begin its configuration. It is also used for maintaining router operation, diagnosing problems, and monitoring the router's basic functionality. The TI is a simple command-line interface and with it, network managers can enable or disable circuits, protocols, lines, and services, provided that the network managers know the Nortel router *Management Information Bases* (MIBs) and the *Simple Network Management Protocol* (SNMP) commands that can change their values.

Being able to access the TI is essential for initially configuring a router. As you may recall from an earlier chapter, we worked with a new router that had no configuration. We connected a PC to the console port of the router and proceeded to configure it with an IP interface. Connecting to the router's console port is called a *local connection* because our connecting device (whether an ASCII terminal or a PC running terminal software) is local to the router. You can also connect to the router via a remote connection to the console port with a modem. Remote connections can also be made over an IP network using the Telnet protocol. After our connecting device is set up with the appropriate communication parameters, we can log into the router and proceed to add the initial IP interface. In previous chapters, we progressed in configuring the router by adding another interface as well as additional protocols and services, but, as you will note, we used the Site Manager tool to make these changes instead of the TI.

The main reason to use Site Manager is that it eases the configuration burden by making the SNMP sets and gets for us. Knowledge of the specific MIB variables is not necessary when setting a parameter. Another reason for using Site Manager over the TI for configuration is that it provides consistency checking. If an incorrect value is entered in one of the fields, Site Manager will balk, whereas the TI will allow the setting, possibly causing a service disruption. Table 5-1 outlines some of the differences between the TI and Site Manager.

Besides initially configuring the router, the TI can be used to maintain its operation. Through the use of predefined scripts, you can stop and start services, check on circuit or line statuses, or view portions of the data that

Table 5-1

Differences
between the TI
and Site Manager

	Technician Interface (TI)	Site Manager (SM)
Location	TI is located in the operating system kernel and is loaded upon router boot.	SM resides on a workstation and it must be installed before it can be executed.
Connection	Sessions to the TI can be established by directly connected devices or through the network.	SM only permits remote connections across a network.
Usage	The TI is a command-line interface. Parameters are entered via cryptic and often long commands.	SM is menu-driven. Options display in a window and are selected with a mouse.
Monitoring Ability	The TI has predefined scripts available for status/statistics polling.	One of the tools available through SM is the Statistics Monitor that enables MIB polling for status or statistics.
Troubleshooting	Besides using predefined scripts, you can view the event log.	Event Viewer is another tool offered in SM that permits event log viewing.

enters or leaves an interface. If you are familiar with the Nortel MIB structure, you can manually enter values, but heed the previous warning about
the TI's incapability to provide consistency checking. Monitoring the
router's basic functionality is an important attribute of the TI. Although the
same functions can be performed through Site Manager, it can usually be
performed quicker through the command-line interface. Again, using predefined scripts and commands called *aliases*, you can rapidly pinpoint a
troubled interface. Scripts and aliases can be created to match your specific
environment. So, if none of the predefined scripts meet your needs, it is
fairly simple to create some that do. Another way of using the TI to diagnose
problems is by using the log facility. The log command allows you to view
the event log, filtering if necessary to isolate a problem.

The TI is a useful tool that provides many functions for keeping your
router healthy and happy. Whichever way you choose to use the TI, you
must be able to establish a connection to the router before you can proceed.
The following sections discuss the various methods of connecting to the
router.

Connections

Out-of-band and in-band connections are the two supported ways of connecting to the router's TI. Direct or dial connections are considered out-of-band because they do not depend on the state of the network for a connection to be established. The connection is made via the console port on the router with an ASCII terminal or a modem. In-band connections rely on the network to establish a remote connection. These connections use the Telnet protocol to establish a session.

Out-of-Band Connections

Local connections to the router's console port require an ASCII terminal or a PC (or laptop) running a terminal emulation program. Remote connections require a modem to be attached to the router console and to the serial port of a PC (or laptop). A dial line is used to establish the TI session.

In Chapter 2, we established a local connection using the terminal emulation program that came with Windows and the following parameters:

- 9600 baud
- Eight data bits
- No parity
- One stop bit

Before we could use the program, we had to connect the laptop to the router console port. We did this using the serial cable that came with the router. Now, for BN routers, the console port is a 25-pin female connector that is located on the SRM-L link module on the backside of the router. The *Access Node* (AN), *Access Node Hub* (ANH), and *Access Stack Node* (ASN) routers have a nine-pin female console port located on the rear chassis panel. Nortel recommends the cables in Table 5-2 to complete the terminal/PC connection.

Using a Modem Connected to the Console   In order to use the modem for a remote connection, set the Modem Enable parameter to Enable in the Console Port parameters. Selecting the Console connector from the Configuration Manager main window lets you access the console port parame-

Table 5-2

Router console
cables

Router	Cable	Part Number
Terminal: Local Connection		
Backbone Node (BN)	25-pin D-sub plug to RS-232 C receptacle	7525
ASN	Nine-pin D-sub plug to RS-232 C receptacle	7526
ANH	Nine-pin D-sub plug to RS-232 C receptacle	7526
PC with Terminal Emulation: Local Connection		
All router models	Nine-pin D-sub plug to RS-232 C modem plug	7527
Note: The nine-pin to RS-232 C cable comes in a kit with a null modem adapter.		
Modem: Local Connection		
BN	25-pin D-sub plug to RS-232 C modem plug	77850
ASN	Nine-pin D-sub plug to RS-232 C modem plug	7825
ANH	Nine-pin D-sub plug to RS-232 C modem plug	7825

ters. Figure 5-1 shows the Configuration Manager main window. Figure 5-2 is the Console Lists window. Use the scroll bar to find the Modem Enable parameter.

In-Band Connections

The Telnet protocol is used to make in-band TI connections. Any PC using a TCP/IP protocol stack and a Telnet client can connect to the router in order to establish a TI session. As you may recall from the last chapter, we enabled the TCP services and specifically the Telnet Server service. It is the Telnet Server service that enables Telnet clients to gain access to the TI and the router's MIB. Actually, proper authentication must be entered before the router enables someone to access its MIB. We will discuss logging into the router in the next section.

Because the TCP Telnet Client service was also activated last chapter, we can connect to the router, using either one of the connection methods previously discussed. We could then use the router's Telnet client to establish an

Figure 5-1
The Configuration
Manager main
window

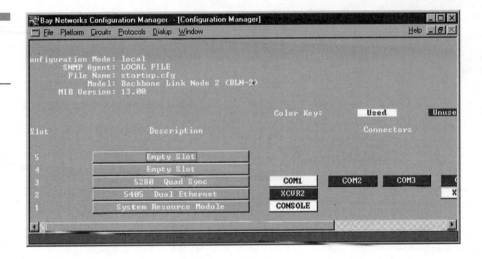

Figure 5-2
The Console Lists
window

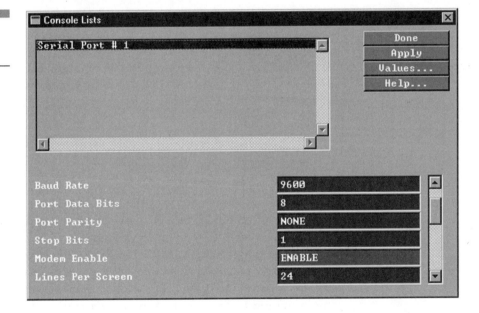

in-band connection to another router. The Telnet Server must be enabled on the other router in order for this to work. So, from one connection, we can administer pretty much all the routers in an enterprise.

Running the TI

The TI is part of the router's operating kernel and is loaded when the router is booted. It runs on the first slot in a router usually to boot, slot 2 for BN routers, slot 1 for AN and ANH routers, and either individually or simultaneously on any slot in an ASN (depending on whether more than one ASN is in a stack). If the current slot that is running the TI is reset, the TI will also reset itself to run on another slot in a multislot router.

Logging In   Access to the TI is barred with a login name and password (if configured). After a connection to the router has been established, a login prompt is presented. Nortel routers only support two login accounts: Manager and User. The Manager account allows full read/write access to the router, whereas the User account is read-only. The login name and password are both case-sensitive, so you must type Manager or User with a capital M or U. To access the login screen, perform the following steps:

1. Start Telnet client.

   For our purpose, we will connect to the router using Windows Telnet client. Use whatever client with which you are familiar. The Window client is limited in features, but it is perfect for our example. To start the Telnet client, click Start: Run > Telnet. Then click **OK** to start the Telnet client.

2. Enter the IP address of the router.

   From Chapter 2, we configured the Ethernet router interface with 172.16.1.200. Select Connect: Remote Session. The Connect window opens, prompting for the connection parameters. Enter the following information in the parameter fields:

   a. Host Name: 172.16.1.200
   b. Port: telnet
   c. Term Type: vt100

Figure 5-3 displays the Telnet client window.

3. Click **OK** to establish a router connection.

4. Log into the TI.

   After a connection is established, the login prompt appears, as shown in Figure 5-4.

Figure 5-3
The Telnet client
Connect window

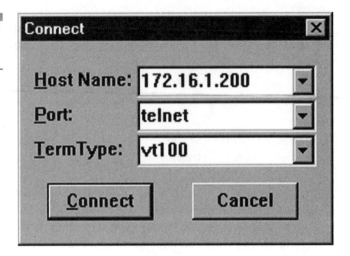

Figure 5-4
The router login
screen within the
Telnet client

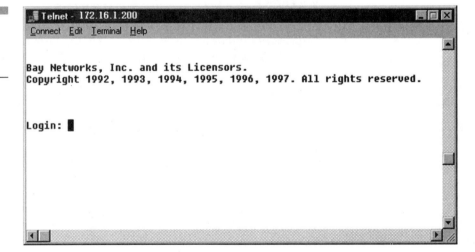

5. Enter "Manager" as the login name and press **Enter** when the password prompt displays. Because a password has not been defined, we do not need to enter one.

After you have successfully logged into the TI on the router, you are presented with the command prompt. The default prompt is two numbers, separated by a colon and encased in brackets, such as the following:

```
[x:y]$
```

The x is the slot number that the TI is currently running on, the y is the port number you are connected to, and the $ is a separator between the prompt and what you type.

Amending the Prompt field among the console parameters in Figure 5-2 can change this prompt. The prompt can consist of no more than 19 characters. The only variable that can be used in the prompt is %slot%. This variable tells the router to insert the slot that the TI session is running on into the prompt. A recommendation for a prompt is to use the router name. If you continually use the router's Telnet client to access other routers, it helps to know on which router you are entering commands. If you choose to have spaces in your prompt, you must encase the text in quotation marks.

A Brief Note on Passwords

Passwords are a great way to secure a router, but sometimes passwords can be lost. If you lose the password on an AN or ASN router, you must call Nortel for help with recovering the lost password. For BN routers, you can perform the following steps to recover a lost password. BN routers distribute a password among its *Fast Routing Engine* (FRE) cards. Thus, if the FRE that currently hosts the TI is reset or fails, security can still be maintained as the TI is hosted on another FRE. So, in order to break the password that is stored on every FRE in the BN, you must use a new FRE or one that has a known password stored on it.

1. Remove the FRE from its slot.

This is to accommodate the new FRE module.

2. Insert the new FRE module.

Remember that this module can be one that has never been used or one that has a known password stored on it.

3. Insert the flash memory card into the FRE module from Step 2.

4. Disengage all other FRE modules in the BN router.

   Do not fully remove these modules. Just remove them so they are not connected to the backplane.

WARNING: *Never run a BN router with all but one FRE module completely removed. Proper airflow must be maintained at all times.*

5. Boot the router.

6. Reinsert the other FRE modules and wait until they reset.

7. Reset the router password. Establish a TI session and enter the Password command at the command prompt. Here's an example:

   ```
   [1:1]$ password Manager
   ```

   This will enable you to set or change the manager's password. After the change is made, the processor module distributes the password to the other modules.

Commands

This section describes the four main categories of TI commands. It is important to note that every command, filename, and password used during a TI session is case-sensitive. If any command is typed incorrectly, the router will issue a "usage:" message that displays the proper syntax when using the command. Lastly, the Enter key must be typed in order to issue any TI command. Here are the four command categories with their respective commands:

- *Operating commands*   help, more, ctrl+c, !, history, exec, and ping
- *File system commands*   compact, cd, copy, delete, dinfo, dir, format, partition, save, tftp, and type
- *Event log commands*   log, save log, clearlog
- *System administration commands*   bconfig, ifconfig, boot, restart, reset, diags, stamp, readexe, prom, loadmap, date, and password

The following sections discuss these commands in detail. You may find that some of the commands fit in more than one category. That's OK. The categories do not prohibit the commands' use. If there is any confusion, simply decide what you want to accomplish and use the appropriate command.

Operating Commands

These commands make working with the TI easier. The *repeat* and *history* commands prevent you from constantly typing long commands by allowing you to replay the last command at the console. Besides making entering commands easier, the *help* operating command gives you information about the many commands that are available to you from the TI. You can even test remote host device's connectivity with the *ping* operating command. The following section goes into more detail about each operating command. Examples are also provided where necessary.

- `help` displays online help text for any of the TI commands. Here is its syntax and some examples follow:

  `help [<command>]`

Command	Description
help	Lists all TI commands
help clear	Displays the help text for the clear command
help-all	Displays all the TI commands and their associated syntax

- `more` pauses the screen output before it scrolls off the screen. Here is its syntax and some examples follow:

  `more -s [on|off] <# of lines>`

Command	Description
more on	Turns screen pause on and prompts you to continue when the screen is filled
more on 24	Limits the screen pause to 24 lines

Note that the -s disables screen output. This option is for use in scripts.

- ctrl + c halts a command.
- ! repeats the previous command a specified number of times. Here is its syntax and some examples follow:

```
! [<repeat count>]
```

Command	Description
!	Repeats the previous command
! 5	Repeats the previous command five times

- history displays a list of the last 20 commands entered from the command line. The default value of the number commands retained is 20 and it can be changed to a maximum of 40 entries. To change this number, modify the TI History Depth parameter located among the console parameters in Figure 5-2 as well as among the Telnet server parameters. The Telnet server parameters are found under the global protocol parameters, as shown in Figure 5-5. Select Protocols: Global Protocols > Telnet Server from the Configuration Manager main window. Here is its syntax and some examples follow:

```
history [<command #>]
```

Command	Description
history	Displays a list containing the last 20 commands entered
history 2	Executes the second command in the list

- ping tests the reachability of network devices. Nortel routers support multiple types of pings depending upon the protocol. Nortel supports the following protocol pings: IP, IPv6, IPX, OSI, Vines, AppleTalk, and APPN. Unless specified, the router will issue an IP ping. In this section, an IP ping will be examined. Here is its syntax:

```
ping -ip <IP address> [-t<timeout>] [-r<repeat count>] [-s<size>]
[-p] [-a<address>] [-v]
```

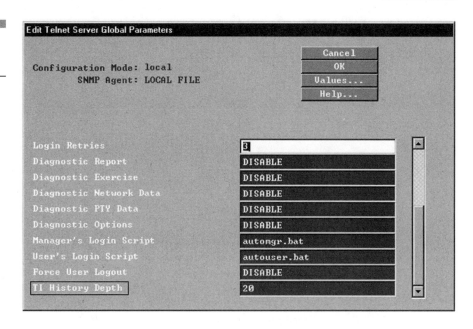

```
Edit Telnet Server Global Parameters

                                              Cancel
   Configuration Mode: local                    OK
            SNMP Agent: LOCAL FILE             Values...
                                               Help...



   Login Retries                    3
   Diagnostic Report                DISABLE
   Diagnostic Exercise              DISABLE
   Diagnostic Network Data          DISABLE
   Diagnostic PTY Data              DISABLE
   Diagnostic Options               DISABLE
   Manager's Login Script           automgr.bat
   User's Login Script              autouser.bat
   Force User Logout                DISABLE
   TI History Depth                 20
```

Its required parameter, <IP address>, is the address of the remote device in dotted decimal notation. The optional parameters are as follows:

- -t<timeout>   This is the amount of time the router will wait for a response. The default timeout for a ping is five seconds.

- -r<repeat count>   This option specifies the number of ping packets the router will send. By default, the router sends only one packet. The valid values for this option are between 0 and 10.

- -s<size>   This option sets the number of bytes to send with each ping. By default, this value is 16 bytes.

- -p   This option generates a path trace report with intervening hops displayed and the time it took to reach them.

- -v   The verbose option generates a statistical report about the echo request including the ping's success rate and the round-trip time.

- -a<address>   This option identifies a source address for a ping and is used to test how different interfaces on the router ping a remote device.

Here are some ping examples:

Command	Description
`ping 172.16.1.200`	Sends a ping to the IP address of 172.16.1.200
`ping -ip 172.16.1.200`	Also sends a ping to 172.16.1.200
`ping 172.16.1.200 -r3`	Sends three pings to 172.16.1.200
`ping 172.16.1.200 -a172.16.2.1 -v`	Sends a ping to 172.16.1.200 from 172.16.2.1 also displaying statistical information

When you issue an IP ping from the TI, you will receive one of the following messages. If you issued an IP ping with a repeat count, one of these messages will accompany each ICMP echo request.

- *An alive message*   This message will be generated when an ICMP echo response is received within the timeout from the target host. Here is a sample message:

  `IP ping: 172.16.1.200 is alive (size = 16 bytes)`

- *A "does not respond" message*   If the router does not receive the ICMP echo response before the timeout, a does not respond message is displayed. Here's an example:

  `IP ping: 172.16.1.200 does not respond.`

- *An ICMP host unreachable from x.x.x.x message*   The router with address x.x.x.x generates this message when it can no longer forward the echo request to the target device. The following is a sample message with x.x.x.x being 192.168.1.200.

  `IP ping: ICMP host unreachable from 192.168.1.200.`

- *A target unreachable message*   This message is generated if a router that has just issued the ICMP host unreachable message receives another ping for the target address within 40 seconds. The ARP will have timed out and could not be resolved. Here's an example:

  `IP ping: 172.16.1.200 is unreachable.`

File System Commands

The File System commands pertain to the *Non-Volatile File System* (NVFS) found on the router flash memory cards. The NVFS is responsible for reading and writing to one or more flash memory cards. NVFS commands enable you to copy or delete files, list directories, view volume statuses, and even format and partition the memory card. Some of the commands support wildcards, which have the same meaning as with Windows:

- * matches any character.
- ? matches a single character.

Before we proceed in discussing the various file system commands, some conventions must be addressed. Please note that volume number refers to the slot number that hosts the memory card. Here are the rules:

- Because a router can accommodate multiple flash cards (BN routers enable one flash card for each FRE module, and ASN routers enable a flash card in router in a stack), the volume number must be used with any file that is to be referenced or created.
- File names must start with a letter; any of the other letters can be alphanumeric. Although no spaces are allowed, the (_) underscore and (.) dot are allowed.
- The length of file names can be no longer than 15 characters. Nortel recommends keeping the file name to eight characters to maintain support for all operating systems.
- File extensions are allowed and must be preceded by a file name and a (.) dot. Again, the total length, with an extension, can be no longer than 15 characters.

Nortel recognizes that maintaining a consistent naming structure helps to distinguish file types. They recommend the following conventions for file extensions:

- *exe* for router image files such as bn.exe, asn.exe, and so on
- *cfg* for alternate configuration files such as startup.cfg
- *al, log, and bat* for aliases, log files, and scripts, respectively

Figure 5-6
Dinfo command
output

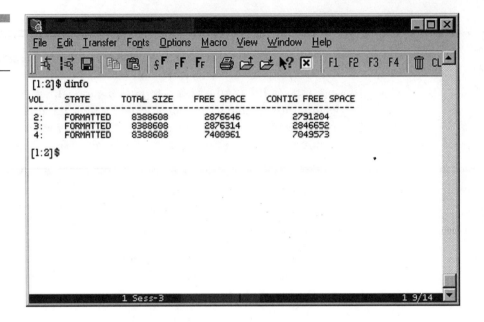

```
[1:2]$ dinfo
VOL    STATE      TOTAL SIZE   FREE SPACE   CONTIG FREE SPACE
------------------------------------------------------------
2:     FORMATTED  8388608      2876646      2791204
3:     FORMATTED  8388608      2876314      2846652
4:     FORMATTED  8388608      7400961      7049573

[1:2]$
```

- *dinfo* displays the status of all flash memory cards installed in a router. Typing this command at the TI produces a table of information about each card. Figure 5-6 is an example of a table produced by the dinfo command.

  The State column tells whether the card is formatted or corrupted. The Total Size contains the total number of bytes in the memory card. This is the total of all used and unused memory space. The Free Space is the amount of unused bytes on the card. As mentioned earlier, the Contiguous Free Space column shows the amount of space available in the largest memory block.

- *dir* lists the directory structure of a volume. The information displayed includes the filename, file size, and the date and time the file was written to the media. As with the `dinfo` command, the Available Free Space and the Contiguous Free Space are listed along with the Total Space allowable on the flash memory card. The wildcards * and ? are also supported (see Figure 5-7).

  Here's an example of dir's syntax and the following table shows some further examples:

Figure 5-7
Example of output from a dir command

```
[1:2]$ dir

Volume in drive 2: is
Directory of 2:

File Name            Size      Date       Day      Time
-----------------------------------------------------------------
bcc_help           170860    09/10/1998   Thurs.   13:57:33
bn.exe            4690999    09/10/1998   Thurs.   13:58:03
debug.al            12319    09/10/1998   Thurs.   14:11:42
freboot.exe        173924    09/10/1998   Thurs.   14:11:44
frediag.exe        238795    09/10/1998   Thurs.   14:12:15
install.bat        206289    09/10/1998   Thurs.   14:12:57
ti.cfg                132    09/10/1998   Thurs.   14:13:34
ymtrans.tbl           371    09/10/1998   Thurs.   14:32:47
ti_notice.txt         145    08/06/0099   Fri.     09:01:33
config1              8860    04/27/2000   Thurs.   12:32:08
config               8860    04/27/2000   Thurs.   12:32:08

  8388608 bytes - Total size
  2876646 bytes - Available free space
  2791204 bytes - Contiguous free space
[1:2]$
```

```
dir <volume:>
```

Command	Description
dir	Lists all the files on the active volume
dir 1:	Lists the files on volume 1
dir *.exe	Lists all the files with an .exe extension on the active volume
dir 2: *.cfg	Lists all the files on volume 2 that have a .cfg extension

■ *cd* changes the active volume. cd is the same command as that found in DOS and Unix, also known as change directory. Here's an example of its syntax and some further examples follow:

```
cd <volume:>
```

Command	Description
cd	Displays the active volume
cd 1:	Changes to volume 1

■ *copy* copies one file to another. A similar command can be found in DOS and Unix. It is important to note that this command does not prompt you if you are about to overwrite a file. Be sure to perform the `dir` command before you copy in order to identify file names. This command also supports the * and ? wildcards. Here's an example of its syntax and some further examples are shown in the following table:

```
copy <volume:><old file> <volume:><new file>
```

Command	Description
copy config config1	Copies the config file to config1 on the same volume
copy 1:config 2:config	Copies the config file on volume 1 to volume 2

■ *delete* removes a file from the active volume. This command has no provision for file recovery. After a file has been deleted, it cannot be undeleted. The `delete` command supports the * and ? wildcards. The following is an example of its usage and some further examples follow:

```
del[ete] <volume:><filename>
```

Command	Description
del config1	Removes config1 from the active volume
del 2:config	Removes the config file from volume 2

■ *compact* retrieves unusable space on a memory card. When files are copied to a flash card in a router, the amount of free space diminishes. A time may arrive when the free space is so limited that no other files can be copied to the flash card. To make room, you should delete files that are no longer needed. Like in the old DOS days, the files still reside on the flash, but they are inaccessible and the free space is still at a minimum. This command is used to retrieve the unavailable space. When using the `dir` or `dinfo` commands, if the Available Free Space is larger than the Contiguous Free Space, you will need to compact the memory card. Here's an example of compact in use and further examples are shown in the following table:

```
compact <volume:>
```

Command	Description
compact 1:	Regains all the available free space on volume 1

■ *format* erases all files on a flash memory card and sets up the media for the reading and writing files. The `dinfo` command can be used to verify that a format is successful. Here's an example of format in use:

```
format <volume:>
```

NOTE: *No unformat command is available. In short, no recovery from a format is possible. It is recommended that you copy all files to another flash card before executing a format command.*

■ *partition* divides a flash memory card into two distinct volumes. Each volume can then be addressed separately. The original volume is referred to by <volume>a, or <volume>, and the new partition as <volume>b. This command can only be used with memory cards four MB or greater and with BayRS™ version 8.10 or later. Because the flash card is divided in half, the original volume must be half the media size. For example, in order to partition a volume that contains files that total five MB on an eight-MB flash card, you would have to delete some files to bring the total used space to four MB or less.

WARNING: *When issuing the partition command to remove a volume, if you do not specify a subvolume, <volume>b will be removed.*

Here's some examples of partition in use, and some further examples are shown in the following table:

```
partition create [<volume:>]
partition delete [<volume:>]
```

Command	Description
partition create 1:	Creates a subvolume on volume 1 named 1b. All files will be stored on 1a.
partition delete 1: or partition delete	Removes volume 1b

■ *type* displays the contents of a file. Here's an example:

```
type [-x] <volume:><filename>
```

type also contains the -x parameter argument that sets the display to hexadecimal. This allows the viewing of nonprintable characters. Here are some further examples of type at work:

Command	Description
type menu.bat	Displays the file menu.bat from the active volume
type 1:debug.al	Displays the debug.al file from volume 1

In the area of file transfers, either an in-band or out-of-band method can accomplish a file transfer to or from a router. The in-band method can be utilized if a valid IP routing path exists on your network. A dial connection must be established in order to use the out-of-band method. The commands for in-band and out-of-band file transfers are `tftp` and `xmodem`, respectively. Here are a couple examples of `tftp`:

```
tftp get <host address> <src volume:><src file>
[<dest volume:>][<dest file>]
tftp put <host address> <src volume:><src file>
[<dest volume:>][<dest file>]
```

The get argument means that you are transferring a file from the host address. The put argument means you are transferring a file to the host address.

`tftp` requires the following parameters:

- *host address*   The address of the device hosting the file transfer

- *src volume*   The volume number of the source volume in relation to the host address

- *src file*   The source filename in relation to the host address

- *dest volume*   The volume number of the destination volume in relation to the host address

- *dest file*   The destination filename in relation to the host address

Here are some further examples:

Command	Description
`tftp get 172.16.1.200` `1:config 1:config1`	Retrieves a copy of the file config from volume 1 on 172.16.1.200 to volume 1 of the router that you are currently connected to and stores it as config1
`tftp get 172.16.1.200` `1:config`	Retrieves a copy of the file config from volume 1 on 172.16.1.200 and stores it with the same name in the current working directory
`tftp put 172.16.1.200` `1:config.bak 1:config`	Sends a copy of the file config.bak from the router that you are currently connected to volume 1 on 172.16.1.200 and stores it as config

- *xmodem* allows for the transfer of files between a workstation and a router when the underlying IP network is not functional. It has the ability to move files via one of the following communication protocols.

- XMODEM/CRC protocol
- MODEM7 batch protocol
- XMODEM-1K block protocol
- YMODEM batch protocol

Even though the previous protocols are supported by the xmodem command, the YMODEM batch protocol is recommended because it offers more versatility. Not only does it support batch transfers; it also automatically converts the file names received during the batch transfers. It provides error detection and file deletion when a transfer is unsuccessful or is canceled. Lastly, the YMODEM protocol transfers binary files intact and without padding. It uses the default packet size of 128 bytes.

```
xmodem [sb | st | rb | rt]<options> <volume:><filename>
<filename>  . . .
```

xmodem requires the following parameters:

Send Binary (sb)   This parameter sends files as they exist on the flash or disk media. No conversion is performed during transfer.

Send Text (st)   This parameter instructs xmodem to send the file(s) as ASCII text.

Receive Binary (rb)   This parameter places files on flash or disk media without conversion. The YMODEM protocol overwrites existing files.

Receive Text (rt)   This parameter instructs xmodem to receive the file(s) as ASCII text.

Options

y   Selects the YMODEM transfer protocol

m   Selects the MODEM7 protocol

k   Uses 1K packets on transfer

c   Selects CRC mode on receive

w   Inserts a 15 second wait before initiating the startup handshake

l   Disables the automatic logging of significant events, errors, and retries. The default for XMODEM & YMODEM protocols is to log events. Logged events are sent to the system log, which can be used for troubleshooting.

p   Allows for the display of information and events during the transfer. This option is only available for Unix stations.

n   Allows for the midstream cancellation of the transfer process by the use of the CAN-CAN (^x^x) abort. By default, YMODEM only allows for the CAN-CAN abort at the beginning of the transfer.

e   Disable EOT verification when transferring files to the router. This option id only available for DOS machines.

System Administration

The commands issued from the TI that pertain to system administration of the router allow for the following functions:

- Booting the router
- Restarting or resetting router slots
- Run diagnostics
- Display router software version number
- Verify and Upgrade software
- View the load addresses and size of applications
- Reset the date and time
- Assign passwords

Before we begin, it will be beneficial to briefly review Chapter 1 in regards to the boot process and the software that resides on each of the processor cards. That will give us a good basis for discussing the previously discussed functions of system administration. As you may recall, on a cold start each processor module executes CPU and backbone diagnostics, and if a link module is present, link diagnostics. Once the diagnostics are completed (successfully or unsuccessfully), the modules then boot. The first module to boot will pull its software image and config file from its local flash card. Once it has loaded, it can now respond to the requests for the router image and config file from other booting modules. The process is similar when the router warm starts; the difference being that the processor modules skip running the CPU, backbone, and link diagnostics. This is indicated by the red DIAG LED on the front panel and on the FRE module. As a point of clarification, power cycling the router or running the `diags` command is considered a cold start. A warm start occurs when the `boot` or `reset` commands are issued. A warm start also occurs when a processor module is removed then reinserted into a slot (hot swap).

The software that exists on a processor module consists of a diagnostics file, bootstrap image file, and the router software image. The diagnostics file is named *frediag.exe* and it is the software that performs the different diagnostic routines. The bootstrap image file, *freboot.exe*, as its name implies boots the processor module and tells it what software image to load. The router software image depends on the type of router. For AN and ANH routers the image file is *an.exe*; likewise ARN and ASN router image files are named *arn.exe* and *asn.exe*, respectively.

The following commands, with their descriptions, can be used to perform the specified system administration functions.

- *boot* boots the entire system using the default image and config file for the router. For BN routers the default software image file is bn.exe with config being the default configuration file name. The `boot` command can be used to specify boot files other than the default files as will be demonstrated.

WARNING: *It is recommended that only one version of the configuration file exist on the router. It is possible for the processor modules to simultaneously load different config files, which may cause service disruption. It is best to create alternate names for configuration files.*

Usage

```
boot <vol:><image_name> <vol:><config_name>
```

Optional Parameters

`<vol:>`	Specifies the volume where the image and/or config file reside
`<image_name>`	The name of the file the contains the router's software image. This can be a valid file name, or "-" which signifies the default image file

`<config_name>`	The name of the file that contains the router's configuration. This can be a valid file name, or "-" which signifies the default config file.

Command	Description
`boot`	Boots the router with the default image and config file from the current volume
`boot 2:bn.exe 2:config`	Boots the router with the "bn.exe" image file with the "config" file found on slot 2
`boot 2:bn.exe 2:startup.cfg`	Boots the router with the "bn.exe" image file with the "startup.cfg" config file found on slot 2
`boot 2:bn.exe 2:-`	Boots the router with the "bn.exe" image file with the default config file found on slot 2

■ *restart* restarts the GAME image on specified slots. It does not restart the processor module with a new router software image.

Usage

```
restart [<slot_no>]
restart [<slot_no>-<slot_no>]
restart [<slot_no>,<slot_no>, ...,]
```

Optional Parameters

`<slot_no>`	This signifies the slot or slots to restart.

Command	Description
`restart`	Restarts the entire system
`restart 3`	Restart the module in slot 3
`restart 2-5`	Restarts the modules in slots 2 through 5
`restart 2,5,8`	Restart the modules in slots 2, 5, and 8

■ *reset*, unlike the `restart` command, causes the router or slots on the router to reload the router software image. What happens is that the GAME operating system on a processor module issues a boot request to all other processor modules in the other slots. Then the following occurs:

1. The first processor module to respond to the request forwards the router image file from its memory.

2. The resetting module receives the image file and executes it. This disrupts service to and from the processor module. The other modules in the router resynchronize their routing tables in response to this failure.

3. The resetting module completes its boot and then transmits a request for the configuration file. The first module to respond forwards the configuration file resident in its memory.

4. The resetting module will then load the config file and start all the services provided by the slot. It is at this point connectivity is reestablished. The module then alerts the other modules that it is able to receive packets.

5. The other modules synchronize their tables accordingly.

Usage

```
reset [<slot_no>]
reset [<slot_no>-<slot_no>]
reset [<slot_no>,<slot_no>, ...,]
```

Command	Description
reset	Resets all slots in the router
reset 2	Resets the module in slot 2
reset 2-5	Resets the modules in slots 2 through 5
reset 2,5,8	Resets the modules in slots 2, 5, and 8

■ *diags* cold starts the entire router or specified slots in the router. The diagnostics consist of CPU, backbone, and link diagnostics. Also, the cold start reboots the router.

Usage

```
diags [<slot_no>]
diags [<slot_no>-<slot_no>]
diags [<slot_no>,<slot_no>, ...,]
```

NOTE: *The system prompts for confirmation when you issue the previous command(s).*

Command	Description
diags	Performs diagnostics and reboots the entire system
diags 2	Performs diagnostics for and reboots the module in slot 1
diags 2-5	Performs diagnostics for and reboots slots 2 through 5
diags 2,5,8	Performs diagnostics for and reboots slots 2, 5, and 8

■ *stamp* displays the current software version as well as the date and time it was created.

Usage

```
stamp
```

■ *readexe* verifies executable software by calculating a file header and image checksum on a file on the file system and comparing it to the checksum within the file. Once the validation is complete, readexe displays the results as well as all the file header information. Figure 5-8 shows the output of the readexe command.

Usage

```
readexe <vol:><filename>
```

Figure 5-8
Sample output
from readexe

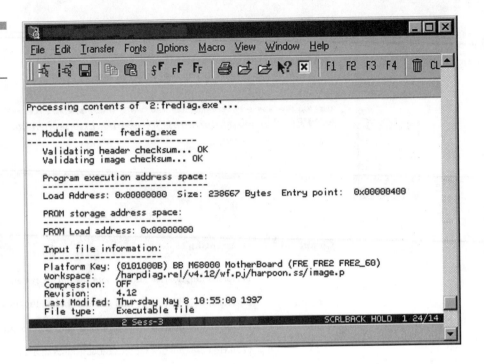

Command	Description
readexe frediag.exe	Validates the file header and image checksum for the file "frediag.exe"

You can see from Figure 5-8 that the system's response to the readexe command contains a lot of information. The following describes some of the information that is displayed:

■ Validating header checksum . . . This indicates if the checksum for the header matches the file found in the file header. A value of OK indicates that they match. A value of BAD indicates the checksums fail to match.

■ Validating image checksum . . . This indicates whether the checksum for the image data matches the checksum in the file. A value of OK indicates that they match. A value of BAD indicates the checksums fail to match.

- Program execution address space This provides information about where the file is loaded in memory. It identifies the memory location and the size of the file.

- Prom storage address space This indicates the location of the diag or boot files in PROM.

- *prom* upgrades the boot and diag proms. In order to use this command you must have "Manager" access to the router. It can also be used to verify the prom upgrade after the upgrade has completed.

NOTE: *If you software is shipped with a PROM upgrade, see the documents that shipped with your software upgrade for instructions on how to perform the PROM upgrade for your router.*

Usage

```
prom [-w | -v] <volume_no:><PROM_source_file> <slot_ID>
```

Required Parameters

-w	Indicates the command will write the upgrade to PROM
-v	Indicates the command will verify the PROM upgrade
<volume_no:>	The volume, or slot, where the PROM source file resides
<PROM_source_file>	Either the boot or diag software image, as in *freboot.exe* or *frediag.exe*
<slot_ID>	The slot to which the upgrade is to applied or verified

Once the prom command has been executed it can not be stopped. The [Crtl]+c key sequence will be disabled until the upgrade has finished. Depending upon the processor module, the upgrade can take between 2 and 10 minutes with approximately 2 minutes for verification.

Command	Description
`prom -w 2:frediag.exe 3`	This erases the diagnostics PROM that is on slot 3 and writes the contents of "frediag.exe" from slot 2 back to the PROM in slot 3.
`prom -v 2:frediag.exe 3`	This verifies the contents of the PROM on slot 3 against the file "frediag.exe" located on slot 2.

■ *loadmap* displays the size of applications in memory and their location.

Usage

```
loadmap [<slot_no>] [<filename>]
loadmap [<slot_no>-<slot_no>] [<filename>]
loadmap [<slot_no>,<slot_no>, ...] [<filename>]
```

Optional Parameter

`<slot_no>` The volume number where the application resides

`<filename>` The name of the file to which the output of the command will be directed. If this option is left blank then the output will be sent to the screen.

Command	Description
`loadmap`	Displays the locations and sizes of all applications on all slots. The output is directed to the screen.
`loadmap 2`	Displays the locations and sizes of all applications that reside on slot 2. Again, the output is directed to the screen.
`loadmap 2-5`	Displays the locations and sizes of all applications that reside on slots 2 through 5. The output is to screen.
`loadmap 2,5,8`	Displays the load information for all applications that reside on slots 2, 5, and 8. The output is to screen.
`loadmap 2:map.dump`	Directs the load information for all applications on all slots to the file "map.dump"

■ *date* displays the current date, time, and *Greenwich Mean Time* (GMT) off-set. The time is based on a 24-hour clock and GMT is based on a direction in hours or minutes. That is the time can be a certain number of hours forward or behind GMT. As an example, *Eastern Standard Time* (EST) is 5 hours behind GMT.

Usage

```
date [<mm/dd/yy hh:mm:ss> [+ | - hh:mm ]]
```

Command	Description
date	Displays the current date and time on the router
date 06/18 /00	Changes the date to be June 18th, 2000
date 09:00:00	Changes the time on the router to 9 A.M.
date 06/18 /00 09:00 -5	Changes the date and time to be June 18th, 2000 at 9 A.M., 5 hours behind Greenwich Mean Time [GMT −5].

■ *password* assigns or reassigns the Manager and User passwords. As with all TI commands and filenames, the password is also case-sensitive. The User password can be changed when logged into the router as either a User or Manager. You must be logged into the router as a Manager in order to change the Manager's password.

Usage

```
password [Manager | User]
```

When the previous command is issued the operating system will prompt you for the old password first before asking for the new one. Once the new password has been keyed, the operating system will prompt you to verify the new password. The password change is successful when the operating system displays "User password changed" or "Manager password changed."

Managing Events

In order to use the TI to manage events on the router, you must be familiar with how events are stored. Each processor module contains a 64KB memory buffer. The operating system on the processor module logs events to this memory buffer on a *first-in, first-out* (FIFO) basis. What this means is as the buffer becomes full, older events are written over to make room for the new log entries. The memory buffer can hold 4,000 entries per processor module. It is the responsibility of the system software to pull all events from all processor modules when a command is issued to display or save the event log. Each entry is sorted in chronological order in order to be displayed or saved. These entries are also protected in the event of a warm start. That is when the `boot` or `reset` commands are issued. Pressing the reset button on the router is also considered a warm start. All event messages will be lost when the router is cold started by either issuing the `diags` command or by power cycling the router. Removing then reinserting a processor module clears the memory buffer for that module only. All other slots will still be actively logging events.

All management of events from the TI is handled with the `log` command. This command allows you to

■ Specify the events to be included or excluded from the event log

■ Specify the event to be displayed

■ Save the event log to a file

■ Display a saved event log

■ Clear all log entries

One more thing that you can do from the TI is configure the router to automatically save the event log to a file. Nortel recommends that this feature be enabled only for troubleshooting.

■ *log* enables the specification of what event messages are to be included or excluded from the event log or event log display. Including and excluding event messages from the event log are handled through "write" filters. "Read" filters are used when including or excluding event messages during display.

Write Filters

Usage

```
log [- i | -x ] [-e<entity>] [-f<severity>] [-s<slot_ID>]
```

Parameters

-i   Include the following options in the event log.

-x   Exclude the following options in the event log.

Options

-e\<entity\> This option allows you to specify the entity (software service) for which the router will include in or exclude in the event log. All entity names must be in upper case and if an entity contains spaces then the entity name must be enclosed in quotation marks.

-f\<severity\> This option allows for the specification of the fault severity levels for which the router will include or exclude in the event log. The fault severity codes are:

f or F for fault

i or I for Informational

t or T for trace

w or W for warning

d or D for debug

NOTE: *You can use more than one severity code in a single log command as will be evident in the following examples.*

-s\<slot_ID\> Using this option specifies the slot number(s) that the router will use to write events to the local log buffer.

Command	Description
log -i -ffw	Include fault and warning events in the log.
log -x -fd	Exclude debug messages from the event log.
log -i -ff -eGAME	Include only fault events for the Gate Access Management entity.
log -x -fi -s2	Exclude informational events on slot 2

Once write filters have been created, you can display them with the `log` command. The following usage displays all write filters across all slots or across the slots you specify.

Usage

```
log -z [-s<slot>]
```

Command	Description
log -z	Displays all write filters across all slots
log -z -s2	Displays all write filters for slot 2

Read Filters

Usage

```
log [volume:log_file] [-d<date>] [-t<time>] [-e<entity>]
[-f<severity>] [-s<slot>] [-p<rate>] [-c<code_no>] [-w]
```

Optional Parameters The `-e`, `-f`, and `-s` parameters are the same as those described previously.

`volume:log_file`	Specifies the location and file name of a previously saved log file
`-d<date>`	Specifies the date from which to begin the log display. The date format is mm/dd/yy.
`-t<time>`	Specifies the time from which to begin the log display. The time format is hh:mm:ss and ranges from 00:00:00 to 23:59:59.
`-p<rate>`	Specifies the polling of the event log. By default, this parameter enables the continuous polling of the log every five seconds.

`-c<code_no>`   Each event has an event code number. This parameter enables filtering on a specific or range of event codes.

`-w`   Enables console output in wide format

Command	Description
`log`	Displays all fault, warning, and informational event messages in memory
`log 2:atm.log`	Displays the event that was saved to volume 2 as atm.log
`log -d07/14/00`	Display the event log starting on 07/14/00 and ending with the present date
`log -t07:30:00`	Displays the event log starting at 7:30am on the current day until the present time
`log -ffw -eIP`	Displays all fault and warning messages associated with the IP entity in memory
`log -p`	Displays all fault, warning, and informational events every five seconds
`log -ffwti -s2 -p10`	Displays all fault, warning, trace, and informational events for slot 2 every 10 seconds
`log -c8`	Displays events associated with event code 8
`log -w`	Displays event log in wide format

NOTE: *Any combination of the previous parameters and in any order can be entered. There is no constraint on which parameter to key first. Also, to cancel any command, press [CRTL] + c.*

■ *save log* allows you to save the current event buffer to file for later retrieval.

WARNING: *There is no duplicate name checking before saves. The system will automatically overwrite a file of the same name on the flash media. Be sure to verify that no file exists on the flash card with the same name as the one you are using for the log file.*

Usage

```
save log <volume:><log_file> [-d<date>] [-t<time>] [-e<entity>]
[-f<severity>] [-s<slot>]
```

Required Parameters

volume   The volume to which the file will be stored

log_file   The name of the file that will store the event log

The optional parameters are the same as those described for the log command.

Command	Description
save log 2:event.log	Saves all the event messages to the file event.log on slot 2
save log 2:event.log -eATM	Saves all the event messages associated with the ATM entity to the file event.log on slot 2
save log 2:6_18.log -d06/18 /99	Saves all events since June 18th, 1999 to the file 6_18.log on slot 2

■ *clearlog* is used when you wish to test a certain configuration change and afterwards examine the log file for any events. The clearlog command will allow you to clear the current event log from a particular slot or from multiple slots.

Usage

```
clearlog [<slot_no>]
clearlog [<slot_no>-<slot_no>]
clearlog [<slot_no>,<slot_no>, ...,]
```

Command	Description
clearlog	Clears all memory buffers of event messages
clearlog 2	Clears event messages from slot 2's memory buffer
clearlog 2-5	Clears the event buffer from slot 2 through 5
clearlog 2,5,8	Clears the event buffer from slots 2, 5, and 8

System Scripts

System scripts are programs that allow you to view and use information from the Nortel MIB. The programs consist of TI commands that let you view routing, configuration, interface and statistical data about a particular service or protocol. In fact the type of information is dependent upon the particular router service or network protocol. The scripts are predefined and are mostly run from batch files that exist on the flash media. You tell a script file by their name designation. Script files are named for the particular protocol that they support as in "ip.bat." The name format for script files is *<protocol_name>*.bat. The method of getting the script files onto the flash media is up to you. A recommended way is to "put" the files onto the router's flash media by using Router Files Manager or FTP. Be sure there is enough space to accommodate all the script files you wish to use. If flash space is of a premium, then place only the scripts that pertain to the services and protocols currently configured on your router.

In addition to the batch file scripts, the router software incorporates several embedded scripts that also display the statistical and configuration information for the various router services and protocols. These embedded scripts are favored over their batch file counterparts because they are more efficient in retrieving the desired information. The embedded scripts included in the router software image cover the following services:

CSMACD	SNMP
FR	SYNC
FTP	TCP
IP	TELNET
MOSPF	TFTP
IP	

Regardless of the type of script (batch or embedded), they are invoked by using the show, monitor, enable, or disable commands. The show and monitor commands perform the same function except that the monitor periodically updates the displayed information. The enable/disable commands enable and disable services and protocols, respectively. Each of these commands is described next.

Before any batch scripts can be used, the router operating system must be made aware of the location of the script files. When you first install a router and connect using the TI you can immediately use the embedded scripts, but in order to use the show or monitor commands to view the batch scripts you must run the setpath command. The setpath command defines the aliases that integrate the scripts into the TI command set. It can be run from a single command line statement, by specifying the volumes to be included, or it can be run to prompt you for the volume numbers. Either way is fine and left up to your prerogative. This example demonstrates the command line statement method.

```
[2:1]$ run setpath "3:"
```

The previous example tells setpath that volume 3 can be searched for script files. Since setpath is a batch file, you must be on the volume that contains it in order to execute the command.

- *show* displays specific driver, protocol, or router service information such as configuration, state, and statistics.

Usage

```
show <subcommand> <option>
```

Required Parameters

<subcommand>   This indicates the protocol or service from which you are interested in retrieving information. The scripts that are supplied with the router software range from AppleTalk to *Xerox Network Service* (XNS). A list of all supported protocols and services can be viewed from the router TI by following the subcommand with a "?" or "help."

<option>   These are the protocol or service specific information that can be polled using the show command, such as configuration, state, and statistics. Use the "?" key or type "help" to view the supported options for the specific protocol or service. If this option is left blank, the show command will automatically display the list of options for the respective protocol or service.

Command	Description
show ip ?	Displays the list of options available for the IP protocol. The available options include, but are not limited to, the ARP table, forwarding table, and route and traffic filters.
show ip arp	Displays the ARP cache

In addition to the variety of protocol and service scripts, you can use the following show commands to get a collective view of status and statistical information:

- show circuits displays the information about all drivers that are running on the router. This command is useful in that you do not need to know the specific driver that runs on a circuit.

- show drivers displays information about the link module type and the slots on which they reside.

- show hardware displays information about the router's hardware, such as information about the backplane, configuration file, image, memory, PROM, and slot.

■ `show protocols` displays the information about all the protocols configured on all slots of the router.

■ `show state` displays the current state information about the services on the router.

■ `show system` displays information about the router's operating system, such as memory, buffers, drivers, and configured protocols.

Most of these commands also support subcommands that detail the statistical and configuration information.

■ *monitor* displays the same type of information as the `show` command. It has the added benefit of being able to periodically refresh its display.

Usage

```
monitor <subcomand> <option>
```

Required Parameters The required parameters are the same as those defined for the `show` command.

Command	Description
`monitor ip stats`	Displays statistical information for all IP circuits configured on the router. The display periodically updates the display every 10 seconds.

■ *enable/disable* enables or disables various router services and protocols.

Usage

```
enable <subcommand> <option>
disable <subcommand> <option>
```

Required Parameters The required parameters are the same as those defined for the show command.

Command	Description
enable ip circuit e21	Enables IP on the Ethernet circuit on slot 2 port 1
disable ip circuit e21	Disables IP on the Ethernet circuit on slot 2 port 1

As an alternative to using the previous show commands, there exists another script command that allows you to access the same information via menus. The command to invoke the menu list of protocols and services is menu. Enter it at the command prompt. Key in the number of the menu item to access its submenus. These are equivalent to the options from the show command. All the information available using the show commands is available using the respective menu option.

SUMMARY

If you have been tasked, or so chose the task of, router management, it is imperative that you become intimate with the *Technician Interface* (TI). The TI can deliver the entire configuration and statistical information that can be gleaned from a router with more efficiency than from its graphical counterpart, Site Manager. Now, its efficiency is an entirely personal preference. For you, the reader might feel that the graphical representation and grouping of the router's MIB variables to of more use and therefore more efficient. While I, on the other hand, prefer to utilize the increased speed at which you can access the MIB variables to be more preferable. Not to mention that the Telnet protocol is a more streamlined communication protocol than SNMP.

The purpose of this chapter was to give you a substantial overview of what the TI is and how to use it, without going into specific detail about every command. What we discovered was that through its simple command line interface, we could view all kinds of information about specific protocols and services configured on a router. Issuing predefined and/or embedded script commands allows us to view a multitude of information. There are a variety of commands that allow us to view information concerning the operating and file system as well as the information about the installed hardware. If a problem surfaces, the router's impressive logging capability can be displayed to aid us in pinpointing the error.

Before you can use any of the commands or scripts, a connection to the router must be made. Nortel routers support two types of connections—inband and out-of-band connections. Inband connections do not rely on the underlying network for transport and they are made using the Telnet protocol. Out-of-band connections bypass the network using physical connections to the router either by a direct-attached terminal or through a modem connected to the router's console port. In either connection type, the router prohibits access to itself by a login and password. One of the important things to remember is that these two items are both case sensitive.

Each of the router's commands and scripts can be grouped into four categories—operating, file system, event log, and system administration commands. A brief look at the more prevalent ones where included in this chapter. A more detailed list can be retrieved from the Nortel web site.

SNMP
Management

As networks grow in size, an issue inevitably arises concerning the ability to manage the devices on the network. Unfortunately, this issue isn't significantly realized until a problem occurs. Now management of the network need not be constrained to preventing or recognizing errors. Network management actually encompasses several areas of concern, among which are configuration and performance management. Generally, five main areas of network management should be addressed and defined:

- *Configuration management* This area is concerned with installing, initializing, and boot loading network hardware and software. It also deals with modifying and tracking configuration parameters to these same network entities.

- *Fault location and repair management* This area deals with the tools that enable you to find faults in equipment, software, and/or provider lines with the capability to fix the said problem or report an outage to a carrier. The tools in this area have strong error and alarm characteristics.

- *Security management* The tools developed in this area are concerned with access control. The tools enable network managers to restrict or grant access to various network resources.

- *Performance management* Performance tools provide operational statistics, real-time or historical, about the network to the network manager. Some of the statistics that can be reported to the network manager might concern bandwidth utilization or the number of packets transmitted, received, or dropped at any given moment.

- *Accounting management* This area deals with the applications that enable managers to define the costs related to various network resources.

Network management's procedures, tools, and applications are a must in order to keep the network operating at its maximum efficiency. But who should define these procedures and tools? If left up to hardware and software manufacturers, we would be stuck in a mire of incompatible products. Imagine the state of the Internet if each manufacturer did not adhere to some semblance of a standard. Would there be an Internet? Fortunately, the *Internet Engineering Task Force* (IETF) recognized these needs and formed a group to handle these management issues. The group was created to develop tools, protocols, and a common database for general network management that is applicable to any TCP/IP network. As a result, the *Simple*

Network Management Protocol (SNMP) was born. Designed in the 1980s, SNMP has gained widespread acceptance.

SNMP is the most commonly used protocol for collecting management data from IP-networked devices. It consists of managers and agents defined in a client/server relationship. The manager, or client program, makes virtual connections to an agent, or a server program, which executes on a remote network device. The agent also controls a database called the *Management Information Base* (MIB). SNMP defines a standard set of statistical and control values that are incorporated in the MIB. Additionally, SNMP enables the MIB to be extended with specific values for a vendor's network devices.

Managers and agents use SNMP's simple request/response communication method to exchange status, configuration, and performance information. A management station issues queries or action requests to an agent. These queries consist of SNMP variable identifiers (called *MIB object identifiers* or *MIB variables*) along with instructions to either get the value for the identifier or set the identifier to a new value. The agent responds back to the manager station with the information requested or performs the requested value change. Agents also have the added responsibility of sending unsolicited messages to managers in the form of a *trap*. When certain network activities occur, such as network bandwidth exceeding a predefined threshold or a faulty interface, the agent would send a trap message alerting the manager.

SNMP, while not the best solution, has gained widespread popularity, which is one of its strengths. Agents can be found for all manner of network devices: routers, hubs, switches, and printers. It is also a flexible and extensible protocol. This is because SNMP agents can be extended to cover device-specific data, and because a clear mechanism exists for upgrading client programs to interface with special agent capabilities. Some of SNMP's weaknesses are its inefficiency and lack of security. It is inefficient in that it wastes bandwidth with needless information and the way its variables are identified leads to needlessly large data handles. Depending on your responsibility, the "simple" in its title is arguable. SNMP is simple to implement if you are an end user. If you are programmer, you could argue that SNMP is not simple, due to its complicated encoding rules.

Two main commercial versions of SNMP are available: SNMPv1 and SNMPv2. Actually, SNMPv2 is more appropriately termed SNMPv2c. Several version attempts have taken place within the lifetime of the protocol, each one improving the security and operational features. The first and most widely used version of the protocol is SNMPv1 and it is defined in RFC 1157. On its heels came the first version 2 flavor, SNMPv2sec. This version added strong security operations to version 1. The security model adopted was based on parties instead of communities as in version 1. SNMPv2sec had a short life and received little or no vendor support. Although short-lived, it did influence the next flavor of the SNMP versions, SNMPv2p. This version adopted the party-based security model from SNMPv2sec. It also refined some of version 1's protocol operations and added some new operations and data types of its own.

As if the updates of version 2p were not enough, SNMPv2c provided updates to the protocol operations and data types of SNMPv2p. The main difference besides the updates is that 2c reverted back to a community-based security model. SNMPv2u kept the protocol operations and data types found in version 2c but changed the security model to one based on users. This protocol also left out any scalability for large networks in the hopes of encouraging rapid deployment of simple agents. In reply to version 2u, the next version *SNMPv2** (SNMPv2star) supported the concurrent standardization of security and scalability features. It wanted to ensure that the security design adequately addressed issues of proxy, trap destinations, discovery, and remote configuration of security. All this leads to the current work regarding the management protocol, that of version 3. This version of the protocol incorporates many aspects of the other versions and is soon to be released as a *Request for Comments* (RFC) on the standards track.

In this chapter, we will discuss the architecture of SNMP and define the three main elements of the protocol: managers, agents, and the MIB. We will also discuss the operation of the protocol as it pertains to Nortel routers. Nortel routers use a SNMPv1 agent that is included in the software image on the flash memory card. This agent responds to commands and queries from SNMP managers. Site Manager is an SNMP manager that is provided by Nortel Networks.

The Architecture of SNMP

SNMP is composed of the following items:

■ *Network elements*   These are hardware devices such as routers, hubs, switches, computers, and printers that comprise the network. In short, these are the devices on the network to be managed.

■ *Agents* An agent is a software program that resides on the particular network element. The job of the agent is to collect and store pertinent information about the managed device.

■ *Managed object* Managed objects are sets of values that describe a manageable characteristic of a device, not to be confused with the actual instance of a managed object. As an example, the number of IP interfaces defined in a router is a managed object, while a specific interface is an instance of the managed object.

■ *MIB* This is the collection of all managed objects for a particular managed device. It resides in a virtual information store on a device where collections of related objects are defined in specific MIB modules.

■ *Syntax Notation* For SNMP, a syntax notation describes a MIB's managed objects. It is derived from the *Open System Interconnection 's* (OSI) *Abstract Syntax Notation One* (ASN.1) syntax language. The main purpose of a syntax notation is to provide a machine-independent format for describing objects.

■ *Structure of Management Information (SMI)* Using ASN.1, the SMI serves as the rules for defining managed objects.

■ *Manager* This issues commands and queries to a managed device. Managers are workstations or servers that run a management application. Site Manager is an example of a management application, as is HP Openview or Nortel's Optivity. The latter two are more robust in monitoring and controlling network elements.

Message Types

Managers and agents communicate by sending messages to each other. Managers send request messages to agents and agents send response messages to managers. Agent-to-agent communication is not defined in SNMP. Four types of SNMP messages are defined in the protocol and are outlined:

■ *get request* These requests exist to return values of a named object. Specific values can be returned by the get request to determine the performance and state of the device.

■ *get next request* These requests exist to return the next name (and value) of the next object supported by a network element given a valid SNMP name. Using the get next request, a network manager can determine all the names and values that an operant device supports.

This can be accomplished by starting with the first SNMP object and getting the next value with a get next and repeating until an error is encountered, indicating that no more MIB object names exist.

■ *set request*   This request sets a named object to a specific value. This provides a way of configuring and controlling network devices.

■ *trap message*   These are defined as messages that notify a network manager of a problem apart from any polling of the device. This requires each network device be configured to issue SNMP traps to one or more network management workstations (or hosts).

Each of these message types is encoded into messages referred to as *Protocol Data Units* (PDUs) that an Agent acknowledges with a get response message or trap to the manager. SNMP is an Application layer protocol that uses the *User Datagram Protocol* (UDP) for transmission. SNMP uses port 161 for all receive messages and dedicates port 162 to the processing of trap messages (see Figure 6-1).

The Management Information Base (MIB)

The MIB is a database that resides on a managed device that contains its characteristics and parameters to be managed. The standard MIB includes various objects to measure and monitor IP activity, TCP and

Figure 6-1
The SNMP message flow. The manager sends a command to the agent (1). The agent queries the managed object (2). The agent then sends the response to the manager (3). In case of an abnormal condition, the agent sends a trap or a event to the manager.

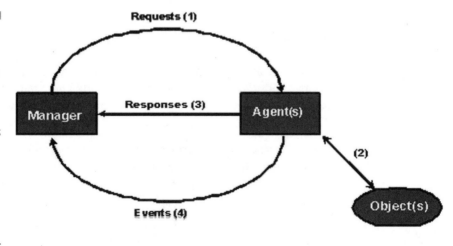

UDP activity, IP routes, TCP connections, interfaces, and general system description. It is arranged in a tree-structured fashion, starting from an unnamed root that is connected to a number of labeled nodes. These nodes are considered children of the root and form the branches of the tree. Each of these nodes in turn may have children, which are labeled. If this is the case, then the node is termed a subtree. The path from the root through a subtree to an object defines that object. This path is called the *Object Identifier* (ID), which is unique to the MIB object and is associated with an official name and a numeric value expressed in dot notation. As an example, if we wanted to access the private MIB objects for Nortel, we would follow the path to `iso.org.dod.internet.private.enterprises.wellfleet` or 1.3.6.1.4.1.18. In Chapter 7, "Nortel Networks MIB," we will discuss the Nortel MIBs in more detail.

Much of the current MIB activity occurs in the ISO branch of the MIB tree in the Internet subtree. In Figure 6-2, we see that four children are under the Internet (1) node. These nodes are administered by the *Internet*

Figure 6-2
Map of standard MIB

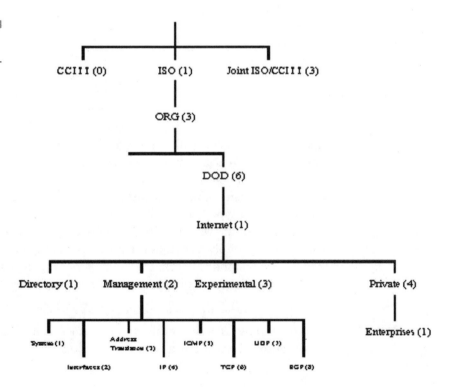

Activities Board (IAB) and are used for varying tasks. The Private (4) node has only one child, Enterprises (1), that is used by vendors for device-specific information. The IAB has delegated administration of this node to the *Internet Assigned Numbers Authority* (IANA) so vendors, like Nortel Networks, must request a node number from them in order to define new MIB objects under this subtree. The IANA is also responsible for assigning numbers to both the Experimental (3) and Management (2) nodes. The Experimental (3) node identifies objects used in Internet experiments, while the Management (2) node is used to identify objects defined in IAB-approved documents. The Directory (1) subtree is reserved for future use.

The Structure of Management Information (SMI)

The *Structure of Management Information* (SMI) defines the rules and formats for adding and/or accessing objects in the Internet MIB. Figure 6-2 shows the seven levels of the hierarchy that are common for every MIB on every device as defined by the *Internet Engineering Task Force* (IETF). As you can see, the root is not labeled and has three children that are administered by the *International Telegraph and Telephone Consultative Committee* (CCITT) and the *International Standards Organization* (ISO). The children are labeled as CCITT (0), ISO (1), and Joint ISO/CCITT (3). The ISO has allocated the ORG (3) node for use by international organizations and of the child nodes, it has given one to the Department of Defense, labeled DOD (6). The SMI is discussed in rfc1155 and from this RFC, the Internet (1) node is assumed to be allocated by the DOD.

Each node, or object, in the SMI is described by a subset of the ASN.1 language and specifies that all objects should have a name, a syntax, and an encoding. Each type of object has a name called the *object identifier*. They also have a syntax, which defines the abstract data structure or data type. The encoding simply describes the presentation of the object's instances for transmission on the network. Three categories make up the SMI data types and they are simple, application-wide, and easily constructed types:

- *Integers* These are positive and negative whole numbers including zero.
- *Octet strings* These contain unique values that are an ordered sequence of zero or more octets. If the octet string is only ASCII

characters, managers display this value as a text string. Otherwise, managers display the type as a sequence of hexadecimal values.

■ *Object IDs*   These data types can contain other SNMP object's identifiers.

Application-wide data types include the following:

■ *Network Address*   These represent an address from a particular protocol family.

■ *Counters*   These are non-negative integers that increment until they reach a maximum value at which time they reset to zero.

■ *Gauges*   These types are also non-negative integers like counters, except that they can increase and decrease and only latch at a maximum value. The length of an output packet queue is an example of a gauge data type.

■ *Time ticks*   Hundredths of a second since an event

■ *Opaque*   This data type holds values of arbitrary encoding, in other words, values that do not conform to the strict data typing used by the SMI.

■ *Integer*   This represents both positive and negative whole numbers including zero.

■ *Unsigned Integer*   This consists of members of the positive whole number set.

Simply constructed data types include the following:

■ *Discrete Objects*   These SNMP objects contain a single piece of management information. They are often denoted by a ". 0" (dot-zero) at the end of their names to be distinguished from the *Table* object type. Many SNMP objects are discrete, meaning that the name of the object is all that is needed to reference the management data. (If the . 0 is omitted, then it will be implied.) One use of discrete objects is to poll a device for summary information.

■ *Table Objects*   These SNMP objects contain multiple pieces of management data. A dot (.) extension is also appended to the end of their names. The extension is to uniquely distinguish a particular value that is being referenced. This object is special in that it enables parallel arrays of information to be supported.

Abstract Syntax Notation One (ASN.1)

ASN.1 consists of the grammatical rules that govern the definitions of protocols and programming languages. It is the OSI standard for describing data structures for representing, encoding, transmitting, and decoding data. For our purposes, ASN.1 is used to determine the precise function of any MIB value. These definitions are textual descriptions of the MIB object in a human-readable form. A network manager can determine the capabilities provided by a private MIB object by reading its definition file. ASN.1 defines an object's type, access, and description. It is a formal language with many nuances. Fortunately, SNMP only uses a simple subset of the notation rules, as described next.

Branch Object Identifiers Branch object identifiers contain no values and act as holders for other objects. These object identifiers are analogous to directories containing files on a PC, but instead of files, they contain other objects, whether they are other branch objects or objects that contain specific values. Branch objects are defined by their object ID as in the following example:

```
wfIpBase      OBJECT IDENTIFIER  : : =  { wfIpGroup  1 }
```

This example defines the directory object called *wfIpBase*. The characters in the brackets are this object's parent branch and a unique identifier for this object.

Scalar Object Definitions A scalar definition is the syntax for declaring an SNMP object. In the following example, the values are left-generic and are described in Table 6-1:

```
(objectname)    OBJECT-TYPE
      SYNTAX    (syntax)
      ACCESS    (access)
```

Table 6-1

*Scalar object
definition example*

Declaration	Description
(objectname)	This is the official name of the SNMP object. By convention, it must begin with a lowercase letter and contain a mixture of both upper and lower case.
OBJECT-TYPE	This is a required keyword and defines the type of ASN.1 declaration.
SYNTAX	A required keyword that defines the type of object
(syntax)	This is the type of the object. Some examples of predefined types are Counter, Gauge, DisplayString, and INTEGER. Each type must begin with an uppercase letter.
ACCESS	A required keyword defining the object's access
(access)	The access of the object that can be read-only, read-write, write-only, or no-access.
DESCRIPTION	This is a required keyword that describes the object defining its functions and features.
(description)	This is the text description of the object. It can be clear and concise or complex and misleading, depending on how well it was written. The description can span multiple lines as long as it is encased in double quotes.
(parent branch)	The directory in which this object resides
(oid)	This object's identifier

```
DESCRIPTION    (description)
: : =  { (parent branch)  (oid) }
```

A real example of a scalar object is shown here:

```
wfIpBaseState           OBJECT-TYPE
    SYNTAX     INTEGER {
               up (1),
               down (2),
               init (3),
               notpres (4)
                        }
    ACCESS     read-only
    STATUS     mandatory
    DESCRIPTION
        "The current state of the entire IP."
```

```
DEFVAL      { notpres }
: : =  { wfIpBase  3 }
```

You may have noticed that this example contains additional keywords. This is not to confuse you, but to point out that optional keywords can be added, depending upon the person (or vendor) that defines the SNMP agent. The previous optional keywords, such as STATUS and DEFVAL, are self-explanatory and are incorporated in Nortel MIBs.

A Note about SYNTAX The ASN.1 specification provides for certain basic types, such as Counter, Gauge, INTEGER, DisplayString, IpAddress, TimeTick, and a few others. The SYNTAX object has special conventions that enable the enumeration of the INTEGER type with specific values and that derive new types based on existing ones.

INTEGER values can be a basic integer over a range of values or, as you may note from the previous real-world example, the INTEGER syntax is enumerated with four values. Each of these values is tagged with a label providing a more descriptive name for an integer value. So, if the value in this INTEGER object is 1, then the object state is up.

Deriving new types can be accomplished by using the convention similar to the convention used for branch objects. The difference is that the OBJECT IDENTIFIER portion is left off, as in the following example:

```
NetworkAddress  : : =  IpAddress
```

What this does is create a new type called *NetworkAddress*. Whenever the MIB compiler encounters the type NetworkAddress, it will substitute the basic type *IpAddress*. This is mainly done for readability's sake as well as for programming of the ASN.1 file.

Table Types Table types are identical to branch types, except that the objects contained in the table can be considered columns rather than scalar objects. The syntax definitions can be confusing, as will be demonstrated, but understanding each facet is not necessary since they are universally implemented.

```
(tablename)         OBJECT-TYPE
    SYNTAX          SEQUENCE of (tabletype)
    ACCESS          not accessible
```

```
             DESCRIPTION      (description)
             : : = { (parent) (oid) }

     (entryname)            OBJECT-TYPE
         SYNTAX     (tabletype)
         ACCESS     not accessible
         DESCRIPTION      (description)
         : : = { (parent) (oid) }

     (tabletype)    : : =  SEQUENCE {
         (column1)          (column1type),
         (column2)          (column2type),
         (column3)          (column3type)   }
```

The following is a real-world example:

```
wfIpBaseRtEntryTable OBJECT-TYPE
        SYNTAX     SEQUENCE OF WfIpBaseRtEntry
        ACCESS     not-accessible
        STATUS     mandatory
        DESCRIPTION
               "The list of elements in IP's routing table"
        := { wfIpGroup 2 }

    wfIpBaseRtEntry OBJECT-TYPE
        SYNTAX     WfIpBaseRtEntry
        ACCESS     not-accessible
        STATUS     mandatory
        DESCRIPTION
               "A description of a route"
        INDEX    { wfIpBaseRouteDest }
        := { wfIpBaseRtEntryTable 1 }

    WfIpBaseRtEntry := SEQUENCE {
            wfIpBaseRouteDest        IpAddress,
            wfIpBaseRouteIfIndex     INTEGER,
            wfIpBaseRouteMetric1     INTEGER,
            wfIpBaseRouteMetric2     INTEGER,
            wfIpBaseRouteMetric3     INTEGER,
            wfIpBaseRouteMetric4     INTEGER,
            wfIpBaseRouteNextHop     IpAddress,
            wfIpBaseRouteType        INTEGER,
            wfIpBaseRouteProto       INTEGER,
            wfIpBaseRouteAge         INTEGER,
            wfIpBaseRouteMask        IpAddress,
            wfIpBaseRouteMetric5     INTEGER,
            wfIpBaseRouteInfo        OBJECT IDENTIFIER   }
```

As you can see, the table type can be confusing. Fortunately, due to the almost perfect universal implementation of this type, we can safely ignore its syntax in lieu of understanding a few basic rules:

- By convention, each SNMP table incorporates the Table keyword. Thus, by its very name, it is a table type object.

- A single branch object exists beneath each table with a Entry keyword. This object contains the table data.

- A series of SNMP objects exists within the Entry branch that contains simple (or complex) indexes to the table rows in dot notation.

Although I state that the table syntax is almost universal in its implementation, the previous rules need not be followed because they are not strictly codified in the SNMP standard.

SNMP Operations

SNMP works by utilizing managers and agents. Agents are software programs that reside on a managed device, report any trouble to a manager, and fill any manager's specific requests. The managers and agents send messages to each other carrying the commands and information. Since agents have full access to an object's configuration and status parameters, security is enabled so that not just any manager can request and receive this privileged information. The way security is implemented in SNMPv1 is through communities. Communities are logical groups containing the agent and one or more managers. The agent validates all requests by verifying that a manager is a member of the group or SNMP community. Locally defined on the agent, the community limits access to the object's MIB variables by granting specific access rights. Two types of access rights exist: read-only and read-write. By defining multiple communities with different rights, you can create more than one level of access for different managers.

Each message that is sent contains a community field and a data field. The community field contains the community name for the specific access right, and the data field contains the SNMP operations to perform. The agent reads the community name from the SNMP header and authorizes the request, verifying that the manager is a member of that community. Figure 6-3 shows the SNMP message format and each field is described in Table 6-2.

From the previous figure, we can understand the Version and Community fields, but a clarification is needed to describe the PDU field. As stated

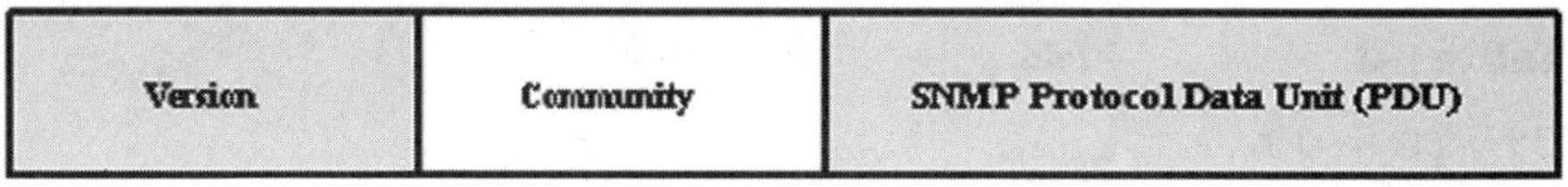

Figure 6-3
SNMpvl message
format

Version	Community	SNMP Protocol Data Unit (PDU)

Table 6-2

SNMpvl message
format fields

Field	Description
Version	The manager and agent must be configured for the same version of SNMP, SNMPv1 or SNMPv2, or messages will be discarded. Version 2 enables bulk requests.
Community	The community name used to validate the manager's request
PDU	The SNMP Protocol Data Unit. This is the GetRequest, GetNextRequest, GetResponse, or SetRequest PDU that contains the operation to be performed or the Trap PDU that contains information about an event.

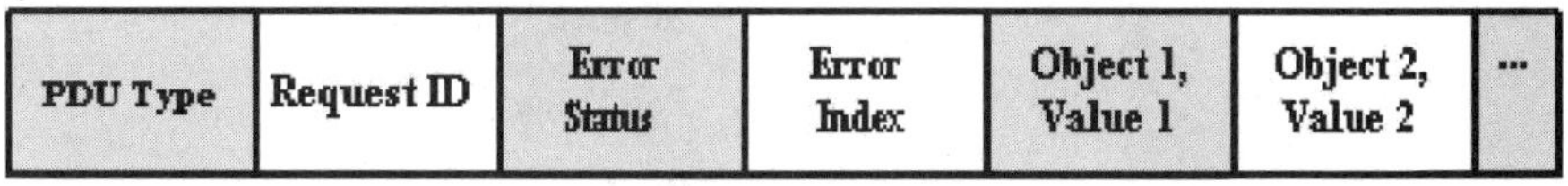

Figure 6-4
PDU format for the
SNMP request and
response data types

PDU Type	Request ID	Error Status	Error Index	Object 1, Value 1	Object 2, Value 2	...

earlier in te chapter, SNMPv1 supports five different PDU types and they are GetRequest, GetNextRequest, GetResponse, SetRequest, and Trap. The PDU field in the SNMPv1 header for the request and response data types has the message format shown in Figure 6-4 and is outlined in Table 6-3. The format of the Trap PDU is shown in Figure 6-5 and is outlined in Table 6-4.

Nortel Implementation

In this section, we'll cover how to start SNMP, how to define agent access, and how to restrict manager access.

Table 6-3

The PDU field in the SNMPv1 header

Field	Description
PDU Type	Specifies the PDU type:
Type	Description
0	GetRequest
1	GetNextRequest
2	GetResponse
3	SetRequest
Request ID	This field correlates the manager's request to the agent's response. This is an integer type.
Error Status	This is an enumerated integer type that indicates a normal or erred status:

Error	Description
0	No Error
1	Too Big
2	No Such Name
3	Bad Value
4	Read Only
5	General Error

Error Index	This identifies the entry within the variable list that caused the error.
Object/Value	The variable binding pair of a variable name and its value

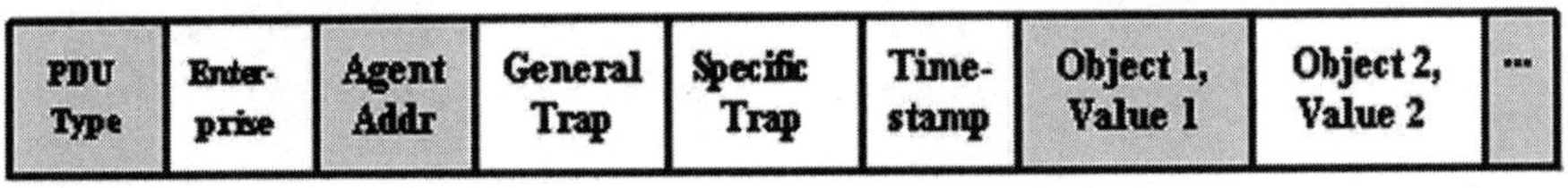

Figure 6-5
The Trap PDU message format

PDU Type	Enter-prise	Agent Addr	General Trap	Specific Trap	Time-stamp	Object 1, Value 1	Object 2, Value 2	...

Starting SNMP and Defining Agent Access   To start SNMP services on a Nortel router, IP must be configured on at least one interface. Open a local copy of the router's configuration file. From the Configuration Manager main window, go to Protocols: IP > SNMP > Global (see Figure 6-6).

Table 6-4

The Trap PDU fields

Field	Description
PDU Type	This specifies the PDU type of 4 (Trap).
Enterprise	This identifies the management enterprise under whose registration authority the trap is defined.
Agent Address	This contains the IP address of the agent.
General Trap	This specifies the event being reported.
Event	Description
0	Cold Start
1	Warm Start
2	Link Down
3	Link Up
4	Authentication Failure
5	EGP Neighbor Loss
6	Enterprise Specific
Specific Trap	This is used to identify a non-generic (enterprise-specific) event.
Timestamp	This holds the value of the sysUpTime object. It is the amount of time between (re-) the initialization and the event.
Object/Value	The variable binding pair of a variable name and its value

The SNMP Global Parameters window now opens. Click **OK** to start SNMP with the default parameters (see Figure 6-7).

Defining agent access is accomplished by creating or modifying SNMP communities. Using the same local copy of the configuration file, follow these steps:

1. Go to Protocols: IP > SNMP > Communities from the Configuration Manager main window.

   This opens the SNMP Communities List, as shown in Figure 6-8.

   BayRS™ defines "public" as the default read/write string. It is recommended that this be changed to read-only. If you are using dynamic mode, do not change this value until after you have added another read/write community string. Otherwise, you would create a

Figure 6-6
The SNMP menu
options

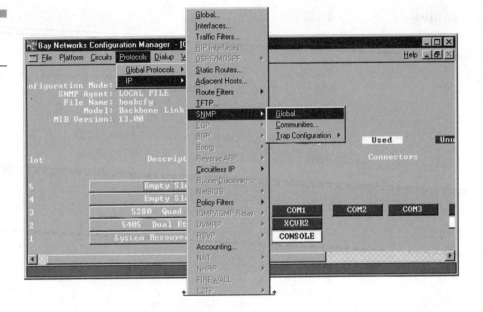

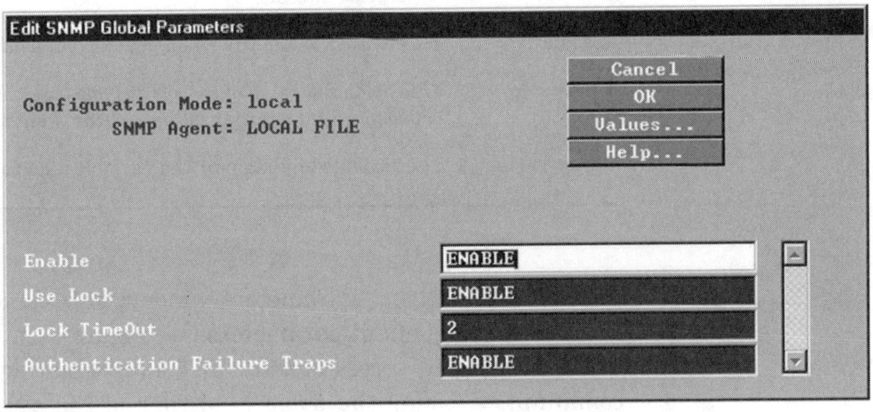

Figure 6-7
The SNMP Global
Parameters window

situation in which you would not be able to make any changes via the
Configuration Manager.

2. Add a Community string.

From Figure 6-8, click on Community, Add Community. Enter a name
in the Community Name field. It can contain no more than 63
characters and spaces can be included (see Figure 6-9).

Figure 6-8
The SNMP
Community List
window

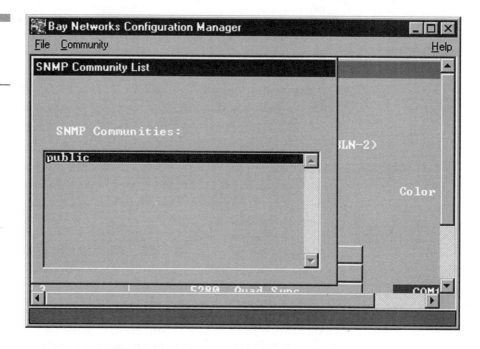

Figure 6-9
The SNMP
Community Add
window

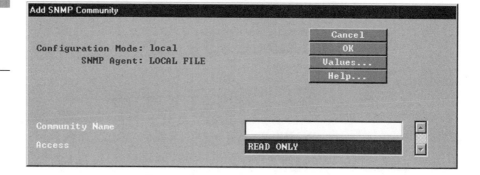

3. Define access to the new community name.

   Once you have entered the new community name, click once into the Access value field. Click **Values . . .** and select the READ/WRITE radio button. Click **OK** to add the new name with read/write access.

4. Repeat the Steps 2 and 3 for all the names you want to add with their specific access rights.

5. If you are using dynamic mode, save the configuration to file and exit Configuration Manager. You will then need to change the connection information for the router, as defined in the Site Manager connection list. Select the router in the Well-Known Connection List and click the **Connection** button. Enter the new name in the Identity (Community name) field and then click **OK** to save.

NOTE: *If you are using a management environment like Openview, you might consider defining at least two communities with read / write access. Use one specifically for the Openview management station and never change it or give it out for use by anyone. This can free you up to change the other one, which you can give to others who might need to access the router for changes. It also gives you a fail-back capability in case you forgot the change you made to the other one.*

Restricting Manager Access   Once the community names have been defined with their respective access rights, you can limit router access to specific managers. Access to the router can be defined by assigning a manager's IP address to a community string. Only the managers you define to the read/write community string will be able to make changes to the router via Site Manager. A value of 0.0.0.0 lets everyone have access in a particular community. In order to limit manager access, you must follow these steps:

1. Access the SNMP Community List.

   From the Configuration Manager main window, click Protocols: IP > SNMP > Communities (refer to Figure 6-8).

2. Access SNMP Managers List.

   Select the community string to which you want to limit access. Click Community: Managers and the SNMP Manager List opens, as shown in Figure 6-10.

3. Define a manager for this community.

   Click Manager: Add Manager from the menu bar and input the IP address of the manager in the "Add SNMP Manager" window (see Figure 6-11).

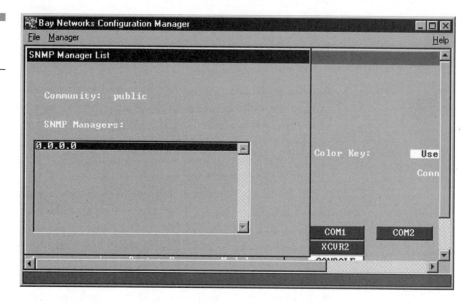

Figure 6-10
The SNMP Manager
List window

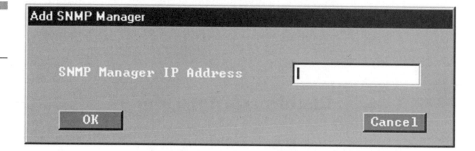

Figure 6-11
The Add SNMP
Manager window

Repeat this step for each manager IP address that you want to define for this community.

4. Click **OK** and then from the SNMP Manager List window select File: Exit.

5. Repeat Steps 1 through 4 for all manager IP addresses you want to restrict.

Security in a Nortel Networks Implementation

As you might have noted from the previous procedure, manager access is limited by only the IP address. If an intruder assumes this IP address (a security violation called *masquerading*), then he or she will have read/write access to the router. He or she will also have access if the correct community strings are known. This is why it is important to make the community strings different than the default read/write strings.

Nortel has a devised a method to stop the masquerading type of violation: the secure mode. The secure mode enables an encryption on SET requests to the MIB variables of the router. A *key* must be input when Site Manager issues its first SET request. The request is sent to the router with an encrypted value of a counter. At the router, the agent compares the encrypted value with its own value plus 1. If the counters match, the SET request is deemed authentic and the agent increments the counter by two, stores it, and then sends it back to the Site Manager application. The secure mode also prevents *message stream modification* in which an intruder reorders, delays, or replays SET requests. Enabling secure mode minimally affects router performance and has no effect on Site Manager's capability to monitor the router or perform SNMP GET requests.

Enabling Secure Mode

By default, the router is placed in *trivial* mode. Placing the router in secure or proprietary mode requires that you start a TI session. Enter the following command at a TI prompt to enable SNMP SET encryption:

```
TI prompt $ wfsnmpmode 3
```

Once in secure mode, you must set a password key to be used. Use the `wfsnmpkey` command to set the six ASCII-character password key:

```
TI prompt $ wfsnmpkey   <key_string>
```

To turn off secure mode and return to the default SNMP community security mode (trivial mode), enter the following command at the TI prompt:

```
TI prompt $ wfsnmpmode 1
```

Specific manager IP addresses must be configured for secure mode to work. It will not work for public communities and manager addresses of 0.0.0.0. It also will not prevent modification of information or disclosure security violations.

SNMP Logging

Any dynamic or remote change to a router's configuration file can be logged. The information is stored in an *audit trail log* and can be saved locally on the management PC or workstation. This SNMP audit feature only stores SET requests from Site Manager to a file of your choosing on the Site Manager workstation. To enable auditing, edit the `audit.cfg` file located in the folder to which Site Manager is installed (c:\wf default on PCs). The parameters to edit are as follows:

- *ROUTER*   The IP address of the router to log
- *AUDIT*   This turns auditing on or off
- *FILE*   The location and file name of the audit trail log file
- *EMAIL*   An Internet e-mail address (Unix workstations only)

If you want to log SET requests for more than one router, enter the previous parameters again, specifying a new router IP address. Then place the new set of parameters below the original and in the same format. It is important to note that changes made in local mode will note be logged. A couple examples of an `audit.cfg` file using single and multiple router logging are provided:

Single-Router Logging

```
ROUTER=172.16.1.200
AUDIT=ON
FILE=c:\wf\fred.adt
EMAIL=fred.jones@sdoo.com
```

Multiple-Router Logging

```
ROUTER=172.16.1.200
AUDIT=ON
```

```
FILE=c:\wf\fred.adt
EMAIL=fred.jones@sdoo.com

ROUTER=172.16.2.200
AUDIT=ON
FILE=c:\wf\daphne.adt
EMAIL=daphne.blake@sdoo.com

ROUTER=172.16.3.200
AUDIT=ON
FILE=c:\wf\velma.adt
EMAIL=velma.hinkley@sdoo.com

ROUTER=172.16.4.200
AUDIT=ON
FILE=c:\wf\shaggy.adt
EMAIL=shaggy.rogers@sdoo.com
```

The following is an example of what is entered into an audit trail file:

```
Fri Jul 07 14:21:54 2000
 142.30.51.200 wfTokenRingCct.1.1 = 3 pcuser dynamic.
Fri Jul 07 14:21:54 2000
 142.30.51.200 wfLineMappingDef.501101 =
312E312E3530313130312E35303A pcuser dynamic.
Fri Jul 07 14:21:54 2000
 142.30.51.200 wfLineMappingCct.501101 = 3 pcuser dynamic.
Fri Jul 07 14:21:54 2000
 142.30.51.200 wfTokenRingLineNumber.1.1 = 501101 pcuser dynamic.
```

SUMMARY

SNMP is the scheme by which network managers can manage their network. Using a combination of client and server programs, network devices can be remotely polled for configuration and performance information. The server program, or agent, acts on behalf of a network device by responding to requests from the client program, known as a manager. The agent retrieves the information desired by querying a local data store called the *Management Information Base* (MIB). It has the added responsibility of sending event messages (or traps) to managers when an adverse situation occurs, such as a down interface or a setting surpasses a specified threshold.

The local data store, or MIB, contains all the management variables defined for a device according to the SNMP standard. The information it contains deals with IP activity as well as information about the device's interfaces. The MIB is set up in a hierarchical tree under an unnamed root. It is from this root that the standard management variables are found. Each branch under the root forms a subtree that branches out until the standard variables are reached. These variables are called MIB objects. These objects are defined by the path through the tree. As an example, the path `iso.org.dod.internet.management.ip` or 1.3.6.1.2.4 in dot notation defines the objects that identify IP activity.

The SNMP standard also enables vendor-specific variables to be incorporated into the MIB. These objects are defined under the `iso.org.dod.internet.private.enterprises` subtree. The MIB objects specific for Nortel will be discussed in the next chapter, although we did discuss how to implement SNMP on a Nortel router in this chapter.

Defining a router for SNMP participation requires access to the router via the TI or through Site Manager. Since Nortel routers utilize SNMPv1, we had to define specific community strings in order to maintain some semblance of security. We also discussed "locking down" these communities to specific workstations or managers. This prevents a user from using any workstation to access the router even if he or she knows the proper community string.

Nortel Networks MIB

From last chapter we learned that the basic tenants of network management involved configuration, fault location and repair, security, performance, and accounting management. All of these areas being handled by a committee commissioned by the *Internet Engineering Task Force* (IETF). This committee defined the basics of what is called the *Simple Network Management Protocol* (SNMP). Through SNMP, management information can be remotely retrieved so that it can be inspected or altered. The main components of the SNMP architecture are as follows:

■ *Managers* These are software programs that reside on a management station or any workstation or PC that receives statistics and control information from an agent on a network device. A manager is considered an SNMP client.

■ *Agents* These are software programs that reside on a network device that respond to queries made by managers. Agents are also responsible for transmitting event messages in the form of a trap when an adverse condition is encountered on the network device. An agent is considered an SNMP server.

■ Management Information Base *(MIB)* This is the information storage database that also resides on a network device. It is where the agent gets the information for the queries from the managers. Agents can also set values according to a manager's request.

The communication process involved among each of the previous entities is straightforward. A manager requests a piece of information (say, a performance statistic such as the number of IP packets transmitted from an interface) from a network device. The agent running on the device receives the request and queries the local data store for the information. Once the information has been retrieved, it sends it to the awaiting manager. It is important to note that provisions exist in the protocol in case an agent is unable to retrieve the requested information. In this case, the agent would send an SNMP packet containing the error status, be it a "no such name" or a "general" error.

The local data store on a device, or MIB, contains plenty of information about the device and its management properties. According to the standard, it contains information concerning IP, TCP, and UDP activity, as well as IP routes and TCP connections. The standard also defines management variables that hold information about a device's interfaces. These management variables are called MIB objects and they are referenced by their object ID.

It may seem confusing, but an object's ID is defined by the path it took to get to it. To clarify, the object ID for the variable that holds the number of discarded datagrams due to an invalid IP address is the following:

```
iso.org.dod.internet.management.ip.ipInAddrErrors
```

or

```
1.3.6.1.2.4.5
```

As you can see, the path can be defined using labels or dot notation. It matters not which syntax is used, suffice it to say that the labels are case-sensitive. The map of the standard MIB, as shown in Chapter 6, "SNMP Management," is repeated below in Figure 7-1. It is presented here to help illustrate the previous concept.

Note how the MIB is fashioned in a hierarchical tree originating from an unnamed root. Each branch, or subtree, is part of the path that defines the MIB object. All the management information is stored under the iso.org. dod.internet.management subtree. That is, all the management variables

Figure 7-1

Map of the standard MIB

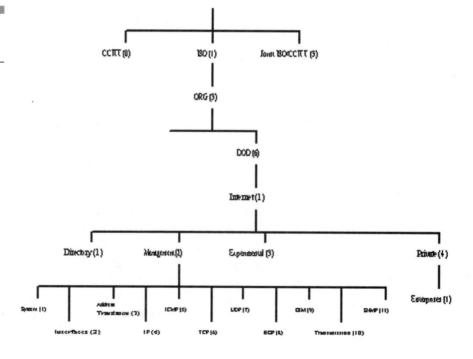

are defined in the standard MIB. The IETF committee knew that these objects would not cover all the bases so they created a branch to handle objects specific to vendors. Now, in order for a vendor to use this extension, it has to request a node number from the IETF. Once a node number is given, the vendor is free to create its own MIB objects for its specific equipment. This brings us to the topic of this chapter: the Nortel router MIB. But before we proceed, a brief note should be addressed concerning the different version of the standard MIB.

MIB-I Versus MIB-II

In the beginning, the creation of a network management solution for the Internet was to be completed in two stages. The SNMP was created and initially rolled out as a short-term solution to the management problem with the long-term solution revolving around the OSI network management framework. SNMP was a hit and because of this, portions of the Internet community were network-manageable. But, upon closer inspection, it was determined that the differences between SNMP and the OSI framework were greater than anticipated. This caused the compatibility requirement between the long-term and short-term solutions to be suspended and in so doing allowed for many needed changes of the MIB. Hence, MIB-II was born and set on to the standards track via rfc1213. Many changes or enhancements have been added to the standard MIB, which are summarized:

- Incremental additions reflect the new operational requirements.
- Improved support exists for multiprotocol entities.
- A textual cleanup has improved clarity.

A main point is to provide upward compatibility with the SMI/MIB and SNMP. The key is to keep the OBJECT IDENTIFIER the same as that in MIB-I as well as make sure that no functionality is lost due to the changes. Figure 7-1 is actually the MIB-II structure. MIB-I did not take into account the different types of transmission media; nor did it define any application-specific variables. Both of these issues are handled in MIB-II by the addition of the transmission and SNMP groups. You can read rfc1213 to learn more about the enhancements made to the standard MIB.

MIB Structure

Nortel Networks' router MIB is an extension to the standard MIB-II, as defined in rfc1213. MIB-II, as we learned earlier, is the second version of the MIB discussed in Chapter 6 and defined in rfc1156. In either MIB, the location of the vendor-specific objects is the same. The vendor-defined objects are located in the Enterprises (1) subtree under the iso.org.dod.internet.private (1.3.6.1.4) branch. Nortel Networks' MIB for version 13.x, BayRS, is defined under the Enterprises (1) subtree as wellfleet (18) and wfSwSeries7 (3). Figure 7-2 displays the MIB with the five object groups defined under wfSwSeries7: wfHardwareConfig, wfSoftwareConfig, wfSystem, wfLine, and wfApplication. These object groups contain the configuration and statistical objects that are used by the router's *Gate Access Management Entity* (GAME) operating system. They also contain the protocol image software

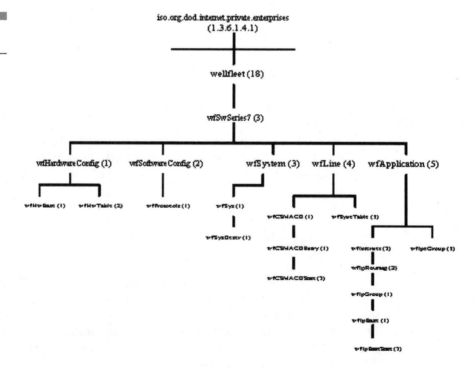

Figure 7-2
Map of Nortel MIB

Table 7-1

wfSwSeries7
Object Groups

Object Group	Description
wfHardwareConfig	This group contains objects that pertain to the router hardware configuration, such as the backplane ID and serial number.
wfSoftwareConfig	This group contains the objects that define the type of protocols and driver software that is to be loaded. The information needed to load the software is also included.
wfSystem	This group contains objects that pertain to the system software, such as the circuit name table and the system record.
wfLine	The objects in this group pertain to the functioning of the drivers that control the data link media, such as Ethernet, Token Ring, FDDI tables, line state, and line traffic.
wfApplication	This group contains the information for LANs, WANs, and bridges defined on the router to include routing tables, packet information, and protocol state information.

that governs the behavior of the router. Table 7-1 gives a brief description of the contents of these objects.

All the protocols supported by Nortel Networks routers are included in the router MIB. Reading from and writing to these MIB objects can be accomplished using Site Manager or the *Technician Interface* (TI) using the SNMP *get* and *set* commands. Also, only the GAME has read or write access to certain MIB objects. Neither Site Manager nor the TI can modify these objects. As the router boots, it is the GAME that takes the config file and creates the active MIB to dictate the router's behavior. In the next sections, we will discuss using Site Manager's Quick Get facility and the TI to access the active MIB.

Quick Get Facility

You can use the Quick Get facility to view the router's active MIB. Quick Get is accessed from the Statistics Manager under Tools, Quick Get. It includes a MIB browser that enables you to scroll through the MIB objects list and select the object that you are interested in. Only 10 MIB objects can be viewed at a single time in the output window. The Quick Get Facility window is shown in Figure 7-3.

Figure 7-3

The Site Manager
Quick Get window

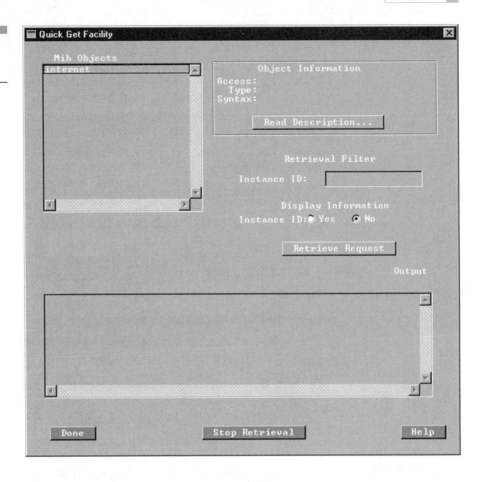

The MIB browser is located in the upper left corner of the window. Selecting a MIB object from this list will query the object's type of access, data type, and syntax. The information queried is displayed in the upper right corner of the window:

- *Access*   Read-only or read-write

- *Type*   Integer, display string, octet string, gauge, or counter

- *Syntax*   The list of values that the object can assume

Using the Quick Get facility enables you to retrieve all instances of selected MIB objects from the router. The instances display in the lower output portion of the Quick Get Facility window. The first time you start Quick

Get, the MIB browser displays the object at the top of the hierarchical tree, Internet. You must navigate through the tree to reach the Wellfleet Series-7 MIB. By clicking once on the top-level object group, Quick Get reveals the object's subordinate groups. You continue down the MIB tree until you reach the individual object you seek. Individual objects differ from object groups by their position in the MIB browser list. Object groups display flush-left within the window, while the individual objects are slightly indented. To move up the MIB tree, click once on the "back" object at the top of the MIB Object list.

Navigating the MIB with Quick Get

The following procedure will step you through viewing the MIB that shows the current state of all IP interfaces. Using this procedure will enable you to view any specific MIB you might be interested in.

1. From the Statistics Manager main window, select Tools: Quick Get.

   The Quick Get Facility window opens, as shown in Figure 7-3.

2. Navigate to the IP Interface Table (wfIpIntfCfgTable).

   In the MIB browser window, go to Internet: private > enterprises > wellfleet > wfSwSeries7. This will bring you to the Wellfleet Series 7 software MIB, as previously discussed, and as shown in Figure 7-4.

   The MIB objects that deal with protocol applications are located in the wfApplication group. Go to wfApplication: wfInternet > wfIpRouting > wfIpGroup. Then click once to access the individual objects under wfIpIntfCfgTable (see Figure 7-5).

NOTE: *You must scroll down to view the Interface Table MIB group.*

3. Select the objects that you want to display.

   To view the state of all IP interfaces, select wfIpIntfCfgState and wfIpIntfCfgAddr. Selecting each one will query the object for its access,

Figure 7-4
The BayRS software
MIB object,
wfSwSeries7

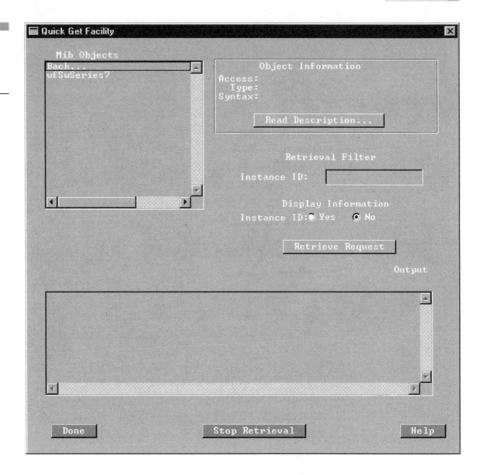

data type, and syntax. To read a description of the MIB object, click on
Read Description. To deselect an object, click on the object again to
remove the highlight. Click on Retrieve Request to display the
information in the Output box.

4. View instance IDs and filtering.

Above the **Retrieve Request** button are the Display Information
options. Selecting "Yes" enables the display of the object's instance IDs
along with the value of any selected MIB object. The "No" option turns
off the instance ID display.

To filter the view for specific instances, type the filter string in the
Retrieval Filter text box. For example, to view only the addresses that

Figure 7-5
The MIB walk to
wfIpIntfCfgTable

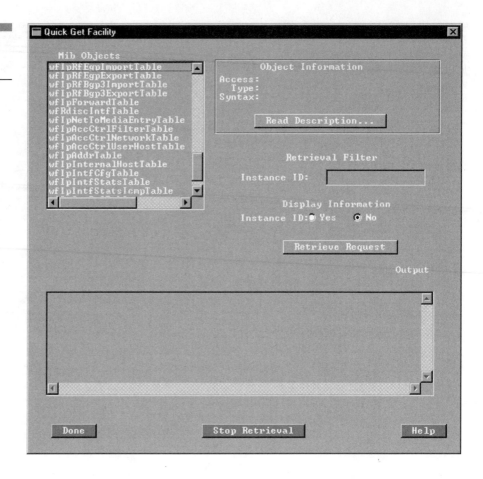

start with 192.168, type 192.168 in the Retrieval Filter text box. Clicking Retrieve Request with the objects selected will display only the object instances that pass the filter.

5. Exit the Quick Get facility by clicking Done.

Using the TI

Viewing the Nortel MIB can be accomplished by using Site Manager and the Quick Get facility (as mentioned previously) or by using the TI. Viewing the MIB requires the *list* and *get* commands. The list command enables you to list all or specific MIB objects and once an object of interest is found, list can be used to view the number of instances the object contains. The get command then can be used to view the attribute or attributes of the object instances. Accessing the MIB objects from the TI is different from using the Quick Get facility. Besides the obvious lack of a graphical interface, the MIB objects are not divided into their five parent object groups. All subordinate MIB objects are listed in ascending alphabetical order. By typing "list," all the objects scroll up your terminal screen. Fortunately, you can use the "*" wildcard to narrow down the amount of objects that scroll past. For example, to view all MIB objects that contain SNMP, you could type list wfS* or list wfSNMP*. The result would be a listing of all the MIBs that begin with S and SNMP, respectively. Note that the prefix "wf" is standard for all Nortel enterprise-specific objects.

Navigating the MIB with the TI

The following steps outline how the TI can be used to view the current state information of all IP interfaces:

1. Locate the MIB object that contains the IP interface table.

   Typing `list wfIp*` will list all the MIB objects that begin with wfIp. In the Quick Get example, we clicked down the MIB tree to reach the wfIpIntfCfgTable. Once we clicked into this group, we accessed the wfIpIntfCfgEntry object to retrieve the IP interface address and state information. That is the same object that we need to access from the TI in order to view the same information.

2. Verify that the object contains the attributes for which we are interested.

   The syntax for viewing an object's attributes is

   ```
   [2:1]$ list <object>      in our case, object is wfIpIntfCfgEntry
   ```

   This command displays all of the object's attributes, as does selecting wfIpIntfCfgTable in the Quick Get facility.

3. View the object's instances.

   Type the following command to list all of the object's instances:

   ```
   [2:1]$ list -i wfIpIntfCfgEntry
   ```

The i is short for instances. Retrieving the instance IDs in this manner will help if you want to view the attributes for a specific instance.

4. View the State information for all IP Interfaces.

Unfortunately, using the TI only allows the retrieval of either one attribute for all instances or all attributes for one instance, unlike the Quick Get facility, which enables you to retrieve up to 10 attributes for all instances. The State information for all instances is located in the wfIpIntfCfgState object under wfIpIntfCfgEntry. Using the list command again with the wfIpIntfCfgEntry as the object, you will find that the state information is the fourth object in this group. You could type out the whole text structure of the objects to retrieve the information

```
[2:1]$ get wfIpIntfCfgEntry.wfIpIntfCfgState.*
```

or you can use a combination of text and numbers:

```
[2:1]$ get wfIpIntfCfgEntry.4.*
```

Both methods will display the list of instances with their state values. Notice how the * wildcard is used to indicate all instances. To view all attributes in this object for a specific instance, you would replace the 4 with an * and you would place an instance ID at the end. Here's an example:

```
[2:1]$ get wfIpIntfCfgEntry.*.instance_id
```

get and set Commands

Now for some brief words on the get and set commands. As we learned in Chapter 6, the get and set commands were defined in the SNMP management model. Their use is simple and straightforward. The get command retrieves the values in a MIB object, while set places values in a MIB object.

The syntax for the get command is

```
get <object>.<attribute>.<instance identifier>
```

and the syntax for the set command is

```
set <object>.<attribute>.<instance identifier> [value]
```

In each command, the arguments are the same are defined:

- `<object>` The MIB branch object name. Under this name is a collection of related objects.
- `<attribute>` A specific object under the above branch object
- `<instance identifier>` An identifier that uniquely identifies a single instance of an attribute. An example would be an IP address.

For the set command, once a value has been changed, it must committed to memory in order for it to take effect. The set and commit commands can be entered on the same line as long as a semicolon follows the set, as shown:

```
set <object>.<attribute>.<instance identifier> [value]; commit
```

The semicolon is the separator between commands.

Aliases

As you can see, using the TI can become quite tedious when long commands need to be entered. Fortunately, we can use a shortcut, called an *alias*, in lieu of typing long or multiple commands. An alias enables you to define a simple word that will invoke the long or multiple command(s). The syntax for defining an alias is

```
alias [ <name> [ ["] <alias_value> ["] ] ]
```

`<name>` is the word that will be used to invoke the TI command defined as `<alias_value>`. If `<name>` already exists, typing `alias <name>` will display any command associated with `<name>`.

`<alias_value>` must be a legal TI command. It can be multiple commands separated by a space and a semicolon. If the command contains spaces, double quotes (" ") must be used around the `<alias_value>`.

To create an alias for checking the current state of all IP interfaces, you would type the following at the command prompt:

```
[2:1]$ alias ipstate "get wfIpIntfCfgEntry.4. *"
```

Aliases can be saved to flash and loaded later for future use. Typing the following command at the command prompt saves the alias to flash:

```
[2:1]$ save alias 1:alias.al
```

Loading an alias into memory from flash can be done with the following command:

```
[2:1]$ source aliases 1:alias.al
```

To remove the alias from memory, type the following at the command prompt:

```
[2:1]$ unalias ipstate
```

Typing alias by itself at the command will display a list of defined aliases.

debug.al

Nortel Networks provides a file that contains predefined aliases that you can use to assist you with debugging common network problems. Loading the file into the router memory is accomplished with the source command:

```
[2:1]$ source aliases 1:debug.al
```

This loads all the aliases defined in that file. Over 30 aliases are defined. A complete list of aliases can be seen by typing the file to view its contents (type `debug.al`) or by entering the alias command by itself after you load the values into memory. Once your troubleshooting has been completed, you can remove the aliases by typing `unalias *` at the command prompt.

Screen Builder Facility

When troubleshooting a network problem or just occasionally viewing the current state of all IP interfaces, perusing the MIB tree can become tedious. You have to continually click down the MIB tree to find the objects you are interested in and retrieve their values. To alleviate the tedium and make accessing the router's MIB objects easier, Site Manager comes with a tool that enables you to save a statistical window for future or continual viewing, Screen Builder. Screen Builder is started from within Statistics Manager and can be used to create custom statistic screens. It contains a MIB browser for perusing the MIB objects and querying each selected object for its access, data type, and syntax. The MIB browser also allows up to nine objects to be included in a window. As with the Quick Get facility, the MIB browser is located on the left with the object information located in the upper right of the facility window. The main difference is the Column Information and Setup frame located at the bottom right (see Figure 7-6).

It is in this frame where the customizing of the headings and formats takes place. You can set the following parameters:

- Column Heading
- Column Width
- Radix (display format)

Once a screen has been built, you can save it to your local management station for viewing. Screen Builder also lets you edit previously created screens. The following procedure takes you through creating a custom screen.

Building a Customized Screen

As in our previous examples in this chapter, we are concerned with the current state of all our router's IP interfaces. The following steps show how to

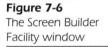

Figure 7-6
The Screen Builder
Facility window

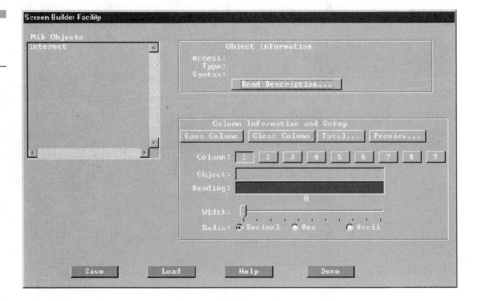

create a customized screen that will enable us to view the IP Interface table more easily. Screen Builder is started by selecting Tools, Screen Builder from the Statistics Manager main window.

1. Navigate the MIB tree to find the IP Interface Table object.

   Using the MIB browser, click on Internet: Private > Enterprises > Wellfleet > wfSwSeries7. This brings you to Wellfleet's Series 7 software MIB object groups. Select wfApplication > wfInternet > wfIpRouting > wfIpGroup > wfIpIntfCfgTable.

2. Select the interface object's address attribute.

   The address is located in the wfIpIntfCfgAddr object. Clicking on this individual object will place it in the object field of column 1 (see Figure 7-7).

3. Define the column.

   Enter a column heading that is representative of the MIB object. In the previous example, you can use the MIB object name as a default or you can input a name like IP State. You will also want to set the column width, which must be at least as wide as the column heading. The previous width was set to 9 to accommodate the heading, even though

Figure 7-7
The Screen Builder window with the wfIpIntfCfgState MIB object selected for column 1

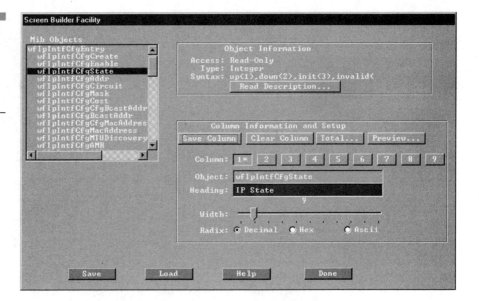

the state is no more than four characters. For IP addresses, you can use a value of 18 for the column width, 15 for the address plus three spaces. Select the appropriate Radix radio button to specify the display format.

4. Save the column changes.

   Once the desired column settings have been made, click **Save Column** to save these values for column 1. An asterisk appears next to the column number.

5. Repeat the previous steps to add more columns to the statistics window.

   Always click on the column number before selecting the individual MIB object. An example of another MIB object to add would be the IP address. If we leave the screen with just the state object defined, when the screen is viewed, there will be no way of correlating the state with an address, although the Launch facility does add the Circuit Index. Figure 7-8 is a completed screen definition for viewing IP state information. If you make any mistakes, you can use the Clear Column button to remove any column parameters for a particular column.

Figure 7-8

The completed screen definition for viewing IP state information

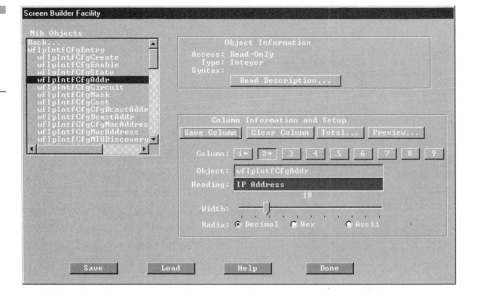

Figure 7-9
The Preview window

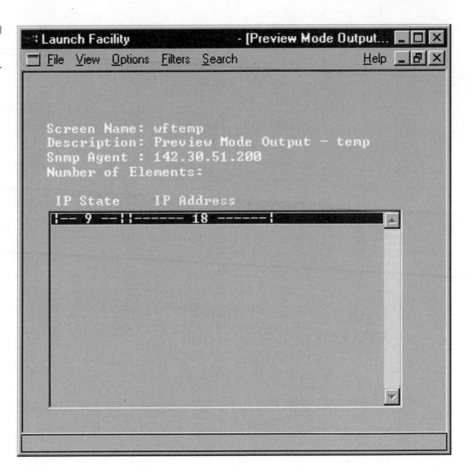

Once the settings have been made, you can preview the screen by clicking the **Preview** button. Figure 7-9 shows the preview screen for the previous screen definition.

To define a column to hold totals, it is required that you select the columns that you want totaled and then click **Totals**. When the Column Totals window pops up, select the column number that will hold the totals. Click **Save** to return back to the Screen Builder main window. In our example, no columns can be totaled, but to give you a clearer picture of this feature, Figure 7-10 shows the Column Total window.

Figure 7-10
The Column Total
window

NOTE: *You must first choose an empty column from the Screen Builder facility to get the total value. In Figure 7-10, I have selected column 3 to sum columns 1 and 2, as described in the equation above the Save button.*

6. Save the new screen.

Once you have saved all the columns for each MIB object, click **Save** to save the screen for viewing. The Statistics Save/Load Screen opens, prompting you for the Screen Name, as in Figure 7-11.

If you are saving this file on a PC, you must follow standard DOS file-naming conventions. You can also enter a description that contains no more than 40 characters. In the previous figure, I used "Displays IP Address and State" as a means for describing what this screen will display. If you want the Statistic Manager to continually poll the values in the window, select Circuit for the screen's orientation. Otherwise, Statistics Manager will gather all the information and display it once. It is important that statistics determine the state or gather traffic information be saved as a Circuit so that the objects can be constantly updated. Finally, the Directory field displays all the screens that have been previous created and saved.

7. Move the new screen into the current screen list for viewing.

You can add screens to the "Current Screen List" by using Screen Manager, which is accessed from the Statistics Manager main window and displays all predefined screens and any user-defined custom screens, as discussed in Chapter 2, "Configure Nortel Networks

Figure 7-11
The Save window for
the Screen Builder
facility

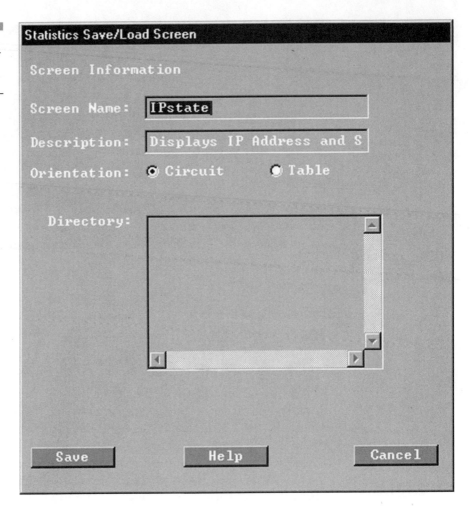

Routers." As a refresher, Figure 7-12 shows the Screen Manager main window.

No statistics screens are available when you first start Statistics Manager. Select a screen from either the Default Screens or User Screens window and then click **Add >>**. Only move the most frequently used screens to the Current Screen List to more efficiently manage the window database.

8. Launch the Statistic view.

Figure 7-12
The Screen Manager main window

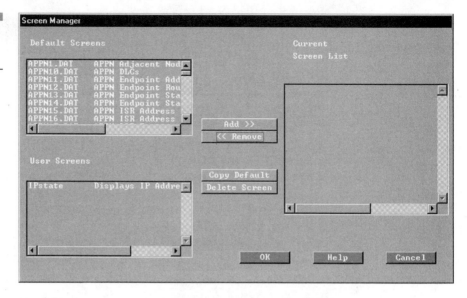

The "Launch" facility enables you to view the current screen list. Selecting a statistic screen from this list will retrieve and display statistics from the router. Figure 7-13 shows the screen list with the IPState screen added.

For more information on the Launch facility, refer to Chapter 2.

SUMMARY

In this chapter, we extended the standard MIB from Chapter 6 by adding the MIB objects proprietary to Nortel equipment. We found that for Nortel routers five object groups contain all the statistical and configuration objects used by the router *Gateway Access Management Entity* (GAME). The groups are wfHardwareConfig, wfSoftwareConfig, wfSystem, wfLine, wfApplication, each of which contain objects specific to their definition. All the IP statistics, addressing, and routes are found under the wfApplication group. It was in this group that we focused most of our attention.

We used a variety of Statistic Manager tools to use the MIB to poll IP state information. Custom screens were defined to assist with the repetitive

Figure 7-13
The current screen list
window

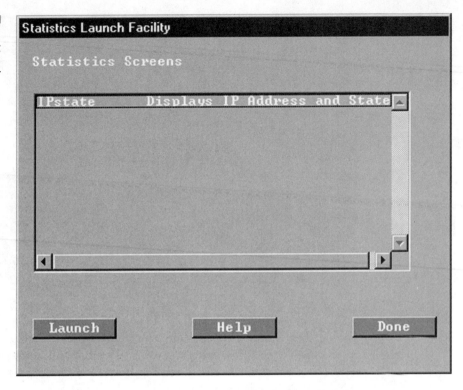

Figure 7-13
The current screen list
window

task of finding the MIB objects that we needed to poll. The Quick Get facility allowed us to use the MIB to examine specific objects and retrieve their values. With Screen Builder, we created a screen that could be saved and launched to perform the work for us. The custom screen we created was added to the Current Screen List using Screen Manager and was launched with the Launch facility that we had previously discussed in Chapter 2.

In addition to using the Statistics Manager tools, we learned how to use the command-line interface or *Technician Interface* (TI). The TI enabled us to use the list, get, and set commands to retrieve information from the MIB objects. It was discovered that typing a get or set command could become quite lengthy due to the involved object labels. Creating aliases allowed us to write a lengthy command to a short name. This made troubleshooting or monitoring easier. Also, aliases can be saved and retrieved for later use.

Internetwork Packet Exchange (IPX) Network Configuration

In the previous chapters, we concentrated on configuring Nortel routers using the TCP/IP protocol suite. Let's take a break and segue briefly to discuss another network layer protocol, the *Internetwork Packet Exchange* (IPX). It was for the most part the flagship protocol for Novell's Netware *Network Operating System* (NOS). It hasn't been until recently, and more specifically on release 5.x, that Novell began to support native IP and all the other open Internet standards that provided LDAP, HTTP, XML, Java, and so on. So why are we going to discuss IPX? Because a substantial installation base of older Netware uses IPX as its chief network protocol.

IPX is a connectionless datagram delivery protocol modeled after the *Xerox Network System* (XNS) protocol by Novell. It is connectionless because it does not establish a connection between communicating nodes. It is also unreliable and therefore does not guarantee packet delivery, leaving the responsibility for reliable delivery to upper layer protocols like *Sequenced Packet Exchange* (SPX) or *Network Control Protocol* (NCP). Like IP, IPX is a Network layer protocol that is responsible for addressing, routing, and switching information packets from one location to another. As the upper layer protocols pass their data units to the network layer, IPX encapsulates the packet for transport across the physical media. The receiving station strips off the encapsulation and passes the data unit up to the awaiting upper layer protocol. For each IPX packet that is transmitted, an IPX acknowledgement packet is sent back. This creates a "back and forth" communication process that may not hinder local traffic too much, but it can cause serious degradation to *wide area network* (WAN) performance. In order to alleviate this problem, a Packet Burst protocol was developed by Novell. Burst mode enables multiple packet fragments, no larger than 64 KB, to be sent without waiting for a reply. Once the last fragment has been received, a single acknowledgment is transmitted showing a list of packets not received. All the sending station has to do is resend the missing packet fragments.

IPX Addressing

The IPX header contains the addressing needed to get the packet to the destination node and socket. Communication on an IPX network relies on a 12-byte, 24-digit hexadecimal number that identifies the network segment, node address, and socket address. Each of these items is discussed in the following section.

Network Address

The network address is a four-byte, eight-digit hexadecimal number that uniquely defines a network segment. This network address (or external network number) is assigned to each network interface and is used by IPX and routers to identify source and destination LANs for each packet of data. This number is arbitrary with valid values ranging from 0x00000001 to 0xFFFFFFFD (hex). It is assigned when the IPX protocol is bound to a network interface card in a server. Now IPX can be bound to a server's network interface using multiple frame types, such as Ethernet 802.2 and/or Ethernet 802.3. Each frame type is considered a logical IPX network and each must have a unique network address associated with it. What this means is that network devices cabled to a network segment that share a common frame type must also use the same network number.

Reserved Network Numbers   Three networks are reserved and cannot be used to identify a specific network. These networks have the following meanings:

- *0x0*   This number represents the local network segment. A router assumes a packet's source and destination nodes are on the same network when it receives a destination network number of 0.
- *0xFFFFFFFF*   This is considered an *all routes request*. A router transmits all the routes it knows to the requesting router when it receives a destination network of all Fs.
- *0xFFFFFFFE*   This represents a *default route*.

Another network address defined for older versions of Netware is the internal network number. This number identifies an individual Netware server defining a logical network that ranges in value from 1 to FFFFFFFE (hex). The internal IPX number must be unique on each server and different from the previous external network number. In version 3 and 4 of Netware, this number is used to advertise services and route packets to the physical networks attached to the server. Its main purpose is to overcome some routing and connectivity limitations that were inherent in version 2.

Node Address

The node address is the hardware address of the network interface card that connects a network device to the network. Commonly referred to as the MAC address, it can be universally or locally administered. The node address is a six-byte, 12-digit hexadecimal number that uniquely identifies an end node, be it a server, workstation, printer, or router. Nortel automatically assigns a unique node value when an IPX interface is created.

Socket Address

The last part of an IPX address is the socket address. It is a two-byte, four-digit hexadecimal number used to represent IPX processes in the destination node. The socket address enables the process to distinguish itself within an IPX network, as do port numbers in an IP network. It is the final destination for a packet. When a node receives a packet, it reads the socket address and passes the message up the protocol stack to the corresponding process. Each socket address is registered and reserved through Novell. Some of the key socket addresses are listed:

- NCP uses socket 0451h
- SAP uses socket 0452h
- RIP uses socket 0453h.
- NetBIOS uses socket 0455h.

A process can use a well-known socket address or one can be assigned dynamically. Dynamic socket addresses range between 0x4000 and 0x7FFF and are used by workstations to communicate with file servers and other devices. Socket addresses are internal to each node, so each node can have its own list of socket addresses independent of other nodes. Figure 8-1 shows an

Figure 8-1
An IPX internetwork
address

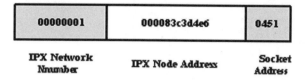

00000001	000083c3d4e6	0451
IPX Network Nnumber	IPX Node Address	Socket Address

example of an IPX Internet address. This address is typically written as 00000001:000083c3d4e6;0451 where the leading zeros can be omitted.

IPX Packet Structure

Novell modeled the IPX packet after the XNS packet, so their structures are identical. The packetheader is 30 bytes long with some of its fields being byte-order sensitive. Also, frame type differences can be seen in the placement of the IPX header. The frame type is the packet data format for a specific media. Some media support multiple formats, such as Ethernet 802.2, Ethernet 802.3, Ethernet II, Ethernet SNAP, Token Ring, and Token Ring SNAP. For each frame type, the IPX header appears in different positions. For Ethernet, the IPX appears for each frame type:

- *Ethernet 802.2* The IPX header follows immediately after the length field.

- *Ethernet 802.3* The IPX header follows immediately after the IEEE 802.2 header (DSAP, SSAP, and Control).

- *Ethernet II* The Type field has a value of 8137 and the IPX header follows immediately after.

- *Ethernet SNAP* The IPX header follows immediately after the five-byte protocol identifier field.

The data portion of an IPX frame is the *Maximum Transmission Unit* (MTU) minus 30 bytes. The MTU is different for each underlying MAC layer protocol. Ethernet supports 1500-byte packets, where 30 bytes is the IPX header and 1470 is the actual data. The content and structure of the data is entirely the responsibility of the application using IPX and can take

Figure 8-2
IPX header format

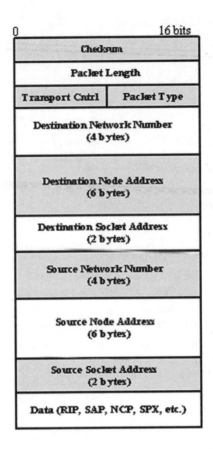

any format. The IPX header is shown in Figure 8-2. Table 8-1 describes each of the 10 fields that are present in the IPX header.

Sequenced Packet Exchange (SPX)

IPX is considered unreliable in delivering a packet from its source to its destination. To bolster the reliability of the IPX, we must look to protocols that exist in the Transport layer. For IPX, that would be SPX. SPX makes sure that IPX packets are received without error and in the proper order. SPX does this is by sequencing, or numbering, the IPX packets. Proper order and transmission verification is maintained by using *sequence* (SYN) and *acknowledge* (ACK) numbers. As two nodes begin to communicate, the SYN

Table 8-1

The IPX header
fields

Field	Description
Checksum	This is an optional field to check the validity of the IPX header. It is normally set to 0xFFFF to signify that no checksum is performed.
Packet Length	This field identifies the length of the IPX datagram in octets (header plus data).
Transport Control	This field keeps track of the number of routers a packet traverses. IPX sets this value to 0 and each router increments it by 1. A value of 16 indicates an undeliverable packet.
Packet Type	This field specifies the packet information or type of service offered or required. Here are some examples:

Type	Definition
0	Hello or SAP
1	*Routing Information Protocol* (RIP)
2	Echo Packet
3	Error Packet
5	SPX/SPXII

Destination and Source Address Fields

Field	Description
Network Node	A network number that uniquely defines a cable segment, as defined above
Number Address	The address that uniquely identifies the network device. This is also referred to as the MAC address.
Socket Address	The location within a node where packets are finally delivered. Sockets define a node process.

and ACK numbers are set to 0 and each device increments the corresponding SPX numbers for each packet. Utilized in this way, SPX mimics TCP by synchronizing the communication between the two nodes.

The communication between the two nodes continues with each transmission of a sequence number being verified by an acknowledge number. The destination node replies to the source node with an acknowledge number that is the next number in the packet sequence and hence "requests" the data packet with the corresponding number.

SPX calls are incorporated in an IPX packet header along with a checksum. SPX checks the packet for errors and reports back to the sending station whether it received the contents successfully. If the checksum fails, a negative acknowledgment is returned and the IPX packet is resent. Lost packets can be detected as follows:

- If the source node sends an SPX data packet and no ACK is received, the packet is retransmitted.

- If the destination node sends an ACK and the subsequent data packet has an unexpected sequence number, the ACK is retransmitted.

SPX Packet Structure

An SPX packet consists of a 42-byte SPX header. SPX works directly with IPX, which manages the forwarding of packets in the network. Since it works with IPX, the 42-byte header is actually comprised of the 30-byte IPX header plus 12 bytes for sequencing, flow control, connection, and acknowledgement information. Figure 8-3 is a representation of an SPX header followed by the description of the fields in Table 8-2.

In 1991, Novell commissioned an SPX development group to improve upon the SPX protocol. Thus, SPX II was born. It provided for larger packet sizes and implemented a windowing protocol. The SPX II header is the same as the SPX described earlier with the following additions:

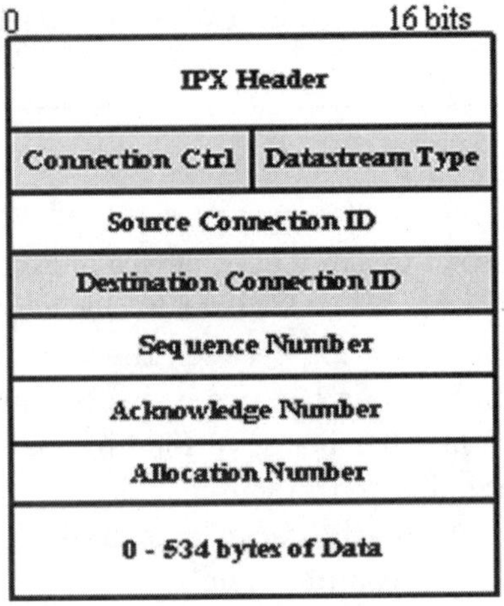

Figure 8-3
The SPX header format

Field	Description
Table 8-2	
The SPX header fields	

Field	Description
Connection Control	This field is comprised of bit-level flags that control the bidirection flow of data across an SPX connection.

Bit	Description
4	EOM: End of Message
6	ACK: Acknowledgement Required
7	SYS: Transport Control

Field	Description
Datastream Type	The field is used to signify an end-of-connection (0xFE) or an end-of-connection acknowledgement (0xFF). All other values are ignored.
Source Connection ID*	This is a 16-bit number generated during the initial connection to identify the source end point.
Destination Connection ID*	This is a 16-bit number generated during the initial connection to identify the destination end point.
Sequence Number	The value in this field represents the number of packets transmitted. This field is managed by SPX and once the value reaches 0xFFFF, it is wrapped to zero.
Acknowledge Number**	The field is used by SPX to represent the sequence number of the next packet expected.
Allocation Number	This field is used by SPX as a means to implement flow control between communicating applications. The receiving node maintains this number.

*SPX uses the source and destination connection ID to demultiplex packets from multiple connections that arrive on the same socket.

**This field is incremented by the receiver to signify that the data was received. If a packet with a sequence number less than the specified acknowledge number is received, SPX drops the packet.

■ *A Connection Control Flag* Two bits are added as stated:

Bit	Description
2	Size negotiation
3	SPX II type

■ *Datastream Type*   An orderly release request (0xFC) and an orderly release acknowledge (0xFD) are added.

■ *An Acknowledgement field*   A two-byte extended field is added.

IPX Routing and Service Advertising

In Chapter 3, "Basic IP Routing," we discussed the purpose of routing in a TCP/IP environment. It is the same for routing in an IPX environment. The capability of workstations and routers to determine the best path from one network to another is of utmost importance in minimizing any network delay. Like IP routers, IPX routers are charged with maintaining the state of each of their connected interfaces by the means of a routing table. Each router must also include a mechanism in which their state information can be transmitted to other routers. IPX routers incorporate two types of routing protocols for propagating and maintaining routing information. The two routing protocols used by IPX servers and routers are as follows:

■ *Routing Information Protocol (RIP)*   RIP is a distance vector protocol used by routers and servers to exchange routing information.

■ *Novell's Link Services Protocol (NLSP)*   NLSP, as its name implies, is a link state routing protocol used by routers to maintain the state of the network. An additional feature of an IPX network is the capability of servers as well as routers to advertise various services that each device may provide. Servers and routers broadcast their services via SAP. SAP is described in more detail later in this section, but a brief description can be found here.

■ *Service Advertisement Protocol (SAP)*   SAP is a distance vector protocol that is used to advertise services, such as file and print services.

Routing Information Protocol (RIP)

IPX RIP works similarly to IP RIP. It enables workstations and routers to exchange route information so that decisions can be made regarding the best path to use to reach a destination. This route information is stored in a table in each router and contains the following information about the IPX network topology:

- The network address
- The number of ticks to a network. A *tick* is a unit of time delay to a network. It is equal to $1/18$ of a second.
- The number of hops to a network. This signifies the number of intermediate routers that must be crossed to reach the destination.
- The address of the next-hop node that will forward the packet to the network

IPX devices participate in maintaining the information in this table by exchanging RIP request and response packets. Two types of RIP requests exist: general and specific. Each type specifies the destination network and is described here:

- *General requests*   These requests are transmitted by routers to discover the fastest route to all networks in an IPX internetwork. A 0xFFFFFFFF in the Network Address field identifies these requests.
- *Specific requests*   These requests are made by routers and workstations in order to determine the fastest route to a specific network. One or more network addresses (except all Fs) can be found in the Network Address field.

Responses to RIP requests are made by routers only and contain network-specific information like the network number as well as the number of ticks and hops to get to the network. RIP response packets can be one of the following types:

- A response to a request
- An informational broadcast that is transmitted periodically (the default is every 60 seconds)
- An informational broadcast that is transmitted when a change occurs. These are sent when parameters like the number of ticks or hops changes or when a route times out.
- An informational broadcast is transmitted when a router's interface is initialized or shutdown.

Each RIP packet contains a maximum of 50 updates and is confined to the router's immediate segments. Routers that share the same immediate LAN segments do not forward RIP packets.

RIP Packet Structure

The RIP packet structure is shown in Figure 8-4. The RIP packet, as with many of the higher layer Novell protocols, is encapsulated within the data portion of the IPX packet. RIP packets are defined in the IPX header as *packet type* 1 and *socket number* 0x453. Table 8-3 describes each field in the RIP packet.

Bringing all this together, each router broadcasts periodic route updates out each of its configured interfaces every 60 seconds. With these updates

Figure 8-4
RIP packet structure

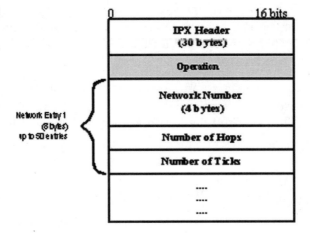

Field	Description
Operation	This field specifies the packet operation. If it contains a value of 1, then it is considered a RIP request. RIP responses place a 2 in this field.
Network Entry	**This section contains the subject of the RIP request of the response.**
Network Number	The IPX network number
Number of Hops	The number of routers that must be traversed to reach the network
Number of Ticks	The time delay associated with the network number. A tick is approximately $1/18$ of a second.
. . . Next Entry	

Table 8-3

RIP packet fields

Table 8-4

IPX Routing Table

Destination Net	Next Hop Network	Next Hop Host	Ticks	Hops	Age
00000001	000000001	0000a20c1d2e	1	0	0
00000002	000000002	0000a20c1d2e	2	0	0
00000003	000000002	0000a20c1d2f	2	1	20

that each router receives, it builds the routing table. This table contains information about all the network segments on an IPX Internet. Table 8-4 shows an example of an IPX routing table.

Table 8-5 describes the fields in the routing table.

The previous example only focuses on the main fields present in the routing table. There may be more or fewer fields, depending upon the router. Nortel routers incorporate additional information, such as the Circuit Index and Method fields. The Circuit Index field is assigned by the router and is used as a reference throughout the router. The Method field indicates whether the route is defined on the router (local) or learned through RIP.

Table 8-5

Routing table fields

Field	Description
Destination Network	The Destination Network address is the hexadecimal address of the destination network.
Next Hop Network	This field represents the network that a packet must traverse to reach the destination network.
Next Hop Host	This field indicates the address of the adjacent router that will pass the packet to the destination network.
Ticks	The time delay to reach the destination network. This value is $\frac{1}{18}$ of a second.
Hops	The number of adjacent hosts that must be traversed to reach the destination network.
Age	This is the time limit for the route. Typically, it is three times the RIP update interval (180 seconds). Every time a router receives information about this route it resets this timer to zero.

NOTE: *When two routes point to the same destination, one route is considered preferred if its tick count is lower than the other. If both tick counts are equal, the preferred route is determined by the fewest hops. Again, if the hop count is equal, the router will send the traffic via the route that it learned first.*

Netware Link Services Protocol (NLSP)

NLSP is based upon the *International Standards Organization's* (ISO) *Intermediate System-to-Intermediate System* (IS-IS) protocol and provides link state routing on IPX networks. Routers configured for NLSP exchange routing information, such as connectivity states, path costs, external network numbers, MTU sizes, throughput, and media types. It is important to note that NLSP is a router-to-router protocol and that the workstation to router information exchange is still performed using IPX RIP. Unlike RIP, NLSP only transmits route information when a change has occurred (or once every two hours, whichever comes first).

As you may recall, a link state protocol is a routing algorithm that routers use to build and maintain a logical map of the entire network. A link state router builds this logical map through a process called *flooding*. Each router transmits a packet that contains all of its link information to other link state routers. The routers use this information to build the network map. When each router has the same view (map) of the network, the network is said to have converged. A NLSP packet is encapsulated within the data portion of an IPX packet and it is defined with a *packet type* of 0x01 and a *socket address* of 0x9001.

How IPX Routing Works

Consider a Netware workstation trying to communicate with a Netware server. If both the workstation and the server share the same IPX network, the workstation sends packets directly to the server hardware address. Each device shares the same IPX network when their external network numbers are identical. If the server's network address is not the same as the workstation's network address, then a router (or routers) must be present to forward the packets along to the correct destination. The workstation must first find the router on its own segment that can forward the packets to the segment on which the server resides.

In order for a workstation to discover a router on its network segment, it must broadcast a RIP packet requesting the fastest route to the destination network. The router with the fastest route to the destination network responds back to the workstation. The router includes its network and node address in the IPX header of the response packet it sends to the workstation.

Now, armed with the router information, the workstation addresses and sends the packets to the destination server as follows:

1. *The workstation inserts the destination server's information into the IPX header* The workstation places the server's network number, node address, and socket numbers into the destination fields in the IPX header.

2. *The workstation inserts its own information into the IPX header* The workstation places its network number, node address, and socket numbers into the source fields of the IPX headers.

3. The router's hardware address is placed into the Destination Address field in the MAC header of outgoing packets.

4. The workstation places its own hardware address into the source field in the MAC header of outgoing packets.

5. The packet is then sent.

Upon receiving a packet, a router will do several things. First, it will check the Transport Control field to determine if it will either forward or drop the packet. RIP routers will drop a packet if the Transport Control field value is greater than 16. Routers running NLSP will discard packets when the value of the Hop Count Limit parameter is exceeded. The router also performs the following checks:

- *Packet Type check* If the router determines that the packet contains NetBIOS information, it must also recheck the Transport Control field value. If this value is 8 or greater, then the router will discard the packet. NetBIOS packets are limited to eight networks.

- *Destination Address check* The router checks the destination network and node addresses as well as the socket numbers to determine the proper way to route the packet. If the packet is addressed to the router, then the router will forward the packet internally to the process defined by the socket number.

NOTE: *The only packets that the router handles internally are those addressed directly to the router and those broadcast to any network segment to which the router is directly connected. The broadcast address for IPX is 0xFFFFFFFF.*

If the router determines that a packet is not destined for one of its internal processes, the router must determine how to forward it. The router can take two options when forwarding a packet:

- If the router is directly connected to the destination network, then
  - The router places the destination node address retrieved from the IPX header into the destination field of the MAC header.
  - The router's interface address is then placed into the source field of the MAC header.
  - The router then increments the Transport Control field value by 1 and forwards the packet onto the physical media.
- If the router is not directly connected to the destination network, then
  - The router places the node address of the next-hop router into the Destination Address field of the MAC header. This information comes from the router's routing information table.
  - The router's own node address is placed in the Source Address field of the MAC header.
  - The router then increments the Transport Control field value by 1 and forwards the packet onto the physical media.

Service Advertising Protocol (SAP)

In an IPX network, a client can be either a workstation or a router. Either one can be assured that its packets will make it to its destination via routes established by the IPX routing protocol, RIP. But a client needs to also know why he is sending something to a destination. It needs to know which service a server provides in order to establish proper communication. In Netware environments, each server that offers a service advertises these services via SAP. These service providers broadcast a SAP packet that contains information identifying the service type and the service location. Routers keep track of these advertisements and make sure other routers are also kept aware. As a router becomes aware of a change in the Internet server layout, it broadcasts this information immediately to all its neighbors. Workstations, on the other hand, use SAP to discover available services and at which IPX address they reside.

Various types of services exist, such as database, communication, and external routers services, with the file and print services being the most common. These services are identified on a server with a socket number, which is then mapped to an IPX address. Each SAP packet can contain as many as seven server names with routing information. A SAP is broadcasted periodically, every 60 seconds, from a server. IPX SAP also utilizes *split horizon* and *triggered updates* in the event of topology changes or failed hardware.

SAP Packet Structure

A SAP packet, like RIP, is encapsulated inside the IPX header. It is used by Netware network services to inform both routers and workstations of their existence. Workstations also use SAP to request network services. They send "nearest-service" queries that request the closet service of a specific type. Figure 8-5 shows the structure of a SAP packet. Table 8-6 describes each field in the SAP packet structure.

Figure 8-5
SAP packet structure

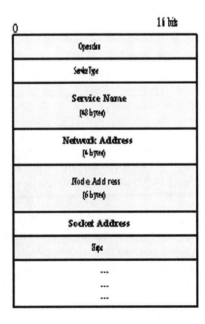

Table 8-6

SAP header fields

Field	Description
Operation	This field specifies the operation the packet will perform. If can be one of the following values:

Value	Description
1	General Service Request
2	General Service Response
3	Nearest Service Request
4	Nearest Service Response

For both SAP requests, the Service Type field follows only. For requests only, the size of a SAP packet is 34 bytes (the IPX header plus the operation and service type fields).

Field	Description
Service Type	This field specifies the type of service performed. Novell servers are assigned unique service type values. A file server advertises itself with a service type of 0x0004. See Table 8-7 for a listing of well-known service types.
Server Name	This field contains the server's name and can be no greater than 48 bytes. Although a SAP packet always allows for the full 48-byte name space, server names seldom utilize its full extent.
Network Address	The four-byte network address of the server
Node Address	The six-byte MAC address of the server where the node resides
Socket Address	The socket number where the server receives service requests
Hops	The number of routers that the packet must pass through to reach its destination. If this value is 16, then the service is not available.

The structure of a SAP request packet includes only the Operation and Service Type fields. Table 8-7 lists some of the well-known service type values.

As a final note, in NetWare 4.x and greater, the use of SAP is considerably reduced. Since the bindery has been replaced with a distributed directory database (NDS), nodes need to only use SAP as a means of locating the nearest NDS server at start time. NDS propagates its service information via direct unicast-based protocols and not by broadcast-based SAP.

Service Type	Description
Table 8-7	**Service Type**	**Description**

Service Type	Description
0x0000	Unknown
0x0003	Print Queue
0x0004	File Server
0x0005	Job Server
0x0007	Print Server
0x0009	Archive Server
0x0021	NAS SNA Gateway
0x0027	TCP/IP Gateway
0x0047	Advertising Print Server
0x8000	Reserved up to

Table 8-7

Well-known service types

Nortel IPX Support

Nortel routers support the following IPX services:

- The dynamic routing of IPX packets
- Multiple interfaces per circuit
- IPX over WAN media
- IPXWAN and IPXCP
- RIP and SAP
- Static and default routes
- Adjacent host and dial-on-demand support

Nortel routers also provide LAN circuit, WAN circuit, and frame format support, as shown in Tables 8-8 and 8-9.

Note that the synchronous circuits support V.35, RS-232/422, X.21, and T1/FT1.

A Nortel router running IPX can be configured four different ways:

- *Multiple-host router configuration*   In this configuration, unique IPX and network addresses are defined for each IPX interface. This is the

Table 8-8

LAN circuits and
frame formats

Circuit Type	Novell Frame Type	Nortel Frame Type
Ethernet	Ethernet_II	Ethernet
	Ethernet_802.2	LSAP
	Ethernet_802.3	Novell
	Ethernet_SNAP	SNAP
Token Ring	Token Ring	LSAP
	Token Ring_SNAP	SNAP
FDDI	N/A	LSAP
		SNAP

Table 8-9

WAN circuits and
frame formats

Circuit Type	Novell Frame Type	Nortel Frame Type
Synchronous	ATM	SNAP
	Frame Relay	SNAP
	PPP	PPP
	SMDS	SNAP
	X.25 Point-to-Point	Ethernet
	X.25 PDN	Rfc 1356
	Nortel Point-to-Point	Ethernet
HSSI	ATM	SNAP
	Frame Relay	SNAP
	PPP	PPP
	SMDS	SNAP
	Nortel Point-to-Point	Ethernet
ISDN	PPP	PPP

Figure 8-6
Multiple-host router
configuration

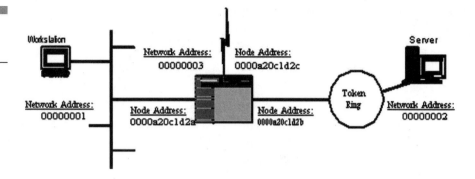

Figure 8-7
Single-host router
configuration

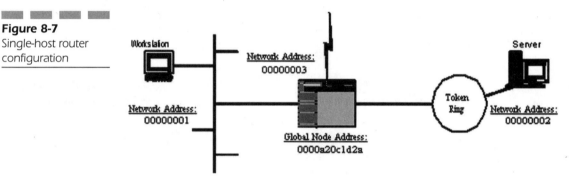

most common configuration for a router. Figure 8-6 is an example of a
network configuration with a multiple-host router.

■ *Single-host router configuration* As with the multiple-host router
configuration, a unique network address is configured according to the
interface. The difference is that each interface shares a global IPX node
address. Figure 8-7 is an example of a network configuration with a
single-host router.

■ *Multiple IPX interfaces per circuit* Nortel routers support as many
IPX interfaces per circuit as there are frame types for each given Data
Link protocol. For an Ethernet circuit, the router would support four
IPX interfaces (refer to Table 8-1). This configuration is used when
migrating from one encapsulation method to another. Figure 8-8
depicts a router with multiple IPX interfaces. Note that the Token Ring

Figure 8-8
Multiple IPX interfaces
on an Ethernet circuit

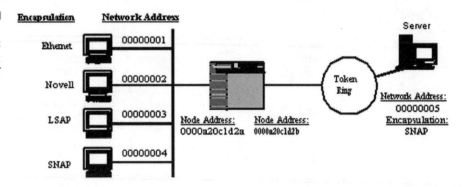

Figure 8-9
Network diagram
with Netware server
running IPX

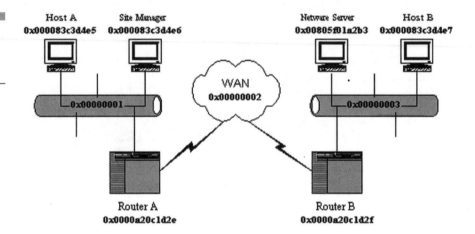

interface on the router need only to support one type of encapsulation method.

■ *Multiple circuits per segment*   These support both concurrent bridging and IPX routing or IPX multilines.

Adding IPX to an Interface

In order to take advantage of Nortel's IPX services, IPX must be added to an interface. The interface can already be configured with another protocol or IPX can reside alone. Figure 8-9 is a modified diagram of our earlier IP-only network. Let's assume that a Novell 3.2 server has been added into our enterprise from a corporate acquisition and it uses IPX for its communication. We need to add IPX to both Router A and Router B so that the clients on both networks will be able to connect to the server.

NOTE: *For the sake of simplicity, the IP information has not been included in Figure 8-9, even though IP is still configured on the routers and workstations as before. The Netware server is only running the IPX protocol at this time.*

Before making any configuration changes on a router, be sure to backup the current configuration so that in case of an error you can recover with a reboot (refer to Chapter 2, "Configure Nortel Networks Routers"):

1. From Configuration Manager, open the backup copy of Router A's configuration file in local mode.

   Start Site Manager and select the address for Router 1 in the Well-known Connection list. Select Tools: Configuration Manager > Local File (F3) and select the backup copy of the config file and click **Save**. If you followed the recommendation from Chapter 2, you named the backup configuration file either config.new or left it as startup.cfg. The Configuration Manager main window opens.

2. Add IPX to the Ethernet interface.

   From the Configuration Manager main window, select the Ethernet interface that we configured for IP in Chapter 2 (XCVR1), as shown in Figure 8-10.

   Once the "Edit Connector" window opens, click Edit Circuit. Figure 8-11 shows the Edit Connector window.

   Adding IPX to this circuit is accomplished by selecting Protocols: Add/Delete and scrolling through the list of available protocols to find the IPX checkbox, as shown in Figure 8-12. Select both the IPX and RIP/SAP checkboxes, and then click **OK**.

3. Input the IPX configuration information.

   The IPX Configuration window prompts you for the configured network number, whether you want to enable RIP/SAP, and the encapsulation method (see Figure 8-13).

   The circuit index is automatically assigned and identifies this circuit within this instance of IPX. The IPX network number can be found

Figure 8-10
The Configuration
Manager main
window

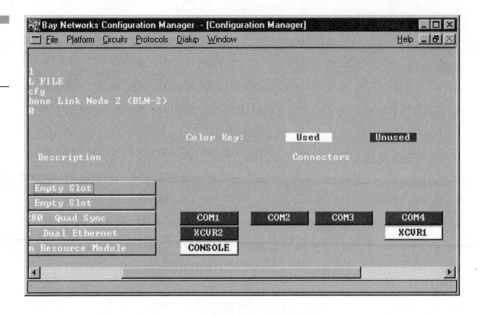

Figure 8-11
The Edit connector
window

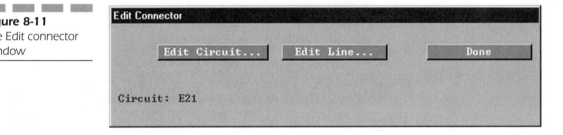

from Figure 8-9 and the encapsulation method we are using is
Ethernet_802.3, which Nortel relates as Novell (802.3). The parameters
are repeated in the following text:

IPX Network Number: 0x00000001 (hex)

Encapsulation Method: Ethernet_802.3

Click **OK** to return to the "Circuit Definition" window. Notice that the
IPX protocol with RIP/SAP is now included in the Protocols list
window, as shown in Figure 8-14. Press F10 to go back to the
Configuration Manager main window.

4. Add IPX to the synchronous interface.

Figure 8-12
The Select Protocols
window

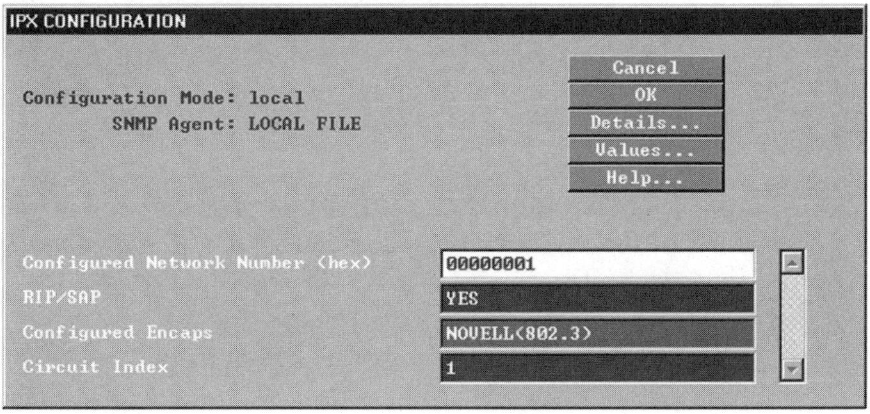

Figure 8-13
The IPX
Configuration
window

Repeat Steps 2 and 3 with the exception of selecting the COM connector that was configured in Chapter 2 (COM1) and use the following IPX information:

IPX Network Number: 0x00000002 (hex)

Encapsulation: PPP

Since the synchronous interface was previously configured as a PPP circuit, only one encapsulation method is available, PPP. Notice also that an additional option is available to us in the IPX Configuration

Figure 8-14
Circuit Definition
window

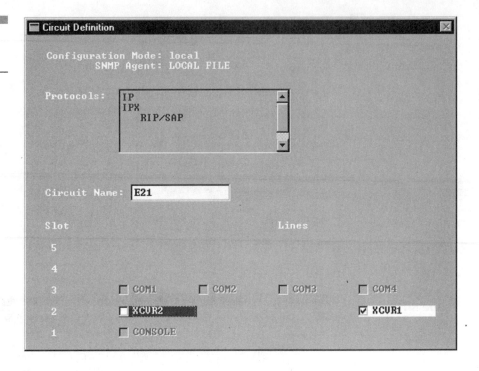

window, IPXWAN. IPXWAN is used when you want the routers to negotiate communication options over WAN media. Leave this value as Disable and click **OK**. Press F10 to exit back to the Configuration Manager main window.

5. Save the configuration and restart the router.

Saving the configuration saves the changes to the backup file.

6. Repeat Steps 1 through 5 for Router B using the IPX information from Figure 8-9.

This IPX network need not have the same encapsulation method as that of Router A, but it is best to be consistent and select Ethernet_802.3 as the encapsulation method.

Once you configure the basic IPX information, the circuits are operational, using default values for their parameters. If you are satisfied with the circuit's operation, you can accept the default values. However, you can customize the IPX configuration with Site Manager. IPX global and interface parameters will be described in the following sections.

Adding an Additional IPX Interface

As mentioned previously, multiple IPX interfaces on a circuit are used when a client needs to communicate with different logical LANs that coexist on the same physical LAN segment. This is usually done when migrating a server from one encapsulation method to another. The following method is for instructional purposes only; an additional IPX interface on the Ethernet circuit in our network is not needed.

NOTE: *Additional IPX interfaces can be added as long as encapsulation types are available. For Ethernet circuits, Nortel routers support four types of encapsulation methods. Therefore, only four IPX circuits can be added to a single Ethernet interface.*

1. Add an additional IPX interface to the Ethernet circuit.

   From the Configuration Manager main window, select the Ethernet connector that already has an IPX interface configured (XCVR1). Click Edit Circuit to open the Circuit Definition window. Select Protocols: Edit IPX > Interfaces from the menu bar to open the IPX Interfaces window (see Figure 8-15).

   Click **Add** to add the information for the second IPX interface on this circuit. The IPX Configuration window opens, as in Figure 8-13. The distinction made between each IPX circuit is via the Circuit Index parameter. This value is incremented with each IPX circuit added to a single interface.

2. Apply the changes and then exit.

   Click **Done** then press F10 to exit back to the Configuration Manager main window.

Multiple-Host and Single-Host Routers   Configuring the router to have a unique IPX node address for each interface is assumed by default. Changing the configuration to a shared, or single-host, address is accomplished through the IPX global parameters. Table 8-10 details the IPX global parameters with specific attention to the multiple and single-host values. From the Configuration Manager main window, select Protocols, IPX, Global.

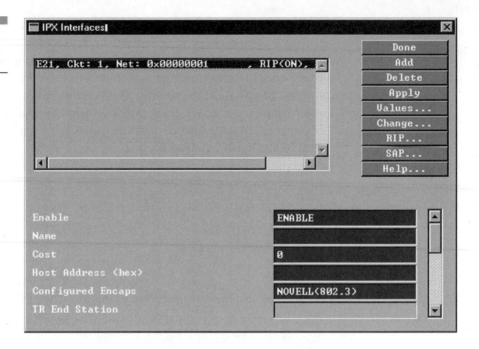

As you can see from Table 8-10, to configure the router as a multiple-host router, you need only leave the IPX parameters at their default values. A multiple-host router has an IPX interface for each circuit and each interface has a unique IPX host address. The router determines the IPX host address by the MAC address in the PROM on the circuit associated with an interface. In order to enable the configuration to share an IPX host address or be configured as a single-host router, you must disable the Multiple Host Address Enable parameter. If you choose to configure the router to share an IPX host address, then you have two options for how the router will select the IPX host address:

- With the Multiple host Address Enable parameter disabled and a blank entry in the Router Host Address field, the host address is based on the serial number of the router backplane.

- With the Multiple Host Address Enable parameter disabled, the host address will be defined by what is entered in the Router Host Address field.

Table 8-10

IPX Global
Parameters

Parameter	Description
Enable	Enables or disables IPX routing on all interfaces depending upon their respective Enable parameters. The default is Enable.
Multiple Host Address Enable	This parameter determines whether the router will assign a unique IPX address to each interface or assign one IPX address for the entire router. Setting this parameter to Disable invokes the single-host mode and the router either uses the IPX address defined in the Router Host Address field or assigns one based on its backplane serial number. The default is Enable.
Router Host Address (hex)	This parameter becomes available when the Multiple Host Address Enable parameter is set to Disable. Enter a valid IPX address or leave it blank to have an address automatically assigned based on the router's backplane serial number. Note that the Token Ring MAC address must agree with this global address when multiple-host addressing is disabled. See the information after this table.
Router Name	This is a symbolic name that must be unique throughout the IPX Internet. IPXWAN uses this value to identify itself to the IPX router at the opposite end of the WAN data link.
Primary Net Number (hex)	A unique IPX number that IPXWAN uses in its link negotiations. This value determines whether the local or remote interfaces become the link master. The highest primary net number determines the link master.

For Token Ring circuits, the host numbers IPX uses are configured independently from the MAC addresses. However, in order for IPX to send and receive data, these addresses must be identical. Keep the following in mind if you choose not to use the default Token Ring and IPX settings. The different ways a router can generate a Token Ring MAC address are discussed in this section. These values can be changed from the Edit Token Ring Line Parameters window, shown in Figure 8-16.

■ *PROM*   This is the default value. This tells the router to use the MAC address defined in the programmable read-only memory on the Token Ring link module.

■ *BOXWIDE*   This parameter instructs the router to generate the MAC address based on the serial number of its backplane.

■ *CNFG*   This enables the user to input a MAC address. A valid 48-bit MAC address must be entered in the MAC Address Override field.

Figure 8-16
Token Ring Line
Parameters window

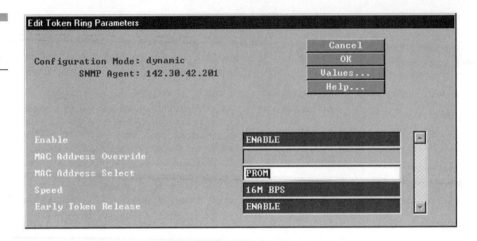

Accessing the Token Ring Line parameters is accomplished from the Configuration Manager main window. Select the Token Ring connector and then click Edit Line.

IPX Traffic Filters

Taking what we learned in Chapter 4, "IP Services," about traffic filters, we can enhance our understanding by expanding our knowledge of the router-filtering capabilities in the IPX protocol. IPX filters bare a purposeful resemblance to the IP filters. Each has a criterion, action, and range that define what is to be accepted, dropped, or logged. The difference being that all IPX filters are based on the reference IPX_Base, which is the start of the IPX header. Inputting an offset and length from the reference point defines the criteria for a filter. Fortunately, most of the criteria for filtering are pre-defined. Table 8-11 is a list of the predefined filter criteria for IPX filters. Each criterion is defined with their respective offset from the reference point IPX_Base and the length (in bits) of the criteria field.

In addition to the previously predefined criteria, you can define your own specific filter using a user-defined criteria filter. All user-defined filters are based on the same reference as earlier, IPX_Base. Both offset and length must be included in all user-defined criteria filters.

Table 8-11

Predefined IPX
filter criteria

Criteria Name	Offset	Length
Destination Network	48	32
Destination Address	80	48
Destination Socket	128	16
Source Network	144	32
Source Address	176	48
Source Socket	224	16

Defining an IPX Filter

IPX filter is defined in much the same way as an IP filter:

1. Select the connector.
2. Access the Protocol menu.
3. Open Traffic Filters window.
4. Define the filter template.
5. Apply the filter.

The subtle difference is the lack of options for defining the IPX filter template. Accessing the IPX template window is accomplished using the following steps:

1. Select the Ethernet connector (from the previous configuration steps) from the main Configuration Manager window shown in Figure 8-5.
2. Select Edit Circuit from the Edit Connector window shown in Figure 8-6.
3. Follow the menu path Protocols: Edit IPX > Traffic Filters. This opens the "IPX Filters" window, shown in Figure 8-17.
4. Click on the Template button to create an IPX filter template.

   This procedure is very much like that pertaining to IP filters. In order to create a filter, you must first create a filter template. It is from this

Figure 8-17
The IPX Traffic Filters window

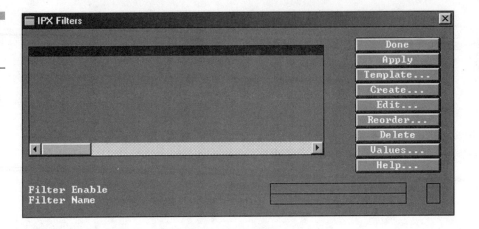

Figure 8-18

IPX Filter Template Management window

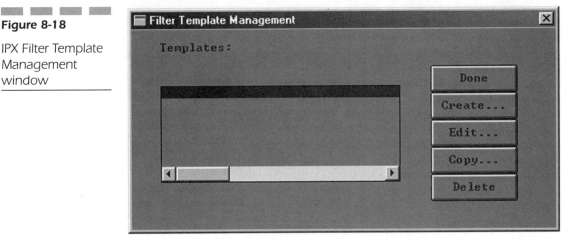

template the actual filter will be created and applied. Figure 8-18 shows the "Filter Template Management" window.

5. Click **Create ...** to open the "Create Template" window, as shown in Figure 8-19.

6. Define the filter template.

   Select the criteria, range, and action that will define your IPX filter template.

7. Apply the filter.

Figure 8-19
The IPX Template
Definition window

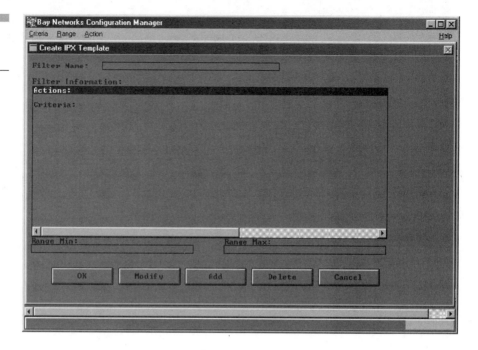

SUMMARY

Our digression from the world of IP into IPX is not entirely complete, yet we did cover enough information to be able to understand how IPX works and how to implement it on a Nortel router. A lot more can be said about the IPX protocol, but should it be? As the world migrates its legacy systems to IP (even Novell offers it as its default protocol with Netware), should we concern ourselves with a more detailed study of IPX? I'll leave that up to you to decide. In this chapter, we began our discussion with a comparison of IPX and IP. In that, we determined that IPX, like IP, is a network layer protocol that provides a connectionless, unreliable delivery service. It is connectionless because it does not establish connections with its counterpart in a destination device's protocol stack. It is also unreliable because it leaves error detection and correction, as well as the sequencing of packets, to upper layer protocols. The upper layer protocol that IPX uses to monitor communication is SPX.

We also discussed the three components that make up the IPX address: the external network address, the node address, and the socket address. The external network address (or network address) defines the network segment where a node resides. The node address is the hardware address of the network device's interface card. This address is defined during manufacturing or it can be manually changed. The socket address defines the end process for a packet, be it a NCP, SAP, or RIP process.

The discussion of IPX ended with a demonstration of how to implement the protocol on a Nortel router. Nortel routers enable IPX to be implemented in several ways, such as multiple-host, single-host, and multiple interfaces per circuit. A multiple-host router is defined by having a unique IPX address for each of its interfaces. Contrarily, a single-host router is defined by a single IPX address. In order to facilitate server migration and upgrades, Nortel routers enable you to define multiple IPX interfaces per circuit, that is, provided each interface has a unique frame type. Four supported frame types are available for Ethernet and two can be used for Token Ring.

Transparent Bridging and the Spanning Tree Algorithm

In this chapter, we are going to digress from our discussion of the routing features of Nortel routers and concentrate on their bridging features. The reason for this digression is to accommodate those legacy systems that use protocols that cannot be routed. IBM's *System Network Architecture* (SNA) and *Network Basic Input/Output System* (NetBIOS) are examples of protocols that do not provide Network layer information. That is, these protocols operate on the first two layers of the OSI Reference Model, the Physical and Data Link layers. It is in the Data Link layer that addressing is done and only by using the hardware or *Media Access Control* (MAC) addresses of each station. As you may recall, all networking boils down to transmitting frames according to the source and destination MAC addresses on a single segment. Thus, an intermediary device is needed to forward these frames onto other segments. That is what a bridge does. Operating at the Data Link layer, a bridge acts as a relay device connecting multiple networks independent of upper layer protocols. Before we proceed, I feel a need to more accurately depict the concept of a *local area network* (LAN).

Believe it or not, what constitutes a LAN is not well defined. There is a consensus, however, that states a LAN has the following qualities:

- It allows for multiple devices to connect to a shared or switched medium.
- It provides high total bandwidth that is shared by all connected devices.
- It exhibits low delays.
- It exhibits a low error rate.
- It has the capability to have a single message reach multiple recipients. This is also called a broadcast or multicast capability.
- It is limited in geography and the number of devices that can be attached.
- It fosters peer relationships among connected devices. All devices are considered equal.

These qualities are in contrast to those that constitute *wide area* (WAN) or *metropolitan area networks* (MAN), yet confusion exists. This can be attributed to the fact that as technologies are discovered, the line that divides LANs and WANs are becoming less and less clear. So, for our sake, let us define a LAN as an entity that devices are attached to and from this attachment, each device can send packets to, and receive packets from, any device that is also attached. But, in all things, control must be maintained. It would not work if all devices decided to talk at the same time. No communication would take place, just a bunch of chatter. Thus, in order to ensure effective communication, only one device is allowed to transmit onto a shared medium at a time (forgoing any conversation involving switched media for a later date). It is also important that each device gets a fair share of the medium's bandwidth with a reasonable access time to the medium.

Fortunately, control can be maintained through several methods. The two most popular are the token-passing and contention schemes. Token-passing schemes come in two flavors: Ring and Bus. Token Ring caught on more so than Token Bus. In either case, a packet, called a *token*, is passed from station to station. Only when the station is in control of the token can it actually communicate on the LAN. The Ring or Bus is just the physical aspect of the token-passing scheme. Token Ring physically connects stations in a ring. Contention schemes enable devices to transmit at will. If two devices transmit at the same time, then their packets will collide. This collision effectively cancels each device's packet and they must try again. Contention schemes are designed so that these collisions do not disrupt communication completely.

IEEE Standards

Many standards define LAN protocols and some of the most relevant fall under the *Institute for Electrical and Electronic Engineers* (IEEE) 802 committee. It is from this committee that what we know as Ethernet and Token Ring have been ratified as standards. One of the things that the 802 committee has done is subdivide the Data Link layer into two sublayers: the MAC and *Logical Link Control* (LLC) sublayer with each sublayer taking on the responsibilities defined for the Data Link layer. Each sublayer is described as follows:

- *MAC sublayer*   This layer is responsible for managing protocol access to the physical medium. It handles addressing as well as issues specific to a particular type of LAN. Some of the issues include channel management algorithms, such as token passing (802.4 and 802.5), binary backoff after collision (802.3), priorities (802.4 and 802.5), error detection, and framing.

■ *LLC sublayer* This layer is responsible for managing the communication between devices over a single link on a network. It supports both connectionless and connection-oriented services to the higher-layer protocols.

In addition to the layer-2 subdivision, the IEEE 802 committee created the following standards:

■ *802.1* This standard covers issues for all 802 LANs such as addressing, management, and bridges.

■ *802.2* This standard defines the LLC.

■ *802.3* The *Carrier Sense Multiple Access with Collision Detection* (CSMA/CD) protocol is defined in this standard. It was derived from the Ethernet LAN protocol invented by Xerox.

■ *802.4* This defines Token Bus.

■ *802.5* This standard defines the Token Ring LAN protocol.

MAC Addressing

In order for a network device to transmit packets to another network device, it must be aware of a recipient's address. Since all devices receive all packets on a shared network, it is imperative that the addresses be unique. This needs to be true not only due to contention (two or more devices vying for the same address), but to also limit software interrupts with every packet. The *Network Interface Card* (NIC) is programmed to drop all packets that it is not destined for; therefore, no needless packets are sent to the *Central Processing Unit* (CPU) for processing. As with the subsequent chapters concerning IP and IPX addressing, the layer-2 address must also uniquely identify the physical network connection. The IP and IPX protocols address devices at the Network layer, or layer 3. In order for packets to cross network boundaries, a layer-3 device is needed, hence a router. But if a protocol is implemented that does not take advantage of the layer-3 addressing functionality, another device must be incorporated to span the different boundaries or bridge segments. This device, or bridge, utilizes the layer-2 addressing that is particular to the LAN segment. The layer-2 address is called the MAC address and it is defined by the IEEE in the MAC sublayer previously defined.

According to the IEEE standard, the MAC address can be one of three sizes: 16-, 48-, or 60-bits long. Fortunately, the 16-bit size was never popular. The size that has been adopted as the de facto size is the 48-bit address. So, for the most part, a MAC address is a 48-bit, six-byte address that uniquely identifies an attached device. This 48-bit address is divided into two 24-bit parts, as shown in Figure 9-1. One part is provided by the IEEE and uniquely identifies a manufacturer or vendor. The address is called the *organizationally unique identifier* (OUI) and must be requested from the IEEE much like an IP address must be requested from the IANA.

The other 24 bits are left for the vendor to assign. In most cases, the vendor uses the serial number of the interface for this number. Both parts of the MAC address are combined and "burned" into the network interface's *read-only memory* (ROM) at the time of manufacture. When the interface initializes, it is copied into the *random access memory* (RAM) of the device.

As I stated previously, the IEEE allocates 24 bits for the OUI, but in actuality it only allocates 22 fixed bits. It designates that the first two least significant bits of the first octet (byte) have specific meaning. One bit represents the *group/individual* (G/I) bit, while the other represents the *global/local* (G/L) bit. The G/I bit enables packets to be addressed to a group of addresses. A group address is also referred to as a multicast address. Changing the bit value from 0 to 1 specifies that the address is a multicast address. The one multicast address that everyone should be familiar with is the broadcast address. Every connected device receives a packet sent to the broadcast address. The G/L bit enables network administrators to change the burned MAC address to suit their networks. The IEEE envisioned that not every manufacturer would be willing to purchase a block of addresses, so it allocated one of the bits in the first octet to be the G/L bit. Changing this bit value from 0 to 1 means that the address is

Figure 9-1
The 48-bit MAC
address

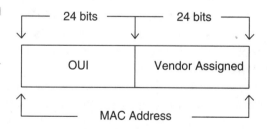

Figure 9-2

Bit representation of the MAC address

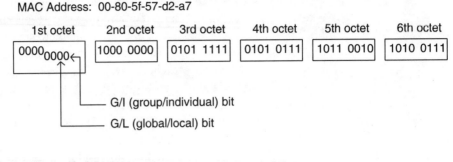

Figure 9-3

Which protocol created the packet?

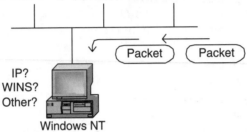

locally administered, and it is the responsibility of the network adminis-trator to manage all locally administered addresses. Figure 9-2 shows the location of the G/I and G/L bits in the MAC address. It also shows the actual binary bits of the MAC address.

Logical Link Control (LLC)

Before we begin the discussion of the LLC, let me preface it with a brief sce-nario and then a question. A Windows NT workstation is currently con-nected to a network (either Ethernet or Token Ring, it does not matter). Its default network protocol is IP and with all Windows NT workstations, it uses Microsoft's *Windows Internet Name Service* (WINS). So how does the workstation know for which protocol a packet received is destined? How does it determine if an arbitrary packet is an IP-only or a NetBIOS packet (see Figure 9-3)?

Another way of asking the question is, how does the workstation deter-mine which protocol created the received packet? Since many computers implement multiple higher layer protocols, how do packets created by them or sent by them get to where they are destined? The question is answered with three letters: LLC. The LLC provides a means for multiple higher layer protocols to share the Data Link layer. The IEEE 802 committee designed the LLC sublayer to provide multiple services. The LLC is defined with the following services:

- **LLC1**: A connectionless service that provides a best-effort delivery of data. It is simply a datagram protocol that transmits frames called *link service data units* (LSDUs) without requiring an acknowledgement from the destination. LLC1 supports point-to-point, multipoint/multicast, and broadcast communications. This service is ideal for upper layer protocols that provide their own addressing, routing, recovery, and sequencing.

- **LLC2**: This service is a connection-oriented protocol that provides a reliable delivery between end points by establishing a connection between communicating devices and tracking message numbers for proper sequencing. It is also responsible for flow control and error recovery.

- **LLC3**: This is a hybrid between LLC1 and LLC2. This means it is a semi-reliable protocol providing connectionless service, but with acknowledgements.

NOTE: *Nortel Networks routers do not support LLC3 service class. For that reason, it will not be discussed further.*

Through these services, there have been defined *service access points* (SAPs). These SAPs act as gateways to a specific protocol. In creating this standard, the IEEE 802 committee modified the Protocol Type field found in the header of the original Ethernet frame format devised by Xerox. The company were also the administrators of the protocol numbers that defined each protocol in the Ethernet frame. What the 802 committee decided was to divide the Protocol Type field into two separate fields: the source and destination SAP fields. They also tacked on a 1 to 2 byte control field. Just as Xerox administered the protocol numbers, the IEEE began to administer the SAP numbers. It would give eight-bit SAP addresses to protocol creators that could be used in the LLC header. A problem arose in that the 802 committee again reserved two bits for the G/I and G/L bits, which function identically to the ones defined for the MAC addresses. The problem was that this only left six bits available for SAP addressing and caused the IEEE to be stingy on the assignments. So, instead of assigning addresses to protocol vendors on a first-come, first-served basis, they created strict rules for the vendors to follow in order to receive a SAP address. For those protocols lucky enough to receive a global SAP, the SAP fields in the LLC header acted like the Protocol Type field as before. But, for the other protocols, this became a problem. The 802 committee had to come up with a more flexible solution.

The IEEE, in order to solve the SAP allocation problem, came up with a universal SAP address that protocols could use that would tell the LLC a protocol type field would follow. The universal SAP is termed the *subnet access protocol* (SNAP) SAP and it equals 10101010 in binary or AA in hex. So, the SNAP SAP (AA) is placed in both the source and destination SAP address fields to alert the LLC services to the presence of a protocol type field. This protocol type field was defined as a five-byte field of which three bytes were IEEE-administered just like the OUI. In fact, it is administered exactly like the OUI. When a vendor requested a block of addresses, it was assigned the three-byte OUI that the vendor could use as the high-order portion in the protocol type field. Figure 9-4 is an example of a vendor-assigned address block and protocol type.

Figure 9-4
Address block and protocol type allocations

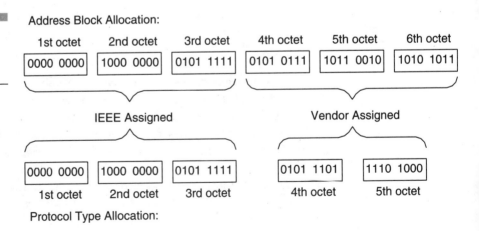

Address Block Allocation:

1st octet	2nd octet	3rd octet	4th octet	5th octet	6th octet
0000 0000	1000 0000	0101 1111	0101 0111	1011 0010	1010 1011

IEEE Assigned / Vendor Assigned

0000 0000	1000 0000	0101 1111	0101 1101	1110 1000
1st octet	2nd octet	3rd octet	4th octet	5th octet

Protocol Type Allocation:

Notice in Figure 9-4 that the address block and protocol type assigned by the IEEE is the same. This gives the vendor the opportunity to assign addresses and protocol types with the three-octet prefix. This only governs the assignment of addresses and protocol types. Suppose a vendor, vendor1, is assigned the address block ABC. It can then assign addresses in the form ABCxyz and protocol types ABCxy. Now suppose another vendor, vendor2, is assigned an address block DDD and it wants to implement vendor1's protocol. Vendor2 would then assign its machine addresses as DDDxyz, but vendor1's protocol would still be addressed as ABCxy inside each machine.

Most of the popular protocols have defined SAP addresses. Table 9-1 is a brief list of some of the defined SAP addresses and their corresponding protocols. Applications use these addresses to send and receive data via the LLC sublayer. It is up to the LLC to sort the frames coming from the MAC sublayer and direct them to the appropriate application or protocol entity.

LLC Format

As stated, the LLC sublayer supports multiple logical links concurrently. It does this through either LLC1 or LLC2 services (These services are also referred to as Type 1 and Type 2 services). The LLC protocols generate and interpret frames called *protocol data units* (PDUs). The LLC (whether Type 1 or Type 2) consists of the following fields:

Table 9-1

Application and Protocol SAP addresses

Application or Protocol Entity	Hex	Dec
Bridge PDU/Spanning Tree	42	66
Global	FF	255
IP	06	06
IPX	E0	224
LAN Manager	F4	260
NetBIOS	F0	256
SNA	04	04
SNAP	AA	170

■ *DSAP* The destination service access point. This identifies the address of the protocol for which the packet is intended. The DSAP address is seven bits long with the least significant bit defined as the G/I bit, as shown in Figure 9-5. The G/I bit specifies the packet is intended for an individual protocol if set to 0. A value of 1 specifies a group protocol address.

■ *SSAP* The source service access point. This identifies the address of the protocol that created the packet. As in the DSAP field, the address is seven bits long with the least significant bit reserved. In this case, the reserved bit indicates the *command/response* (C/R) bit, as shown in Figure 9-6. This feature will be explained later. A value of 0 in the C/R bit location specifies the LLC PDU is a command PDU. The C/R bit specifies a response PDU if its value is set to 1.

■ *CTL* The control field that contains control and response information as well as sequence numbers when necessary. It is one or two bytes long, depending upon the type of PDU. For a Type 1 PDU, the CTL field is always one byte long and can be one of three values:

　■ *UI* Unnumbered Information

　■ *XID* Exchange Identification. A C/R PDU that conveys the types of LLC services supported along with the receive window sizes. The command PDU is transmitted to the destination with the previous information about the source. The destination sends the response with its information.

　■ *Test* This is also a C/R PDU. Its purpose is to test the LLC-to-LLC connection. The command PDU initiates the establishment of an LLC1 connection. The response confirms this establishment.

Figure 9-5
DSAP bit designation

Address Desgination Bit

DSAP

| DDDDDDD | G/I |

Figure 9-6
SSAP bit designation

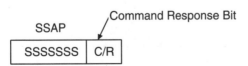

Command Response Bit

SSAP

| SSSSSSS | C/R |

For a Type 2 PDU, the CTL field can be one or two bytes long. The following values require a two-byte CTL field:

- *I*   Information
- *RR*   Receiver Ready
- *RNR*   Receiver Not Ready
- *REJ*   Reject

The following values of the Type 2 LLC PDU only need a one-byte CTL field:

- *SABME*   Set Asynchronous Balanced Mode Extended
- *DISC*   Disconnect
- *DM*   Disconnected Mode
- *FRMR*   Frame Reject
- *UA*   Unnumbered Acknowledgment

Reasons for Bridges

This section is not meant to state the reasons for bridges over routers. Instead, it is meant to point out some of the limitations that are present with several of the Data Link protocols and how a bridge can be used to overcome them.

Basically, the following summarizes the limitations for a couple of the 802.x protocols:

- *The number of stations*   Especially with 802.5 Token Ring, a limit exists on the number of stations that can be on the ring. As this number increases, issues include clock jitter and a loss of phase lock loop. The problems surface due to increased contention for the media as the number of stations increase for 802.3.

- *Extended length restriction*   This is more prevalent a problem for 802.3 than 802.5, because as the length of the bus increases, the round-trip time also increases, thereby prohibiting proper collision detection.

- *Amount of traffic*   Since all stations on a LAN share the total bandwidth, the more stations that are transmitting, the less share of the bandwidth there is.

So, because of the previous limitations, as networks grow, the single LAN model becomes insufficient. If protocols are implemented on workstations on the network that adhere to the single LAN model and they do not have provisions in the network layer (no routing information), then a device is needed to connect LANs together such that packets can be forwarded from one LAN to another. These devices are known as *bridges*.

Bridge Types

Four types of bridges exist: transparent, source routing, translation, and encapsulation. Each of these types is outlined in this section. Transparent bridges will be discussed in more detail later in this chapter, while source routing bridges are covered in Chapter 10, "Source Route Bridging."

- *Transparent bridge*   This is also called the *learning bridge* because it learns about the stations on each of its network interfaces. It provides network connections to LANs that employ identical Data Link layer protocols (an example would be Ethernet to Ethernet). It places no burden on end stations and it does not participate in route discovery or selection (see Figure 9-7).

- *Source routing bridge*   This bridge type has been developed for transporting packets across Token Ring networks. It does not learn about end-stations; instead, it relies on information in the packet to determine proper routing. Route discovery and retention is left in the hands of the end stations (see Figure 9-8).

- *Translation bridge*   This bridge is designed to forward packets across the boundaries of dissimilar Data Link layer protocols (such as Ethernet to Token Ring). The bridge must be able to convert frame formats from one media type to the frame formats of another (see Figure 9-9).

Figure 9-7
An example of a transparent bridge

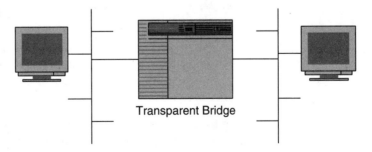

Transparent Bridge

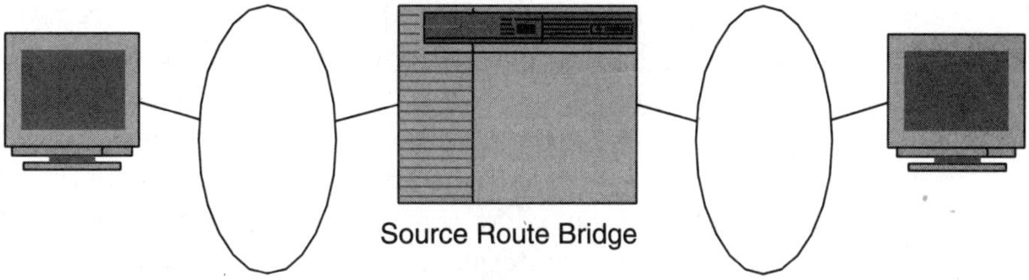

Figure 9-8
An example of a source route bridge

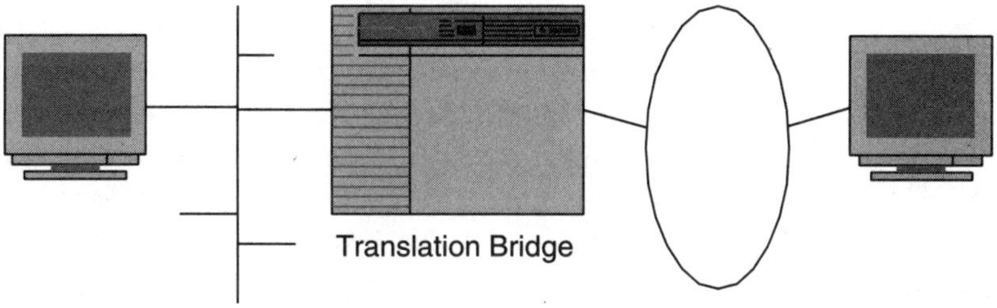

Source Route Bridge

Figure 9-9
An example of a translation bridge

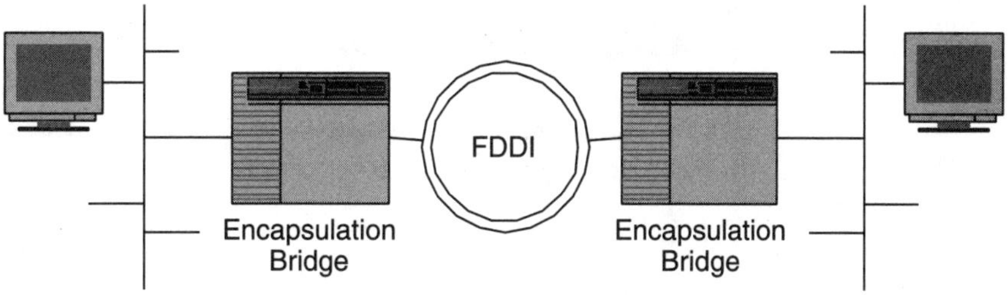

Translation Bridge

Figure 9-10
An example of an encapsulation bridge

FDDI

Encapsulation Bridge

Encapsulation Bridge

■ *Encapsulation bridge*   This bridge's primary use is with backbones that connect like networks. For example, suppose you have two Ethernet networks connected via a FDDI backbone. These bridges encapsulate the Ethernet packet into a FDDI envelope for transport across the backbone (see Figure 9-10).

Transparent Bridging

By far, the two most prevalent types of bridges are the transparent and the source route bridges. Actually, they both competed to be incorporated as the 802.1 standard. Of course, transparent bridges won out, leaving source route bridges to seek out another standards committee. In a similar vein, we will seek out another discussion of the details of source route bridges in Chapter 10.

The basic tenant of a transparent bridge is that it receives and examines all frames that are transmitted on the network. The main stipulation is that the networks that the bridge connects to must be of the same Data Link layer protocol. That is, a transparent bridge can only connect similar LANs like Ethernet to Ethernet or Token Ring to Token Ring. It is from these frames that the bridge learns about the end stations.

How the bridge learns about all the end stations on the network is by inspecting the frames it receives and noting the source address. It correlates the source address with the interface for which it was received and documents the pair into its *station cache*. The station cache is also called a *forwarding table*. So, when a transparent bridge receives a packet on one of its interfaces, it looks into its forwarding table to determine a course of action. That is, should it be dropped or forwarded?

Bridge Operation

The following outline describes the operation of a transparent bridge. A more detailed example will follow.

- A transparent bridge receives every packet by listening promiscuously on the network. This basically means that every packet received is placed back on to the network unchanged.

- It will note the source MAC address in the packet and store it along with the interface designator from which it was received in the forwarding table.

- It will check the destination MAC address in the received packet and compare it to addresses already in the forwarding table. Depending upon an address match, the bridge will do the following:

  - If the destination address is not already in the table, the bridge will forward the packet out every interface except the one from which it was received. This process is called *flooding*. The bridge's forwarding table will be updated with the interface designator corresponding to the interface from which the response is received.

  - If the address has a match in the forwarding table, then the bridge will forward the packet out the specified interface. If the specified interface is the same as the interface from which the packet was received, then the bridge will drop or filter the packet.

▪ A transparent bridge also ages entries in its forwarding table. After a specified amount of time, the bridge will delete an entry if packets are not received with that entry's address as a source address. This specified amount of time is the *aging time*.

As an example, look at Figure 9-11 and let's assume that the bridge knows nothing about stations A, B, and C.

Now, suppose station A transmits a packet that is destined for station C. The packet will be of the form

DA	SA		Data

or specifically

C	A		Data

where DA and SA stand for destination and source address, respectively. The bridge notes the source address from the packet and also that it receives it on port 1. Since the bridge does not know where station C is located, it floods all ports with station A's packet. In our example, the bridge only has two ports. Thus, it will transmit A's packet onto the network connected to port 2. The bridge's forwarding table will look like the following:

Port	Address
1	A

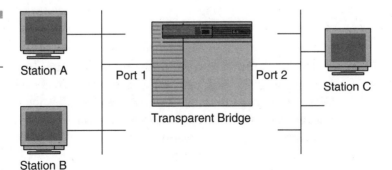

Figure 9-11
The operation of a transparent bridge

Station A

Station B

Port 1

Transparent Bridge

Port 2

Station C

Suppose station C responds to station A's packet. Station C's packet will look like the following:

A	C	Data

The bridge would again note the source address in the packet and that it was received on port 2. So, it now knows that station C resides on the network connected to port 2. It will update its table to be the following:

Port	Address
1	A
2	C

The bridge already knows station A's location and it will forward station C's response out port 1. Let's take this a step further and suppose B sends a packet to A. From Figure 9-11, we see that both stations A and B reside on the same network. What this means is that both station A and the bridge will receive station B's packet. The bridge, as before, will note the source address and receiving interface and will update its forwarding table as follows:

Port	Address
1	A
2	C
1	B

The bridge will then search the table to see if it has already learned the location of station A. Upon finding the match, the bridge notes the interface that can be used to reach A is the same as that for which it received the packet from B. The bridge will then drop the packet.

This scenario can be extended for bridges that have more than just two ports. But what about networks with more than one bridge? How does the bridging operation work when two or three bridges connect networks? The

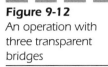

Figure 9-12
An operation with three transparent bridges

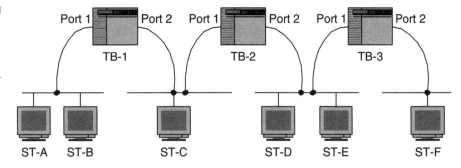

Port	Address
1	ST-A
1	ST-B
2	ST-C
2	ST-D
2	ST-E
2	ST-F

Port	Address
1	ST-A
1	ST-B
1	ST-C
2	ST-D
2	ST-E
2	ST-F

Port	Address
1	ST-A
1	ST-B
1	ST-C
1	ST-D
1	ST-E
2	ST-F

answer is the same, but the perception by each bridge will be different. Take a look at Figure 9-12. This figure shows three bridges connecting three distinct networks. After each station has transmitted, each bridge will have populated its own forward table, as shown.

Conceptually, bridge TB-1, TB-2, and TB-3 will have their own respective view of the network. Each bridge will believe only two LANs exist. Bridge TB-1, for example, would believe that it connects two LANs with the ST-A and ST-B on port 1 and ST-C, ST-D, ST-E, and ST-F on port 2 (see Figure 9-13).

Similarly, TB-2 and TB-3 will only be aware of two LANs with the stations divided per their forwarding table. These are shown in Figures 9-14 and 9-15, respectively.

The process the transparent bridge performs to learn about the location of the end stations works quite well for all tree-type topology networks. That is, no more than one path exists between any two end stations. But what would happen if another interface were added to TB-1 and it was connected to the same LAN occupied by TB-3's port 2? We will cover this scenario when we come to the discussion of the Spanning Tree protocol.

Figure 9-13
Bridge TB-1's
conception of
attached devices

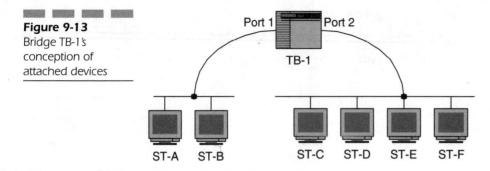

Figure 9-14
Bridge TB-2's
conception of
attached devices

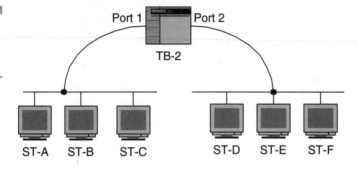

Figure 9-15
Bridge TB-3's
conception of
attached devices

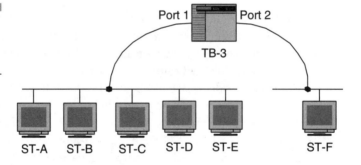

Nortel Implementation

Implementing bridging functions on a Nortel router interface is exceedingly simple. This is especially true if you are not implementing the Spanning Tree protocol. For the sake of an example, we will be configuring an interface on the router for bridging in order to accommodate an IBM cluster controller that has just been added to the network. The controller is a Token Ring-attached 3174 controller using the IBM SNA protocol. The configuration starts like all previous configuration examples, from the Configuration Manager main window. The steps for configuring the bridge service are outlined as follows.

Configuration Steps

1. Select the connector to which the bridging service is to be implemented.

   From the Configuration Manager main window, select either an unconfigured connector or one that already contains circuit information. The Configuration Manager main window is shown in Figure 9-16.

   Select the **Token1** connector on slot 2. This is the network segment where the controller is connected. The "Add Circuit" window opens with the default name of the circuit, O21. You can change the name of this circuit to a more descriptive name if you want, as was done in Figure 9-17.

   Click **OK** to continue.

Figure 9-16
The Configuration Manager main window

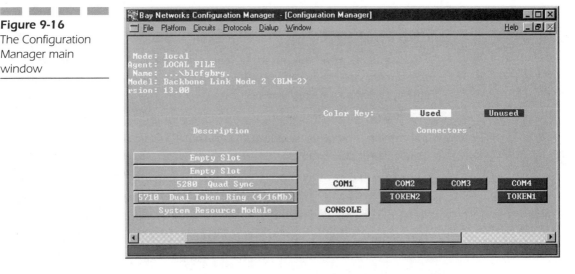

Figure 9-17
The Add Circuit
configuration
window

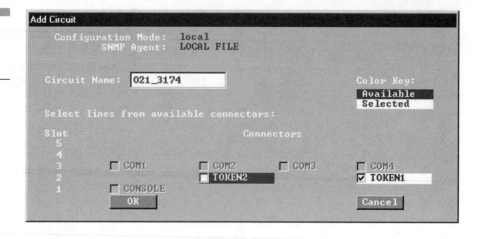

Figure 9-18
The Site Manager
ring speed warning
window

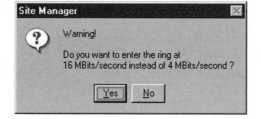

2. Choose ring speed for this Token Ring interface.

Site Manager pops up a warning message prompting you to choose whether or not the interface will enter the ring at 16 Mbps. Figure 9-18 shows the popup warning message.

3. Select the Bridge protocol from the list of available protocols.

The "Select Protocols" window in Figure 9-19 lists the available protocols for this interface.

Click **OK** to continue. Since we are not configuring Spanning Tree, we are returned to the Configuration Manager main window (that is, if no other protocol is being added at the same time).

The default values for the bridging service should be sufficient enough that they need not be modified. The bridge parameters will be covered in the following section.

Figure 9-19
The Select Protocols
window

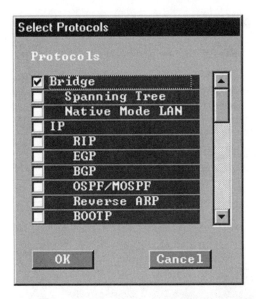

Figure 9-20
The transparent
bridge global
parameters window

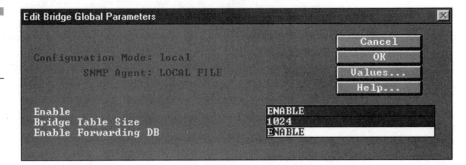

Transparent Bridge Parameters

Since bridges are very intelligent devices, not many parameters need to be modified. The parameters that configure the bridge service can be grouped as global or local. The global parameters are displayed in Figure 9-20 and deal with the size of the forwarding table and whether or not the service is enabled throughout the whole router.

Only three parameters can be changed that will affect the bridging service for the entire router. Table 9-2 describes each parameter.

The local bridging parameters are accessed via the Interface option under the bridge protocol. Figure 9-21 shows the Bridge Interfaces window.

Chapter 9

Table 9-2

Bridge Global
parameters

Parameter	Description
Enable	Enables or disables bridging for the entire router
Bridge Table Size	Sets the maximum number of MAC addresses that the forwarding table can contain. The default is 1,024 but can be as high as 131,072. This parameter has specific settings, so in order to change it, you must select the Values button. Be advised that increasing this number will utilize more of the router's memory.
Enable Forwarding DB	Setting this field to Enable allows you to view the forwarding table entries from a copy in the router's *Management Information Base* (MIB). The default value is Enable.

Figure 9-21
The Bridges
Interfaces window

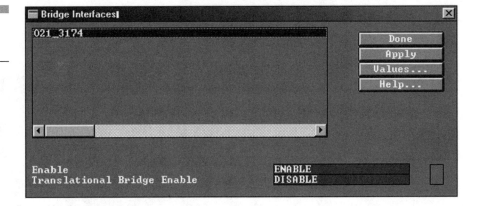

Only two parameters can be changed, Enable and Translational Bridge Enable. As we defined earlier, the translational bridge lets you bridge networks with different Data Link protocols.

Spanning Tree Algorithm

The Spanning Tree algorithm has been developed to eliminate problems associated with redundant links in an extended network. This ensures that the network is loop-free and that only one path exists between any two end stations. You may recall that at the end of our discussion concerning the operation of the transparent bridges, I posed a question about modifying the topology of Figure 9-12. To reiterate, what would happen if an additional interface were added to TB-1 and it was connected to the LAN already connected by TB-3, port 2? To answer this question, I will simplify the scenario to that of two bridges in parallel, as in Figure 9-22.

Suppose that workstation A transmits a packet destined for any device on LAN 2. Let's assume that no frames have been sent from the device to which A's packet is destined. Since both bridges have an interface onto LAN 1, they will both receive A's packet. Both BR1 and BR2 will make an entry into their forwarding tables for A in the direction of LAN 1. Looking in their forwarding table, they note that no entry exists for the destination device and they flood A's packet out onto LAN 2.

The first thing you will note is that the destination device will now receive two identical packets. This increases the traffic on LAN 2, contributing to an insufficient use of the available bandwidth. The second thing that will happen is that both bridges will receive each other's flooded packet. That is, BR1 will receive A's packet from BR2, and BR2 will receive A's packet from BR1. Both bridges will modify their forwarding tables to reflect that A now resides on LAN 2 while transmitting the packets out their LAN 1 interfaces. The cycle continues. Both bridges again receive each other's packet, noting A in the direction of LAN 1 and then transmitting onto LAN 2. This process will continue until the buffers in each of the bridges overflow and effectively shut down. What does this loop do to workstation A? It will continually receive the same packet it transmitted and get

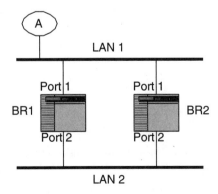

Figure 9-22
Parallel bridge
problem

thoroughly confused. Just imagine what could happen if this were extended to many bridges across a wide area. Fortunately, this is what the Spanning Tree Algorithm is designed to prevent.

The Spanning Tree Algorithm works by having all the bridges discover a subset of the topology that is loop-free with just enough connectivity to provide a single path to each LAN. This creates a logical tree topology out of an arrangement of bridges, the Spanning Tree. The way the bridges discover this tree topology is by transmitting configuration messages with each other called *Bridge Protocol Data Units* (BPDUs). The BPDUs contain the information needed to elect a central bridge and a single, best path to it from all the other bridges. The idea of a single path should not cause any worry because the algorithm is highly fault-tolerant. It enables the automatic reconfiguration of the Spanning Tree in the event of a failed bridge or data path. It also converges quickly to minimize the unavailability of services.

The exchange of the BPDUs between bridges is what builds the Spanning Tree. These BPDUs contain the information that allow the bridges to perform the following tasks:

- Elect a root bridge from all the bridges on all the LANs. This will be the bridge with the lowest priority. If two bridges have the same priority, then the bridge with the lowest MAC address will be chosen.

- Determine the root path cost. This is the shortest path from them to the root bridge.

- Elect a designated bridge for each LAN from among the bridges residing on that LAN. The designated bridge is determined by its closeness to the root bridge. It has the responsibility of forwarding packets from the LAN to the root bridge.

- Select a port based on the best path from themselves to the root bridge. This port is called the *root port*.

- Designate ports to be included into or excluded from the Spanning Tree.

Spanning Tree Terms

In order to proceed with our discussion of the Spanning Tree Algorithm, it is necessary to define a few important terms. Table 9-3 contains the main values used when describing the Spanning Tree Algorithm.

	Term	Definition
Table 9-3	Bridge priority	This is a value assigned by the network manager that enables him or her to influence the selection of the root bridge and the designated bridge. The lower the priority, the more likely the bridge will be elected as root.
Spanning Tree terms and definitions	Root bridge	This is the bridge that sits at the top of the Spanning Tree hierarchy. It is from this bridge that all other bridges base their path and port costs.
	Path cost	This is the cost taken from the circuit that points to the root bridge.
	Designated bridge	A bridge on a LAN shared by another bridge that is responsible for forwarding packets to the root bridge. The bridge with the lowest path cost to the root bridge is deemed the designated bridge.
	Root port	This is the port on a bridge that has the lowest cost path to the root.
	Designated port	Any ports on a bridge, besides the root port, that offer the best path to the root.
	Root cost	This is the sum of all the costs associated with each link in the path toward the root bridge.

Bridge Protocol Data Unit (BPDU) Format

BPDUs are the configuration messages used by bridges to ensure that physical looping in the network topology does not lead to logical looping of the network traffic. Using the BPDUs, the Spanning Tree Algorithm defines a single bridge as a reference (the root bridge) and switches one of two bridges forming a network loop into backup or standby mode. This establishes a single path through which traffic will pass. When the path breaks down due to an error or reconfiguration, the standby bridge is available to resume forwarding traffic. This is determined by continually examining the BPDUs. The structure of a BPDU is shown in Figure 9-23. Table 9-4 outlines the fields in the BDPU format.

Root Bridge Selection

The first thing that needs to happen in order to construct a Spanning Tree is to have all the bridges decide on a single bridge that will become the root

Figure 9-23
BDPU format

Protocol Identifier - 2 bytes
Protocol Version ID - 1 byte
BPDU Type - 1 byte
Flags - 1 byte
Root Identifier - 8 bytes
Root Path Cost - 4 bytes
Bridge Identifier - 8 bytes
Port Identifier - 2 bytes
Message Age - 2 bytes
Max Age - 2 bytes
Hello Time - 2 bytes
Forward Delay - 2 bytes

bridge. The way the bridges in the Spanning Tree elect a root bridge is through the reception of BPDUs. Each bridge initially assumes that it is the root bridge and will transmit a configuration message (BPDU) out each of its interfaces, relating a root path cost of 0. Each bridge will then compare configuration messages that it receives on its ports as well as configuration messages that it would send out each of its ports to determine the best configuration message. The best message is determined by the following ways.

Given two configuration messages, C1 and C2

- C1 will be considered better than C2 if it has a lower priority than C2.

- If the priorities are equal, then C1 is better than C2 if its root path cost is lower.

- If it happens that their path costs are also equal, then C1 is preferred if its MAC address is numerically lower than that of C2. The bridge's MAC address is taken from the Bridge ID field in the BPDU. The Bridge ID is comprised of a two-byte priority and a six-byte MAC address. The priority bytes are added in front of the most significant byte of the MAC address.

- If all three of the previous parameters are equal, then it falls to the port priority as the tiebreaker.

Table 9-4	Field	Description
The BDPU fields	Protocol Identifier	Identifies the Spanning Tree Algorithm and protocol
	Protocol Version ID	Identifies the version of the protocol
	BPDU Type	Identifies the BPDU type
	Value	Type
	00000000	Configuration
	10000000	Topology change notification
	Flags	Currently only two bits are used as flags
	Value	Flag
	bit 1	Topology Change
	bit 8	Topology Change ACK
	Root Path Cost	This is the total of all costs associated with the path leading from the bridge that sent the configuration BPDU to the root bridge. It is an unsigned binary number.
	Bridge Identifier	This designates the bridge priority. The lower the bridge ID, the more likely it will be selected as the root bridge. It is an unsigned binary number.
	Port Identifier	This designates the port priority. The lower the priority, the more likely it will be included in the Spanning Tree.
	Message Age	Two octets that represent the amount of time since the BPDU's transmission. The estimated time is in 1/256ths of a second.
	Max. Age	Two octets that represent the time in 1/256ths of a second, at which time this BPDU should be deleted
	Hello Time	Two octets that represent the time in 1/256ths of a second between BPDUs from the root bridge
	Forward Delay	Two octets that represent the length of time a BPDU must wait before transitioning from blocking to forwarding

Once the root bridge is determined, then each bridge calculates the best path to the root. Also, if two or more bridges share a single LAN, then a designated bridge for that LAN must be selected as well as a root port and any other ports that offer a best path to the root bridge. The Spanning Tree process is best described using the following example.

Spanning Tree Example

Suppose you have set up the bridged network shown in Figure 9-24.

Each path has the same cost value of 10 and the port IDs are defined in the following format:

Port ID = XXYY

XX = Port priority, which is set to 128 hex

YY = Circuit number assigned at its creation

Bridge C will be elected as the root bridge because it has the lowest priority. The other bridges must determine their root ports and whether any other ports need to be designated. The following describes how the other bridges determine which of their ports are to be a part of the Spanning Tree.

Figure 9-24

An example bridge network

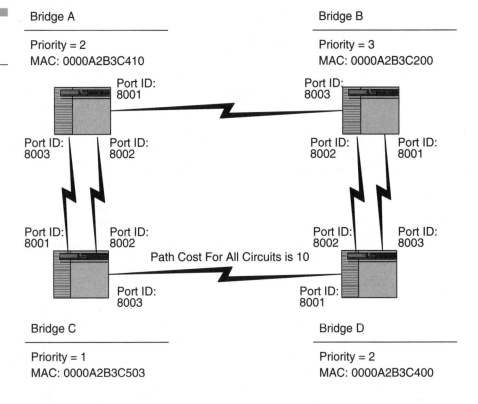

Bridge A

Priority = 2
MAC: 0000A2B3C410

Port ID: 8001

Port ID: 8003

Port ID: 8002

Port ID: 8001

Port ID: 8002

Bridge C

Priority = 1
MAC: 0000A2B3C503

Port ID: 8003

Path Cost For All Circuits is 10

Bridge B

Priority = 3
MAC: 0000A2B3C200

Port ID: 8003

Port ID: 8002

Port ID: 8001

Port ID: 8002

Port ID: 8003

Bridge D

Priority = 2
MAC: 0000A2B3C400

Port ID: 8001

Bridge A The two paths pointing to the root bridge have equal costs. Since they are both connected to the root bridge, they both share the same bridge priority and MAC address. The root bridge has even set the port priorities to the same value. So, the only metric that is left that will determine the root port for A is the port number. Bridge A blocks the port that it received a BPDU for from the root with a higher port number (see Figure 9-24a).

Bridge B For bridge B, a comparison takes place between the BPDUs received from bridge A and bridge D. The first thing that is checked is the bridge priorities, which are equal. One of the two paths pointing to bridge D is chosen due to bridge D having a lower MAC address than A. So, bridge B blocks the path toward bridge A. As with bridge A, bridge B has two equal cost paths to the root through the same bridge. Bridge B determines that its port 2 is the best path to the root (see Figure 9-24b).

Bridge D This bridge will be considered the designated bridge for bridge B. Therefore, it will not block any ports.

Logical Network The Spanning Tree has created a loop-free topology for the example network in Figure 9-24. The logical (loop-free) network is shown in Figure 9-24c.

If the two links connecting bridge B with bridge D are not of the same bandwidth, then there could be a problem with performance as the Spanning Tree Algorithm determines the port to designate. Suppose the line

Figure 9-24a
Bridge A discovery process

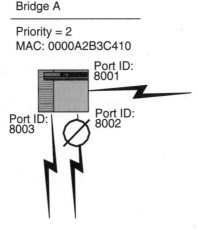

Bridge A

Priority = 2
MAC: 0000A2B3C410

Port ID: 8001

Port ID: 8003

Port ID: 8002

Figure 9-24b
Bridge B discovery
process

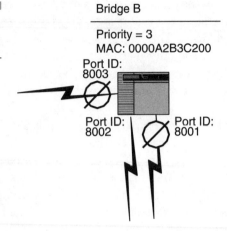

Bridge B

Priority = 3
MAC: 0000A2B3C200

Port ID: 8003

Port ID: 8002

Port ID: 8001

Figure 9-24c
The logical network
view

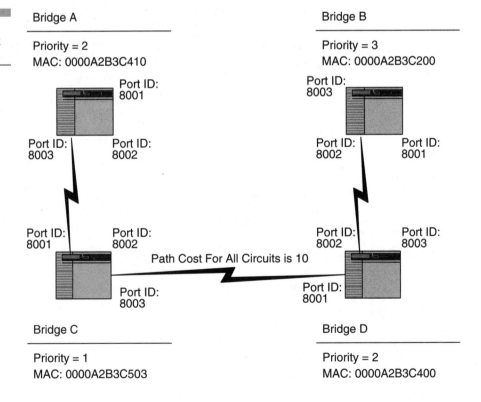

Bridge A

Priority = 2
MAC: 0000A2B3C410

Port ID: 8001

Port ID: 8003

Port ID: 8002

Bridge B

Priority = 3
MAC: 0000A2B3C200

Port ID: 8003

Port ID: 8002

Port ID: 8001

Port ID: 8001

Port ID: 8002

Port ID: 8002

Port ID: 8003

Path Cost For All Circuits is 10

Port ID: 8003

Port ID: 8001

Bridge C

Priority = 1
MAC: 0000A2B3C503

Bridge D

Priority = 2
MAC: 0000A2B3C400

selected between B and D in the previous example is only a 9.6K line and the other one that is blocked is a 56K line. You can see how the less efficient line could be chosen. So, how do you make sure the 56K line gets picked for the Spanning Tree? You could either lower the path cost to D on the 56K line or decrease the port priority on the 56K line on D.

Spanning Tree Parameters

At the beginning of this chapter, we learned how to configure the router to be a transparent bridge. In order to provide a loop-free topology, we must add the Spanning Tree protocol to our bridge configuration. Figure 9-19 shows the Select Protocols window and from there you can select the Spanning Tree protocol. To open this window, you must first select the Token Ring connector that is configured as the transparent bridge from the Configuration Manager main window. This will open the Edit Connector dialog box, as shown in Figure 9-25.

Select the **Edit Circuit ...** button, which brings up the "Select Protocol" window, as shown in Figure 9-19. Once you check the box next to the Spanning Tree protocol and click **OK**, the Spanning Tree Autoconfiguration parameter window opens (see Figure 9-26). You can also access this window by following the menu path: Protocols: Bridge > Spanning Tree > Global.

The parameters for the Spanning Tree Algorithm were defined earlier in this chapter. The only addition is the Bridge MAC Address field in Figure 9-26. This field defaults to a value of 12 zeros (000000000000). This means the MAC address will be taken from the interface to which the Spanning Tree protocol was added. This address is appended to the bridge priority to create the bridge ID. The bridge priority occupies the most significant 16 bits of the bridge ID. Conversely, the MAC address occupies the other 48 bits.

Figure 9-25
The Edit Connector window

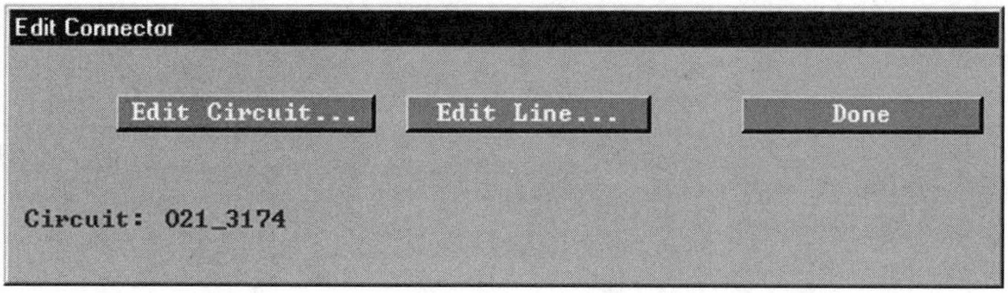

Edit Connector

Edit Circuit...   Edit Line...   Done

Circuit: 021_3174

Figure 9-26
Configuration
parameters for
the Spanning Tree
protocol

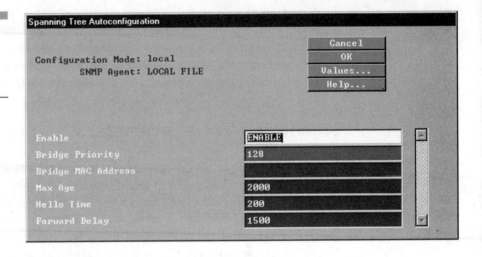

Figure 9-26
Configuration
parameters for
the Spanning Tree
protocol

Figure 9-27 shows the interface parameters that can be modified to enhance or direct the traffic flow on specific ports. By setting the port priority and the path cost, you can direct the Spanning Tree Algorithm using preferred ports as designated ports back to the root.

Bridge Traffic Filters

Nortel routers configured to act as bridges support a variety of filtering encapsulations. They support four such encapsulations:

- Ethernet
- IEEE 802.2 LLC
- IEEE 802.2 LLC with SNAP
- Novell Proprietary

NOTE: *Not every interface supports these encapsulations. For instance, FDDI and Token Ring obviously do not have a need for the Ethernet encapsulation method. They do not support the Novell Proprietary encapsulation either.*

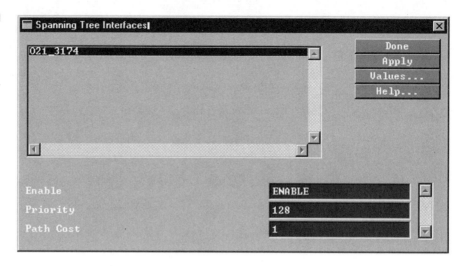

Figure 9-27
Spanning Tree
Interfaces parameters
window

Each of these encapsulation methods has predefined criteria. Table 9-5 lists the predefined criteria for each encapsulation method.

If none of the previous predefined criterion suit your needs, you can create your own filter by specifying specific user-defined criteria. Specifying your own bridge filter enables you to filter on almost any data pattern. The structure of user-defined criteria is basically the same as the predefined ones. The difference is that it is up to you to define the filter's reference, offset, and length:

■ *Reference*   This is the starting point in the frame where the offset is referenced (see Figure 9-28). Only two options for bridge filters are available:

   ▪ *MAC*   This reference points to the first byte of the MAC destination address.

   ▪ *DATA_LINK*   This starting point is after the Length/Type header field.

   Figure 9-28 shows the reference points in a header.

■ *Offset*   This is the length from the reference point to the position of the bit pattern to be filtered.

■ *Length*   This is the length of the bit pattern.

Table 9-5

Predefined criterion listed by encapsulation

Encapsulation Method	Criterion Name	Reference Field	Offset (bits)	Length (bits)
All	MAC Source Address	MAC	0	48
MAC Destination Address	MAC	48	48	
Ethernet	Ethernet Type	MAC	96	16
IEEE 802.2 LLC	Length			
(Ethernet/802.3 & PPP)	MAC	96	16	
SSAP	DATA-LINK	0	8	
DSAP	DATA-LINK	8	8	
Control	DATA-LINK	16	8	
IEEE 802.2 LLC with SNAP	Length	MAC	96	16
Organizational Code (Protocol ID)	DATE-LNK	24	24	
Ethernet Type	DATA-LINK	48	16	
Novell Proprietary	Novell	MAC	112	16

Figure 9-28

User-defined reference points

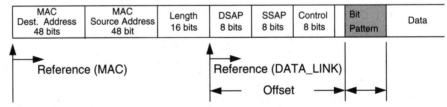

After specifying the reference, offset, and the length, you must also specify the range of values for which you will filter. The range must at least consist of a minimum numeric value.

Lastly, you must specify the action to take for all the frames that match your filter specification. The bridge can take five actions upon matching an incoming frame with your filter. These consist of the standard Accept, Drop, and Log filter actions, as well as two defined specifically for the transparent bridge:

- *Flood*   This specifies that a frame that matched your filter will be flooded out every interface except the one for which it was received.

- *Forward to Circuit List*   This action has the bridge forward any matching frames to every circuit in a circuit list that you define. The circuits in the list are case-sensitive. If you specify a circuit as e21 when the bridge defines it as E21, the filter will not work.

SUMMARY

In this chapter, we discussed the underlying mechanisms for which bridges operate. We spent the better part of the first several sections detailing the two sublayers that are found in the Data Link layer. The IEEE 802 committee has taken the OSI layer-2 definition and subdivided it among a *Medium Access Control* (MAC) and *Logical Link Control* (LLC) sublayer. The MAC sublayer is responsible for managing protocol access to the physical medium. It is the first stop (after the physical layer) on the way up the protocol stack. From the MAC sublayer, it is handed to the LLC so that proper routing can be made to the upper layer protocols. I say routing here because it is the duty of the LLC to make sure that the packet gets to the right upper layer protocol. It does this by managing the *service access points* (SAPs) for these protocols. Three types of LLC exist: Type 1, Type 2, and Type 3. Types 1 and 2 define connectionless and connection-oriented communication, while Type 3 s a hybrid between the two: connectionless with acknowledgments.

This chapter's main purpose was to shed some light on the various types of bridges while focusing on the transparent type. A transparent bridge is one that is invisible on a network. Workstations connected to a network with a transparent bridge operate as if no bridge is connected, hence the name transparent. A transparent bridge achieves its transparency by listening promiscuously on the network. It sees all packets that are on the network and it stores information about the transmitters into a local data store called a station cache, or a forwarding table. The bridge makes decisions on packets it receives by consulting its forwarding table. If the source address of a packet can be matched, then the packet is forwarded out the appropriate interface. Otherwise, it is either flooded out all interfaces or dropped.

When the source MAC address does not match any entry in the bridge's forwarding table, the bridge sends a copy of the packet out each of its interfaces (except the one from which it was received) in the hopes that the destination will respond. If the destination responds, the bridge updates its forwarding table with the destination's address. The bridge drops the packet if it determines that the destination is on the same network as the one where the packet originated.

One of the main principles governing transparent bridges is that there must be a loop-free topology. If loops exist, the possibility of packets getting forever forwarded without reaching a destination is highly likely. Since physical loops in a network can be desirable, a method has been developed to dynamically configure the topology to provide for the removal of logical loops. This method is the Spanning Tree Algorithm. It works by having all bridges elect a root bridge that all traffic will be directed through. Once the root bridge is determined, each subsequent bridge will calculate which port has the best cost path to the root. That port is then designated as part of the Spanning Tree while the other ports may be blocked. After we discussed an example of the Spanning Tree Algorithm, you were shown how to add the protocol to a port and modify any parameters by using Site Manager.

CHAPTER 10

Source Route Bridging

In the last chapter, we spent some time defining certain aspects of the Data Link layer. From that discussion, we developed the concept of bridges and why they are needed. Specifically, we focused our discussion on transparent bridges and the Spanning Tree protocol. In this chapter, we will extend that discussion to incorporate *source route bridges* (SRBs). But before proceeding with any new subject, you must always spend some time in review.

As a brief review from the last chapter, we will note that certain protocols cannot be routed. That is, some protocols have no provision for addressing in the network layer. For this reason, devices like bridges must be used to forward packets across network boundaries. Bridges operate in the Data Link layer, forwarding packets based on the destination and source MAC addresses. The MAC address being a 48-bit, six-byte address that uniquely defines a network device. As you may recall, this address is composed of a three-byte *organizationally unique identifier* (OUI) assigned by the IEEE and a three-byte vendor assigned address.

NOTE: *Since this chapter deals with bridges, the use of the term address is taken to mean MAC address.*

Transparent Bridge Operation

The way a bridge, or a transparent bridge, operates is by comparing a packet's destination address with addresses that it has stored in its local cache. Based on this comparison, the bridge either forwards the packet onto its destination or it drops it. The process starts when the bridge initializes and begins to listen on the network. The main responsibility of a bridge is to listen to every packet on every interface connected to the network. With every packet received on an interface, the bridge performs the following operations:

- It correlates the source address from the packet and the interface from which it was received. This information is stored in a local table called the *station cache*.

- It then searches the station cache for an address that matches the packet's destination address. Depending upon whether a match is found in the station cache, the bridge does one of the following:

- If the address match is not found, the bridge transmits the packet out every interface except the one from which it was originally received. This is called *flooding*.

- If the address match is found, since the station cache keeps track of address/interface pairs, upon matching the destination address the bridge will know to which interface the packet is destined. If the interface is the same as the one it was received on, then the bridge will drop the packet. Otherwise, the packet is sent out the respective interface.

- It also keeps track of the age of each entry in the station cache. After a specified amount of time, if a packet is not received with an address matching an already cached source address, the entry in the cache is purged.

To illustrate the point, let's take look at Figure 10-1, which is a diagram showing two networks (or *local area networks* [LANs]) connected with a bridge.

If the bridge is functioning correctly, then all the frames on LAN1 will be isolated from LAN2 and vice versa. In this figure, the bridge creates a station cache consisting of workstations A and B connected to interface 1 and workstations C and D connected to Interface 2. Table 10-1 is a representation of the bridge's station cache. This is also called the *forwarding table*.

If workstation A transmits a packet, the bridge will forward or drop it depending on the packet's destination. If the packet is destined for workstation B, the bridge will drop the packet because the interface (INT1) that received the packet is the same one it is destined for (INT1). Since every workstation on a network sees every packet transmitted on that network, workstation B will have already received the packet. Thus, there is no need

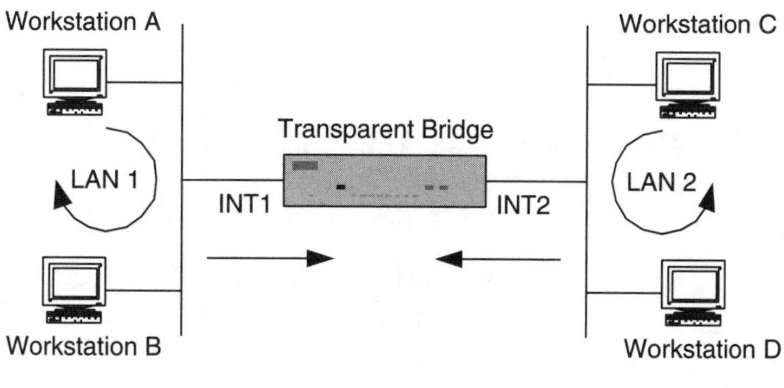

Figure 10-1
Bridge network operation

Table 10-1

Bridge station
cache

MAC Address	Interface
A	INT1
B	INT1
C	INT2
D	INT2

for the bridge to retransmit the packet back onto the same wire. If the packet is destined for workstation C, the bridge will forward the packet out INT2 and onto workstation C after checking the station cache.

Source Route Bridge Operation

The way an Source Route Bridge operates is very different than that described previously. Used in Token Ring environments, SRBs forward packets based upon the Route Identification field located in the header of the packet. The responsibility of router discovery belongs to the source end station (hence the name source route). An SRB does not maintain an address forwarding table, so the decision to forward or drop a frame is based on the data present in the frame.

Source route bridging differs from transparent bridging in two respects.

- *The toleration of multiple paths*   As transparent bridges require that the network topology be loop-free, SRBs have considerably more tolerance for loops in the physical network layout.

- *No forwarding tables*   SRBs rely on the end stations to provide the delivery information instead of keeping the forwarding tables up to date.

Source Route Bridge (SRB) Overview

The SRB specification has been around for a long time. It was in direct competition with the transparent bridge specification for the 802.1 standard. Of course, as we know, the IEEE 802.1 committee chose the transparent bridge specification over the source route specification for its standard. It was then that the source route proponents began courting the 802.5 committee for acceptance as the standard way of connecting 802.5 LANs. The IEEE 802.5 committee adopted source route bridging as its standard way of connecting 802.5 LANs. As source route bridging was developed, so too did transparent bridging develop, albeit independently.

After a time, it was deemed necessary to be able to connect each type of LAN. The devised method was to connect these LANs via a source route-to-transparent bridge. This method proved complex and it was finally mandated that all standard bridges support transparent bridging with a source route option. Bridges that perform both transparent bridge and SRB functions are called *source route transparent* (SRT) bridges.

The basic premise behind source routing is that the packet header contains the routing information needed for it to reach its destination and that the source end station inserts this route. The process is simple in that the source end station discovers a route by transmitting a special packet that replicates when faced with route decisions. When a packet arrives at a bridge with multiple interfaces, a copy of the packet is sent out each interface. As the packets traverse their paths to the destination, they keep diaries of their travels. The destination makes a choice of which path to use as it receives all incoming frames. Once a path is chosen, the destination formulates a response and sends it down the chosen path. The source will then cache this route for use in subsequent communications with the destination.

In order for source routing to work in an extended network, you must designate special identifiers for each bridge and LAN segment. These identifiers are explained here:

- *Bridge ID* This is a unique, network-wide value that defines all Nortel routers in the network. Assigning an ID to a bridge must adhere to the following guidelines:
  - Unless bridges are operating in parallel, assign each Nortel bridge the same Bridge ID.
  - The Bridge IDs assigned to Nortel bridges must be unique among all other bridges on the network.
  - Assign different Bridge IDs to bridges from third-party vendors.

  If you are operating parallel bridges, then a unique ID must be entered for each parallel bridge. Also, you must enter each bridge ID into each

Figure 10-2
Parallel bridge
identification

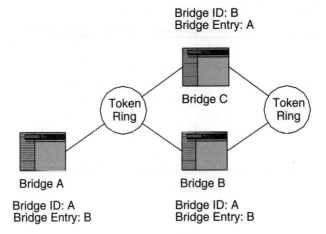

bridge's entry list. Take a look at Figure 10-2. Bridges A and B are given the Bridge ID, A. Since bridge C is parallel to bridge B, it must receive a different bridge ID. It is then given the bridge ID, B. Also, each bridge must have an entry in the bridge entry list for each other.

■ *Internal LAN ID*   This is a Nortel-specific ID that is designed to overcome a shortcoming with the Token Ring chipset. This ID creates a virtual ring internal to a Nortel bridge that enables multiport bridges to operate in a source routing network. This ID must be globally unique and can be thought of as a ring within the bridge to which each port connects. An internal LAN ID adds two hops to the total hop count because each port acts as a mini-bridge connecting the outside ring with the internal ring.

■ *Group LAN ID*   This parameter is proprietary to Nortel bridges and must be globally unique. It helps the source routing bridges identify the destination end stations. Each bridge in the network must have the same Group LAN ID, which must be different from all Internal LAN IDs or ring IDs.

■ *Source route ring number*   This specifies a ring number with a specific LAN segment or circuit number.

These configuration parameters define a bridge for participation in a source routing network. As an end station seeks a path to a destination end station, these field values populate a route header field called a *Routing Information Field* (RIF). Information about the RIF will be provided later in this chapter. For now, we will discuss how the end stations discover a path to a destination, which is called *route discovery*.

Route Discovery

Each end station on a source routing network is responsible for maintaining the routing table that contains the routes to all the nodes with which it communicates. If a path to a destination is not in its routing table, then the end station must discover it. Once the route is discovered, it is then added to the cache or routing table. The sequence of events is as follows:

1. A source end station determines a destination station is not on the local ring.

2. It checks its route table for a path to the destination. Two situations will arise:

    a. If a route exists, it will contain a list of ring/bridge ID pairs, and the source will transmit packets via this route.
    b. If a route does not exist, the source must send an explorer frame to discover the route.

3. The first SRB receives the frame and adds the following information to the RIF:

    a. The ring number from which the frame was received
    b. Its assigned bridge ID
    c. The ring number of the ring where the frame is to be forwarded

    The bridge then forwards the frame out all ports except the one from which it was received.

4. Each subsequent bridge appends its bridge ID and the ring number that the frame is being forwarded to the frame for.

5. Once the destination receives the frame, it responds back using the route that is contained in the header. It sets a bit in the RIF that informs each bridge to read the route in reverse.

6. These bridges read the RIF and forward the packet to the next bridge in the RIF.

7. Once the source end station receives the response frame, it updates its routing table and uses the information for subsequent communication with that node.

Three frame types are used to discover routes in a source route network:

- An *All Routes Broadcast* (ARB), which can be an
  - *All Routes Explorer* (ARE)
  - *All Paths Explorer* (APE)
- A *Spanning Tree Broadcast,* which is referred to as a *Spanning Tree Explorer* (STE)
- A *Specific Routed Frame* (SRF)

All Routes Broadcast (ARB)   When an end station is configured to use an ARE frame to discover a route, multiple frames are generated that traverse all paths to the destination. The bridges receive the broadcasted frame and add their appropriate information to the RIF. The information identifies the incoming ring number, bridge ID, and outgoing ring number. The bridges then flood the frame out all the ports. Once received at the destination end station, it contains a sequence of routing designators for which a response frame can be returned.

NOTE: *The way SRB handles loops is by having the originating bridge drop received packets that are the same as those transmitted.*

Spanning Tree Broadcast (STB)   When an end station is configured to use an STE frame to discover a route, a single frame is generated that follows a loop-free path to the destination. The bridges in the Spanning Tree forward the STE out all active (nonblocked) ports except for the one from which it was received.

Specific Routed Frame (SRF)   This frame type is generated by the destination in response to either an ARE or STE. The SRF traverses the path defined in the RIF. As long as bridges are included on the path, they will forward the frame. Once the source receives the SRF, it strips the routing information out and stores it in its routing table for future communication with the destination. If a source end station has a defined path to a destination end station, then it too will also transmit an SRF.

Routing Information Field (RIF)

In the previous sections of this chapter, there has been a lot of talk about the RIF. But just what is this field? To explain, look at Figure 10-3. This is the basic format of the data link header of a frame.

In order to use this frame to transmit routing information, additional fields will need to be added. However, you can't just add fields and hope it all works out. A method needs to exist that will tell the bridges how to distinguish normal frames from those that contain routing information. Well, it just so happens that an unused bit in the source address field is used to for this purpose, the multicast bit. If this bit is set, then a routing information field is present. This is represented in Figure 10-4. Otherwise, the value will be zero, signifying a normal frame.

When a RIF is present in a frame, it is located directly after the source address of an 802.5 frame. It is composed of two sections, the control fields and the route designators. The control fields contain information about the type of frame, its length, and the direction of the path. The route designators are further divided into a LAN number and a bridge number. As the

Figure 10-3
The basic data link header format

Destination Address	Source Address	Data

Figure 10-4
A modified data link header format

Destination Address	Source Address	RI	Data

Figure 10-5
The RIF in a Token
Ring frame

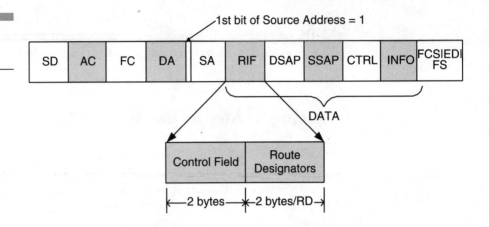

Figure 10-6
The two parts
of the RIF

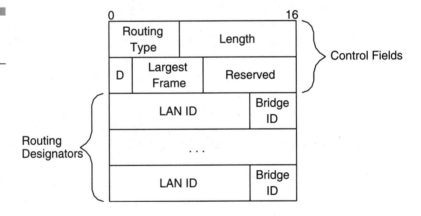

frame traverses bridges, route designators are appended. Each designator
is two bytes. The RIF in a 802.5 frame is shown in Figure 10-5.

The RIF Format   Figure 10-6 shows the two parts of the RIF. The control fields occupy two bytes of the RIF while the routing designators can
occupy two bytes per designator. Table 10-2 outlines the RIF format.

When the path in the RIF is being traversed, the last bridge ID will equal
zero. This is because the bridges on the next ring are unknown. The RIF can
contain no more than 14 routing designators.

Table 10-2

The RIF format

Field	Size (bits)	Description
		Control Fields
Routing Type	3	This specifies the type of source route frame.
		Value Type
		0xx SRF
		10x ARE
		11x STE
Length	5	Specifies the total length of the RIF in bytes. The RIF can be from 2 to 30 bytes.
D (Direction) bit	1	This bit field specifies if the route should be read from the source to the destination or from the destination to the source. This bit is usually set in SRFs to signify the reverse, from the destination to the source.
Largest Frame	3	Specifies the largest size of a frame. Sizes can be 516, 1,500, 2,052, 4,472, 8,144, 11,407, 17,800, 65,535.
Reserved	4	Reserved for future use
		Routing Designators
LAN ID	12	Specifies a network ring number
Bridge ID	4	A number that identifies the bridge in the network. This number need not be unique unless the bridges are parallel.

Nortel Implementation

This section is going to detail how the Nortel Bridge handles both an an ARB frame and a SRF. The way Nortel bridges handle these frames is dependent upon the bridge's position in the Token Ring network. We will also describe the global and interface parameters for the Source Route protocol. This section will end with a brief discussion on end station support by Nortel bridges. Figure 10-7 shows an example of a bridged network that will be used in our discussion of Nortel's bridge implementation.

As you may recall, if the end station does not have a route to the destination in its routing table, it will broadcast an explorer frame in the hopes

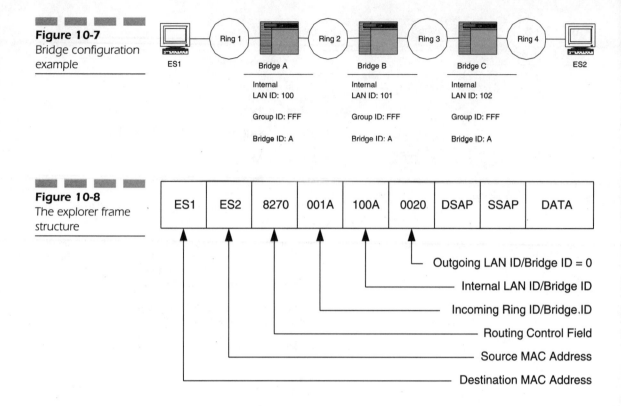

Figure 10-7
Bridge configuration example

Figure 10-8
The explorer frame structure

that it can discover the route. The destination, upon receiving the explorer frame, will respond with an SRF. The following sections track the explorer frame from ES1 to ES2 and then the response from ES2 back to ES1.

All Routes Broadcast (ARB) Frame

Let's say ES1 has a desire to transmit packets to ES2. ES1 checks the local segment for ES2 and finds that it is not there. After checking its routing table, ES1 must broadcast an explorer packet to try and locate the path to ES2. The following tasks are then performed:

1. ES1 broadcasts an ARE. It should be noted that the multicast bit is set in the source address to indicate that this frame has a RIF.

2. Bridge A receives the broadcast and performs the following RIF update operations (see Figure 10-8):

   a. It adds the incoming Ring ID/Bridge ID.

   b. It adds the Internal LAN ID/Bridge ID.

   c. It sets the outgoing Ring ID/Bridge ID. Since this is the first bridge, the Bridge ID here is set to 0.

3. The next bridge to receive the frame, Bridge B, performs the following RIF update procedure (see Figure 10-8a):

   a. It removes the last internal LAN ID.

   b. It replaces the bridge ID of 0 with its bridge ID.

   c. It adds its own internal LAN ID/Bridge ID to the RIF.

   d. It adds the outgoing Ring ID/Bridge ID. Again, the bridge ID is 0.

4. Bridge C follows the same process as Step 3 (see Figure 10-8b).

Specifically Routed Frame (SRF)

Once ES2 receives the explorer frame from ES1, it sends an SRF in response. As you can see in the previous figures, the RIF tracks the path through each bridge until the final LAN segment reaches the destination end station, ES2. Since the route is already present in the frame, all ES2

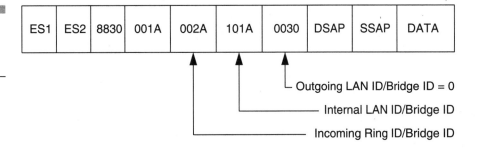

Figure 10-8a
The explorer frame structure as set by Bridge B

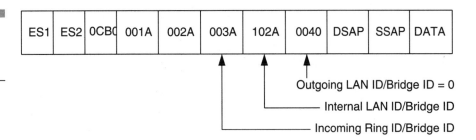

Figure 10-8b
The explorer frame structure as set by Bridge C

has to do is set the direction bit in the RIF as well as change the Route Type field to reflect an SRF:

1. ES2 responds to the ARE frame by sending an SRF back to ES1. Before it can do that, ES2 must change the Routing Type to SRF and set the Direction bit to reverse.

2. Bridge C receives the frame and makes some modifications to the RIF header:

   a. It changes the destination address to the Nortel group address of C000A2FFFFFx. The x is a placeholder for the bridge ID of the next Nortel bridge in the RIF.

   b. It then removes its internal LAN ID/Bridge ID and inserts the group ID before the last incoming ring and bridge ID listed in the RIF.

   c. It then copies the destination MAC address into the data portion of the frame.

   Recall the frame from Figure 10-8. This is the frame that will be received by bridge C. Figure 10-9 is the frame as sent by bridge C.

3. Bridge B receives this frame from ring 3 and, before it transmits it onto ring 2, it must do the following:

   a. Locate the bridge ID, which is at the end of the group address.

   b. Change this ID to the bridge ID of the next bridge in the RIF. Since all bridge IDs are the same, the frame is unmodified. So, bridge B transmits the same frame as that shown in Figure 10-9a.

4. Since bridge A is the last bridge to be traversed, it has to move the copied destination address from the data portion to its proper location.

Figure 10-9
The explorer frame structure as set by bridge C onto Ring 3

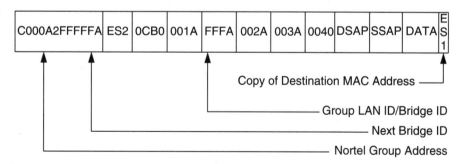

Figure 10-9a
The explore frame
structure as set by
bridge A onto ring 1

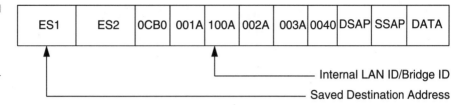

| ES1 | ES2 | 0CB0 | 001A | 100A | 002A | 003A | 0040 | DSAP | SSAP | DATA |

Internal LAN ID/Bridge ID

Saved Destination Address

It has to also remove the group ID and replace it with its Internal LAN ID/Bridge ID.

5. ES1 will store the route in its routing table for future communication with ES2.

Source Route Parameters Nortel routers and, subsequently, bridges provide a plethora of parameters that govern the operation of a source routing network. For most cases, and ours specifically, you can accept the default values or the parameters. The ones that are of most concern are the ones that played so heavily in the previous examples. These parameters can be found by accessing the global and interface parameters of the SRB. Both the global and interface parameters are displayed in the following section, but before we get to the available parameters, we must first enable the protocol on the bridge.

To enable a bridge to participate in a source routing network, you have to assign the protocol to each respective interface or port. The procedure is very much like the procedure for assigning transparent bridging to an interface from Chapter 9, "Transparent Bridging and the Spanning Tree Algorithm."

Assigning a Port for Source Routing Before enabling the source routing protocol on a bridge, you must first select an interface from the Configuration Manager main window:

1. From the Configuration Manager main window, select an available Token Ring port.

   You can add the source routing protocol to an interface that is currently running IP or IPX. Figure 10-10 shows an available Token Ring port on slot 2 of the BLN.

2. Add the Token Ring circuit.

Figure 10-10
The Configuration
Manager main
window

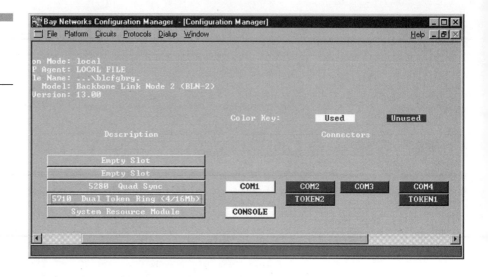

Figure 10-10
The Configuration
Manager main
window

Figure 10-11
Ring speed warning

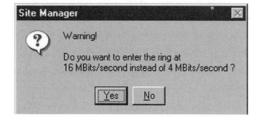

The "Add Circuit" window opens after selecting the available Token Ring port. Modify the name of the circuit if you want. Changing the name or adding a description is always helpful when troubleshooting a problem. Click **OK** to add the circuit.

3. Select the Source Routing protocol.

Once you click **OK** to add the Token Ring circuit, Configuration Manager prompts you with a warning (see Figure 10-11). It wants you to verify the ring speed for this circuit. Click Yes for 16 Mbps.

When the "Select Protocols" window opens, scroll down the list of available protocols to find the Source Routing protocol. Check its box and then click **OK** to add the Source Routing protocol to your circuit, as shown in Figure 10-12.

Figure 10-12
The Select Protocols
window

Figure 10-13
The Source Routing
Global Parameters
dialog box

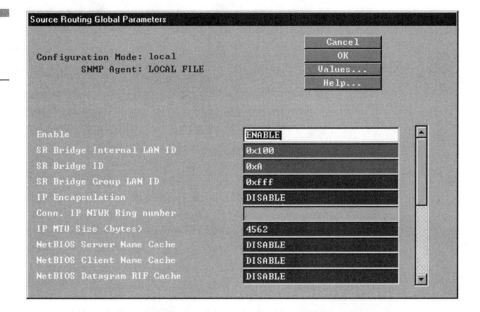

4. Set the global parameters for the bridge to match those of your
network.

The global parameters for source routing are the internal LAN ID, the
bridge ID, and the Nortel-specific group ID. After selecting the Source
Routing protocol, the "Source Routing Global Parameters" window
opens (see Figure 10-13).

5. Set the source routing interface parameters.

These parameters have not been discussed as much as the global parameters. Again, pretty much all of these parameters can be left at their default values. Figure 10-14 shows the "Edit *Source Routing* (SR) Interface" window. Table 10-3 describes the fields of the window.

Figure 10-14

The Edit Source Routing (SR) Interface window

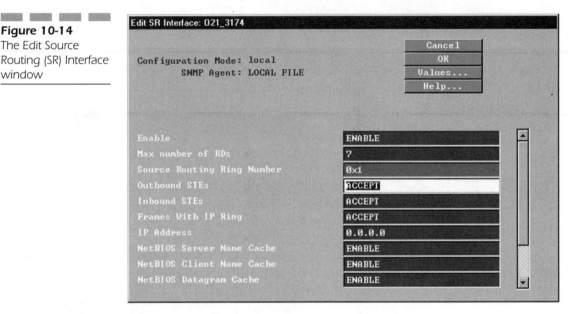

Table 10-3

Edit Source Routing (SR) Interface fields

Field	Description
Enable	This parameter enables or disables source routing.
Maximum number of RDs	This specifies the number of routing designators that can be in the RIF. Seven is the default and the maximum value.
Source Routing Ring Number	The ring number to which this circuit is attached
Outbound STEs	Specifies that the bridge should drop single-route explorer packets outgoing from this circuit
Inbound STEs	Specifies that the bridge should drop single-route explorer packets received on this circuit

6. Click **OK** to save the configuration.

If at any time you need to change the parameters, you can do so through the Protocols menu option. To access the global parameters, go to Protocols: Source Routing > Global. To access the interface parameters, go to Protocols: Source Routing > Interfaces.

End Station Support

In source routing, end stations must accept the responsibility of managing the routes between themselves and other devices. So, in order for a router to route across a source routing network, it must also act as an end station. This is necessary when a path between two devices includes a routing network. Figure 10-15 shows an example of when you would enable end station support.

This feature is configured for each individual routing protocol running on a per-circuit basis. Currently, Nortel supports this feature in IP, IPX, XNS, AppleTalk, and Vines. As ES1 transmits to ES2, the first IP router will add the necessary RIF information to the packet's MAC header and send the packet out onto the network where it is source routed toward its next hop. The peer router must then strip off the RIF information and route the packet accordingly.

To enable this feature, access the respective routing protocol's interface parameters. For the following example, we are connecting our network via

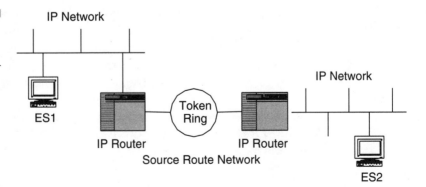

Figure 10-15

A source route end station example

Figure 10-16
Token Ring end
station support
through IP

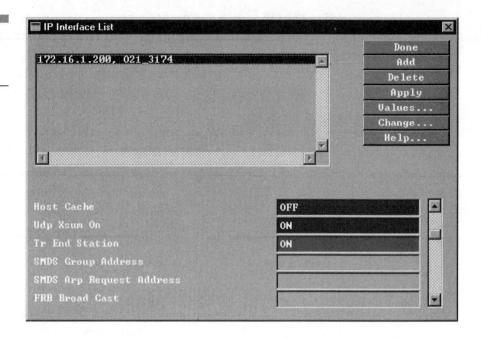

IP. Figure 10-16 shows the IP Interfaces window. In order to enable the end station support, you must enable the TR End Station field. You find this field by using the scroll bar on the right of the interface options.

SRB Traffic Filters

The source route filtering capabilities enable users to select predefined criteria that can be used to create a filter. It is important to note that the filters created will affect both explorer and specifically routed frames. However, one exception exists and that is a filter using the next ring as a criterion, because only routed frames have the next ring reference.

NOTE: *Filters are applied only after the packet has been processed. This means the router/bridge will first update the RIF before applying any of the filters.*

Table 10-4

Predefined
criterion for SRB
inbound filters

Criterion Name	Reference Field	Offset (bits)	Length (bits)
Next Ring	Next_Ring	0	12
Destination MAC Address	Header_Start	0	48
Source MAC Address	Header_Start	48	48
DSAP	Data_Link	0	8
SSAP	Data_Link	8	8
Destination NetBIOS Name	Data_Link	120	120
Source NetBIOS Name	Data_Link	240	120

The predefined filter criteria have been compiled for you in Table 10-4.

In order to use the Source or Destination NetBIOS Name filter, you must enter a NetBIOS name (in ASCII characters) using the first 15 characters of the name. If the NetBIOS name is less than 15, you must pad the filter in order to make the 15. To pad the name field, use the ASCII code for a space, 0x20.

User-Defined Criteria

If the predefined criteria do not suit your circumstance or filtering needs, you can create your own using a user-defined criterion. Three reference points can be used to create your specific filter:

■ *Header_Start*   This references the first bit in the destination MAC address.

■ *Data_Link*   This references the first bit in the DSAP field.

■ *Next_Ring*   This references the LAN ID field located in the RIF. If you recall, the RIF is divided between the control field and the routing designators. This reference point is at the beginning of the first routing designator.

From these reference points, you can specify the offset and the length of the bit pattern to filter. To complete a custom filter, the last thing to specify is the range of values that each incoming packet will be tested against.

SRB Actions

SRB has the same functions as all other inbound traffic filters: accept, drop, and log. Yet it also has two additional actions that can be used: direct IP explorers and forward to circuits. The direct IP explorers action enables you to direct explorer packets to a specific IP address. IP encapsulation must be configured in order to use this action. The forward to circuits enables you to specify that the frames that match the filter be forwarded to a number of circuits that you define.

SUMMARY

In this chapter, we continued our discussion of the bridging capabilities of Nortel routers. To begin with, we reviewed the operation of a transparent bridge so that we could compare it to the operation of a source routing bridge. We found that the source routing bridge is more tolerant when multiple paths exist between bridges and that they do not require any type of forwarding table.

Source routing networks were adopted by the IEEE 802.5 committee as the standard for connecting 802.5 devices. The way they work is by requiring end stations to manage all routes between themselves. The bridges only forward packets received by reading a special routing field called the *routing information field* (RIF). End stations populate the RIF by broadcasting explorer frames throughout the network. When the intended destination receives the frame, it responds with a directed frame called a *specific routed frame* (SRF) back to the source. The RIF contains the complete path from the source to destination. Source end stations cache this information in their local routing tables.

When configuring bridges to operate on a source routed network, you must become familiar with several terms that are extremely important if you want your bridges to function properly. Some of the more important terms covered were as follows:

- *Incoming ring number*   This is the source routing ring number for a LAN. It must be unique throughout the entire LAN.

- *Bridge ID*   This identifies the bridge or bridges in the source routing network. Nortel recommends giving all Nortel bridges the same bridge ID unless the bridges act in parallel.

- *Internal LAN ID*   This ID identifies an internal LAN or ring that each configured interface is connected to in order to forward source routed traffic.

Using Site Manager and an understanding of your own network, you configure your bridges using the previous parameters plus several others.

APPENDIX A

The information in this Appendix outlines the many processor and link modules for each of the discussed router families.

Access Node Products

Access Node (AN)

Order Number	Description
	Ethernet-Based
AE1001006	BayStack AN with one Ethernet interface, two synchronous interfaces, and 4 MB of DRAM memory (110/220 V)
AE1001007	BayStack AN with one Ethernet interface, two synchronous interfaces, and 8 MB of DRAM memory (110/220 V)
AE1001008	BayStack AN with one Ethernet interface, two synchronous interfaces and 16 MB of DRAM memory (110/220 V)
AE1001038	BayStack DC AN with one Ethernet interface, two synchronous interfaces, and 4 MB of DRAM memory
AE1001039	BayStack DC AN with one Ethernet interface, two synchronous interfaces, and 8 MB of DRAM memory
AE1001040	BayStack DC AN with one Ethernet interface, two synchronous interfaces, and 16 MB of DRAM memory
AE1001010	BayStack ANH with eight Ethernet hub ports (single segment), two synchronous interfaces, and 4 MB of DRAM memory (110/220 V)
AE1001011	BayStack ANH with eight Ethernet hub ports (single segment), two synchronous interfaces, and 8 MB of DRAM memory (110/220 V)
AE1001012	BayStack ANH with eight Ethernet hub ports (single segment), two synchronous interfaces, and 16 MB of DRAM memory (110/220 V)

Token Ring-Based

AE1101002	BayStack AN with one Token Ring interface, two synchronous interfaces, and 4 MB of DRAM memory (110/220 V)
AE1101003	BayStack AN with one Token Ring interface, two synchronous interfaces, and 8 MB of DRAM memory (110/220 V)
AE1101004	BayStack AN with one Token Ring interface, two synchronous interfaces, and 16 MB of DRAM memory (110/220 V)

Mixed LAN Media-Based

AE1101006	BayStack AN with one Ethernet interface, one Token Ring interface, two synchronous interfaces, and 4 MB of DRAM memory (110/220V)
AE1101007	BayStack AN with one Ethernet interface, one Token Ring interface, two synchronous interfaces, and DRAM memory (110/220 V)
AE1101008	BayStack AN with one Ethernet interface, one Token Ring interface, two Synchronous interfaces, and DRAM memory (110/220 V)

Access Node Hub (ANH)

Order Number	**Description**

Ethernet-Based

AE1001010	BayStack ANH with eight Ethernet hub ports (single segment), two synchronous interfaces, and 4 MB of DRAM memory (110/220 V)
AE1001011	BayStack ANH with Ethernet hub ports (single segment), two synchronous interfaces, and 8 MB of DRAM memory (110/220 V)
AE1001012	BayStack ANH with Ethernet hub ports (single segment), two synchronous interfaces, and 16 MB of DRAM memory (110/220 V)

AE1001042	BayStack DC ANH with Ethernet hub ports (single segment), two synchronous interfaces, and 4 MB of DRAM memory
AE1001043	BayStack DC ANH with Ethernet hub ports (single segment), two synchronous interfaces, and 8 MB of DRAM memory
AE1001044	BayStack DC ANH with Ethernet hub ports (single segment), two synchronous interfaces, and 16 MB of DRAM memory
AE1001014	BayStack ANH with 12 Ethernet hub ports (single segment), two synchronous interfaces, and 4 MB of DRAM memory (110/220 V)
AE1001015	BayStack ANH with 12 Ethernet hub ports (single segment), two synchronous interfaces, and 8 MB of DRAM memory (110/220 V)
AE1001016	BayStack ANH with 12 Ethernet hub ports (single segment), two synchronous interfaces, and 16 MB of DRAM memory (110/220 V)

Advance Remote Node (ARN)

Order Number	Description
CV1001002	BayStack ARN with one Ethernet interface and 4 MB of DRAM memory (110/220 V)
CV1001003	BayStack ARN with one Ethernet interface and 8 MB of DRAM memory (110/220 V)
CV1001004	BayStack ARN with one Ethernet interface and 16 MB of DRAM memory (110/220 V)
CV1001005	BayStack ARN with one Ethernet interface and 32 MB of DRAM memory (110/220 V)
	Token Ring-Based
CV1101002	Baystack ARN with one Token Ring interface and 4 MB of DRAM memory (110/220 V)
CV1101003	BayStack ARN with one Token Ring interface and 8 MB of DRAM memory (110/220 V)

CV1101004	Bay Stack ARN with one Token Ring interface and 16 MB of DRAM memory (110/220 V)
CV1101005	BayStack ARN with one Token Ring interface and 32 MB of DRAM memory (110/220 V)

WAN Adapter Modules

CV0004001	Serial adapter module
CV0004002	ISDN BRI S/T (without NT1) adapter module
CV0004003	ISDN BRI U (with NT1) adapter module
CV0004004	56/64 K DSU/CSU adapter module
CV0004005	V34 Modem adapter module (North America only)

Expansion Modules

CV0004011	Tri-serial expansion module
CV0004012	Ethernet expansion module
CV0004013	Ethernet plus Tri-serial expansion module
CV0004015	Token Ring plus Tri-serial expansion module

Access Stack Node (ASN)

Order Number	Description
AF0002?08	ASN2 base unit with 8 MB of DRAM, nonredundant power
AF0002?09	ASN2 base unit with 16 MB of DRAM, nonredundant power
AF0002?10	ASN2 base unit with 32 MB of DRAM, nonredundant power
AF0002?11	ASN2 base unit with 8 MB of DRAM, AC redundant power
AF0002?12	ASN2 base unit with 16 MB of DRAM, AC redundant power
AF0002?13	ASN2 base unit with 32 MB of DRAM, AC redundant power
AF0002A14	ASN2 base unit with 8 MB of DRAM, 48 V redundant power

AF0002A15	ASN2 base unit with 16 MB of DRAM, 48 V redundant power
AF0002A16	ASN2 base unit with 32 MB of DRAM, 48 V redundant power

Backbone Node Products

Backbone Link Node and Backbone Concentrator Node (BLN and BCN)

Order Number	Description
72000	BLN Base Unit that includes a four-slot BLN chassis with a single SRM-L, a single Flash memory card, and an integral 620 watt
71000	BLN-2 Redundant Base Unit that includes a four-slot BLN-2 chassis with a single SRM-L, a single Flash memory card, two 620-watt power supplies, and documentation. The system software includes a system software suite
71001	BLN-2 Redundant DC Base Unit that includes a four-slot BLN-2 chassis with a single SRM-L, a single Flash memory card, two 48 VDC power supplies, and documentation. The systems software includes the system software suite
71004	BLN-2 Non-Redundant Base Unit that includes a four-slot BLN-2 chassis with a single SRM-L, a single Flash EPROM card, a 620-watt power supply, and documentation. The system software includes a system software suite

Backbone Concentrator Node

73000	BCN Base Unit that includes a 13-slot BCN chassis with a single SRM-L, a single Flash memory card, a single 620-watt power supply, and documentation The system software includes the system software suite

System Hardware Redundancy Options

75010	Redundant System Resource Module (SRM-F)
75020	Additional BCN/BLN-2 AC power supply
75021	Additional BCN DC power supply
75006V###*	Redundant 4-MB Flash memory card

Interfaces

100BASE-T Fast Ethernet Interfaces

Order Number	Description
7404408/16/-32	Dual 100BASE-T with 8-MB/16-MB/32-MB FRE 040-2 processor module
AG2204001	Dual 100BASE-T with 16-MB FRE 060 processor module
AG2204002	Dual 100BASE-T with 32-MB FRE 060 processor module
AG1004005	Dual 100BASE-T with 64-MB FRE 060 processor module

Net Modules

34010	100BASE-T

Ethernet Interfaces

Order Number	Description
74005-08/-16/-32	Quad Ethernet with 8-MB/16-MB/32-MB FRE 040-2 processor module
74006-08/-16/-32	Quad Ethernet with 8-MB/16-MB/32-MB FRE 040-2 processor module and high-speed filters
74008-08/-16/-32	Dual Ethernet/dual synchronous with 8-MB/16-MB/32-MB FRE 040-2 processor module
74010-08/-16/-32	Dual Ethernet/dual synchronous with 8-MB/16-MB/32-MB FRE 040-2 processor module and high-speed filters

AG1004012	Dual Ethernet/dual synchronous with 16-MB FRE 060 processor module
AG1004013	Dual Ethernet/dual synchronous with 32-MB FRE 060 processor module and high-speed filters
AG1004010	Dual Ethernet/dual synchronous with 32-MB FRE 060 processor module
AG1004011	Dual Ethernet/dual synchronous with 32-MB FRE 060 processor module and high-speed filters
AG1004008	Dual Ethernet/dual synchronous with 64-MB FRE 060 processor module
AG1004009	Dual Ethernet/dual synchronous with 64-MB FRE 060 processor module and high-speed filters
AG1004001	Quad Ethernet with 16-MB FRE 060 processor module
AG1004002	Quad Ethernet with 16-MB FRE 060 processor module with high-speed filters
AG1004003	Quad Ethernet with 32-MB FRE 060 processor module
AG1004004	Quad Ethernet with 32-MB FRE 060 processor module with high-speed filters
AG1004006	Quad Ethernet with 64-MB FRE 060 processor module
AG1004007	Quad Ethernet with 64-MB FRE 060 processor module with high-speed filters
	AN/ANH Adapter Modules
AE004003	AN/12-port ANH second Ethernet interface
AE004007	Eight-port ANH second Ethernet interface
	ASN Net Module
34000	Dual Ethernet

Token Ring Interfaces

Order Number	Description
74002-08/-16/-32	Dual Token Ring with 8-MB/16-MB/32-MB FRE 040-2 processor module

74003-08/-16/-32	Single Token Ring/Dual Synchronous with 8-MB/16-MB/32-MB FRE 040-2 processor module
74021-08/-16/-32	Quad Token Ring with 8-MB/16-MB/32-MB FRE 040-2 processor module
AG1104011	Single Token Ring/dual synchronous with 16-MB FRE 060 processor module
AG1104009	Single Token Ring/dual synchronous with 32-MB FRE 060 processor module
AG1104007	Single Token Ring/dual synchronous with 64-MB FRE 060 processor module
AG1104010	Dual Token Ring with 16-MB FRE 060 processor module
AG1104008	Dual Token Ring with 32-MB FRE 060 processor module
AG1104005	Dual Token Ring with 64-MB FRE 060 processor module
AG1104003	Quad Token Ring with 16-MB FRE 060 processor module
AG1104004	Quad Token Ring with 32-MB FRE 060 processor module
AG1104006	Quad Token Ring with 64-MB FRE 060 processor module

Net Modules

34002	Dual Token Ring

FDDI Interfaces

Order Number	Description
74012-08/-16/-32	Multimode FDDI with 8-MB/16-MB/32-MB FRE 040-2 processor module and high-speed filters
74013-08/-16/-32	Single-mode FDDI with 8-MB/16-MB/32-MB FRE 040-2 processor module
74016-08/-16/-32	Single-mode FDDI with 8-MB/16-MB/32-MB FRE 040-2 processor module and high-speed filters

74014-08/-16/-32	Hybrid single-mode/multimode FDDI with 8-MB/16-MB/32-MB FRE 040-2 processor module
74017-08/-16/-32	Hybrid single-mode/multimode FDDI with 8-MB/16-MB/32-MB FRE 040-2 processor module and high-speed filters
74015-08/-16/-32	Hybrid multimode/single-mode FDDI with 8-MB/16-MB/32-MB FRE 040-2 processor module
74018-08/-16/-32	Hybrid multimode/single-mode FDDI with 8-MB/16-MB/32-MB FRE 040-2 processor module and high-speed filters
74036-16/-32	Multimode FDDI with 16-MB/32-MB FRE 060 processor module
74037-16/-32	Multimode FDDI with 16-MB/32-MB FRE 060 processor module and high-speed filters
AG1204001	Multimode FDDI with 64-MB FRE 060 processor module
AG1204002	Multimode FDDI with 64-MB FRE 060 processor module and high-speed filters
74038-16/-32	Single-mode FDDI with 16-MB/32-MB FRE 060 processor module
74039-16/-32	Single-mode FDDI with a 16-MB/32-MB FRE 060 processor module and high-speed filters
AG1204003	Single-mode FDDI with a 64-MB FRE 060 processor module
AG1204004	Single-mode FDDI with a 64-MB FRE 060 processor module and high-speed filters
74040-16/-32	Hybrid single-multimode FDDI with a 16-MB/32-MB FRE 060 processor module
74041-16/-32	Hybrid single-multimode FDDI with a 16-MB/32-MB FRE 060 processor module and high-speed filters
AG1204005	Hybrid single-mode/multimode FDDI with a 64-MB FRE 060 processor module
AG1204006	Hybrid single-mode/multimode FDDI with a 64-MB FRE 060 processor module and high-speed filters

74042-16/-32	Hybrid multimode/single-mode FDDI with a 16-MB/32-MB FRE processor module
74043-16/-32	Hybrid multimode/single-mode FDDI with a 16-MB/32-MB FRE 060 processor module and high-speed filters
AG1204007	Hybrid multimode/single-mode FDDI with a 16-MB/32-MB FRE 060 processor module
AG1204008	Hybrid multimode/single-mode FDDI with a 16-MB/32-MB FRE 060 processor module and high-speed filters

Net Modules

AF1204001	Dual attached multimode FDDI
AF1204002	Single-mode FDDI
AF1204003	Hybrid single-mode/multimode FDDI
AF1204004	Hybrid multimode/single-mode FDDI

ATM Interfaces

Order Number	Description
AG1304001	SONET/SDH multimode fiber with 8 MB of DRAM and 1 MB of SRAM
AG1304002	SONET/SDH multimode fiber with 16 MB of DRAM and 3 MB of SRAM
AG1304003	SONET/SDH multimode fiber with 32 MB of DRAM and 6 MB of SRAM
AG1304004	SONET/SDH single-mode fiber with 8 MB of DRAM and 1 MB of SRAM
AG1304005	SONET/SDH single-mode fiber with 16 MB of DRAM and 3 MB of SRAM
AG1304006	SONET/SDH single-mode fiber with 32 MB of DRAM and 6 MB of SRAM
AG1304007	DS3 with 8 MB of DRAM and 1 MB of ARE
AG1304008	DS3 with 16 MB of DRAM and 3 MB of ARE
AG1304009	DS3 with 32 MB of DRAM and 6 MB of ARE
AG1304010	E3 with 8 MB of DRAM and 1 MB ARE

AG1304011	E3 with 16 MB of DRAM and 3 MB of ARE
AG1304012	E3 with 32 MB of DRAM and 6 MB of ARE

Synchronous Interfaces

Order Number	Description
74000-08/-16/-32	Quad synchronous with 8 MB/16 MB/32 MB of FRE 040-2 processor module
74045-08/-16/-32	Octal synchronous with 8 MB/116 MB/32 MB of FRE 040-2 processor module
AG2104035	Quad synchronous with 16 MB of FRE 060 processor module
AG2104036	Quad synchronous with 32 MB of FRE 060 processor module
AG2104043	Quad synchronous with 64 MB of FRE 060 processor module
AG2104009	Octal synchronous with 16 MB of FRE 060 processor module
AG2104040	Octal synchronous with 64 MB of FRE 060 processor module
	ASN Net Modules
34001	Dual Synchronous
AF2101006	Quad Synchronous
	AN / ANH Adapter Modules (All Bay Stack AN and BayStack ANH routers come with two synchronous interfaces)
AE004000	AN/12-port ANH third synchronous interface
AE004005	Eight-port ANH third synchronous interface

HSSI Interfaces

Order Number	Description
74001-08/-16/-32	Single HSSI with 8 MB/16 MB/32 MB of FRE 040-2 processor module
74035-16/-32	Single HSSI with 16 MB/32 MB of FRE 060 processor module

AG2104039   Single HSSI with 64 MB of FRE 060 processor module

ISDN PRI, MCT1/MCE1 Interfaces

Order Number	Description
74019-08/-32	Single multichannel T1 with 8-MB/32-MB FRE 040-2 processor module
74020-08/-32	Dual multichannel T1 with 8-MB/32-MB FRE 040-2 processor module*
AG2104001	Quad multichannel T1 DB-15 with 8-MB FRE 040-2 processor module*
AG2104002	Quad multichannel T1 DB-15 with 32-MB FRE 040-2 processor module*
AG2104019	75-ohm single multichannel E-1 (MCE1-ll) for 75-ohm leased line with 8-MB FRE 040-2 processor module
AG2104020	75-ohm single multichannel E! (MCE1-ll) for 75-ohm leased line with 32-MB FRE 040-2 processor module
AG2104016	75-ohm dual multichannel E-1 (MCE1-ll) for a 75-ohm leased line with 8-MB FRE 040-2 processor module
AG2104017	75-ohm dual multichannel E1 (MCE1-ll) for 75-ohm RE 040-2 processor module
AG2104022	120-ohm single multichannel E1 (MCE1-ll) for 120-ohm ISDN PRI and 120-ohm leased line with 8-MB FRE 040-2 processor module*
AG210423	120-ohm single multichannel E1 (MCE1-ll) for an 120-ohm ISDN PRI and 120-ohm leased line with 32-MB FRE 040-2 processor module*
AG2104013	120-ohm dual multichannel E1 (MCE1-ll) for an 120-ohm ISDN PRI and 120-ohm leased line with 8-MB FRE 040-2 processor module*
AG210414	120-ohm dual multichannel E1 (MCE1-ll) for 120-ohm ISDN PRI and 120-ohm leased line with 32-MB FRE 040-2 processor module*

74031-16/-32	Single multichannel T1 with 16-MB/32-MB FRE 060 processor module*
AG2104048	Single multichannel T1 with 64-MB FRE 060 processor module
74032-16/-32	Dual multichannel T1 with 16-MB/32-MB FRE 060 processor module*
AG2104049	Dual multichannel T1 and 64-MB FE 060 processor module*
AG2104003	Quad multichannel T1 DB-15 with 32-MB FE 060 processor module*
AG2104004	Quad multichannel T1 DB-15 with 64-MB FRE 060 processor module*
AG2104021	75-ohm single multichannel E1 (MCE1-ll) for 75-ohm leased line with 32-MB FE 060 processor module
AG2104047	75-ohm single multichannel E1 (MCE-ll) for 75-ohm leased line with 64-MB FRE 060 processor module
AG2104018	75-ohm dual multichannel E1 (MCE-11) for 75-ohm leased line with 32-MB FRE 060 processor module
AG2104024	120-ohm single multichannel E1 (MCE1-ll) for 120-ohm ISDN PRI and 120-ohm leased line with 32-MB FRE 060 processor module*
AG2104045	120-ohm single multichannel E1 (MCE-ll) for 120-ohm ISDN PRI and 120-ohm leased line with 64-MB FRE 060 processor module*
AG2104015	120-ohm dual multichannel E1 (MCE-ll) for 120-ohm ISDN PRI and 120-ohm lease line with 32-MB FRE 060 processor module*
AG2104044	120-ohm dual multichannel E1 (MCE-11) for 120-ohm ISDN PRO and 120-ohm leased line with 64-MB FRE 060 processor module*
AG2104054	Quad port multichannel T1 and DSOA (QMCT1 and DSOA) DB15 FRE2-040 32 MB ILI
AG2104055	Quad port multichannel T1 with DSOA (QMCT1 and DSOA) DB15 FRE2-060 32 MB ILI

AG2104056   Quad port multichannel T1 with DSOA (QMCT1 and DSOA) DB15 FRE2-060 64 MB ILI

Net Modules

AF2104013   Dual MCT1*

AF2104004   Single MCE1*

APPENDIX B

Event Manager

One of the ways in which you can monitor your router's health and functionality is by regularly viewing its event messages. A router uses event messages to alert you to problems, such as a downed interfacet, the misconfiguration of an entity, and/or when unauthorized access is attempted. Not all messages need be bad. Some messages are presented just for information.

All event messages are collected by the router and stored in a file called the event log. This file can be in memory or on the local router's flash card. You could use the TFTP protocol to transfer the file to your local Site Manager workstation. Regardless, you view the messages in the log by using the Events Manager. The Events Manager retrieves the event log for viewing through your Site Manager workstation. This view is not dynamic. Although the router continually logs events, when you retrieve them for display you are only retrieving a single instance of the log. Figure B-1 shows

Figure B-1
Event Manager View window

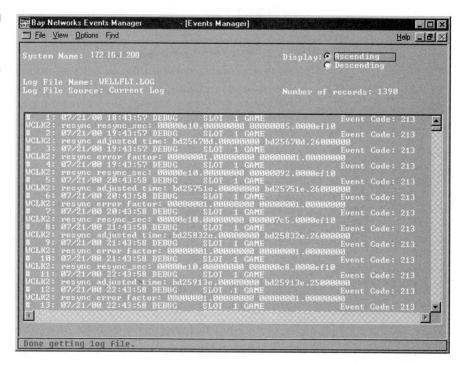

the Event Manager View window. It is accessed from Site Manager by selecting Tools: Event Manager . . . or by clicking the **Events** button.

The Event Manager View window is divided into several parts. The menu bar is located at the top and contains the options—file, view, options, and find. Directly under the menu bar is an information section that relates information about the log, the router for which you are connected, and the number of events in the display or message window. The information section also allows you to change the current ordered state of the display, whether the messages are displayed from oldest to most recent (ascending) or from the most recent to the very oldest (descending).

The display or message window is the largest section and it is located right in the middle of the View window. This is where the message details are displayed. At the bottom of the View window is the status bar. Status messages are displayed in red and they can relate to successes as well as any failures when using the Event Manager.

The event logs can be classified under three types depending upon where they reside. The three types of event logs are as follows:

■ *Current Log* This is the event log that is currently in the router's memory. To view the details of this log, it must be retrieved from the router's memory.

■ *Remote Log* A remote log is one that has been previously saved on a router's flash memory card.

■ *Local Log* A local log is similar to the remote log in that it resides on a physical medium. But, instead of the router's flash storage, it is stored on the local Site Manager workstation. Actually, it does not really matter where the local log resides. It can still be "loaded" using the Event Manager.

Each of these logs can be viewed using the File menu option. Only one log from one router can be viewed at one time. When the event messages populate the message view they are displayed in columnar format. Table B-1 details each of the events messages columns as they can be viewed from left-to-right in the message view window.

Retrieving the Log Files

To retrieve a router's event log you must first make a connection to the router. This is done by selecting the router in the Well-known Connections

Table B-1

*Details of event
messages*

Column	Description
Event Number	The event's place in the event log
Timestamp	The date and time the event occurred
Severity	The severity level of an event—fault, warning, info, trace, & debug
Slot	The slot where the entity that generated the event message is being hosted
Entity	The name of the entity that generated the event. Some of the names are abbreviated.
Event Code	The event's code
Description	A textual description of the event

list in Site Manager. Once the router has been selected, either click on the menu options Tools: Event Manager . . . or click the **Event** button. This will bring up the View window as seen in Figure B-1. To retrieve the log files follow this procedure:

1. Retrieve current log file.

   Select File: Get Current Log File to retrieve the event log from router memory.

2. Load a remote log file.

   Select File: Get Remote Log File. This opens the "Load Remote Log File" window as seen in Figure B-2.

   Select the logfile from the list and click **Open**.

3. Load a local log file.

   Select File: Load Local Log File. This opens the "Load Local Log" window as seen in Figure B-3.

Filter Options

From the View menu on the menu bar, you can access the filter parameters to narrow down the messages. Focusing on specific types of event can only

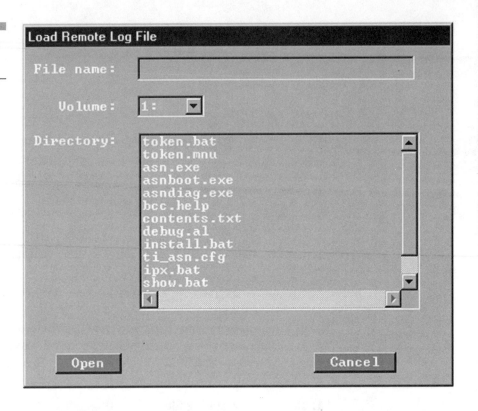

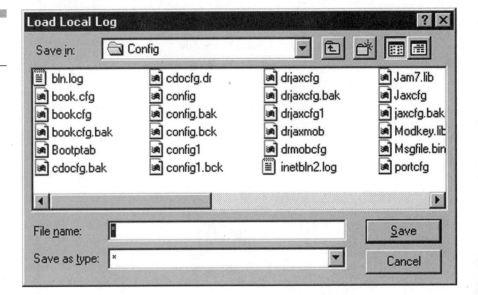

Figure B-4

Filtering parameters
window

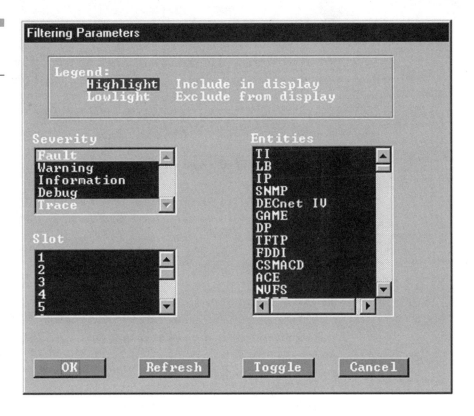

Figure B-4

Filtering parameters
window

help you determine any cause of problem. Figure B-4 shows the "Filter Parameters" window.

This window allows you to filter the event messages on the severity type, which slot the event took place, and the type of entities. The entities are the protocols and services provided by the router. Select your filter preference then click **Refresh** to enact. When you are done click **OK** to exit.

Saving the Event Log

To save the event log to the local disk select File: Save Output To Disk. This will save an ASCII version of the event log on your local Site Manager workstation.

Refresh Display

When you retrieve the current event log from router memory you are pulling a single instance of events. Viewing the event log through the Event Manager does not display in real time. So, in order to update you must occasionally refresh your screen. To refresh the display select View: Refresh Display.

Clearing the View

To start over with a blank message view window, you will need to clear the window. To clear the window select View: Clear Window.

Searching

The event log can contain a large amount of messages and it can be tedious to sort through an extremely long log. Fortunately, the Event Manager has a search facility to help us locate any event for which we may be looking. To access the search facility, select Find from the menu bar. Select Find once more (or pressing F2) to open the "Find Text Pattern" window as shown in Figure B-5.

Enter the pattern of text to search for and click **Find**.

Clearing the Event Log

If you are rolling out a new config for a router, you may want to monitor the event messages just to be sure that the changes have no adverse affect.

Figure B-5
Find text pattern
window

Since the event log can be extremely large, you might want to clear it so that viewing it for problems will no be hard. Clearing the event log is done through the Site Manager main window. Select Administration: Clear Event Log . . . . Click **OK** at the confirmation prompt to clear the event log.

Trap Monitor

Similar to event messages, trap messages allow for the management of Nortel routers and the assurance of their functionality. The main distinction between the two is that trap messages are displayed in real-time. Actually, the differences are really just presentational. Trap messages are event messages in succinct form. As the router generates an event message, it creates a detailed message that is saved to the event log. When the router is configured to also generate traps, you are just telling it to send the shorten form of the event message. Of course, the trap is sent to a SNMP manager instead of the router's memory. To view these messages you use the Trap Monitor.

Trap Monitor is a tool that comes with Site Manager. Its main purpose is to display the unsolicited traps sent by a router or routers. After initialization of a stored `trap history file`, the Trap Monitor displays the trap messages in real-time. SNMP traps are categorized as either generic or enterprise specific, as defined in RFC 1157. Generic traps are general traps of which there are six.

- coldStart
- warmStart
- linkUp
- linkDown
- authenticationFailure
- egpNeighborloss

Nortel identifies enterprise traps as being any event that is sent to the event log. These traps are identified by an entity and event code.

Configuring Trap Messages

To configure a router's SNMP agent to send traps to an SNMP manager, you must first define the SNMP manager in the router's configuration. Once defined you can then specify the types of traps to send. There are three trap criteria which instruct the router to which traps to send.

■ *Category*   This identifies the type of traps, generic or specific. You can also specify that all or no traps are to be sent.

■ *Protocol Entity*   This identifies specific protocol entity events to be sent. This criterion must be accompanied with the Event Severity criterion.

■ *Event Severity*   This specifies the severity of a particular event, fault, warning, trace, information, and or debug. This criterion must accompany the Protocol Entity criterion.

There is one more criterion, if you will, that can be specified—the trap exception. A trap exception is a particular entity and event code that is sent (or not) regardless of defined criteria.

Adding an SNMP Manager   From the Configuration Manager main window:

1. Select Protocols: IP > SNMP > Communities . . .

   This opens the "SNMP Communities" window with the default string "public" highlighted. This is shown in Figure B-6.

2. Open "Manager List" window.

   Select Community: Managers . . . to open the "Manager List" window. The "Manager List" window is shown in Figure B-7.

3. Add the address of the Manager that will receive the traps.

   Select Manager: Add Managers . . . from the menu bar. This will open the "Add SNMP Manager" dialog box where you can input the IP address of the SNMP Manager. Click **OK** to enter the address into the Manager list.

4. Define the Trap Category for the Manager

   You need to specify whether this Manager will receive generic, specific, or all trap messages. To do this you need to "edit " the Manager. Select the Manager's entry from the list then select Manager: Edit Manager . . . from the menu bar. Figure B-8 shows the widow where you can edit the Manager's parameters.

   The Trap Port lets you define an alternate port for which the Manager can receive traps. IP port 162 is the default port for SNMP traps. The Trap types are All, Generic, Specific, None.

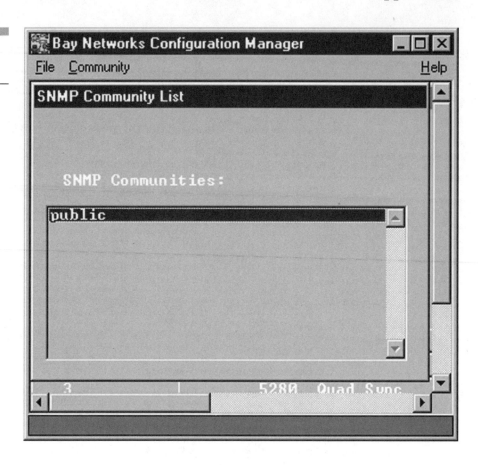

5. Click **OK** to save.

6. Exit both the Manager and Community windows.

   Select File: Exit twice to exit both windows and return to the Configuration Manager main window.

7. Save the configuration file.

Specify Trap Criteria   Once you define the Manager to receive traps, you then can specify the type of traps that will be sent. So, from the Configuration Manager main window:

Figure B-7
SNMP Managers
window

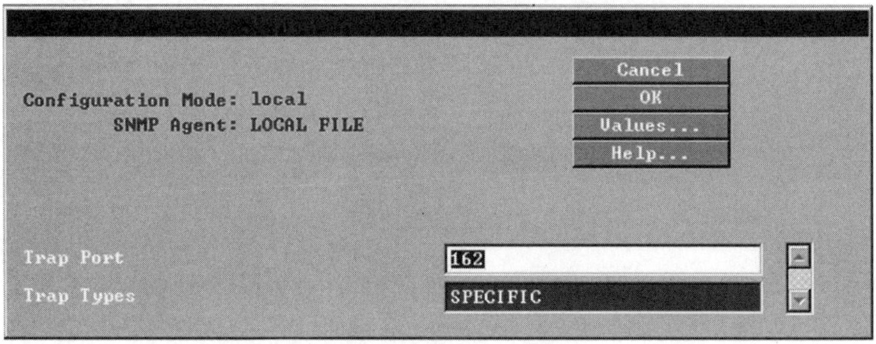

Figure B-8
Manager parameters
window

1. Open the Trap Configuration screen.

   From the main menu, select Protocols: IP > SNMP > Trap Configuration > Interfaces . . . . The configuration screen where you assign the protocol entity and severity traps, opens. This screen is shown in Figure B-9.

   This window is subdivided into "Available Entities" and "Current Entities." Select the protocol entities for which you wish to send traps, from the "Available Entities" list, and move them to the "Current Entities" list by clicking the **Update** button. To remove them from the list, select them and click **Remove**.

   The protocol entities can not be made current unless a severity has also been chosen. The five severity options for each particular protocol entity is located above the buttons near the bottom of the window. Select a check corresponding to a either the fault, warning, debug, trace, and/or info severity.

   The last option to set is the slot number. Since each processor card in a slot generates a separate event log, you must specify the slot for which the protocol entity events are to monitored.

Figure B-9
Trap Configuration window

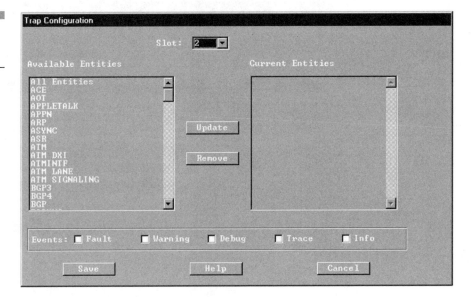

2. Click **Save** to return to the Configuration Manager main window.

Trap Exceptions:

Suppose you are interested in a specific event from a particular protocol. You can configure the router's SNMP agent to always or never send the trap by configuring a trap exception.

3. Access the Trap Exceptions List.

From the Configuration Manager main window, select Protocols: IP > SNMP > Trap Configuration > Exceptions . . . . This will open the exceptions list window shown in Figure B-10.

4. Add Exception information.

Click **Add** to open the "Add Trap" dialog. Enter the protocol entity and event code for the specific trap. These codes are documented in the `Event Messages for Routers` document located on the Nortel's web site. Figure B-11 shows the "Add Trap" window.

Specify, also, whether or not you want to send this trap.

5. Click **OK** to return to the exception list.

6. Click on **Apply**.

7. Click on **Done** to return to the Configuration Manager main window.

8. Save your configuration changes.

Figure B-10
Trap Exception List

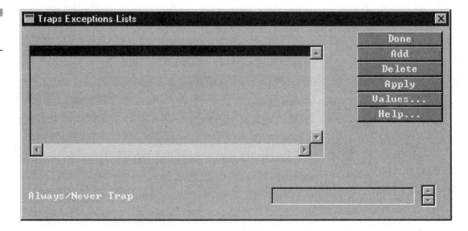

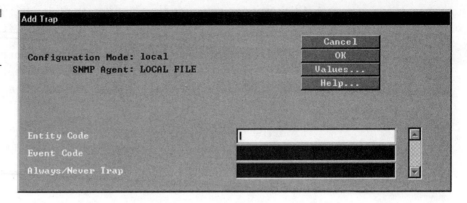

Viewing Trap Messages

In order to view the trap messages sent from the router, you need to run the Trap Monitor. Trap Monitor is accessed from within Site Manager and it dynamically displays traps sent to it from any SNMP agent on the network. The Site Manager workstation saves traps in a history file whether or not you are currently viewing them. To start the monitor you select Tools: Trap Monitor from the Site Manager menu bar or click the **Traps** button. Figure B-12 shows the Trap Monitor window.

As you can see the window has a big viewing area for which to view the incoming trap messages. The traps are displayed in columnar format with the following column meanings.

- *Timestamp* This is the date and time the Site Manager workstation received the message.
- *Node* This is the IP address of the router that generated the message.
- *Slot* This refers to the slot that is hosting the entity the generated the event.
- *Entity* This is the abbreviated name of the entity the generated the message.
- *Severity* This is the single letter designation of the severity, (F)ault, (W)arning, (I)nformation, (D)ebug, and (T)race.
- *Description* A textual description of the message

Figure B-12
Trap Monitor

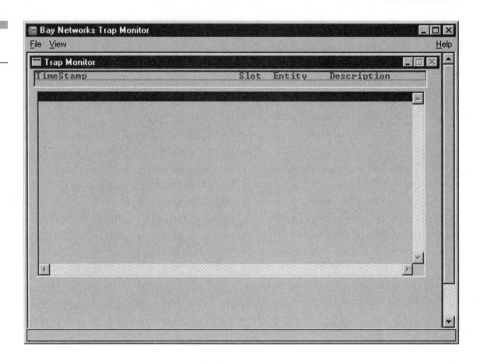

Once you start the Trap Monitor, you need to load the history file. This present the traps that were cleared from the previous display.

`Load History File`

Select File: Load History File from the Trap Monitor menu.

After you have loaded the trap messages, you can filter the messages you view in the viewing area. Filtering in no way interferes with what traps are sent by the router's SNMP agents. You can filter trap messages on either the severity or IP address. Figure B-13 shows the severity filter window.

Choose one or more of the severity types. Figure B-14 shows the IP address filter window. You can specify a full IP address of a partial one. The address 0.0.0.0 means all IP addresses. The address 255.255.255.255 is just a placeholder. It has no meaning in this context.

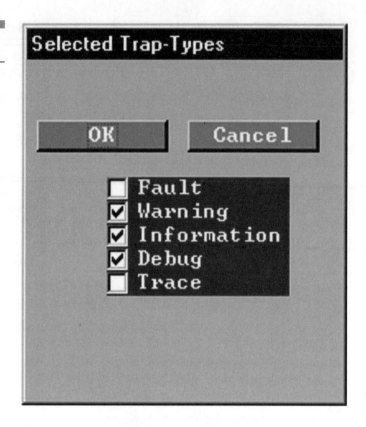

Saving Traps

The Trap Monitor allows you to save the trap messages currently displayed to an ASCII file. You can later view or print this file.

Select File: Save Traps

This will open the "Save Traps to File" dialog box. Enter the path and file name for which you wish to save messages.

Clearing the Trap Window

The Trap window can be cleared by selecting View: Clear Window. This will erase all traps in the current viewing window. But, because the Trap Monitor constantly updates this window, new message appear right away.

Figure B-14
Address Filters

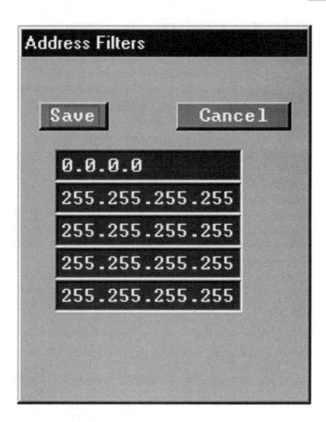

Figure B-14
Address Filters

Clearing the History file

The history file can only store a certain number of messages before the old ones begin to be overwritten. You can clear the history file in order to start a new list of traps. To clear the history file, select File: Clear History File. Again, the history file is immediately written to because of its dynamic monitoring.

Image Builder

This tool is a special customizing tool for the router software image. Now, you may recall that the router software image is made up of a group of executable files that contain a version of the router software. What this means is that the router software image contains various components which can be executed by the router hardware and other software components. These executables are the protocol entities and for the most part end in `.exe` except for ATM protocol entities, which end in `.ppc`. The image type depends upon the router. Table B-2 shows the relationship between the router and the type of software image for which it runs.

To modify any part of these images you must be able to use the Image Builder tool. This tool comes with Site Manager and it allows you to perform the following:

- Remove protocols that will not be used
- Add protocols that were previously removed
- View the image components and their information
- Convert the image to work with a different router.

By letting you modify the components that comprise a router's software image you can create a customized image that suits you and your company's requirements. The Image Builder tool is shown in Figure B-15. It is accessed by selecting Tools: Image Builder . . . .

Table B-2

Relationship between router and type of software image

Router	Software Image
AN	an.exe
ANH	an.exe
ARN	arn.exe
ASN	asn.exe
BLN	bn.exe
BCN	bn.exe

Figure B-15

Image Builder main
window

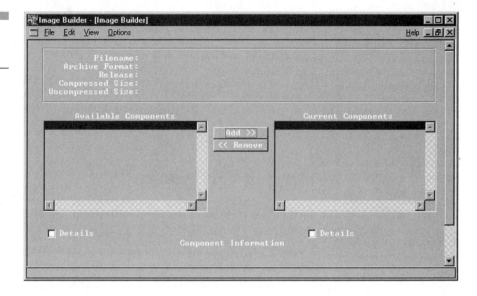

Anatomy of the Image Builder Window

The main window for the Image Builder tool has three distinct parts (not counting the menu bar). Information about the router software image is located at the top part of the window. It contains information such as:

- Filename
- Archive format
- Version
- Compressed and uncompressed size

The Available Components list is located along side of the Current Components list. The Available Components list specifies all the software components that comprise the router software image. The Current Components list is merely a subset of the router software image. The components listed in these windows are the respective groups of executable files. They are grouped under a common entity or service. Under each list is a "Details" checkbox. Placing a check in this box expands all the components in the list, thereby displaying all the executables that comprise each component. The bottom of the window is the Component Information box. This area specifies the information for a selected component.

Loading the Image File

In order to load a router software image file into the Image Builder tool, you must have first purchase the image. To load it into the tool, you select File: Open. The image will be copied to the `builder.dir` folder then loaded into the Image Builder tool. As you can see in Figure B-16, the image file components get placed into the Current Components list.

Modifying the Image

One of the nice things about the router's image is that you can remove pieces that are not needed. This is a great boon if you are running low on flash memory space. Using Image Builder you can remove the protocols and services that are not needed in your environment. You will not be allowed to remove essential components and executables. So, there is no need to worry about creating an incomplete image. The router's baseline software cannot be removed from the Current Components list because it is an

Figure B-16
Image Builder with loaded image

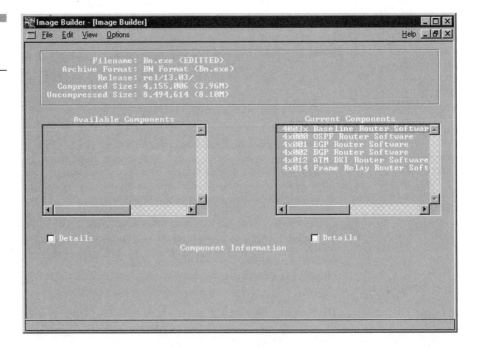

essential part of the image. If you select "Details" you can remove some nonessential executables from the baseline component.

Removing Components and Executables   To remove a component

1. Select the component and click the << Remove button that appears, see Figure B-17.

2. Click << Remove to remove the component from current to available.

   Once you remove the component from the Current list it now becomes available.

3. Remove an executable.

   The executables can be removed by checking the "Details" box below one of the list boxes. Under Current Components, check the "Details" box. This will expand the component to show the executables that lie within. If the executable is not deemed essential, then the

Figure B-17
Image Builder with remove button

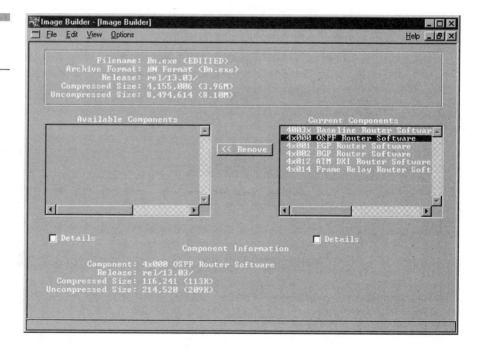

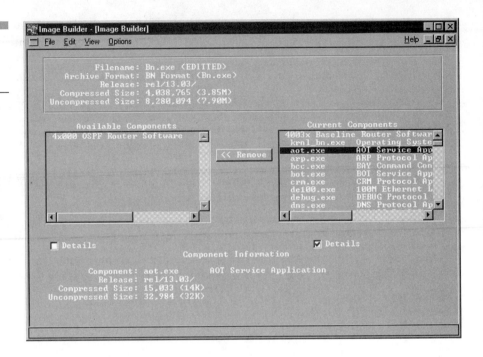

<<Remove button will display. Figure B-18 shows the Image Builder window with the current components expanded.

Remove all unnecessary components and executables.

4. Save Router Image

The modified image can now be saved. Select File: Save. This will save the image to your current directory. To save the file in another directory and/or with another name, use the File: Save As option.

5. Exit Image Builder.

Converting an Image for Other Router Types

If you created an image that you wanted to run on different types of routers, all you would need to do is convert it for the different routers in your network.

NOTE: *You can only convert to a router image that has already been run in the Image Builder tool.*

Convert bn.exe image for use on an ASN router.

1. Load bn.exe

   Load the bn.exe image file into the Image Builder tool.

2. Convert file for ASN use

   In order to convert for use with an ASN you must first have run the asn.exe image through the Image Builder.

   Select File: Change Format > <router_format>

   The router_format is the format for which you wish to convert. If the image for which you wish to convert to is dimmed, then you need to load that image into Image Builder first.

3. Save the modified image.

Converting an Image for Other Software Versions

In a likewise manner to the router type conversion, you can change the version of the software image. The same rule applies: you must first load the software version into Image Builder before you convert any software to that version.

Convert bn.exe version 13.03 to 12.02

1. Load bn.exe version 13.03 into the Image Builder tool.

2. Select version from list.

   Select File: Change Release > <image_version>

   The image_version is the version to which you wish to convert the image.

3. Save modified image.

Saving the Contents of the Current Components list

To keep track of a created image's components, you can save the component list to an ASCII file. The file gets saved to the Site Manager workstation with the name CONTENTS.TXT. This is a feature that gets turned on via an Options menu item. Select Options: Generate CONTENTS.TXT when saving. This will save the ASCII contents of the image along with the binary image to the local drive. The CONTENTS.TXT is saved to the same directory as the image.

NOTE: *No confirmation will display when the contents file is saved.*

GLOSSARY

10Base-T A variant of Ethernet (IEEE 802.3) that enables stations to be attached via twisted pair (telephone) cable. *See* Ethernet, twisted pair, 802.x.

802.1 The committee responsible for issues common across all 802 LANs.

802.2 This committee defines the LLC.

802.3 This committee deals with issues concerning the *Carrier Sense Multiple Access with Collision Detection* (CSMA/CD) LAN.

802.4 This committee deals with Token Bus.

802.5 This committee deals with four-Mbps and 16-Mbps Token Ring.

802.x The set of IEEE standards for the definition of LAN protocols.

abstract syntax A description of a data structure that is independent of machine-oriented structures and encoding. *See* transfer syntax.

ACK Acknowledgement. A type of message sent to indicate that a block of data arrived at its destination without error. A negative acknowledgement is called a NAK.

address mask A bit mask used to select bits from an Internet address for subnet addressing. The mask is 32 bits long and selects the network portion of the Internet address and one or more bits of the local portion. Sometimes called subnet mask.

address resolution A means for mapping Network Layer addresses onto media-specific addresses. *See* ARP.

an.exe Router software that contains the executables that are used to boot the AN or ANH routers.

anonymous FTP Enables a user to retrieve documents, files, programs, and other archived data from anywhere in the Internet without having to establish a user ID and password. By using the special user ID of anonymous, the network user will bypass local security checks and will have access to publicly accessible files on the remote system. *See* archive site and FTP.

ANSI American National Standards Institute. The U.S. standardization body. ANSI is a member of the *International Organization for Standardization* (ISO).

API   Application Program Interface. A set of calling conventions defining how a service is invoked through a software package.

APPC   Advanced Program-to-Program Communications. Part of IBM's *Systems Network Architecture* (SNA).

AppleTalk   A networking protocol developed by Apple Computer for communication between Apple Computer products and other computers. This protocol is independent of what network it is layered on. Current implementations exist for LocalTalk (235 Kbps) and EtherTalk (10 Mbps).

Application layer   The topmost layer in the OSI Reference Model providing such communication services as email and file transfers.

Archie   A system that provides lists of anonymous FTP archives. Archie is one of the many neat new applications on the Internet. *See* Gopher, Prospero, WAIS, and *World Wide Web* (WWW).

archive site   A machine that provides access to a collection of files across the Internet. An anonymous FTP archive site, for example, provides access to this material via the FTP protocol. *See* anonymous FTP, archie, Gopher, Prospero, WAIS.

ARP   Address Resolution Protocol. The Internet protocol used to dynamically map Internet addresses to physical (hardware) addresses on LANs. Limited to networks that support hardware broadcasts. *See* RARP.

ARPA   Advanced Research Projects Agency. Now called DARPA, the U.S. government agency that funded the ARPANET.

ARPANET   A packet switched network developed in the early 1970s. The grandfather of today's Internet, ARPANET was decommissioned in June 1990.

ASCII   American Standard Code for Information Interchange. A standard character-to-number encoding widely used in the computer industry. *See* EBCDIC.

ASN.1   Abstract Syntax Notation One. The OSI language for describing abstract syntax. *See* BER.

asn.exe   Router software image that contains the executable files used to boot ASN routers.

ATM   Asynchronous Transfer Mode. The SONET standard for a packet switching technique that uses packets (cells) of fixed length. Also referred to as BISDN and Cell Relay.

attribute Properties or functional aspects of a configurable MIB object.

autonomous system Internet (TCP/IP) terminology for a collection of gateways (routers) that fall under one administrative entity and cooperate using a common Interior Gateway Protocol (IGP). *See* subnetwork.

backbone The primary connectivity mechanism of a hierarchical distributed system. All systems that have connectivity to an intermediate system on the backbone are assured of connectivity to each other. This does not, however, prevent systems from setting up private arrangements with each other to bypass the backbone for reasons of cost, performance, or security. *See* core gateway.

baseband Characteristic of any network technology that uses a single-carrier frequency and requires all stations attached to the network to participate in every transmission. *See* broadband.

BER Basic Encoding Rules. Standard rules for encoding data units described in ASN.1. Sometimes incorrectly lumped under the term ASN.1, which properly refers only to the abstract syntax description language, not the encoding technique.

big-endian A format for storage or transmission of binary data in which the most significant bit (or byte) comes first. The reverse convention is called little-endian.

bn.exe Router software that contains the executables that are used to boot the BLN or BCN routers.

BOC Bell Operating Company. More commonly referred to as *Regional Bell Operating Company* (RBOC). The local telephone company in each of the seven U.S. regions.

BootP Boot Protocol. This enables an Internet node to discover certain startup information such as its IP address.

bridge A device that connects two or more physical networks and forwards packets between them. Bridges can usually be made to filter packets, that is, to forward only certain traffic. Related devices are repeaters that simply forward electrical signals from one cable to another, and full-fledged routers that make routing decisions based on several criteria. In OSI terminology, a bridge is the Data Link Layer. *See* repeater, router, intermediate system.

broadband   Characteristic of any network that multiplexes multiple, independent network carriers onto a single cable. This is usually done using frequency division multiplexing. Broadband technology enables several networks to coexist on one single cable. Traffic from one network does not interfere with traffic from another since the "conversations" happen on different frequencies in the "ether," rather like the commercial radio system. *See* baseband.

broadcast   A packet delivery system where a copy of a given packet is given to all hosts attached to the network. An example would be Ethernet. *See* multicast.

broadcast storm   A condition that can occur on broadcast-type networks such as Ethernet. This can happen for a number of reasons ranging from a hardware malfunction to configuration errors and bandwidth saturation.

caching   A form of replication in which information learned during a previous transaction is used to process later transactions.

CCITT   International Consultative Committee for Telegraphy and Telephony. A unit of the *International Telecommunications Union* (ITU) of the United Nations. An organization with representatives from the PTTs of the world. CCITT produces technical standards, known as Recommendations, for all internationally controlled aspects of analog and digital communications. *See* X Recommendations, OSI.

Cell Relay   *See* ATM.

CIDR   Classless Inter-Domain Routing. A method for using the existing 32-bit Internet Address Space more efficiently.

circuit   A communication path between two hosts over a packet-switched, cell-switched, dial, or leased-line connection.

circuit switching   A communications paradigm in which a dedicated communication path is established between two hosts and on which all packets travel. The telephone system is an example of a circuit switched network. *See* connection-oriented, connectionless, packet switching.

client   A computer system or process that requests a service of another computer system or process. A workstation requesting the contents of a file from a file server is a client of the file server. *See* client-server model, server.

client-server model   A common way to describe network services and the model user processes (programs) of those services. Examples include the nameserver/nameresolver paradigm of the DNS and fileserver/file-client relationships such as NFS and diskless hosts.

CMIP   Common Management Information Protocol. The OSI network management protocol.

CMOT   CMIP Over TCP. An effort to use the OSI network management protocol to manage TCP/IP networks. CMOT is historical, not implemented.

connectionless   The model of interconnection in which communication takes place without first establishing a connection. Sometimes (imprecisely) called a datagram. Examples include Internet IP and OSI CLNP, UDP, and ordinary postcards.

connection-oriented   The model of interconnection in which communication proceeds through three well-defined phases: connection establishment, data transfer, connection release. Examples include X.25, Internet TCP and OSI TP4, and ordinary telephone calls.

connector   The physical and electrical means to interconnect an interface module in a network device to a physical medium.

core gateway   Historically, one of a set of gateways (routers) operated by the Internet Network Operations Center at BBN. The core gateway system forms a central part of Internet routing in that all groups must advertise paths to their networks from a core gateway using the *Exterior Gateway Protocol* (EGP). *See* EGP, backbone.

CSMA/CD   Carrier Sense Multiple Access with Collision Detection. The access method used by LAN technologies such as Ethernet.

DARPA   Defense Advanced Research Projects Agency. The U.S. government agency that funded the ARPANET.

Data Link layer   The OSI layer that is responsible for a data transfer across a single physical connection, or a series of bridged connections, between two network entities.

DCA   Defense Communications Agency. The government agency responsible for the *Defense Data Network* (DDN).

DCE   Distributed Computing Environment. An architecture of standard programming interfaces, conventions, and server functionalities (naming, distributed file systems, and remote procedure calls) for distributing applications transparently across networks of heterogeneous computers. It is promoted and controlled by the *Open Software Foundation* (OSF), a vendor consortium. *See* ONC.

DDN Defense Data Network. Comprises the MILNET and several other DoD networks.

DECnet Digital Equipment Corporation's proprietary network architecture.

Direct Netboot The procedure used by Nortel routers for receiving router image and configuration files from a TFTP server.

DISA Defense Information Systems Agency, which is the new name for DCA. *See* DCA.

DNS Domain Name System. The distributed name/address mechanism used on the Internet.

domain On the Internet, a part of a naming hierarchy. Syntactically, an Internet domain name consists of a sequence of names (labels) separated by periods (dots), such as tundra.mpk.ca.us. In OSI, domain is generally used as an administrative partition of a complex distributed system, as in MHS *Private Management Domain* (PRMD), and *Directory Management Domain* (DMD).

dotted decimal notation The syntactic representation of a 32-bit integer that consists of four eight-bit numbers written in base 10 with periods (dots) separating them. This is used to represent IP addresses in the Internet, as in 192.67.67.20. Also called dotted quad notation.

EBONE European Backbone. A pan-European network backbone service.

EGP Exterior Gateway Protocol. A reachability routing protocol used by gateways on a two-level Internet network. EGP is used in the Internet core system. *See* core gateway.

Electronic Frontier Foundation (EFF) A foundation established to address social and legal issues arising from the impact on society of the increasingly pervasive use of computers as the means of communication and information distribution.

Electronic Mail (email) A system whereby a computer user can exchange messages with other computer users (or groups of users) via a communications network.

email address   The domain-based or UUCP address that is used to send email to a specified destination. For example, an email address is `steve@mentor.lgc.peachnet.edu`.

encapsulation   The technique used by layered protocols in which a layer adds header information to the *protocol data unit* (PDU) from the layer above. As an example, in Internet terminology, a packet would contain a header from the physical layer, followed by a header from the network layer (IP), followed by a header from the transport layer (TCP), followed by the application protocol data.

encryption   The manipulation of a packet's data in order to prevent anyone but the intended recipient from reading that data. Many types of data encryption are available, and they are the basis of network security.

ES-IS   End system to Intermediate system protocol. The OSI protocol used for router detection and address resolution.

Ethernet   A 10-MB/s standard for LANs, initially developed by Xerox, and later refined by Digital, Intel, and Xerox (DIX). All hosts are connected to a coaxial cable where they contend for network access using a *Carrier Sense Multiple Access with Collision Detection* (CSMA/CD) paradigm. *See* 802.x, Local Area Network, Token Ring.

EZ-Install   The default procedure used by Norel AN, ANH, ARN, and ASN routers to receive configuration files from a BootP server using the router's serial interface.

FDDI   Fiber Distributed Data Interface. An emerging high-speed networking standard. The underlying medium is fiber optics, and the topology is a dual-attached, counter-rotating Token Ring. FDDI networks can often be spotted by the orange fiber cable. The FDDI protocol has also been adapted to run over traditional copper wires.

finger   A program that displays information about a particular user, or all users, logged on the local system or on a remote system. It typically shows full name, last login time, idle time, terminal line, and terminal location (where applicable). It may also display plan and project files left by the user.

FIPS   Federal Information Processing Standard.

FIX   Federal Internet Exchange. A connection point between the North American governmental internets and the Internet. The FIXs are named after their geographic region, as in FIX West (Mountain View, California) and FIX East (College Park, Maryland). *See* CIX and GIX.

flame   To express strong opinion and/or criticism of something, usually as a frank inflammatory statement in an electronic message.

Flash memory   The removal PCMCIA memory card that holds the routers *nonvolatile file system* (NVFS). The NVFS is also called the local file system.

FNC   Federal Networking Council. The body responsible for coordinating networking needs among U.S. federal agencies.

fragmentation   The IP process in which a packet is broken into smaller pieces to fit the requirements of a given physical network. The reverse process is termed reassembly. *See* MTU.

frame   A frame is a datalink layer packet that contains the header and trailer information required by the physical medium. That is, network layer packets are encapsulated to become frames. *See* IP datagram, encapsulation, packet.

Frame Relay   A recently developed switching interface that operates in packet mode. Generally regarded as the future replacement for X.25.

FRICC   Federal Research Internet Coordinating Committee. Now replaced by the FNC.

FTP   File Transfer Protocol. The Internet protocol (and program) used to transfer files between hosts. *See* FTAM.

GateD   Gateway Daemon. A popular routing software package that supports multiple routing protocols. Developed and maintained by the GateDaemon Consortium at Cornell University.

gateway   The original Internet term for what is now called router or, more precisely, IP router. In modern usage, the terms "gateway" and "application gateway" refer to systems that do a translation from some native format to another. Examples include X.400 to/from RFC 822 email gateways. *See* router.

GIX   Global Internet eXchange. A common routing exchange point that enables pairs of networks to implement agreed-upon routing policies. The GIX is intended to enable maximum connectivity to the Internet for networks all over the world. *See* CIX and FIX.

Gopher   The Internet Gopher is a distributed document delivery system. It allows a neophyte user to access various types of data residing on multiple hosts in a seamless fashion. *See* archie, Prospero, WAIS, World Wide Web.

header   The portion of a packet, preceding the actual data, containing the source and destination addresses and error-checking fields. This also be used to describe the part of an email message (or Usenet news article) that precedes the body, although one usually talks about headers (plural) in that case.

hop   A term used in routing. A hop is one data link. A path from the source to destination in a network is a series of hops. This is often used to measure the number of routers that a packet must traverse. For instance, "BARRnet is seven hops away from our LAN."

host   A term used in the Internet community to describe any device attached to the network that provides an application level service (a machine that you can log in to and do useful work). A router is not a host.

http (HyperText Transport Protocol)   The protocol for moving hypertext files across the Internet. It requires a HTTP client program on one end and an HTTP server program on the other. HTTP is the most important protocol used on the Web.

hypertext   Generally, any text that contains links to other documents. Words or phrases in the document can be chosen by a reader and cause another document to be retrieved and displayed.

IAB   Internet Architecture Board. Formerly called the Internet Activities Board. This is the technical body that oversees the development of the Internet suite of protocols (commonly referred to as TCP/IP). It has two task forces (the IRTF and the IETF), each charged with investigating a particular area.

IANA   Internet Assigned Numbers Authority. The entity responsible for assigning numbers in the Internet Suite of Protocols.

ICMP   Internet Control Message Protocol. The protocol used to handle errors and control messages at the IP layer. ICMP is actually part of the IP protocol.

IEEE   Institute of Electrical and Electronics Engineers.

IESG   Internet Engineering Steering Group. The executive committee of the IETF.

IETF   Internet Engineering Task Force. One of the task forces of the IAB. The IETF is responsible for solving short-term engineering needs on the Internet. It has over 60 working groups.

IFIP   International Federation for Information Procession. A research organization that performs substantive pre-standardization work for OSI. IFIP is noted for having formalized the original *Message Handling System* (MHS) model.

IGP   Interior Gateway Protocol. The protocol used to exchange routing information between collaborating routers in the Internet. RIP and OSPF are examples of IGPs.

interface   A data link/physical layer connection to a physical network transmission medium. An interface includes media-specific driver software.

intermediate system   An OSI system that is not an end system, but which serves instead to relay communications between end systems. *See* repeater, bridge, router.

Internet   (note the capital "I") The largest Internet network in the world consisting of large national backbone nets (such as MILNET, NSFNET, and CREN) and myriad regional and local campus networks all over the world. The Internet uses the Internet protocol suite. To be on the Internet, you must have IP connectivity or, in other words, be able to Telnet to, or ping, other systems. Networks with only email connectivity are not actually classified as being on the Internet.

internet   A collection of networks interconnected by a set of routers that enable them to function as a single, large virtual network.

Internet address   A 32-bit address assigned to hosts using TCP/IP. *See* dotted decimal notation.

Internet Society (ISOC)   A non-profit organization that fosters the voluntary interconnection of computer networks into a global communications and information infrastructure. The ISOC is the umbrella organization for the IAB, IETF, and IRTF.

interoperability   The capability of software and hardware on multiple machines from multiple vendors to communicate meaningfully.

IP   Internet Protocol. The network layer protocol for the Internet protocol suite.

IP datagram   The fundamental unit of information passed across the Internet. It contains source and destination addresses along with data and a number of fields that define such things as the length of the datagram, the header checksum, and flags to say whether the datagram can be (or has been) fragmented.

IPng IP Next Generation. A collective term used to describe the efforts of the Internet Engineering Task Force to define a new version of the *Internet Protocol* (IP) that can handle larger IP addresses to cope with the explosive growth of the Internet. At the time of this writing, there were three candidate protocols for IPng: CATNIP, TUBA, and SIPP. By the summer of 1994, the IETF is scheduled to have chosen Ipng.

IPX Internetwork Packet Exchange. The Novell NetWare protocol that provides a datagram delivery of messages. A router with IPX routing can interconnect LANs so that Novell Netware clients and servers can communicate. *See* Local Area Network.

IRTF Internet Research Task Force. One of the task forces of the IAB. The group responsible for research and development of the Internet protocol suite.

ISDN Integrated Services Digital Network. An emerging technology that is beginning to be offered by the telephone carriers of the world. ISDN combines voice and digital network services in a single medium, making it possible to offer customers digital data services as well as voice connections through a single wire. The standards that define ISDN are specified by CCITT.

IS-IS Intermediate system to Intermediate system protocol. This is the OSI protocol by which intermediate systems exchange routing information.

ISO International Organization for Standardization. You knew that, right? It is best known for the seven-layer OSI Reference Model. *See* OSI.

Jughead A gopher search engine similar to Veronica. The difference is that Jughead searches one server at a time.

KA9Q A popular implementation of TCP/IP and associated protocols for amateur packet radio systems.

Kerberos The security system of MIT's Project Athena. It is based on symmetric key cryptography. *See* encryption.

Kermit A popular file transfer and terminal emulation program.

Knowbot An experimental directory service. *See* white pages, WHOIS, X.500.

LATA   Local Access and Transport Area. A telephone company term that defines a geographical area. It normally, but not always, corresponds to an area code.

line   A physical medium that comprises a circuit path, identified typically by slot, connector, and media type.

little-endian   A format for the storage or transmission of binary data in which the least significant byte (bit) comes first. *See* big-endian.

Local Area Network (LAN)   A data network intended to serve an area of only a few square kilometers or less. Because the network is known to cover only a small area, optimizations can be made in the network signal protocols that permit data rates up to 100 MB/s. *See* Ethernet, FDDI, Token Ring.

Local boot   The procedure in which a router receives its image and configuration file from the local file system.

LocalTalk   A LAN protocol developed by Apple Computer. This network is designed to run over twisted pair wire and has a data rate of 235 Kbps. All Macintosh computers contain a LocalTalk interface. *See* AppleTalk.

mail exploder   Part of an email delivery system that enables a message to be delivered to a list of recipients. Mail exploders are used to implement mailing lists. Users send messages to a single address (`hacks@somehost.edu`) and the mail exploder takes care of the delivery to the individual mailboxes on the list. A machine that connects two or more email systems (especially dissimilar mail systems on two different networks) transfers messages between them. Sometimes the mapping and translation can be quite complex, and generally it requires a store-and-forward scheme whereby the message is received from one system completely before it is transmitted to the next system after suitable translations.

Martian   A humorous term applied to packets that turn up unexpectedly on the wrong network because of bogus routing entries. It is also used as a name for a packet that has an altogether bogus (non-registered or ill-formed) Internet address.

MBONE   Multicast Backbone. A collection of Internet routers that support IP multicasting. The MBONE is used as a broadcast (actually multicast) channel on which various public and private audio and video programs are sent. Examples include audio/video transmissions from the IETF meetings. At a recent IETF meeting, there were as many participants listening in on the MBONE as there were people present at the meeting itself.

MIB Management Information Base. A collection of objects that can be accessed via a network management protocol. *See* SMI.

MILNET MILitary NETwork. Originally part of the ARPANET, MILNET was partitioned in 1984 to make it possible for military installations to have reliable network service, while the ARPANET continued to be used for research. *See* DDN.

MIME Multi-purpose Internet Mail Extensions. This is the standard for multimedia mail contents in the Internet suite of protocols.

modem (MOdulator, DEModulator): A device that you connect to your computer and to a phone line that enables the computer to talk to other computers through the phone system. Basically, modems do for computers what a telephone does for humans.

MTU Maximum Transmission Unit. The largest possible unit of data that can be sent on a given physical medium. For example, the MTU of Ethernet is 1,500 bytes. *See* fragmentation.

multi-homed host A computer connected to more than one physical data link. The data links may or may not be attached to the same network.

multicast A special form of broadcast where copies of the packet are delivered to only a subset of all possible destinations. *See* broadcast, MBONE.

NAK Negative Acknowledgement. *See* ACK.

name resolution The process of mapping a name into the corresponding address. *See* DNS.

NetBIOS Network Basic Input Output System. The standard interface to networks on IBM PC and compatible systems.

Netboot The procedure where Nortel routers receive their startup files from a BootP server in an IP network.

network Any time you connect two or more computers together so that they can share resources you have a computer network. Connect two or more networks together and you have an Internet.

network address *See* Internet address or OSI network address.

network byte order   The Internet-standard ordering of the bytes corresponding to numeric values.

Network File System (NFS)®   A distributed file system developed by Sun Microsystems that enables a set of computers to cooperatively access each other's files in a transparent manner. *See* RFS.

Network layer   The OSI layer that is responsible for routing, switching, and subnetwork access across the entire OSI environment.

Network Time Protocol (NTP)   A protocol built on top of TCP that assures accurate local time-keeping with reference to radio and atomic clocks located on the Internet. This protocol is capable of synchronizing distributed clocks within milliseconds over long time periods.

NIC   Network Information Center. Originally, there was only one, located at SRI International that served the ARPANET (and later DDN) community. Today many NICs are operated by local, regional, and national networks all over the world. Such centers provide user assistance, document service, training, and much more.

NIST   National Institute of Standards and Technology. (Formerly NBS). *See* OIW.

NMS   Network Management Station. The system responsible for managing a network. The NMS talks to network management agents that reside in the managed nodes via a network management protocol. *See* agent.

NOC   Network Operations Center. Any center responsible for the operational aspects of a production network. These tasks include monitoring and control, troubleshooting, user assistance, and so on.

node   Any single computer connected to a network.

NREN   National Research and Educational Network. This network is still on the drawing board. It is expected to become a state of the art high-speed network for research and education in the U.S. In recent years, the NREN has become synonymous with the National Information Infrastructure, often referred to as the Information Superhighway.

NSAP   Network Service Access Point. The point where the OSI network service is made available to a transport entity. The NSAPs are identified by OSI network addresses.

NSF   National Science Foundation. The sponsors of the NSFNET.

NSFNET   National Science Foundation NETwork. A collection of local, regional, and mid-level networks in the U.S. tied together by a high-speed backbone. NSFNET gives scientists access to a number of supercomputers across the country.

octet   An octet is eight bits. In networking, this term is often used (rather than byte) since some machine architectures employ bytes that are not eight bits long.

ONC(tm)   Open Network Computing. A distributed applications architecture promoted and controlled by a consortium led by Sun Microsystems. *See* DCE.

OSF   Open Software Foundation. The group responsible for the *Distributed Computing Environment* (DCE) and the *Distributed Management Environment* (DME). *See* DCE.

OSI   Open Systems Interconnection. An international standardization program to facilitate communications among computers from different manufacturers. *See* ISO and CCITT.

OSPF   Open Shortest Path First. A proposed standard IGP for the Internet. *See* IGP.

packet   The unit of data sent across a network. This is a generic term used to describe a unit of data at all levels of the protocol stack, but it is most correctly used to describe application data units. *See* IP datagram, frame.

packet switching   A communications paradigm in which packets (messages) are individually routed between hosts with no previously established communication path. *See* circuit switching, connection-oriented, connectionless.

PCI   Protocol Control Information. The protocol information added by an OSI entity to the service data unit passed down from the layer above, all together forming a *Protocol Data Unit* (PDU).

PDU   Protocol Data Unit. This is OSI terminology for a "packet." A PDU is a data object exchanged by protocol machines (entities) within a given layer. PDUs consist of both *Protocol Control Information* (PCI) and user data.

Physical layer   The OSI layer that provides the means to activate and use physical connections for bit transmission. In plain terms, the

Physical layer provides the procedures for transferring a single bit across a physical media.

physical media   Any means in the physical world for transferring signals between OSI systems. This is considered to be outside the OSI model and therefore is sometimes referred to as Layer 0. The physical connector to the media can be considered as defining the bottom interface of the Physical layer, or the bottom of the OSI Reference Model.

ping   Packet Internet groper. A program used to test the reachability of destinations by sending them an ICMP echo request and waiting for a reply. The term is used as a verb: "Ping host X to see if it is up!"

Point of Presence (POP)   A site where there exists a collection of telecommunications equipment, usually digital leased lines and multi-protocol routers.

port   The identifier (a 16-bit unsigned integer) used by Internet transport protocols to distinguish among multiple simultaneous connections to a single destination host. *See* selector.

Post Office Protocol (POP)   A protocol designed to enable single user hosts to read mail from a server. Three versions are available: POP, POP2, and POP3. Latter versions are not compatible with earlier versions. *See* Electronic Mail.

PPP   Point-to-Point Protocol. The successor to SLIP, PPP provides router-to-router and host-to-network connections over both synchronous and asynchronous circuits. *See* SLIP.

Presentation layer   The OSI layer that determines how application information is represented (such as encoded) while in transit between two end systems.

Prospero   A distributed directory service and file system that enables users to construct customized views of available resources while taking advantage of the structure imposed by others. *See* Gopher, WAIS, World Wide Web.

protocol   A formal description of messages to be exchanged and rules to be followed for two or more systems to exchange information.

protocol converter   A device/program that translates between different protocols that serve similar functions (TCP and TP4).

proxy   The mechanism whereby one system fronts for another system in responding to protocol requests. Proxy systems are used in network management to avoid having to implement full protocol stacks in simple devices, such as modems.

proxy ARP   The technique in which one machine, usually a router, answers ARP requests intended for another machine. By faking its identity, the router accepts responsibility for routing packets to the real destination. Proxy ARP enables a site to use a single IP address with two physical networks. Subnetting would normally be a better solution.

PSN   Packet Switch Node. The modern term used for nodes in the ARPANET and MILNET. These used to be called *Interface Message Processors* (IMPs). PSNs are currently implemented with BBN C30 or C300 minicomputers.

queue   A backup of packets awaiting processing.

Quick Start   The procedure used to configure the initial IP interface for a Nortel router.

RARP   Reverse Address Resolution Protocol. The IP a diskless host uses to find its Internet address at startup. RARP maps a physical (hardware) address to an Internet address. *See* ARP.

RBOC   Regional Bell Operating Company. *See* BOC.

reassembly   The process by which an IP datagram is put back together at the receiving host after having been fragmented in transit. *See* fragmentation, MTV.

repeater   A device that propagates electrical signals from one cable to another without making routing decisions or providing packet filtering. In OSI terminology, a repeater is a Physical-layer intermediate system. *See* bridge, intermediate system, gateway, router.

replication   The process of keeping a copy of data either through shadowing or caching. *See* caching, shadowing.

RFC   Request for Comments. This document series, begun in 1969, describes the Internet suite of protocols and related experiments. Not all (in fact, very few) RFCs describe Internet standards, but all Internet standards are written up as RFCs. This glossary is based on RFC1209.

RFS   Remote File System. A distributed file system, similar to NFS, developed by AT&T that is distributed with their UNIX System V operating system. *See* NFS.

RIP   Routing Information Protocol. An *Interior Gateway Protocol* (IGP) supplied with Berkeley UNIX.

rlogin   A service offered by Berkeley Unix that enables users of one machine to log into other Unix systems (that they are authorized for) and interact as if their terminals are connected directly. It is similar to Telnet.

router   A system responsible for making decisions about which paths of network (or Internet) traffic will follow. To do this, it uses a routing protocol to gain information about the network, and algorithms to choose the best route based on several criteria known as routing metrics. In OSI terminology, a router is a Network-layer intermediate system. Historically, routers were called gateways in Internet terminology. *See* gateway, bridge, repeater.

routing   The process of selecting the correct interface and next hop for a packet being forwarded. *See* hop, router, EGP, IGP.

RPC   Remote Procedure Call. An easy and popular paradigm for implementing the client-server model of distributed computing. A request is sent to a remote system to execute a designated procedure using arguments supplied, and the result is returned to the caller. Many variations and subtleties can be done, resulting in a variety of different RPC protocols.

RTFM   Read The Fantastic Manual. This acronym is often used when someone asks a simple or common question. The work "Fantastic" is usually replaced with one much more vulgar.

SAP   Service Access Point. The point where the services of an OSI layer are made available to the next higher layer. The SAP is named according to the layer providing the services and transport services are provided at a *Transport SAP* (TSAP) at the top of the Transport layer.

server   A provider of resources (such as file servers and name servers). *See* client, DNS, Network File System.

Session layer   The OSI layer that provides a means for dialog control between end systems.

SGMP   Simple Gateway Management Protocol. The predecessor to SNMP. *See* SNMP.

SIPP   Simple Internet Protocol Plus. One of the three IPng candidates. *See* Ipng.

Site Manager   A graphical, SNMP-based router management tool used to configure and maintain Nortel routers.

SLIP   Serial Line IP. An Internet protocol used to run IP over serial lines such as telephone circuits or RS-232 cables interconnecting two systems. SLIP is now being replaced by PPP. *See* PPP.

SMDS   Switched Multimegabit Data Service. An emerging high-speed networking technology to be offered by the telephone companies in the U.S.

SMI   Structure of Management Information. The rules used to define the objects that can be accessed via a network management protocol. *See* MIB.

SMTP   Simple Mail Transfer Protocol. The Internet email protocol. It is a server-to-server protocol, so other protocols are used to access the messages.

SNA   Systems Network Architecture. IBM's proprietary network architecture.

SNMP   Simple Network Management Protocol. The network management protocol of choice for TCP/IP-based internets.

SNMPv2   SNMP version 2. The second-generation SNMP.

socket   A pairing of an IP address and a port number. *See* port.

SQL   Structured Query Language. The international standard language for defining and accessing relational databases.

subnet mask   *See* address mask.

subnetwork   A collection of OSI end systems and intermediate systems under the control of a single administrative domain that is utilizing a single network access protocol. Examples would be private X.25 networks or a collection of bridged LANs. *See* autonomous system.

TCP   Transmission Control Protocol. The major transport protocol in the Internet suite of protocols providing reliable, connection-oriented, full-duplex streams. It uses IP for delivery. *See* TP4.

Technical Interface (TI)   The command-line interface used by administers to manage Nortel routers.

Telnet   The virtual terminal protocol in the Internet suite of protocols. It enables users of one host to log into a remote host and interact as normal terminal users of that host. *See* VT.

terminal emulator   A program that enables a computer to emulate a terminal. The workstation thus appears as a terminal to the remote host.

terminal server   A device that connects many terminals to a LAN through one network connection. A terminal server can also connect many network users to its asynchronous ports for dial-out capabilities and printer access. *See* Local Area Network.

three-way handshake   The process whereby two protocol entities synchronize during a connection establishment.

TN3270   A variant of the Telnet program that enables one to attach to IBM mainframes and use the mainframe as if you had a 3270 or similar terminal.

Token Ring   A type of LAN with nodes wired into a ring. Each node constantly passes a control message (or token) on to the next; whichever node has the token can send a message. Often, Token Ring is used to refer to the IEEE 802.5 Token Ring standard, which is the most common type of Token Ring. *See* 802.x, Local Area Network.

topology   A network topology shows the computers and the links between them. A network layer must stay abreast of the current network topology to be able to route packets to their final destination.

transceiver   Transmitter-receiver. This is the physical device that connects a host interface to a LAN, such as Ethernet. Ethernet transceivers contain electronics that apply signals to the cable and sense collisions.

transfer syntax   A description on an instance of a data type that is expressed as a string of bits. *See* abstract syntax.

Transport layer   The OSI layer that is responsible for reliable end-to-end data transfers between end systems.

Trojan Horse   A computer program that carries within itself a means of allowing the creator of the program access to the system using it. *See* virus, worm.

tunneling   This refers to the encapsulation of protocol A within protocol B, such that A treats B as though it were a datalink layer. Tunneling is used to get data between administrative domains that use a protocol that is not supported by the Internet connecting those domains. *See* administrative domain.

twisted pair   A type of cable in which pairs of conductors are twisted together to produce certain electrical properties.

UDP   User Datagram Protocol. A transport protocol in the Internet suite of protocols. UDP, like TCP, uses IP for delivery, but, unlike TCP, UDP provides for the exchange of datagrams without acknowledgements or a guaranteed delivery. *See* CLTP.

Unix   A computer operating system that is the basic software running on a computer underneath things like word processors and spreadsheets. Unix is designed to be used by many people at the same time and has TCP/IP built-in. It is the most common operating system for servers on the Internet.

URL (Uniform Resource Locator)   The standard way to give the address of any resource on the Internet that is part of the Web. An example is `http://www.berkeley.edu`. The most common way to use a URL is to enter it into a Web browser program, such as Netscape.

Usenet   A collection of thousands of topically named newsgroups, the computers that run the protocols, and the people who read and submit Usenet news. Not all Internet hosts subscribe to Usenet and not all Usenet hosts are on the Internet.

UUCP   Unix-to-Unix Copy Program. A protocol used for communication between consenting Unix systems. Today the term is more commonly used to describe the large international network that uses the UUCP protocol to pass news and electronic mail. *See* Electronic mail, Usenet.

Veronica   Very Easy Rodent-Oriented Net-wide Index to Computerized Archives. Developed at the University of Nevada, Veronica is a constantly updated database of the names of almost every menu item on thousands of gopher servers. The Veronica database can be searched from most major gopher menus.

virus   A program that replicates itself on computer systems by incorporating itself into other programs that are shared among computer systems.

VT   Virtual Terminal. The OSI Virtual Terminal Service that is similar to Telnet.

WAIS   Wide Area Information Server. A WAIS allows users to search and access different types of information from a single interface. The WAIS protocol is an extension of the ANSI Z39.50 information retrieval protocol. *See* Gopher, Prospero, World Wide Web.

white pages   The Internet supports several databases that contain basic information about users such as email addresses, telephone numbers, and postal addresses. These databases can be searched to get information about particular individuals. Because they serve a function akin to the telephone book, these databases are often referred to as white pages. *See* Knowbot, WHOIS, X.500.

WHOIS   An Internet program that enables users to query a database of people and other Internet entities, such as domains, networks, and hosts, kept at the DDN NIC. The information for people shows a person's company name, address, phone number, and email address. *See* DDN, white pages, Knowbot, X.500.

World Wide Web (WWW)   An easy but powerful global information system based on a combination of information retrieval and hypertext techniques. *See* Gopher, Prospero, WAIS.

worm   A computer program that replicates itself and is self-propagating. Worms, as opposed to viruses, are meant to spawn in network environments. Network worms were first defined by Shoch & Hupp of Xerox in ACM Communications (March 1982). The Internet worm of November 1988 is perhaps the most famous. It successfully propagated itself on over 6,000 systems across the Internet. *See* Trojan Horse, virus.

X   The name for TCP/IP-based network-oriented window systems. Network window systems enable a program to use a display on a different computer. The most widely-implemented window system is X11, a component of MIT's Project Athena.

X.500   The CCITT and ISO standard for electronic directory services. *See* white pages, Knowbot, WHOIS.

XDR   eXternal Data Representation. A standard for machine-independent data structures developed by Sun Microsystems that is similar to BER.

X/Open   A group of computer manufacturers that promotes the development of portable applications based on Unix. They publish a document called the X/Open Portability Guide.

X recommendations   The CCITT documents that describe data communication network standards. Well-known ones include the X.25 Packet Switching standard, X.400 Message Handling System, and X.500 Directory Services.

X Window system (TM)   A popular window system developed by MIT and implemented on a number of workstations.

Yellow Pages (YP)   A service used by Unix administrators to manage databases distributed across a network.

zone   A logical group of network devices (AppleTalk).

INDEX

ABOUT THE AUTHOR

Jean-Pierre Comeau is currently a Senior Network Engineer for a major automotive distributor. He has been troubleshooting networks for over seven years and has gained an impressive knowledge of Ethernet, Token-Ring, and ATM networks. He previously worked at Alliance Mortgage Company in Jacksonville, Florida where he managed their multi-state Frame Relay network. He started out as a graduate from the University of Florida (Go Gators!) earning a Bachelor of Science degree in Mechanical Engineering. His knowledge includes multiple protocol analysis and network management of enterprise networks using Nortel Networks routers, hubs and switches. He also conducts interdepartmental training on related issues.